T0364607

Indian Journalism in a New Era

Indian Journalism in a New Era
Changes, Challenges, and Perspectives

Edited by
Shakuntala Rao

OXFORD
UNIVERSITY PRESS

OXFORD
UNIVERSITY PRESS

Oxford University Press is a department of the University of Oxford.
It furthers the University's objective of excellence in research, scholarship,
and education by publishing worldwide. Oxford is a registered trademark of
Oxford University Press in the UK and in certain other countries.

Published in India by
Oxford University Press
2/11 Ground Floor, Ansari Road, Daryaganj, New Delhi 110 002, India

First Edition published in 2019

ISBN-13 (print edition): 978-0-19-949082-0
ISBN-10 (print edition): 0-19-949082-1

ISBN-13 (eBook): 978-0-19-909761-6
ISBN-10 (eBook): 0-19-909761-5

Typeset in Minion Pro 10.5/13
by Tranistics Data Technologies, Kolkata 700 091
Printed in India by Nutech Print Services India

CONTENTS

ACKNOWLEDGEMENTS

· ·

No project, of this size, is complete without the input of many people. The authors who contributed essays to this academic volume are also friends and colleagues in and outside of the academy who often, sometimes proactively, sometimes at my behest, shared ideas, expertise, and knowledge. The book is an outcome of their collective effort, intellectual energy, and patience. In particular, I thank Daya Thussu, Prasun Sonwalkar, Radhika Parameswaran, and Mohan Dutta for their kind words and boundless enthusiasm for the topic each time we conferred. The book received enormous support from the editorial staff at Oxford University Press. I have colleagues at my home institution who deserve mention and gratitude for creating an environment in which I write, edit, and teach. Those colleagues are Kirsten Isgro, Deborah Altamirano, Linda Luck, Timothy Clukey, Jin Kim, and Bridget Haina. In the larger home of Indian journalism, I have gained much from intellectual conversations, over the years, with Vipul Mudgal and Paranjoy Guha Thakurta. The Department of Communication at the University of Hyderabad has become a de facto academic home in India for me, and the faculty there have become long-distance colleagues, friends, and powerhouse intellectual resources for everything that pertains to Indian journalism. They must all be thanked publicly: Vinod Pavrala, Vasuki Belavadi, E. Sathyaprakash, V. P. Sanjay, Anjali

Gupta, Madhavi Ravi Kumar, Usha Raman, and Kanchan K. Malik. For the past decade, my true intellectual home has been the scholarly field of media ethics research. Scholars at this 'home' have given me unique intellectual perspectives and I have gained much from conversations with them about journalism ethics. From this group, I express my gratitude to Stephen Ward, Clifford Christians, Herman Wasserman, Patrick Plaisance, Ginny Whitehouse, Lee Wilkins, and Muhammad Ayish.

The book is dedicated to Joe and Aedan, the two who provide love, laughter, and dinners.

ABBREVIATIONS

AAP	Aam Aadmi Party
ABP	Ananda Bazar Patrika
ABVP	Akhil Bharatiya Vidyarthi Parishad
BJP	Bharatiya Janata Party
BRICS	Brazil, Russia, India, China, and South Africa
CCTV	China Central Television
CGTN	China Global Television Network
CPJ	Committee to Protect Journalists
CSE	Centre for Science and Environment
DD	Doordarshan
FEJI	Forum of Environmental Journalists in India
ILIA	Indian Language Internet Alliance
IRS	Indian Readership Survey
NBSA	News Broadcasting Standards Authority
NCRB	National Crime Records Bureau
NDTV	New Delhi Television
NGT	National Green Tribunal
NRI	non-resident Indian
NWICO	New World Information and Communication Order
PCI	Press Council of India
PIL	public interest litigation

PREAL	Project in Radio Education for Adult Literacy
RNI	Registrar of Newspapers for India
RT	Russia Today
SITE	Satellite Instructional Television Experiment
TERI	The Energy Research Institute
TRP	television rating points
UGC	University Grants Commission
UNESCO	United Nations Educational, Scientific and Cultural Organization
UPA	United Progressive Alliance

CHAPTER ONE

Introduction

SHAKUNTALA RAO

. . . .

In the ever-changing information environment of the early twenty-first century, citizens and journalists alike are eagerly adapting to new technologies. India is no different. The country's communication revolution, in the post-liberalization era, has been well documented. Beyond the explosion of newspaper and magazine sales, television and new media have played a powerful role in the country's transformation. With 660 million viewers, India now claims to be the second largest television market in the world. Sixty per cent of Indian households, approximately 119 million, have a television, and 42 per cent of those have cable services. The growth of internet and social media, small in comparison to China and the United States, has been impressive with an 89 per cent increase in connectivity in the five years leading up to 2012 (Parthasarthi et al. 2012). Some are predicting that India's social media users will number approximately

370 million by 2022 (Chaffey 2018). In 2019, it is estimated that there will be around 258 million social network users, up from close to 168 million in 2016. These approximate numbers are driven by the increasing popularity of social network apps such as WhatsApp and Snapchat and sites such as YouTube and Facebook. India had 825 registered television channels in all languages and over 80,000 newspapers as of 30 May 2017, according to official figures released by the Registrar of Newspapers of India and the Telecom Regulatory Authority of India (TRAI 2017). The country now boasts more than 300 24/7 news channels broadcasting in 16 languages. India's media business is among the most profitable in the world, with each of the top 10 media companies growing at least twice in size in the five-year period between 2003 and 2008. According to FICCI-KPMG (2017), the media and entertainment sector has registered a continuous growth of almost 12 per cent since 2013 to touch INR 918 billion (US$14 billion). The media industry is dominated by the television segment, which accounted for 44 per cent of the revenue share in 2016 expected to grow further to 48 per cent by 2021. Print media, which is continuing to flourish, is the second largest sector in the overall media industry, generating revenues worth US$4.51 billion in 2017.

Such a massive media market in the context of the world's largest functioning democracy also continues to struggle with multiple contradictions: how prosperity can coexist with poverty, and how the services sector can live side by side with a failing agrarian system; how patterns of poverty and social exclusion along the lines of caste, class, region, and gender often reproduce themselves in relative isolation from the overall patterns of economic transformations; and why, while prosperity has not yet touched the lives of millions, the big story in the international media is about India's prospering classes. Recent changes in the media suggest a growing contradiction: a desire for advocacy of the politics of redistribution and giving voice to the voiceless on the one hand, and the growing power of business in politics and media on the other. For the last two decades, the Indian state has increasingly prioritized economic growth, and the economic and political importance of indigenous business groups within and outside India has grown. The Indian business sector has successfully and lucratively invested in the media business. As the media environment has become corporatized and commercialized, some media outlets have tried to foster a culture of investigative journalism and have tried to hold the powerful accountable and give voice to the marginalized; this is particularly true for e-journalism, which has started to flourish with the rise of internet use. Other media outlets have gone down-market and emulated Western tabloid-style journalism by exclusively focusing on, in Thussu's (2005: 54) words, the 'three Cs of Indian journalism … cricket, crime and cinema'. It can be debated whether corporatization of India's media has led to an exclusive desire for the lowest common denominator with a view to maximizing profits and increasing ratings, and whether such a desire has destroyed established norms of ethical journalism, but it is clear that corporatization of news has led to radical changes in what is covered and what is not. Drèze and Sen (2013: 263) do not mince words when they write that Indian media can now be marked as 'celebratory media dominated by breathless gossip about cricketers, billionaires and Bollywood stars and point-scoring among the political elite'.

The explosion and ubiquity of media has raised some important questions about journalistic training, professionalism, ethics education, and pedagogy. There is now global hand-wringing about the changing nature and future of journalism, especially in democratic societies. This has been occasioned by the seismic shift characterized by new forms of journalism, global connectivity, multi-directional flows of information, instantaneous reporting, multimedia content, and extreme content customization. The barrage of information one can receive via handheld mobile phones has raised serious questions about authenticity of content, source verification, accuracy, and truth. While one can argue that it is digital connectivity which has led to this moment, the answer perhaps is more complicated. Changes in global economic systems, individual governments pushing neoliberal and deregulatory practices especially in media ownership, the blending of news with opinion, and low-cost global forums have impacted old and established professional practices of 'shoe-leather reporting'. Indian journalism faces some of the same changes and challenges, its growth marked by both inclusivity and exclusions. While the explosion of regional-language news channels, magazines, and newspapers has given some people a voice in the national arena hitherto unseen, the content of many of these outlets is poor in quality, journalistically unsound, and, at times, sensational and crude. Professional journalism education and training have grown precipitously, but the quality of the training remains substandard (except at some elite universities and private media schools), and the quality of content reflects the education and training gap.

Exacerbating the situation are overall trends towards media polarization in content, partially driven by economic relations, between urban and rural India. Mudgal (2011) in his seminal study finds that the top-circulating Hindi and English newspapers devote a miniscule portion (only 2 per cent) of their coverage to rural India's crises and anxieties and almost entirely ignore issues of malnutrition, hunger, displacement, or farmers' suicides. India, between 1991 and 2011, witnessed the highest increases in poverty since independence, with the top 1 per cent of earners increasing their share of the country's wealth from 36.8 per cent to 53 per cent, and the top 10 per cent owning 76.3 per cent of the country's wealth (Motiram and Sarma 2011). When one looks at India's rural–urban polarization in terms of wages and consumption, one can observe that it has been rising since the 1980s, but has increased at a very rapid pace since the 1990s. It may not be a coincidence that among the various cleavages that exist in Indian society, such as caste, gender, and religion, the rural–urban cleavage is characterized by the most significant and increased polarization (Bandyopadhyay 2013). This polarization extends to digital technology where, as recent news reports suggest, only 8 per cent of Indians have regular access to the internet and about 19 per cent have occasional access (Chopra 2017). Urban India has close to 60 per cent internet penetration, reflecting a significant level of saturation, but there are 750 million users in rural India who remain disconnected from the digital sphere (Wu 2016). While Prime Minister Narendra Modi's recent efforts at e-governance have been lauded by diasporic and urban Indians, preliminary research shows that it has made almost no impact on the lives of the rural Indian in municipality or *gram panchayat* (village) governance (Chatterji 2017). India may be an information technology powerhouse for the rest of the world, but its projects under successive governments to bridge the gap between digital haves and have-nots have fallen woefully short of stated targets.

Complicating economic equations and ever-evolving professional practices are also the government's moves towards curtailing freedom of press and a media driven by deep political biases. Increasingly, both print and television journalists report feeling pressure from management to refrain from criticizing the government or supporters of Hindu nationalist groups who have attacked people and damaged the property of those whom they perceive as having been insulting or disrespectful to Hinduism. Although the minister of information and broadcasting promised that the government would not interfere with the freedom of the press, the administration attempted to institute (and later retracted) a one-day ban of Delhi-based cable news channel NDTV on spurious charges of national security violation. Clampdown on conflict zone journalists, working in areas such as Kashmir or Chhattisgarh, is now expected. Beyond outright censorship, the rise of outrage media, best exemplified by Arnab Goswami among others, has meant that news has come to resemble a blood sport, engaging in not information but insult trading, not neutral anchoring but one long, exhausting, hectoring, and mocking diatribe. Alternately referred to as 'pop journalism' or 'Arnab's reality show', these news shows have been described by critics as food fights rather than sustained discussions about serious civil, economic, and political matters (Khorana 2012; Torri 2015). With mass digitization of information, journalists face expectations and pressure to be active on various social media platforms; the underbelly of this has been the rise of online threats, harassment, and bullying of journalists, especially women who report and write about politics and critical social issues. With the assassination of Bengaluru-based senior journalist Gauri Lankesh in 2017, the safety of journalists and free speech have become important topics of discussion. India's rank in the press freedom index stands at 136 out of 180 countries, one of the lowest among democratic societies (Reporters without Borders 2017).

Amidst such interlinked contraries and crises, there remains a dearth of serious scholarly research on the role of journalists or on the dramatically changing journalism practices. While a few scholars have written about the specifics of journalism practices in India, far more research and analysis remains to be done. For instance, as the state broadcaster (Doordarshan) weakens and fails to provide the essential scaffolding for an informed democratic society, can the new media take its place as the vanguard of the public good and reasoned deliberation? Can the plethora of privately run cable news channels provide the discursive space needed to strengthen the 'practices of democracy', and not just information regarding results from the ballot boxes? Can neoliberal media ownership patterns provide space for a critical and free journalistic culture to evolve? What are the ethical challenges editors and journalists face on a day-to-day basis in a media industry which has exploded? And what role, if any, does the expanding social media play in the future of Indian journalism practices?

Despite the breadth and scope of India's media and journalism, there is very little meaningful and scholarly literature available about Indian journalism. It is only recently that scholarly journals like *Journalism Studies, Asian Journal of Communication, Journalism Practice*, and *South Asian Popular Culture* have begun focusing on Indian journalism and media history, practices, and influence. There is also a complete lack of integration of or interest in studies about Indian journalism in Euro-American scholarly books and textbooks. The most comprehensive of journalism studies handbooks and anthologies do not include chapters on Indian journalism or journalism practices stemming from India and other non-Western contexts. This book will be the first of its kind, bringing together 21 Indian and global scholars and journalists writing informatively and critically about Indian journalism. In trying to answer some of the questions posed previously, the contributors in this volume focus on the changes in journalism practices within the context of India's long history of journalism, the socio-economic conditions of the Indian state, and minority politics. While it is impossible to capture all elements of Indian journalism, this volume is divided into four parts, each addressing one relevant aspect: the history of journalism and its evolving changes; social media and e-journalism; marginalization; and pedagogy, ethics, and the public sphere. Underlying the chapters is a theoretical focus on how to address and analyse the enormous and precipitous changes taking place in journalism, media technology, and global relations.

CHAPTERS

The chapters in this book, purposefully, have no single theoretical trajectory. The scholarly task is to present a multi-modal, multidimensional, and multi-platform reading of the history and contemporary state of Indian journalism. Given the cultural and linguistic diversity of India, it would be difficult to provide a coherent record of journalism in the country. Due to the particular historical circumstances and the linguistic borders involved, a national approach is perhaps the best one and is adopted by many of the authors. Even within the socio-linguistic diversity among the English, Hindi, and vernacular media, there have been reciprocal influences and synergy. If there is one thread that weaves through these chapters, it is a critical look at the commercialization of journalism and journalistic practices. Commercialization has impacted every facet of Indian media, including the content, production, and dissemination of news. The path to commercialization of media has been viewed with both optimism and fear. Some see the deregulation of broadcast media— or the delinking of radio and television from direct state control—as potentially aiding the emergence of community radio and other forms of more democratic, participatory communication. Others despair that Indian audiences have been inundated with partisan and entertainment-oriented news content in contrast with public service broadcasting. Over the last four decades, the state's forays into development communication, the ruling communication paradigm during that time, have been significant. But the successes of the Satellite Instructional Television Experiment or the Kheda Communication Project have been offset by the phenomenal failures of other projects such as PREAL (Project in Radio Education for Adult Literacy), and, in the long run, have been undermined by the vacillating fortunes and commitments of changing governments. Today's vastly altered media scenario calls for a recasting of scholarship in journalism. Authors in this anthology wish to go beyond the anachronistic development communication model in studying Indian journalism to adopt a more global, technology-friendly analytical approach, while at the same time casting a critical eye on the commercialization of news and news practices.

The first part begins with Prasun Sonwalkar's chapter, focused on the colonial history of Indian journalism. Sonwalkar suggests that there was no complete eclipse of earlier forms of communication as print culture proliferated across colonial India, as demonstrated by the continuity between the *akhbarat* (newsletters of the Mughal period) and early print journalism. He argues that journalism scholars must understand Indian journalism history not merely as an offshoot or as derivative of the first English journals, but rather in terms of pre-established reading publics with their own rituals and modes of information which were integrated into the new, burgeoning colonial print culture. In the next chapter, Deb Aikat gives a historical account of how important the period of Emergency (1975–7) was for India's media, and how this brief period changed the way Indian journalism evolved thereafter. Most importantly, for Aikat, this critical period finally affirmed the press's watchdog role in postcolonial democracy and inspired journalists to question authority. The chapters by Daya Thussu and Radhika Parameswaran, Sunitha Chitrapu, and Roshini Verghese address two absences. For Thussu, the study of global media has been marked by an absence of the study of Indian news makers and, subsequently, news *about* India. Given the size of India's media, Thussu laments the lack of India's voice and distinctive perspective on the world's media stage. While India could easily be an important source of information on global forums like the United Nations Educational, Scientific and Cultural Organization, the International Telecommunications Union, and the World Intellectual Property Organization on such diverse and contested issues such as multiculturalism, intellectual property rights in the digital environment, and safeguarding of media plurality, India's presence and media voice have, thus far, been limited. Thussu argues that globalization of Indian journalism must include a concerted effort by varied actors to have their voices heard in the global media marketplace, via increased distribution, dissemination, and consumption. Parameswaran, Chitrapu, and Verghese address the absence of any serious and scholarly study of the history of Indian magazine journalism and the impact magazine journalism has had on Indian journalistic culture as a whole. By charting the rich history of magazine journalism, the authors suggest that instead of dying as some scholars had long predicted, Indian magazines have adjusted well to economic and technological challenges and readers' changing tastes and practices and have come to provide spaces for sustained analyses of news events, dissent against the state and corporate power, experimentation with long-form narrative styles and visual storytelling, and cultivating a new generation of journalists.

In part two, the chapters by Taberez Neyazi, Kalyani Chadha and Prasanth Bhat, Smeeta Mishra, Saayan Chattopadhyaya, and Monica Chadha give readers a broad-ranging and comprehensive account of emerging news culture with the proliferation of new media. These chapters also point to linguistic fragmentation of audiences, changing journalistic practices and ownership patterns, online forums as alternative news sites, and, alongside and inevitably, changing ideologies. Neyazi addresses a topic largely ignored in new media literature: the vernacularization of the internet and its implications for journalism. The use of the internet and mobile phones to mobilize groups and communities against each other has been accentuated with internet vernacularization, as platforms like WhatsApp and Facebook introduce multiple-language delivery and translations and substantial numbers of people from rural areas and small towns enter the digital space. While advocating digital literacy to develop more informed and educated internet users is on the government's agenda, placing a check on the disinformation economy is no easy task. With internet vernacularization, warns Neyazi, there have been growing cases of fake news and online propaganda which have resulted in riots, deaths, and lynchings. For Chadha and Bhat, online websites and forums have emerged as critical and crucial building blocks in establishing a right-wing ecosystem, and are constituting a parallel discursive arena where conservative activists are not only able to articulate their core principles, but can also define their own identity and develop oppositional discourses, challenging what they consider to be a biased mainstream media narrative. These online forums have become important alternatives to the mainstream public sphere and, as the authors' analysis of the 2014 general election shows, serve to articulate a rhetorical assault against mainstream news media. While Chadha and Bhat suggest that the impact of these sites is currently limited to urban, English-speaking elites, this situation is likely to change with rapid increase in the number of internet users. In her chapter, Mishra gives a panoramic view of the upheaval caused by the changing nature of news production and dissemination as the news industry transforms to meet the needs of an ever-interactive audience which demands social media connectivity. The result, Mishra writes, has been a growing practice of 'tweet first and work on the story later'. Even as news organizations struggle to identify suitable revenue models for their digital operations, according to the author, it will take time for the frenzy of social media usage in journalism to settle and for clear professional patterns to emerge. Meanwhile, reporters have to keep up with the speed of social media, with events being reported faster and involving global audiences. Through interviews with digital news startup owners, Chadha in her chapter explores the reasons why these sites were started. Her interviews reveal that the owners viewed themselves as a digital vanguard that wanted to publish stories that mainstream media failed to produce and, thus, target the very audiences the latter catered to. The founders looked at Western companies as exemplars, but knew that they would have to work towards developing a voice, brand, and content that specifically resonated with their Indian audiences. Chattopadhyaya explores mobile apps in the context of the 2014 general elections to show the ways in which news apps have connected to new content and produced new experiences and patterns of engagement with citizens and consumers. New media ecologies, Chattopadhyaya writes, have resulted in new opportunities in the distribution of and access to news within a rising culture of mobility. Such potentialities have been the result of interrelated factors, including the availability of cheap mobile devices, significant reduction in data charges, and rising demand for mobile-ready regional content backed by emerging app entrepreneurs in India. But such changes must be juxtaposed, the author suggests, with new centres of agency, interactions, and desires, and also the consolidation of a system for societies of control. Chattopadhyaya concludes that there has been an ideological shift in the way news is commodified, and while these mobile apps exploit the power of social media, big data analytics, and mobility to give the user a sense of control, they also function as 'modalities of control'.

No book on Indian journalism can be complete without discussions of marginalization and inequality. The third part is devoted to chapters which address marginalization, and address topics that are often marginalized in studies of Indian journalism. The outcry over the December 2012 rape of Jyoti Singh in Delhi, if nothing else, highlighted the deficiencies and strengths of the Indian media's coverage of gender issues. Dhiman Chattopadhyaya discusses how India's newsrooms treat stories about gender-related crimes such as rapes, and extends the discussion to the larger issue of gender imbalance in Indian newsrooms. Much has to change in Indian news practices, Chattopadhyaya writes, to regain public trust in the media to report on gender violence in a fair and accurate way. As an experienced journalist himself, the author makes various practical recommendations, for example, greater sensitivity training, increased research, gender balance in the newsroom, and focus on credibility and accuracy for editors and reporters when they report on gender issues. Like Chattopadhyaya, Arif Hussain Nadaf focuses on a topic which has escaped critical scrutiny among scholars: journalism in Kashmir. Kashmir is ubiquitously in the news, but little if any research exists which provides an in-depth, thoughtful, and critical look at the quality and nature of news about and from Kashmir. Nadaf undertakes this difficult task by analysing the coverage of the Kashmir conflict and regional politics in three different media sites—local Kashmiri media, Indian media, and Pakistani media. His findings ought not to surprise any student of South Asian journalism; Nadaf finds that both Indian and Pakistani media provide nationalistic interpretations of the conflict, exclusively through their own (patriotic) rhetorical visual lens and narratives. It is only the local Kashmiri media, according to Nadaf, which provides the closest, ear-to-the-ground coverage of events, even as these journalists face threats, harassment, and assassination attempts from insurgents and the military alike. Another topic largely ignored or merely given lip service in Indian journalism studies is environmentalism. If one thinks about the environmental costs of the sleek high-rises and serpentine highways which now dot the landscape of every major Indian city, one will recognize that mismanagement and overuse of India's once abundant forests have resulted in desertification, contamination, and soil depletion throughout the subcontinent. Environmental degradation thus has serious repercussions for the livelihoods of hundreds of millions of Indians who live off the land. Ram Awtar Yadav and Kanchan Malik get to the heart of why environmental journalism is important in India and how the so-called 'green beat' must be prioritized, even though in practice it has been marginalized. The chapter draws attention to the complexity of environmental reporting and how it is not just about covering natural disasters; that there are challenges and difficulties that journalists encounter in writing accurate narratives about topics which require interdisciplinary expertise and ethical and political commitment.

In the final section of the book, authors discuss the varied peda-gogical, ethical, and critical implications of evolving journalism practices. The section opens with a chapter by Usha Raman on the importance of a serious discussion about pedagogy in journalism studies. The author notes that the pragmatic aspect of the field seems to supersede any pedagogical engagement, as journalism courses are increasingly treated akin to assembly-line production work to feed an industry. Raman suggests that such a view of journalism education must change and that we need to have more classroom ethnographies and examination of individual teaching philosophies, which could give us further insights into how journalism pedagogy can improve and train future journalists, both intellectually and in development of skills. Mohan Dutta and Ashwini Falnikar's essay studies the way in which the 24/7 English news cycle operates as spectre of neoliberal violence, circulating as 'normal' the various forms of violence. According to Dutta and Falnikar, these instances of violence are presented as part and parcel of the neoliberal project being carried out across India in the name of growth, progress, and development. The authors conclude that the narratives of an unfet-tered free market and economic growth are used uncritically across news frames, offering a framework of trickle-down economics, and marking India as a site of aspirations toward the global free market, while simultaneously marking as the threatening 'other' any sites of resistance. Specifically examining religious violence and lynch-ings, Dutta and Falnikar conclude that India's neoliberal ambitions are 'perpetuated and made palatable' through the 24/7 news cycle, whose audiences are exclusively the aspiring urban middle classes who, on most occasions, do not critically engage in resisting such ideologies. Anup Kumar focuses on the evolving public sphere of Indian-language media. Kumar suggests that the English and the Hindi media foster different subcultures of news and function as a split public sphere. Indian-language media has more power to foster social action and mass agitation, while the English-language media has remained focused on building agendas and framing issues con-sequential to the elite power structure. Finally, Geeta Seshu's chapter is a thorough analysis of the everyday ethics of journalism practices with an emphasis on individual privacy. The author uses a case study approach to distinguish between what the public has a right to know, needs to know, and wants to know, the ways in which journalists go around gathering such information, and what implications this has for individuals. Seshu connects the pitfalls of violations of individual privacy with the parallel efforts by the state to increase surveillance and to control information.

These chapters represent a balance sheet of wide-ranging research about Indian journalism. As a caveat, it is important to say something about the omissions from the collection. Given the size, scope, and diversity of the field, it was impossible to include chapters on every aspect of Indian journalism, and thus this book can only give readers a bird's-eye view. Much needs to be mined regarding the multilingual, multidimensional nature of journalism practices as India's media expands and changes. The chapters are organized based on similar queries about the state of journalism, though some authors disagree with others about certain outcomes, practices, and conditions. Along with variations, readers will also note significant overlaps in methodologies and findings. Across the wide-ranging gamut of topics, authors most critically explore the three Ds of a new informational ecosphere, 'digitized, decentralized, and democratized' (Kaul 2011). It should be emphasized that the larger task is to produce a cohesive work on Indian journalism beyond the footnotes that the research gets in global media literature and among Euro-American scholars. Indian journalists face unique challenges and bring unique perspectives to academic discussions of global journalism. This academic volume, one of many to come, one hopes, can begin to fill the gap.

REFERENCES

Bandyopadhyay, S. (2013). 'Why Inequality in India Is on the Rise'. Retrieved from http://blogs.lse.ac.uk/southasia/2013/03/27/why-inequality-in-india-is-on-the-rise/ (accessed on 1 July 2016).

Chaffey, Dave (2018). 'Global Social Media Research Summary 2018', 28 March. Retrieved from https://www.smartinsights.com/social-media-marketing/social-media-strategy/new-global-social-media-research/.

Chatterji, T. (2017). 'Digital Urbanism in a Transitional Economy: A Review of India's Municipal e-Governance'. *Journal of Asian Public Policy*. doi.org /10.1080/17516234.2017.1332458.

Chopra, A. (2017). 'Number of Internet Users in India Could Cross 450 Million by June: Report'. Retrieved from http://www.livemint.com/

Industry/QWzIOYEsfQJknXhC3HiuVI/Number-ofInternet-users-in-India-could-cross-450-million-by.html (accessed on 1 July 2016).

Drèze, Jean and Amartya Sen (2013). *An Uncertain Glory: India and Its Many Contradictions*. Princeton: Princeton University Press.

FICCI-KPMG (2017). 'Indian Media and Entertainment Industry Report'. Retrieved from https://home.kpmg.com/in/en/home/insights/2017/03/ficci-media-industry-trends.html (accessed on 15 October 2017).

Kaul, V. (2011). 'Globalization and Media'. *Journal of Mass Communication and Journalism*. Retrieved from https://www.omicsonline.org/open-access/globalisation-and-media-2165-7912.1000105.php?aid=3360&view=mobile (accessed on 27 July 2017).

Khorana, S. (2012). 'Orientalizing the Emerging Media Capitals: The Age on India TV's "Hysteria"'. *Media International Australia*, 145(1): 39–49.

Motiram, S. and N. Sarma (2011). *Polarization, Inequality and Growth: The Indian Experience*. Retrieved from http://www.ecineq.org/milano/WP/ECINEQ2011-225.pdf (accessed on 11 July 2016).

Mudgal, V. (2011). 'Rural Coverage in the Hindi and English Dailies'. *Economic and Political Weekly*, 46(35): 2–11.

Parthasarthi, V., Alam Srinivas, Archna Shukla, Supriya Chotani, Anja Kovacs, Anuradha Raman, and Siddharth Narain (2012). 'Mapping Digital Media: India'. Retrieved from http://www.opensocietyfoundations.org/sites/default/files/mapping-digital-media-india-20130326.pdf (accessed on 15 July 2013).

Reporters without Borders (2017). World Press Freedom Index. Retrieved from https://rsf.org/en/ranking (accessed on 2 October 2017).

Thussu, D. (2005). 'Media Plurality or Democratic Deficit? Private TV and the Public Sphere in India'. In *Journalism and Democracy in Asia*, eds A. Romano and M. Bromley, pp. 54–65. London: Taylor and Francis.

Torri, M. (2015). 'The "Modi Wave": Behind the Results of the 2014 General Elections in India'. *International Spectator: Italian Journal of International Affairs*, 50(2): 56–74.

TRAI (Telecom Regulatory Authority of India) (2017). *Overview of Telecom and Broadcasting Sectors, Annual Report*. Retrieved from https://trai.gov.in/sites/default/files/AnnualReportEng16032018.pdf (accessed 11 September 2018).

Wu, H. (2016). '900 Million Indians Can't Get Online'. Retrieved from http://money.cnn.com/2016/03/09/technology/india-internet-access/index.html (accessed on 11 December 2016).

PART ONE

History and Evolving Changes in Journalism

· ·

CHAPTER TWO

From *Akhbarat* to Print

The Hybridity of News Culture in Early Indian Journalism

PRASUN SONWALKAR

. . . .

The civilized world affords no similar instance in the rise and culture of the arts, and to such perfection as Calcutta this day affords.... In splendor London now eclipses Rome ... and in similar aspects, Calcutta rivals the head of empire. But in no respect can she appear so eminently so, as in her publications.... If in Europe, the number of publications gives the ground to ratiocinate the learning and refinement of particular cities, we may place Calcutta in rank above Vienna, Copenhagen, Petersburg, Madrid, Venice, Turin, Naples or even Rome.

—William Duane, editor of *The World*, Calcutta, 15 October 1791

German historian Reinhart Kosseleck's theory of *sattelzeit*—referring to the 'saddle time' of about 1750 to 1850, when concepts took on their contemporary modern meaning—has been a useful device to unpack several ideas that developed during that defining period and influenced the course of global history. It was also 'saddle time' in colonial India, when the old was giving way to the new in complex ways, when the English East India Company that arrived to trade, went on to capture power and rule over millions across the subcontinent. Modern journalism began and developed during this crucial period in Indian history; many press laws in force today were enacted in their original incarnation during this period, when India became the site of the first fully formed print culture outside Europe and North America (Dharwadker 1997: 112). During this period, print journalism became the 'workshop' for experiments in prose style and literature in various Indian languages that had acquired, or were in the process of acquiring, a script; journalism was seen as the advanced third stage in the evolution of script, prose, and literature:

> All Indian languages did not pass through the three stages, namely, production of pedagogical materials, socio-religious debates and journalism in this period, but all of them finally had to go through these phases. The last two phases overlap one another as the religious debates were often carried through newspapers and periodicals.... Most of the important writers of this period, as well as of the periods that followed, were either journalists or served their apprenticeship in journals. (Das 1991: 75, 77).

A close study of this period of Indian journalism can enrich an understanding of contemporary realities, such as the domination of politics as a theme in news discourse despite the dumbing down of news since the early 1990s (Sonwalkar 2002); or the idea of 'paid news', which is not a recent phenomenon but was evident even in the first flush of English newspapers published from colonial Calcutta from 1780 onwards. The phrase 'change and continuity' has become something of a cliché in academic discourse, but like most such oft-repeated phrases, it reflects some realities. There is much in Indian journalism today that can be seen as a continuation of the early impulses, as well as changes that complement the continuities. There was adoption of the print-based British model of journalism (such as it was in the late eighteenth century), and also its adaption to Indian idioms, languages, and codes. If modern print journalism began in the colonial crucible, when the East India Company consolidated its rule in India through wars, conquest, and other means, the period also witnessed the Indian response to the new print-based mode of social communication that, until then, had been based on oral cultures of bazaar gossip, community plays, placarding, *mehfils*, and ballads. A significant site in the Indian response to colonial ideas and the then new print culture was the discourse of religion, best exemplified in the personality and writings of Rammohun Roy (1772–1833). Roy straddled the language-cultures of Bengali, Persian, Sanskrit, and English, and used print to challenge attacks on Hinduism by colonial writers and officials, for example, by countering claims in publications of the Baptist missionaries from Serampore, and later launching journals (the *Brahmunical Magazine, Sambad Kaumidi, Mirat-ul-Akhbar*) to present the Indian response.

However, as this chapter suggests, the idea of news and information was not new in India. It was not introduced by the British, but had a key role in the public sphere during the reign of the Mughal and Maratha empires, and several kingdoms. Information gathering by rulers has long existed in India and elsewhere, blurring the boundaries between surveillance and political intelligence, but it acquired an organized form during the reign of Emperor Akbar (1556–1605), when the system was expanded to record, check, and disseminate every action in the empire, however small. Central to the system was the Persian handwritten *akhbarat* (newsletter), a compilation describing events during a day or a week in some detail. It was a feature of almost all princely states and empires in precolonial India; a large number of 'akhbarats' preserved in libraries and archives in India, Britain, and France provide a rich resource for research. In the eighteenth century, Maratha rulers based in Poona used the services of a Delhi-based firm called Khemkaran Mansaram, which functioned as what Kulkarni (2005) called the world's first news agency, selling news to customers in Persian across the subcontinent, collected from its gatherers based in various parts of north India—long before the first modern news agency was set up (Havas, in 1835). In a landmark study of pre-colonial and colonial modes of social communication, Bayly concludes that 'print in itself did not create an information revolution. Rather, it speeded up the velocity and range of communication among existing communities of knowledge' (1996: 243).

I have elsewhere explored early Indian journalism in terms of its ethical roots (Sonwalkar 2015a) and how journalism itself became the focus of a largely forgotten chapter in Indian political history (Sonwalkar 2015b). This chapter looks at three interconnected aspects of early Indian journalism: the pre-colonial news system before print journalism began in English from 1780 onwards in Calcutta; the beginning and take-off of print-based journalism, first in English and later in Bengali, Persian, Hindi, Marathi, and other languages; and an example of continuity and collision of religious and linguistic worlds in the early nineteenth century in print, sparked by the use of the word *tursa* in a news item in Roy's Persian journal, *Mirat-ul-Akhbar* (Mirror of News). As Pernau and Jaffery suggest, 'the break between the akhbarat and the printed newspapers is by no way as deep as contemporary British sources would have it' (2009: 31). Much remains to be mined from this early period, as evident from the surviving print journals (some of them digitized) and extensive records of the East India Company in archives in Britain, India, and elsewhere. The three aspects are characteristic of the 'sattelzeit' of Indian journalism. There were impulses of continuity between the pre-colonial and postcolonial worlds at least until the Mutiny of 1857, as journalism progressively became the site of sustained cultural and political encounters that involved renegotiation of and adaptation to new realities by the colonizer and the colonized.

THE WORLD OF *AKHBARAT*

Before *akhbarat* (derived from the Persian-Arabic *khabr* for news) was elaborately expanded during the Mughal Empire, court proceedings and information were routinely chronicled across the subcontinent, for example, the *buranji* that compiled information during the thirteenth century Ahom rule in Assam, and the eighteenth century *bakhar*, for which Maratha rulers had news writers who described events and developments, the best known being the rhetorical description of the Maratha debacle in the third battle of Panipat in 1761 (some scholars believe bakhar was inspired by akhbarat). Information gathering was institutionalized during Akbar's rule, permitting exchange between the imperial and regional courts through news writers. It was the first instance of information being systematically used as an advance warning system by those in power, with arrangements to counter-check information sent by news writers (*waqai nigar* and *waqai navis*) by a parallel channel of reporting by spies (*khufiya navis* and *harkara*s) (see below). According to Pernau, under the akhbarat system,

> [L]etters from the imperial envoys at the nobles' courts on the one hand, and the record of the emperor's daily proceedings on the other hand were compiled into a daily account which was then publicly read out during the durbar. The envoys of the nobles in turn took notes of this information and sent it back to their patrons. In contrast to the gathering of information by spies—which went on side by side with it—these news-writers were the central institution of a system guaranteeing an open flow of information between the emperor and the nobles, and at times also among the peripheral courts. (2003: 107)

Several scholars have explored the rich resource of akhbarat, mainly Jadunath Sarkar,[1] S. C. Sanial (1911, 1928), C. A. Bayly (1996), Abdus Salam Khurshid (1988), Jagadish Narayan Sarkar (1967), G. H. Khare (1967), B. D. Verma (1949), and Margrit Pernau and Yunus Jaffery (2009). A large number of akhbarats from various periods are based in the British Museum, Royal Asiatic Society Library, Rajasthan State Archives (Bikaner), Panjab University Library, Bodleian Library (Oxford), Bharat Itihas Sanshodhak Mandal (Pune), and the Bibliothèque Nationale de France (Paris). Their studies have rarely figured in research into journalism or media history, but demonstrate that every provincial and subdivisional headquarters under Mughal rule had recorders of events; in the capital, an imperial news writer recorded court events. The network outside the capital was complemented by a parallel network of spies and runners (harkaras) dispatched under the charge of a head postmaster (*daroga-i-dak*). The newsletters from the reign of Ahmad Shah (1751–2) were described by Verma:

> These ... are in Persian and are of uniform size, 8½ × 4 inches and are written on both sides of the paper which is of a brown colour, with great economy, and every inch of the paper is meticulously utilised, so as to minimise the cost and weight. They have been written in the variety of script called in Persian *Shikastah*, which is very difficult to decipher. (1949: ii–iii)

They were written and produced either daily or on a bi-weekly basis.

The system had four categories of personnel, who sent two kinds of reports to the capital, written, and oral. There were three categories of writers and one category of oral reporters, but this distinction was not always maintained: waqai navis or waqai nigar (also known as *akhbar navis*, a writer or surveyor of events), *sawanih navis* or *sawanih nigar* (also a recorder of events), khufiya navis (secret writer), and harkara (literally a courier of news but also a spy who carried oral news and sent secret newsletters). The writers, posted in various parts of the empire (including military stations), were encouraged to report facts without fear of antagonizing the ruler. The sawanih nigar was intended to act as a check on the waqai navis, because the latter was often suspected to be corrupt and in collusion with local officers, which affected the credibility of his dispatches. Most of the contents of the official akhbarats were of a routine, mundane nature, set down in bare-bones prose, such as setting out details of the emperor's health, who he met, when he awoke and rested, the petitions he received and the decisions taken. But those sent to the capital from different parts of the empire contained much more. Sarkar (1967) lists several examples of Akbar punishing governors or asking for explanations from them on issues that came to his notice through the akhbarat. The vast majority of the newsletters met the requirements of the empire's administration, but some were of literary value, such as the diary of the conquest of Cooch Behar and Assam in the seventeenth century by Mir Jumla's waqai navis Ibn Muhammad Wali Ahmad, author of *Fathiyya-i-ibriyya*, in which he is considered to have risen to the level of a historian.

Many newsletters were written for British representatives in Indian courts. As the Mughal Empire was on the decline in the mid-eighteenth century and the East India Company moved to acquire power, the latter made efforts to tap native sources of information and intelligence to consolidate its rule. Khurshid notes that the gradual deterioration of the state newsletters and the growing British presence led to the creation of private akhbarats, sponsored mainly by the erstwhile news writers who were out of jobs; several private newsletters transformed into sites of opposition to British rule, exhorting Hindus and Muslims to unite against 'the low wretches of

Europeans who had usurped sovereignty of the country' (Khurshid 1988: 84). The system of newsgathering finds mention in written notes and accounts of East India Company officials; they were the focus of at least two notes by George Eden (Lord Auckland), who was the governor-general of India from 1836 to 1842, and by Thomas B. Macaulay.

At a time when print journalism had proliferated beyond Calcutta and the akhbarat continued to coexist in the new environment, Eden wrote:

> Princes and others who can afford it have their news writers, or employ people established in that line where they think it of sufficient importance to see intelligence. Fabricators and collectors of nonsense, of gossip, of intelligence, and of lies, exist probably in all great towns. The manuscript papers derived from these sources are private; anything may be inserted in them without scruple, and in critical times ... the most absurd reports and mischievous misrepresentations were made to agitate men's minds, and to produce evil which might have been better prevented or guarded against if the circulation had been effected by printed papers. (Quoted in Khurshid 1988: 86)

Macaulay agreed with Eden:

> The character of the manuscript gazettes is, I believe, what the Governor-General describes it to be. They are filled with trivial details, with idle reports and often with extravagant falsehood suited to the capacity of ignorant and credulous readers. They are often scurrilous far beyond any papers that appear in print either in English or in any native languages. They often contain abuse of the Government and its servants and sarcasms on our national character and manners.... The number of manuscript gazettes daily dispatched from the single town of Delhi cannot ... be precisely known, but it is calculated ... at hundred and twenty. Under these circumstances it is perfectly clear that the influence of the manuscript gazettes on the native population must be very much more extensive than that of the printed papers (in the native languages whose circulation in India by dawk (post) does not now—1836—exceed three hundred. (Quoted in Khurshid 1988: 86-7)

The lines of continuity were evident when the pre-colonial form of communication continued to influence public discourse after the East India Company acquired power over almost the entire subcontinent by the early nineteenth century. As the next section shows, the akhbarat continued to be a major source of news and information when print journals proliferated from 1780 onwards. Colonial officials had their own arrangements to acquire local information, but they also monitored private newsletters that appeared in the public domain, often read out to groups of people in bazaars and other public places. Irritation and frustration were expressed in official notes over their contents, but the restrictions imposed on print journals from 1799 could not be applied to the akhbarat.

The next section traces the lines of continuity from the era of the akhbarat to the early years of print journalism, which transformed colonial India's public sphere and provided a vigorous site for the expression of early Indian nationalism.

THE ONSET OF PRINT JOURNALISM

Several studies (such as Barns 1940; Ahmed 1965; Sankhdher 1984) have chronicled the introduction and growth of the Indian press since the first publication of *Hicky's Bengal Gazette or the Original Calcutta General Advertiser* in 1780. The origin of modern journalism in India presents a unique case study of the idea of 'British journalism abroad', of how the ways of doing journalism travelled from England to various colonies of the British Empire, how the 'model' was received, adopted, and constructively adapted by the local elites, and how journalism of this period prepared the groundwork for the use of the press as a powerful weapon during India's freedom struggle. According to standard historical accounts, Indian nationalism began in 1885 with the formation of the Indian National Congress, or during the preparatory phase of agitation politics in the preceding decade. However, the vast material comprising handwritten records of the East India Company and surviving publications suggest that, as early as 1835, print journalism had emerged as a site where the first impulses of Indian nationalism were being expressed. Journalism had also become an effective tool for social and religious reform. By 1835, Indians were already using print journalism to lecture to the British on how to run their empire, and writing extensively about the Irish and the revolutionary struggles in Spain and Italy as part of veiled attacks on the Company's rule in India.

Calcutta became the setting and crucible of the first sustained cultural encounter between Indian intellectuals and the West. In the late eighteenth century (1780), the white population in the town was less than 1,000; in the 1837 census, 3,138 English were returned, with soldiers forming the main element of the community. A part of Calcutta came to be known as the 'white town', where the British based themselves and sought to recreate British cultural life through news, goods, music, theatre, and personnel that arrived and left for England by sea. As Marshall (2000: 324) notes, 'White Calcutta sustained a remarkable number of newspapers and journals in English. Between 1780 and 1800, 24 weekly or monthly magazines came into existence.... The total circulation of English-language publications was put at 3000.... These are astonishing figures for so small a community.' It was the era of the journalist as publicist, as editors—in England and in colonial India—stamped their personalities on their journals, often entering into vicious attacks against rival editors and officials of the East India Company.

Some historians see Christian missionaries and the first English journals as the two 'unofficial Westernizing influences' in early colonial India. The English journals, according to Spear (1978: 279), 'were the unofficial apostles of western influence and all the more effective for being unofficial. Further they stimulated the development of a genuine Indian press, at first in the local languages and then in English.... from gossipy and irresponsible beginnings, the press came to exercise an important influence on Indian life.' But, alert to the dangers of Jacobinism, officials of the East India Company were uneasy with the proliferation of journals, and matters first came to a head on the issue of press freedom during the governorship of Richard Wellesley (1798–1805). In 1799, he introduced regulations for the press which stipulated that no newspaper be published until the proofs of the whole paper, including advertisements, were submitted to the colonial government and approved; violation invited deportation to England. Until 1818, the regulations applied only to the English journals, because until that year there were no journals in Indian languages. Indian-language journals emerged from 1818 onwards, first in Bengali and soon after in Persian, Hindi, Marathi, and other languages. Editors of English journals, such as James Silk Buckingham (*Calcutta Journal*), encouraged the growth of the 'native press'. In 1823, as one of the first Indians in journalism, Rammohun Roy led the famous response in the form of two memorials against severe press restrictions imposed by the acting governor-general, John Adam.

The proliferation of print journalism—first in Calcutta and later in Madras, Bombay, and other towns of British India—led to the Company government focusing on regulating the press. This was formalized in rules and regulations promulgated in 1799, 1818, and 1823. In 1835, the acting governor-general, Charles Metcalfe, aided by Macaulay, removed licensing and other restrictions on the press through Act no. XI. These regulations and laws formed the basis of subsequent colonial era press laws until India became independent in 1947; some of them continue to be in force in amended form in India today. By 1835, the idea of a free press had been much debated and immortalized in the Metcalfe Hall, a major landmark in Calcutta, which was built with public subscription in the style of imposing empire architecture in honour of Metcalfe.

However, less focus has been devoted in studies of the Indian press to the continuing salience of the akhbarat in the then burgeoning print culture. It is important not to exaggerate the role of the akhbarat vis-à-vis the print journals, but in north India, in particular, the newsletters played the role of a news agency, providing much content to print journals. As Indian or 'native' news increased in the English journals, the akhbarat proved a rich source of information, even if it was not the only source. After the East India Company consolidated its hold over most of India by the early nineteenth century following the decline of the Mughal Empire, newsletters continued to be produced and dis-tributed by various Indian courts, as well as privately by former news writers. Not only did print journals draw from the akhbarat, the latter also reproduced content from the former.

Pernau and Jaffery (2009) reproduce an akhbarat of 1830 that has several references to the print journals published from Calcutta. One reference states: 'Through the English newspapers it became known that these days the Honourable Lord Lough Sahib Bahadur had set on a journey to visit all the countries the British "sarkar" had subdued'; another adds: 'Through the French newspapers it became known that the king of France had sent 340 battleships with colourful flags to subdue the islands of al Bahrain' (Pernau and Jaffery 2009: 364). It was not a simple case of a homogenous 'West' imposing perspectives of the 'Orient', but involved blurring of boundaries:

> Neither the *akhbarat* nor the English and vernacular newspapers existed in isolation. The exchange of complimentary copies among the newspapers and extensive quotations from one another—usually in a separate column—were the rule, thus linking the local publics and creating a network of common knowledge and opinion on current affairs, which extended, if not to an all-India level, at least across Bengal and Hindustan. (Pernau and Jaffery 2009: 25)

Contents of the akhbarat dominated the first print journals in Persian and Urdu, following not only its genre and form, but also what constituted news. *Jam-i-Jahan Numa*, the first printed Persian journal published in Calcutta from May 1822, had most of its contents derived from the akhbarat of courts in Delhi, Lucknow, Jaipur, Poona, Lahore, and the Holkar camp. The first issue of its Urdu supplement launched in December 1824, for example, was almost entirely devoted to an akhbarat from Jaipur. The newsletters were also reflected prominently in English journals. The first issue of *Calcutta Gazette* published in 1784 had on its first page the court newsletter of the Mughal emperor in Delhi under the title 'Khulasa-i-Darbar-i-Mualla ba Dar-ul-Khilafat Shahjahanabad'. The English version appeared on the opposite page, and the practice continued for several weeks. On 22 April, the journal reported: 'The Hindustan newspapers (akhbars) received since our last publication remove all doubt as to the occupation of Attock by the forces of Runjeet Singh' (quoted in Khurshid 1988: 89).

The Mughal system of newsgathering was favourably cited by Roy in the lengthy second 'memorial' to make the case against Adam's press restrictions of 1823 (see Sonwalkar 2015b). Using the rhetorical strategy of mixing fulsome praise with caution, warning, and criticism, the memorial sent to London recalled world history and put it to the king:

> Notwithstanding the despotic power of the Mogul princes who formerly ruled over the country, and that their conduct was often cruel and arbitrary, yet the wise and virtuous among them always employed

two intelligencers at the residence of their Nawabs or Lord Lieutenants, Ukhbar-nuvees, or news-writer, who published an account of whatever happened, and a Khoofea-nuvees, or confidential correspondent, who sent a private and particular account of every occurrence worthy of notice; and although these Lord Lieutenants were often particular friends or near relations of the price, he did not trust entirely to themselves for a faithful and impartial report of their administration, and degraded them when they appeared to deserve it, either for their own faults, or for their negligence in not checking the delinquencies of their subordinate officers; which shows, that even the Mogul princes, although their form of Government admitted of nothing better, were convinced, that in a country so rich and so replete with temptations, a restraint of some kind was absolutely necessary to prevent the abuses that are liable to flow from the possession of power. (Sen 1990: 80)

Thus, contrary to claims by some colonial officials and scholars that the Indian-language journals that appeared from 1818 were derivatives of the English journals launched since 1780, the reality was complex. The Mughal system of newsgathering not only featured prominently in the print-based news discourse, but also figured in a minute dated 10 October 1822, by W. B. Bayley, chief secretary, highlighting what he saw as the dangers of a free press in India: 'I believe it is pretty well known, that as far as native feeling is concerned regarding the Press, the impression … is that Mr Buckingham is an Akhbar Nuvees or News Writer stationed by the King of England in Calcutta, to report and deliver his opinions freely respecting the conduct of the local government. This is ridiculous enough at present….'[2] C. A. Bayly makes the wider point that 'the information order of colonial India retained distinctly Indian features, even while it was absorbing and responding to the profound influences set in motion by the European rulers' (1996: 9). The next section presents an example of the contrast and confluence of Indian and Western impulses in the colonial cauldron through the use of the Persian word 'tursa' in a news item in Roy's *Mirat-ul-Akhbar*.

ROW OVER 'TURSA'

The last week of August 1822 was a relatively peaceful period. By this time, most of the subcontinent had been brought under the influence of the East India Company through a series of conquests and battles beginning with the Battle of Plassey (1757) and a controversial system of indirect rule through alliances with regional powers. However, a small news item published on 29 August on the front page of the Calcutta-based English daily, *Bengal Hurkaru*, caused ripples for several days. It was symbolic of the complex matrix of religion, power, language, tradition, modernity, and the texts and context in which print journalism began in colonial India. On that Thursday, the *Bengal Hurkaru* followed a pattern that, by 1822, had become a template: its contents included a summary of news and extracts from American and British newspapers lately arrived by ship, some local news items, government notifications, poetry, and pages of advertisements offering goods from home that promised to recreate the 'British world' in India.

The day's issue had a summary of newspapers that had arrived on the *George* from Salem, an extract from 'that ably conducted paper Scotsman', news about 'Lancaster Assizes', 'Manchester Transactions', and three news items on the front page translated from *Mirat-ul-Akhbar*, which had been launched in Calcutta in April of that year. The three items were: (*a*) three boats belonging to Moteechund Sahookar being robbed on the Ganges on 25 July; (*b*) a three-storey house near a cemetery in Patna collapsing, killing at least 23 people; and (*c*) a widow's son drowning in nearby Serampore (a Danish colony). At a time when the contents of a journal were freely reproduced by rival and other publications, the English translation of the news from Patna was reproduced the next day by *Calcutta Journal*:

> *Fatal accident.* The three-storey house of Mohummed Hossain Khan, which stood near the burial-ground of the Infidels, fell down and 15 persons (passengers and those who lived near its bottom) were killed outright by this unexpected event, and six of other seven men, who were with great difficulty taken out half dead from the ruins, died subsequently. After a few days, when they removed the bricks, they found one woman still alive with a dead child by her, but she was rendered so feeble that there was scarcely any hope of her recovery. Two persons who were passing by, died by the fall of the wall. The family experienced no danger, nor any great loss, except in glass and other such articles of furniture as are most apt to be injured. It is a matter

of astonishment that a house so firmly founded should fall, except by constant showers of rain, or the ravages of time. (*Calcutta Journal*, 30 August 1822)

Much was lost in translation when the Persian word 'tursa' in the original news item in *Mirat-ul-Akhbar* was rendered as 'infidels' in English ('burial-ground of the Infidels'). It provoked much criticism from the editor and readers of another journal, the Tory *John Bull in the East*, which had a history of sparring with the liberal *Calcutta Journal*. 'It appears to us', wrote the *John Bull* in an editorial, 'that the word *tursa* was not originally used in any other than a degrading sense, and that it cannot be respectfully employed to our countrymen in India, however low their condition may be' (Banerji 1931: 507). In turn, the *Bengal Hurkaru* ridiculed *John Bull*, while the *Calcutta Journal* pointed out that it was not responsible for the original translation, nor did the news item first appear in its columns. The row soon led to one of the first major counter-narratives asserting the Indian world view in the English language by Roy, who had earlier countered attacks on Hinduism by Baptist missionaries in print.

In two long letters to the editor of the *Calcutta Journal*, Roy explained, politely but firmly, quoting chapter and verse from ancient Persian texts, that 'tursa' 'does not signify Infidels, but according to the general usage of the word, it means Christians' (Banerji 1931: 508). Refuting *John Bull*'s criticism (published on 31 August) of the word's alleged derogatory use, he wrote that he 'felt indeed surprised and shocked at this *groundless, illiberal* and *hurtful* charge of the Editor, in a Public Paper' (italics in original), and went on to state why the charge was groundless, illiberal, and hurtful. Several British residents in Patna and Calcutta joined in, writing to the journals quoting more Persian texts to support or refute the contention that 'tursa' had been used in a derogatory way.

To ward off criticism, Roy wrote in his first letter of 3 September 1822 to the editor of *Calcutta Journal*, quoting from 'Boorhani Qatiu, A Dictionary of the Persian Language' by Thomas Roebuck that had been published in Calcutta in 1818:

> I quote the standard Dictionary of the Persian language, which was some time ago printed by the late Capt. Roebuck, with the assistance

of the *principal officers of the College of Fort William,* (page 236) after giving the meanings derivable from the root, to wit, 'fearer, fearful, fancy-sick', the author says, 'it also signifies Christians and worshippers of fire', without confining the application to a degraded sense.... The Editor of JOHN BULL concludes with the following remark, in a triumphant tone, 'It the word Tursa cannot be respectfully employ(ed) to our *countrymen in India* however low their condition might be!' But JOHN BULL should know that there *are* countries where neither the Conductor of an English nor of a Persian Paper would feel himself at liberty to sue disrespectful or insolent expressions towards persons of any faith or complexion, of *whatever country* they might be, in violation of the rules of politeness, and of that courtesy and liberality which are reciprocally due from persons of all creed and climes. (Banerji 1931: 508; italics in original)

As mentioned previously, religion was one of the sites of controversy in early Indian journalism. The tursa controversy was symbolic of the multiple levels at which the early colonial cultural encounter unfolded. It was significant for its many texts, subtexts, and context, the use of different language-worlds (Persian, English, Bengali), religions (Islam, Christianity, Hinduism), politics (Tory, Whig), and power dynamics between the colonizer and the colonized. It also exposed the dangers of a news culture in which content is uncritically reproduced, particularly that translated from Indian-language journals into English. In earlier counterarguments, Roy had adopted the ancient Indian debating style of *purvapaksha*—('if it is said/then the reply is')—but in the two letters to *Calcutta Journal* written in near-Addisonian English, he used the English academic style, quoting with chapter-verse citations and direct quotations, a style he had become familiar with from the theological writings of John Locke and other Unitarian writers.

Roy's *Mirat-ul-Akhbar* also figured prominently in Bayley's lengthy minute, citing a report in it of the death of Thomas Middleton, the bishop of Calcutta:

After some laudatory remarks of his learning and dignity the article concludes by stating that the Bishop having been now relieved from the cares and anxieties of this world, had 'tumbled on the shoulders of the mercy of God, the Father, God the Son, and God the Holy Ghost'....

the editor's known disposition for theological controversy had led him to seize an occasion for publishing remarks on the Trinity, which, although covertly and insidiously conveyed, strike me as being exceedingly offensive.... The expression coming from a known impugner of the doctrine of the Trinity, could only be considered as ironical.... In the paper of the 19th July he enters into a long justification of his obituary notice and affectedly misunderstanding the real purport of the objection taken to his introduction of the mention of [the] Trinity, he makes use of observations which in my mind constitute an aggravation of the offence.[3]

* * *

The limitations of the binary of 'West' and 'Orient' or 'the rest' is being increasingly recognized and addressed in recent media research as well as in the 'connected histories' strand of research in history. This chapter seeks to contribute to studies that show the impact of Western models, frames, and notions in non-Western setting are anything but clear and linear, but present complexities of adoption, adaption, and hybridity. As Murdoch (2011: 137, 138) states,

> It is indisputable that much communication scholarship has been based, either openly or by default, on the assumption that accounts developed to address Western experiences and ambitions have universal applicability.... Not only does the simple oppositional contrast between West and East ignore the complexities and contradictions of cultural formations in continual movement, it reproduces the dualistic thinking that critics see as the major limitations of Western world-views.

In short, this chapter suggests that the *sattelzeit* of Indian journalism was a complex project marked by permeability; there was no complete switch-off of earlier forms of social communication as the print culture proliferated across colonial India. The early print journals in English and Indian languages demonstrated more complexity than has been acknowledged; they were not merely offshoots or derivatives of the first English journals. The less acknowledged work in the discourse of media history of scholars named above suggests the continuities in social communication that coexisted with the new forms introduced by the British, initially in colonial Calcutta and later across the subcontinent.

NOTES

1. Jadunath Sarkar's English translation of *Oudh Akhbarat* (1786) is available in the National Library, India; S.C. Sanial (1911) 'The History of the Press in India—Manuscript Newspapers', *The Calcutta Review*, 1–47; S.C. Sanial (1928) 'The Newspapers of the Later Mogul Period', *Islamic Culture*, Vol. II, No. 1, January; Bayly (1996); Khurshid (1988); J.N. Sarkar (1967) 'Newswriters in Mughal India', in S.P. Sen (ed.) *The Indian Press*, Calcutta: Institute of Historical Studies; G.H. Khare (1967) 'Newsletters of the Medieval Period', in S.P. Sen (ed.) *The Indian Press*; Verma (1949); Pernau and Jaffery (2009).
2. Bengal Public Consultations, P/10/55, British Library.
3. Bengal Public Consultations, P/10/55, British Library.

REFERENCES

Ahmed, A. F. S. (1965). *Social Ideas and Social Change in Bengal, 1818–1835*. Leiden: E. J. Brill.

Banerji, B. N. (1931). 'Rammohun Roy as a Journalist', *Modern Review*, May, 507–s15.

Barns, M. (1940). *The Indian Press: A History of the Growth of Public Opinion in India*. London: G. Allen and Unwin.

Bayly, C. A. (1996). *Empire and Information: Intelligence Gathering and Social Communication in India, 1780–1870*. Cambridge: Cambridge University Press.

Das, S. K. (1991). *A History of Indian Literature, 1800–1910: Western Impact, Indian Response*. New Delhi: Sahitya Akademi.

Dharwadker, V. (1997). 'Print Culture and Literary Markets in Colonial India'. In *Language Machines: Technologies of Literary and Cultural Production*, eds J. Masten, P. Stallybrass, and N. J. Vickers, pp. 108–33. London: Routledge.

Khare, G. H. (1967). 'News-Letters of the Medieval Period'. In *The Indian Press*, ed. S. P. Sen. Calcutta: Institute of Historical Studies.

Khurshid, A. S. (1988). 'Newsletters in the Orient, with Special Reference to the Indo Pakistan Sub-Continent'. National Institute of Historical and Cultural Research, Islamabad.

Kulkarni, G. T. (2005). 'M/s Khemkaran Mansaram: The World's First Ever News Selling Agency during the Eighteenth Century Maratha Rule'. In *Webs of History: Information, Communication and Technology from Early to Post-Colonial India*, eds A. K. Bagchi, D. Sinha, and B. Bagchi, pp. 145–63. New Delhi: Manohar.

Marshall, P. J. (2000). 'The White Town of Calcutta under the Rule of the East India Company'. *Modern Asian Studies*, 34(2): 307–31.

Murdoch, G. (2011). 'Journeys to the West: The Making of Asian Modernities'. In *De-Westernizing Communication Research*, ed. G. Wang, pp. 137–56. New York: Routledge.

Pernau, M. (2003). 'The Delhi Urdu Akhbar: Between Persian Akhbarat and English Newspapers'. *Annual of Urdu Studies*, 18: 105–31.

Pernau, M. and Y. Jaffery (2009). *Information and the Public Sphere: Persian Newsletters from Mughal Delhi*. Oxford: Oxford University Press.

Sanial, S. C. (1911). 'The History of the Press in India: Manuscript Newspapers', *Calcutta Review*, 1–47.

——— (1928). 'The Newspapers of the Later Mogul Period', *Islamic Culture*, vol. II, no. 1, January.

Sankhdher, B. M. (1984). *Press, Politics and Public Opinion in India*. New Delhi: Deep and Deep.

Sarkar, J. N. (1967). 'Newswriters in Mughal India'. In *The Indian Press*, ed. S. P. Sen. Calcutta: Institute of Historical Studies.

Sen, A. K. (1990). *Raja Rammohun Roy: The Representative Man*, 3rd edn. Calcutta: Calcutta Text Book Society.

Sonwalkar, P. (2002). 'Murdochization of the Indian Press: From By-Line to Bottom-Line'. *Media Culture and Society*, 24(6): 821–34.

———. (2015a). 'For the Public Good: Rammohun Roy and His Tryst with Journalism Ethics'. In *Media Ethics and Justice in the Age of Globalisation*, eds S. Rao and H. Wasserman, pp. 155–73. London: Palgrave Macmillan.

———. (2015b). 'Indian Journalism in the Colonial Crucible: A Nineteenth Century Story of Political Protest'. *Journalism Studies*, 16(5): 624–36.

Spear, P. (1978). *The Oxford History of Modern India, 1740–1975*. New Delhi: Oxford University Press.

Verma, B. D. (1949). *Newsletters of the Mughal Court*. Bombay: Government Central Press.

CHAPTER THREE

An Inexorable Watchdog of Democracy

Theorizing Press Censorship in 1975–7 as a Watershed Media Moment in India

DEB AIKAT

. . . .

A Government that has to rely on the criminal law amendment Act and similar laws, that suppresses the press and literature, that bans hundreds of organisations, that keeps people in prison without trial and that does so many things that are happening in India today, is a Government that has ceased to have even a shadow of a justification for its existence.

—Jawaharlal Nehru (1889–1964) in his April 1936 speech as president of the Indian National Congress party in Lucknow.

Deriding India's British rulers for 'deprivation of civil liberties', Jawaharlal Nehru exhorted the people of India in 1936 to wrest unconditional freedom from British rule (Nehru 1936). Eleven years later, in 1947, India attained independence from British rule. As the first prime minister of independent India, Nehru gained renown as democracy's dedicated defender, deeply committed to press freedom among other democratic values. Nehru's 1936 expression of derision towards the British government has profound relevance for the period of press censorship in India in 1975–7, as this chapter will argue.

As a prominent institution of democracy, India's media function as an inexorable watchdog that informs the community and safeguards freedom. India's press, empowered by a rising readership, an avid audience, dedicated journalists, and fearless whistleblowers, has survived egregious assaults on press freedom rights. The quest for free speech in India dates back to the trials and tribulations of the press under British rule in the eighteenth century. In later years, the pursuit of free speech has persisted despite endemic assaults on press freedom rights. The first and only Emergency imposed in India in the twentieth century disbanded democracy, suspended civil liberties, and jailed opposition leaders.

In more than four decades since the 1975–7 Emergency in India, several journalists, historians, and novelists have authored their interpretations of the period in books such as *The Emergency: Indian Democracy's Darkest Hour* (Prakash 2017), *The Emergency: A Personal History* (Kapoor 2015), *Emergency Retold* (Nayar 2013), *JP Movement, Emergency, and India's Second Freedom* (Devasahayam 2012), *A Fine Balance: A Novel* (Mistry 1997), *Indira Gandhi and Her Power Game* (Thakur 1979), and *Two Faces of Indira Gandhi* (Vasudev 1977). In a 1987 study, Ramaprasad compared *New York Times* reportage on India over three periods—pre-censorship, the 21-month Emergency period, and post-censorship. Western concern about news from a country during a period of censorship suggests that the *Times*'s coverage of India would be more favourable during the mid-1970s period of press censorship in India. However, Ramaprasad's study found no differences, in slant or topics, over the periods studied. Barring some books cited in this chapter and the Ramaprasad study, scholarly analyses of the Emergency, are sparse, at best. This chapter seeks to bridge that gap in the scholarly literature.

Based on case study research into the misuse of media during the Emergency, and on the subsequent rise of media and journalism, this chapter explores the media's role as watchdog of India's democracy during and after the Emergency and concludes that press censorship during the Emergency constituted a watershed in the history of Indian media. The Emergency energized free speech norms and inspired a new breed of journalists who continue to engage, entertain, educate, enrich, empower, and enlighten India's democratic society.

With a surging population of over 1.3 billion people, India is the world's largest democracy and an important global player in business, politics, and the media. By scope and definition, India's media comprise news, information, and entertainment products and media platforms in traditional and digital formats. While the traditional media include print, radio, and television, digital media encompass news blogs, online videos, social media, mobile media, and other media content created, viewed, distributed, modified, archived, and curated in digital formats.

India has gained distinction as a nation where 'print is king', but 'digital is coming on strong' (Kilman 2015). Since digital media were virtually non-existent during the 1975–7 Emergency, this chapter's qualitative case study sets aside analysis of digital media to concentrate on traditional media. As a venerable guardian of democracy, India's media foster free speech by serving as an inexorable watchdog. The next section analyses the impact of press censorship during the 1975–7 Emergency.

MISUSE OF MEDIA DURING EMERGENCY, 1975–7

Nehru's 1936 criticism of the British government, reproduced in the epigraph to this chapter, represents a poignant defence of free speech. The Government of India's 1977 white paper on the misuse of mass media during the 1975–7 Emergency featured, as the first of three epigraphs, Nehru's quotation in its frontispiece (GoI 1977). The second epigraph featured the twentieth-century British lawyer Sir Ivor Jennings's reasoned analysis in 1959 of the British statesman Oliver Cromwell's aperçu, 'Not a dog barked', upon dissolving the Long Parliament in 1653. The third and final epigraph accentuated the line '[Adolf] Hitler was never told the uncomfortable truth', in a brief excerpt from the German Conservative Revolutionary

Hermann Rauschning's 1939 book, *Hitler Speaks: A Series of Political Conversations with Adolf Hitler on His Real Aims* (GoI 1977).

Truth be told, the Government of India had rarely published white papers on free speech violations since independence from British rule in 1947. Besides that rarity extraordinaire, government white papers seldom present a medley of epigraphs about Nehru, Cromwell, and Hitler on the same page, let alone on the frontispiece of a prominent government report. The epigraphs in the 1977 white paper implicitly convey an important lesson about the role of the press as a watchdog of democracy. They embody a searing rebuke and contain the impish irony that Nehru's daughter, Indira Gandhi (1917–1984), serving as India's third prime minister, promulgated in 1975 the nation's first and only Emergency that resulted in the disbanding of democracy, suspension of civil liberties, and incarceration of opposition leaders (Hart 1976).

Reacting to opposition leaders' threat to rebel, Indira Gandhi asked the then obeisant President Fakhruddin Ali Ahmed to declare a state of emergency on 25 June 1975 (Nayar 1977; Thakur 1977). In succeeding hours, authorities shut off the electricity to stop the presses of major newspapers in New Delhi, the capital of India and seat of all three branches of the Government of India (Thakur 1977; Vasudev 1977). In a surreptitious move, the police arrested opposition leaders, journalists critical of the ruling party, members of Parliament, and political activists (Nayar 1977; Mehta 1978). The harsh action intimidated government officials. The sudden declaration of Emergency surprised the Union Cabinet ministers who were not consulted about the Emergency. The ministers learned about the Emergency through phone calls and media reports, like the common people (Dhar 2000; Tarlo 2001; Chandra 2003).

The Emergency imposed monumental restrictions on free speech. Over July–August 1975, Indira Gandhi abolished the Press Council, merged the major news agencies into one agency, modified advertisement policy, withdrew housing facilities to journalists, and warned foreign correspondents of deportation if they failed to follow the rules of censorship (GoI 1977: Appendix, pp. 1–6). During the mid-1970s, the news media in India mainly comprised newspapers, magazines, and government-owned broadcast media. The next section outlines the chilling effect of the Emergency on journalists and media publishers.

'WHEN ASKED TO BEND, YOU CRAWLED': THEORIZING THE MEDIA'S WATCHDOG ROLE

The strict censorship of the press during the Emergency had a chilling effect on journalists and media publishers. Fearing retribution, journalists, editors, and publishers complied with the rule of censorship and succumbed to the reign of terror. Political leaders like Lal Krishna Advani, Bharatiya Janata Party co-founder and prominent political activist, later admonished the compliant press and obsequious journalists (Chandra 2003; Devasahayam 2012).

'When asked to bend, you crawled,' Advani assailed journalists for their officious obedience. Journalists were not alone in their acquiescence. The repressive measures intimidated news executives who were forced to dutifully abide by press censorship diktats. They relented, fearing more restrictions on media privileges.

True to their role as watchdogs of democracy, defiant journalists and editors of some prominent publications opposed the censorship. Newspapers such as the *Indian Express* and the *Statesman* fiercely opposed the harsh censorship laws. The *Indian Express* proprietor Ramnath Goenka and *The Statesman* Editor-in-Chief Cushrow Russi Irani fearlessly defied the censors and passionately decried the repressive action. Joining them were crusading journalists and publishers of prominent publications such as *Freedom First, Himmat, Opinion*, and *Thuglaq*, who fought the censorship restrictions (Nayar 2013; Kapoor 2015; Prakash 2017).

During the Emergency, the government's officially appointed apparatchiks vetted major news reports to strictly censor the press, and resorted to other excesses. These apparatchiks often occupied offices that were adjacent to the newsroom. In other Emergency actions harsher than censorship, government officials seized 38 printing presses and arrested more than 8,200 persons after raids and searches of the presses from July 1975 to January 1977. These repressive measures restricted the dissemination of alternative publications. This was a major blow to free speech because these publications enriched India's democracy by contributing to the marketplace of ideas. The Emergency excesses stifled them.

The misuse of media during the Emergency dominated international news, with reports condemning Indira Gandhi for the draconian measures. In a 22 June 1977 report submitted to Parliament, an enquiry committee confirmed that it had received 217 complaints of media misuse (GoI 1977: 1). The complaints comprised 45 instances of 'misuse of censorship provisions', 103 events of 'harassment of journalists', 8 'allegations about unfair practices in film certification', 23 cases of 'manipulation of Mass Media including news agencies', and 38 complaints about other 'incidental matters' (GoI 1977:1).

The enquiry committee also received complaints of egregious excesses and wanton restrictions on press freedom from eminent journalists like Chanchal Sarkar, doyen of Indian journalism and the founder-director of the Press Institute of India, B. G. Verghese, who served between 1966 and 1969 as information advisor to Indira Gandhi and editor of the *Hindustan Times* from 1969 to 1975, Kuldip Nayar, veteran journalist of the *Indian Express*, which emerged as an anti-establishment newspaper during the Emergency, C. Raghavan, former editor-in-chief of India's leading news agency, the Press Trust of India, and Nikhil Chakravartty, founder-editor of the venerable current affairs weekly, *Mainstream*, which briefly suspended publication in January 1977 in the concluding months of the Emergency to oppose the arbitrary pre-censorship regulations. Chakravartty, who founded *Mainstream* on 1 September 1962, assiduously defended press freedom through his insightful columns during the Emergency days.

Other complainants comprised prominent journalists' associations like the Indian Federation of Working Journalists, founded on 28 October 1950 as independent India's first trade union for media persons and a professional body of working journalists, and the worldwide National Union of Journalists' India wing, which was established in January 1972 to represent the voice of journalists and journalism in India. The enquiry committee's 1977 white paper concluded that India had 'witnessed misuse of mass media totally inconceivable in a democracy' with the disappearance of 'the distinction between party and government' during the Emergency (GoI 1977: v).

The government-owned radio network Akashvani and the state-owned television channel Doordarshan became 'propaganda instruments of the ruling party and peddlers of a personality cult' (GoI 1977: v). The white paper reported that even non-press entities such as films, which were considered outside the strict control of government, were 'made to dance to the tune' of the government (GoI 1977: v).

The 'ruthless exercise of censorship powers' and 'enactment of a set of draconian laws' disrupted democratic norms and 'reduced press freedom to nought', the white paper concluded (GoI 1977: v). Media misuse also entailed 'an unabashed abuse of authority' in 'disbursing advertisements, allocation of newsprint and release of raw stock for films' (GoI 1977: v).

The Emergency excesses marked the darkest days of democracy in independent India (Grover and Ranjana 1997). Some international journalists compared the assault on civil rights to the oppression inflicted on journalists during the 190-year-long British rule in India. The international press reports contributed to worldwide outrage and influenced public opinion against the draconian censorship of the press. The international press thus fulfilled a crucial watchdog role during the Emergency by supporting India's battered press.

The Emergency stifled democratic dissent, imposed intense censorship, suspended fundamental rights, including elections, and jailed journalists, among other steps to restrain the press. In a twist of irony, the press survived the Emergency to report Indira Gandhi's defeat in the 1977 general elections.

The media attributed Indira Gandhi's sudden defeat to the excesses of the Emergency, and celebrated the newly-formed Janata Party government led by independence activist Morarji Desai, who was among the opposition leaders arrested and detained on 26 June 1975, the day after Emergency was declared. Desai was sworn in as India's fourth prime minister on 24 March 1977, three days after the Emergency officially ended on 21 March 1977. The newly elected government led by the Janata Party instituted, on 21 May 1977, a committee to enquire into the misuse of media during the Emergency.

The end of Emergency unleashed a spirit of freedom and conferred on the press an increased prominence as the watchdog of democracy, as the next section explicates.

THE EMERGENCY AS A WATERSHED FOR INDIAN MEDIA

Joyous celebration marked the end of Emergency on 21 March 1977. Unshackled from the draconian excesses of the Emergency, citizens called for institutional reforms and greater government accountability (Ryan 1977; Tully and Masani 1988; Anant and D'Harnoncourt 1997). The experience of the dark days of 1975–7 galvanized people to celebrate the end of Emergency with a spirit of freedom that fostered a rare culture of candour (Thakur 1977, 1979; Kapoor 2015; Prakash 2017). The media regained public trust in the aftermath of the Emergency. An overbearing fear of conflict with the government had restrained most media entities from opposing the Emergency. This section presents a select list of newspapers, magazines, news television, and other journalism initiatives that have contributed to a media boom in India in the 1970s and early 1980s.

The country's leading news magazine *India Today* released its first print issue in the midst of the Emergency in December 1975. During the Emergency, *India Today* thrived because its fortnightly issues cogently summarized the news. After the Emergency, *India Today* refined its news magazine model to grow into India's most widely read magazine, with a circulation of 1.1 million every week and a readership of more than 15 million for multiple language editions in English, Hindi, Tamil, Malayalam, Kannada, and Telugu.

The India Today Group aggressively diversified in the 1970s and 1980s by launching multifaceted media brands, catalysing the group's media success in the twenty-first century. The commercial success of *India Today* magazine evolved into the twenty-first century media juggernaut that constitutes the India Today Group, based on rapid expansion to areas beyond its flagship magazine. In 2017, the India Today Group's media mix of multilingual and multifarious media fare recorded a combined reach of 110 million consumers. The India Today Group has accomplished this rapid growth by hosting 36 leading magazines like *Business Today* (launched in 1992) and *Gadgets & Gizmos*, and Indian editions of international publications like *Cosmopolitan, Harper's Bazaar, Good Housekeeping, Golf Travel Plus, Harvard Business Review*, and *Men's Health*.

The India Today conglomerate owns prominent media brands like the *Mail Today* tabloid newspaper, 17 radio stations including the *Oye! 104.8* FM radio channel, 10 websites, three mobile portals, the Music Today classical Indian music label, and the Thomson Press for commercial printing. The group's initiatives also cover education, retail, yellow pages, and book publishing. The India Today Mediaplex headquarters in Noida Film City, Uttar Pradesh, has enabled the group to capitalize on its proximity to New Delhi and ignite public conversations through media forums and conferences.

The post-Emergency media boom heralded the rise of private television channels. Prannoy Roy, former economics professor at University of Delhi, and his wife Radhika Roy founded, in 1988, the country's first 24-hour English-language news and current affairs television channel, New Delhi Television Limited (NDTV). NDTV's big break occurred when the government's Doordarshan television network featured during prime time NDTV's televised news magazine *The World This Week*, which focused on international news and entertainment. NDTV triumphed with its insightful analysis of the 1989 Tiananmen Square protests in China and the fall of the Berlin Wall on 9 November 1989 in widely watched *World This Week* segments that riveted the national television audience.

Several print media entities also diversified into television. The India Today media conglomerate launched in December 1998 its prominent 24-hour Hindi news television channel Aaj Tak (meaning 'Until today' in Hindi); the English news television channel India Today (called Headlines Today until May 2015, originally founded in April 2003); and localized channels like Dilli and Tez television news channels.

The Emergency inspired media entrepreneurs to establish new media genres that interpreted the complex worlds of finance, business, economics, and commerce and translated them into intelligible insights for general readers. Oxford-educated lawyer Ashok Hotchand Advani launched in February 1978 the country's first mainstream business magazine, *Business India*, as a family venture with his two brothers, Cambridge-educated lawyer Hiroo Advani and entrepreneur Rajkumar Advani.

The post-emergency media ecosystem signified a rise in feminist political commentary, in-depth feminist analysis of national and global issues, feminist cultural criticism and action, feminist responses to popular culture, and women's first-person narratives. Indian academics Madhu Kishwar and Ruth Vanita founded *Manushi*, a journal about women and society, in 1978. In succeeding years, *Manushi* morphed into an organization at the forefront of many struggles for the rights of marginalized and vulnerable groups with a special focus on women, minorities, and the self-employed poor.

The media boom after the Emergency prompted traditional media publishers to expand and enhance. Traditional newspaper publishers upgraded their publishing systems with computerized innovations and launched news publications with national and international aspirations. Major English newspapers such as the *Times of India, Hindu, Hindustan Times,* and *Indian Express* reinforced their national status with multi-city editions to target readers in remote parts of the country. Newspapers, big and small, incorporated media innovations to facilitate multi-city editions that targeted a national audience. During the late 1990s, India's satellite and cable television channels emulated the print media's multi-city media model to customize content for specific audience segments in India's diverse society.

The rapid rise of regional media innovations has been an intriguing feature of the post-Emergency media boom, as discussed in the next section.

THE METEORIC RISE OF REGIONAL MEDIA BRANDS

The post-Emergency media boom germinated an impressive range of sustained innovations that facilitated the rise of regional media publishers. Some regional media brands accomplished a meteoric rise by launching English publications that targeted a national audience. They also strengthened their local-language publications to reinforce their regional dominance.

Eastern India's publishing giant, the Ananda Bazar Patrika (ABP) Group, launched in 1976 India's first weekly political news magazine, *Sunday*, with a 25-year-old M. J. Akbar as its editor. With inscrutable zeal, Akbar led *Sunday* news magazine to national prominence by pioneering a tradition of adept reporting from distant parts of the country, judicious news analysis, and a competitive low cover price of one rupee. Enthused with the success of *Sunday* (now defunct news magazine), ABP launched the daily newspaper *Telegraph* on 7 July 1982 in Calcutta. By 2008, the *Telegraph* emerged as among the largest circulating English daily in eastern India with simultaneous daily editions from four cities, Guwahati (for the North-East region), Siliguri (for north Bengal and Sikkim), and Jamshedpur and Ranchi (for Jharkhand state). Media publishing firms in India's other regions also thrived with a targeted media fare, as enunciated later in this chapter.

The ABP Group conceived the media novelty of hiring celebrities to edit publications. In the 1970s, the group launched the *Sportsworld* magazine (now defunct sports magazine) with legendary cricketer and former Indian cricket team captain Mansoor Ali Khan Pataudi as its editor. Targeting an audience of sports fans, *Sportsworld* emerged as an instant hit with its memorable ad pitch: 'Take a look at sport from people who've played the game.' Besides its niche branding, *Sportsworld* manifested the marvels of media technology of the late 1970s and early 1980s. Technology innovations empowered Pataudi to remotely edit *Sportsworld* by interacting with his editorial team and employers via telecommunication links. After retiring in 1975 as a cricketer, Pataudi edited *Sportsworld* from his Bombay office, communicating by telephone and telex with his team of journalists in *Sportsworld's* editorial offices in Calcutta (located 1,200 miles from Mumbai). The *Sportsworld* magazine was printed in Madras (1,200 miles from Kolkata). Innovations in media technology enabled such bridging of distant process points. Other publishers replicated such tech innovations to revolutionize India's media boom.

The ABP Group expanded its team of celebrity editors by launching, on 31 July 1986, the popular Bengali magazine *Sananda* with filmmaker and actress Aparna Sen as its editor. Unlike most celebrity editors, Sen went beyond just lending her name to the magazine. She wrote editorials, actively engaged in editorial decisions for each issue, and planned picture pages with punctilious precision. Sen edited *Sananda* for nearly 20 years, from 1986 through 2005, when she quit *Sananda* for other media ventures.

The media boom also engaged regional media entities in the south. Kerala's leading publication house, Malayala Manorama, expanded its array of eponymous publications by launching the *Week*, a popular news magazine, on 26 December 1982. The competition among southern Indian magazine publishers heated up with Tamil Nadu's Hindu group launching *Sportstar* sports magazine in 1978, and *Frontline* news magazine in December 1984 from Madras (now Chennai). The proliferation of news magazines continued into the 1990s, when the journalist, editor, and political commentator Vinod Mehta launched *Outlook* in October 1995, under the financial tutelage of the realty conglomerate Rajan Raheja Group that was diversifying into manufacturing, financial services, and media.

The media proliferation of the 1970s and early 1980s generated a plethora of magazines that thrived on targeting specific audience segments. Bombay-based advertising executive turned publisher Nari Hira epitomizes the magazine boom of this period. In 1971, Hira's Magna Publishing successfully launched the leading Bollywood news and gossip magazine *Stardust* in Bombay. *Stardust* initiated a national phenomenon of glossy magazines, spawning an array of sister publications like women's magazine *Savvy*, launched in 1984. In succeeding decades, Magna Publishing emerged as a twenty-first-century leader in entertainment media for over 20 million readers worldwide. Magna's media fare in India featured an array of publications on films, celebrities, television, health, food, architecture, design, lifestyle, fashion, women, people, and places. Besides magazines, Magna diversified into multimedia platforms like e-mags, websites, and mobile media.

Capitalizing on the media boom in the aftermath of the Emergency, renowned media companies invested in state-of-the-art publishing technologies that spawned for decades new publications and intensified competition in print media. Besides attracting readers nationwide, Indian media products—print, television, and digital—enjoy a worldwide presence in the Indian diaspora, estimated at over 31 million people according to 2017 estimates by the Ministry of External Affairs (Kuthiala 2018). The United Nations estimated in 2017 that India's diaspora comprised 16.6 million Indian citizens living outside the country's borders (UN DESA 2017: 12). This media surge legitimized journalism and reinforced the media's watchdog role, among other important trends that marked the aftermath of censorship in 1975–7, as the next section shows.

THEORIZING MEDIA TRENDS IN THE AFTERMATH OF EMERGENCY

The Indian media accomplished its watchdog role by publishing powerful media reports and news analyses that influenced public opinion against the Emergency. Through the exploration of the effects of the 1975–7 censorship, five significant media trends may be identified:

1. *Post-Emergency journalism reaffirmed the centrality of media in India's democratic society*: The media boom after the Emergency reaffirmed the centrality of media's watchdog role

in restoring democracy. In the aftermath of the Emergency, journalists began investigating the truth behind Emergency excesses. They published news reports of flagrant violations of civil liberties, such as coercive sterilizations for birth control and wanton demolition drives that rendered thousands of people homeless, and were euphemized as beautification initiatives. The Emergency excesses piqued renewed interest in journalism. For the first time since the independence struggle, news reports from India gained a worldwide readership and indignation. The people of India and the Indian diaspora worldwide devoted special attention to news and the facts behind news events. Several new publications were launched to capitalize on the surge in the interest in news and reliable information. During the Emergency, several journalists were jailed or harassed, similar to the height of the struggle for independence, when freedom fighters had challenged the British rulers with their crusading journalism. Journalists opposing the Emergency took inspiration from figures such as Bal Gangadhar Tilak, who in 1881 founded two newspapers, the *Kesari* in Marathi and the *Mahratta* in English, and Madan Mohan Malaviya, who launched the English daily, the *Leader*, along with Motilal Nehru in 1909. Similar to media messages of activism during British rule, the widespread abomination of authoritarian excesses bolstered free speech and forged an indomitable spirit to sustain democracy and fight corruption. Journalism thrived in this media milieu.

2. *The Emergency fostered media pluralism and enriched democratic values*: In the aftermath of the Emergency, the proliferation of media and journalism ventures fostered media pluralism, with enriching effects on the nation's democratic values. Niche publications from the 1970s through the 1990s accelerated India's media growth. The news media, in its print, broadcast, digital, and mobile manifestations, fostered an unwavering commitment to protecting civil liberties, sustained a dogged fervour for free expression, engaged citizens in a vibrant public sphere, and strived for equitable, inclusive, and participatory practices in disparate communities that were riddled by divisions in class, caste, religion, and race. In stark

contrast to the US or European news stories that dominated the news agenda, Indian media consumers appreciated news stories based on ingenious insights from local communities. These developments redefined the search for truth in India's pluralistic society.

The wide array of press entities and media products enabled the people to distinguish opinion from fact in news content, appreciate the quest for objective truth in journalism, and inspired citizens to pursue their varied interests. The efficacy of India's vibrant democracy was enhanced by the superabundance of media outlets that encouraged citizens to either expound or restrain ideas in seeking a common ground. The proliferation of various media platforms also enabled a well-informed community and civil society that fostered a democratic discussion of important ideas and issues.

3. *Emergency excesses motivated journalists to question authority*: The Emergency inspired journalists to question authority, to report truth with accuracy, and to persevere in their pursuit of free speech by speaking truth to power. Journalists legitimized their role of speaking truth to power and used that power to speak out. The end of Emergency in March 1977 and discussion of its excesses intensified the spirit of investigative journalism in India. Readers were intrigued by investigative reports and considered them searing indictments of autocratic oversight and the suspension of democracy. In the aftermath of the Emergency, long-form journalism witnessed a resurgence, with renowned journalists such as Kuldip Nayar and Khushwant Singh writing about Emergency excesses with startling revelations about the people who perpetrated them. Investigative journalism quickly shifted, in later years, to generating painstaking reporting of communal riots, misuse of authority, and rampant corruption.

Like most civil societies, India's democratic society has engaged in debate and dissent. The media have sought to satiate the information needs of their audiences by engaging in civil discourse and respectful exchange of disparate views that facilitate democratic aspirations. By cultivating diverse perspectives, the media celebrate the people's right to dissent and thereby enshrine the power of free speech. These aspects have strengthened Indian democracy, which has been consistently threatened by bigotry, abuse of women, poverty, and corruption, with dismaying regularity since the nation attained independence from British rule in 1947.

4. *Media technologies empower truth telling and better journalistic practices*: The mid-1970s marked an era of technology transforming India's media. Technological innovations, such as improved telecommunications, multimedia systems, improved newsgathering tools, sophisticated printing processes, and desktop publishing enabled the proliferation of media and journalism that enabled the expression of truth to power. Journalists assiduously adopted evolving media technologies such as computerized publishing systems, data analysis, and improved communication modes to find and report important news developments. Using ingenious ways to report news, journalists empowered voices of dissent to enhance the democratic marketplace of ideas. The Emergency and related developments highlighted the power of the media to topple people in power. Journalists were also inspired by international events, such as the Watergate scandal. In a significant exposé by US journalists, the Watergate scandal, which began with the 17 June 1972 break-in at the Democratic party's Watergate office headquarters in Washington, D.C., led to the resignation of President Richard Nixon on 9 August 1974. Millions of people in India among other nations worldwide watched the 1976 film, *All the President's Men*, which delineated the puissant impact of two *Washington Post* journalists Bob Woodward and Carl Bernstein, as they untangled the Watergate scandal with the help of a mysterious source, nicknamed Deep Throat. Besides highlighting the importance of journalism, events such as the Emergency excesses and the Watergate scandal inspired generations of aspiring journalists and motivated young people to pursue journalism as a career. In his 1977 book, *All the Prime Minister's Men*, veteran journalist Janardan Thakur narrated the misuse of power and corrupt practices of politicians and officials under Prime Minister Indira Gandhi's regime and during the Emergency (Thakur

1977). Such developments led to an exalted legitimacy of journalism as a profession in India and inspired journalists to bolster truth and trust by clever use of technology among other journalistic tools. That trend has been sustained in the twenty-first century rise of social media's diverse channels, which have motivated journalists to pursue free expression, to aspire for a more inclusive society, and to encourage citizens to engage with the media in the digital age.

5. *The Emergency legitimized journalism and reinforced media's watchdog role*: Increased media investments, rising advertising revenues, and audience support have enabled the media to legitimize journalism as a profession and reinforce their watchdog role. Such developments have contributed to the dignified distinction of journalism as a noble and influential profession in India.

The government responded to the media proliferation with significant initiatives to improve the working conditions of journalists. On 9 February 1979, the government reconstituted the Palekar Wage Board, which was the third wage board since 1956 to stipulate consistent compensation for working journalists and non-journalist newspaper employees. Several media companies adopted the Palekar Wage Board's recommendations for equity and parity in salaries of journalists and non-journalist employees. With improvements in working conditions, the news industry attracted well-educated professionals who contributed to better-quality journalism. The print media thrived with increased advertising revenues. Newspapers and magazines enjoyed the lion's share of advertising in the absence of significant competition from television, which was primarily in black-and-white format until 1982, when mainstream colour television arrived in India.

To conclude, these five post-Emergency trends contributed to a watershed moment for journalism in India. In their pursuit of full, accurate, contextual truth, journalists have learned an important lesson: the audience expects journalists to verify facts before publication because, if they do not, other media outlets will call them out, and this invariably leads to deprecation in social media and beyond. This important lesson attained increased significance in 2005 when India introduced the Right to Information Act that authorized citizens to request information from a 'public authority', which must reply 'expeditiously or within 30 days'. The act also stipulates that public authorities should computerize their records for wide dissemination and proactively publish certain categories of information. With the crusading zeal of a perpetual adversary, the media campaigned and influenced public demand for this right with fervent calls for free flow of information.

The 1975–7 Emergency manifested a watershed media moment that reinforced journalistic values. The analysis of trends in India's press in this section has been enhanced with perspectives and predictions of the Emergency's societal effects, as discussed in this chapter's concluding section.

* * *

With compelling examples and theoretical insights into the rise of news media, this chapter analysed the 1975–7 press censorship as a watershed media moment in India. As an influential economic powerhouse in South Asia, India's status as the world's largest democracy has been ratified time and again by the nation's free press. In theorizing the effects of the 21-month Emergency, this study derives important lessons. The misuse of news media during 1975–7 represented some of the darkest days that undermined cherished democratic ideals. Faced with impetuous censorship, vehement arrests of renowned journalists, among other flagrant violations of democratic tenets, India's press was under severe attack, but survived to endure and report the end of Emergency excesses. Such media moments deepened the spirit of free press and the power of responsible journalism.

Media coverage commemorating anniversaries of the Emergency identify two conflicting perspectives and predictions. The first perspective involves the consistent conjecture that the Emergency's excesses will never recur in the twenty-first century's pluralistic media milieu of round-the-clock social media updates and news websites that provide up-to-the-minute news. The second prediction relates to ominous prognostications that evoke intimations of the draconian days of authoritarian rule. While the veracity of these disparate declarations can only be confirmed with time, the Emergency is widely considered as a watershed in the evolution of media and journalism in India. This chapter has offered ample evidence that proves that the deleterious effects of the Emergency enriched democratic values instead of debilitating them.

This chapter featured succinct analyses of events that depict a shining moment for journalism in India and imparts a new understanding of the evolving role of India's free press. The authoritarian acts during the 21-month Emergency and its aftermath witnessed the rise of media brands that thrived on innovative media content, journalistic integrity, and an aspiration for accurate, ethically responsible journalism. The changing media landscape led audiences to trust India's press and to expect balanced news reporting. This chapter concludes that the media misuse during the 1975–7 manifested a landmark media milestone that reinforced journalistic values. The Emergency strengthened free speech norms and inspired journalists to inquire, investigate, inform, invoke, improve, and impact India's democratic society. These media trends germinated a sustained bond between the journalists and the people they serve. News organizations, such as newspapers, magazines, television, radio, and other media outlets, reinforced their commitment to serve their community with reliable news and relevant information every day.

With the power of robust reporting during the Emergency and news insights in succeeding decades thereafter, India's media matured as a vibrant arm of democracy by establishing its critical role in sustaining democratic norms and free expression. In India's twenty-first century media landscape, news consumers continue to favour journalists with stellar standards for unbiased, independent, and ethical journalism. The watchdog role of the Indian press began in the eighteenth century when the British ruled India. Since independence from British rule in 1947, the press has endured endemic assaults on its freedom rights, assaults that have persisted in the twenty-first-century digital era. Over the years, the media have undergone trials and tribulations that have strengthened journalism practices in India. Journalists and the media have shown a consistent propensity to survive seemingly insurmountable troubles to report about corruption among other ills, much to the chagrin of perpetrators and to the admiration of audiences.

REFERENCES

Anant, V. and A. D'Harnoncourt (1997). *India: A Celebration of Independence, 1947–1997.* New York, NY: Aperture.

Chandra, B. (2003). *In the Name of Democracy: JP Movement and the Emergency.* New Delhi: Penguin Books.

Devasahayam, M. G. (2012). *JP Movement, Emergency, and India's Second Freedom.* New Delhi: Vitasta Publishing.

Dhar, P. N. (2000). *Indira Gandhi, the 'Emergency', and Indian Democracy.* New Delhi: Oxford University Press.

GoI (Government of India) (1977). *White Paper on Misuse of Mass Media During the Internal Emergency, August 1977.* Delhi: Controller of Publications.

Grover, V. and A. Ranjana (1997). *India: Fifty Years of Independence.* New Delhi: Deep & Deep.

Hart, H. C. (1976). *Indira Gandhi's India: A Political System Reappraised.* Boulder, CO: Westview Press.

Holloman, C. (2013). *The Social Media MBA in Practice: An Essential Collection of Inspirational Case Studies to Influence Your Social Media Strategy.* Chichester, UK: Wiley.

Kapoor, C. (2015). *The Emergency: A Personal History.* New York, NY: Penguin.

Kilman, L. (2015). *Digital Media India: Where Print is King, Digital is Coming On Strong.* WAN-IFRA news release. Retrieved from http://www.wan-ifra.org/press-releases/2015/02/12/digital-media-india-where-print-is-king-digital-is-coming-on-strong (accessed on 17 August 2018).

Kuthiala, T. (2018). 'Overseas Indians in 208 Countries, Zero in Pakistan'. *Connected to India*, 12 April. Retrieved from https://www.connectedtoindia.com/overseas-indians-in-208-countries-zero-in-pakistan-3914.html (accessed on 11 September 2018).

Mehta, V. (1978). *The Sanjay Story: From Anand Bhavan to Amethi.* Bombay: Jaico.

Mistry, R. (1997). *A Fine Balance: A Novel.* New York, NY: Vintage Books.

Nayar, K. (1977). *The Judgment: Inside Story of the Emergency in India.* New Delhi: Vikas.

———. (2013). *Emergency Retold.* New Delhi: Konark Publishers.

Nehru, J. (1936). Presidential address, Indian National Congress, 49th session, Lucknow, 23 April. Retrieved from http://celebratingnehru.org/english/nehru_speech34.aspx (accessed on 17 August 2018).

Prakash, A. S. (2017). *The Emergency: Indian Democracy's Darkest Hour.* Gandhinagar: MeghNirghosh Media.

Ramaprasad, J. (1987). Pre-, during and Post-Censorship Coverage of India by the New York Times. *Newspaper Research Journal* 9(1): 19–29.

Ryan, N. (1977). *India: Nationalism and Independence*. Kuala Lumpur: Longman.

Tarlo, E. (2001). *Unsettling Memories: Narratives of the Emergency in Delhi*. Berkeley, CA: University of California Press.

Thakur, J. (1977). *All the Prime Minister's Men*. New Delhi: Vikas.

———. (1979). *Indira Gandhi and Her Power Game*. Ghaziabad: Vikas.

Tully, M. and Z. Masani (1988). *India: Forty Years of Independence*. New York, NY: G. Braziller.

UN DESA (2017). *International Migration Report 2017*. New York: Department of Economic and Social Affairs of the United Nations Secretariat. Retrieved from http://www.un.org/en/development/desa/population/migration/publications/migrationreport/docs/MigrationReport2017_Highlights.pdf (accessed on 11 September 2018).

Vasudev, U. (1977). *Two Faces of Indira Gandhi*. New Delhi: Vikas.

CHAPTER FOUR

A Missing Voice

India in the Global News Space

DAYA THUSSU

. . . .

Despite the extraordinary growth of international and national news media in the past two decades, India remains perhaps the only major nation without any significant presence within the global news space. This chapter aims to explore why this is the case and the implications of not having a voice in the international arena for a country which harbours ambitions of being a global power. Unlike most other developing countries, India has a highly developed and professional news media. With nearly 400 round-the-clock dedicated news channels—many of these in English, the language of global communication in commerce—and a strong tradition of English-language journalism, India should have been an early adopter of global journalism. However, the Indian state broadcaster Doordarshan remains one of the few major state news networks not available on television screens in key markets at a time when global television news in English has expanded to include channels from countries where English is not widely used, including China, Japan, and Iran.

THE GLOBAL CONTEXT OF INTERNATIONAL NEWS

The global news sphere has traditionally been dominated by what Tunstall once called the 'US-UK news duopoly' (Tunstall 1977). One reason for the American domination of global media—from news agencies and television news agencies (Associated Press and Associate Press Television News) to international news networks (CNN International and CNBC, to name the prominent ones)—is that the country has always followed a commercial model for its media industry, supported by the US government. With the economic and technological globalization and deregulation of the 1990s, the US-inspired commercial model of broadcasting has also been globalized. The US continues to dominate and define the global media scene as the largest exporter of media content distributed across a digitized globe. Sales of US copyright materials in 2015—recorded music, motion pictures, television and video, software publishing, and other publications including newspapers, books, and periodicals—were approximately $177 billion (Siwek 2016: 13). Companies based in the US own the infrastructure of global communication from satellites to undersea cables, to telecommunication hubs and cyberspace, as well as multiple networks and production facilities. From news (CNN, CNBC, *New York Times*) to documentary (Discovery); from sport (ESPN) and film, popular music, gaming, and entertainment (Hollywood) to online communication (Google, Facebook, Twitter), the US presence is formidable (Boyd-Barrett 2014; Thussu 2018).

However, this global expansion of media through multichannel networks, together with digital communication technologies in broadcasting and broadband, have given viewers across the world the ability to access simultaneously a vast array of international, national, regional, and local channels in various genres. In particular, the last decade has witnessed an exponential growth in the number of international 24-hour news channels around the world (Cushion and Sambrook 2016). This has dramatically changed the international news landscape, challenging the US-UK duopoly with a range of new voices and perspectives, particularly from the global South.

Russia has raised its international broadcasting profile by entering the English-language news world in 2005, with the launch of the Russia Today (RT) network which, apart from English, also broadcasts 24/7 in Spanish and Arabic, claiming to have a global reach of more than 550 million people. Ironically, while the channel covers international affairs generally from an anti-US perspective and questions the dominant Western media discourse—its tag line is 'question more'—when it comes to domestic Russian political issues, RT is cautious, as it does not want to upset the Kremlin, where the ultimate editorial control rests.

Qatar's Al Jazeera English—which reaches 260 million homes in 130 countries—and Iran's English language network, Press TV, are other players, though the latter is perceived, accurately, as a propaganda channel reflecting the viewpoints of the Iranian government. Al Jazeera's coverage of the NATO-led invasion of Libya in 2011 and the campaign against the Syrian regime in 2012–17, as well as support for Hamas in Gaza and the Muslim Brotherhood in Egypt, shows how it has used its media power to influence Middle Eastern politics. Al Jazeera English claims to privilege the global South in its coverage of international affairs, and its emergence as a broadcaster of substance has not only changed journalistic culture in the region, but also provided a space for a wider conversation in the global communication arena (Figenschou 2014).

Arguably the most significant development in terms of the 'rise of the rest' is the growing presence on the international news scene of Chinese news in English for a global audience, part of China's 'going global' project, promoting the Chinese model of development with an intensive programme of external communication (Sinha-Palit 2017). More than a decade and half have passed since the launch of CCTV-9, China's first English-language news network in 2000. Since then, an estimated $7 billion were earmarked for external communication, including the expansion of the state-funded 'central media'—China Central Television (CCTV), which in 2016 changed its name to China Global Television Network (CGTN), Xinhua News Agency, China Radio International, *People's Daily*, and the English-language *China Daily* (see the essays in Thussu et al. 2018).

The examples of news outside the Anglo-American sphere mentioned above provide interesting sites for an emerging alternative discourse on global issues: RT's coverage of the war in Syria is strikingly different from the dominant US-UK media discourse (the only naval base that the Russians have in the strategically significant Middle East is in Syria); Al Jazeera English, with its focus on the global South, has contributed to improved coverage of Arab issues as well as of other developing countries, while CGTN has given greater prominence to stories from Africa.

In an era of visually driven global geopolitics, the importance of news in a country's external communication strategy cannot be over-emphasized. Unlike other established and emerging powers, India's presence in the international news arena is characterized by private rather than public broadcasters. This is ironic, given India's traditional role in articulating Southern concerns in international forums, most notably during the contested and often acrimonious debates of the 1970s within UNESCO (the United Nations Educational, Scientific and Cultural Organization) and beyond about the need to create a New World Information and Communication Order (NWICO). Under Prime Minister Indira Gandhi, India was a leading exponent of NWICO, deploying its considerable international influence within such organizations as the Non-Aligned Movement to demand redressing of the existing imbalances in international news flows (Boyd-Barrett and Thussu 1992). The Press Trust of India (India's leading national news agency) was a nodal point for the Non-Aligned News Agencies Pool set up to encourage South–South news exchange to mitigate dependence on Western news organizations for international news and to enhance news from Asia, Africa, and Latin America so as to reach a global audience (Boyd-Barrett and Thussu 1992).

Much has changed since then. The champion of protectionism in foreign trade and investment and the articulate voice of 'Third World solidarity' has today become an ardent promoter of the free market. As India has emerged as an economic and political power—in purchasing power terms, it surpassed Japan in 2015 to become the world's third largest economy after China and the US—its news priorities too seem to have altered beyond recognition. Following the liberalization, privatization, and deregulation of the media and communication sector, news has become a commodity to be bought and sold in an increasingly competitive and crowded market. While the all-news channels in India have only been in existence for a decade, their pro-business agenda was well formed from the start. Journalism in India no longer aspires to be the voice of the global South but increasingly echoes the US-dominated market-driven news culture, dependent on Bollywoodized infotainment.

TELEVISION NEWS IN INDIA

Television in India has grown exponentially in the past decade: from Doordarshan—a state monopoly until 1991—to more than 800 channels, including 400 dedicated news networks, making it home to the world's most competitive news arena, catering to a huge Indian audience and indeed the South Asian diaspora. In the late 1990s and early 2000s, India's news television sector saw an extraordinary increase in the number of dedicated news channels, most of which were national, but many international in reach, while some catered to the regional markets. Dedicated news networks now operate in a dozen of the 18 state-recognized languages, several of which have large geo-linguistic constituencies, both within the country and among the 25 million strong South Asian diaspora. As elsewhere, the Indian news space has been reconfigured by what Hallin and Mancini have described as the 'triumph of the liberal model' (2004: 251) of media, partly 'because its global influence has been so great and because neo-liberalism and globalization continue to diffuse liberal media structures and ideas' (2004: 305). Deregulation and a fiercely market-driven agenda has transformed journalism in India, notably broadcast journalism, as mostly US-based media conglomerates tap into the burgeoning middle-class market of 300 million (Kohli-Khandekar 2013; FICCI-KPMG 2017).

India's news in English is available globally via such channels as NDTV 24×7, part of New Delhi Television Group, which has been operating for a quarter of a century as a news provider to Doordarshan and international news networks such as the BBC and CNN, and since 2003 as a 24/7 operation; CNN News 18, part of the TV-18 group; India Today Television (part of Living Media—publishers of the country's leading news magazine *India Today*); and Times Now (owned by the Times of India group—one of India's biggest media corporations); WION (World Is One News) owned by the Zee network; Republic TV (fronted and partly owned by Arnab Goswami,

Table 4.1 Leading English-Language TV News Networks in India

Channel	Owner	In Operation Since
NDTV 24×7	New Delhi Television	2003
CNN News 18	Reliance Corporation	2005
India Today Television	Living Media Group	2003
WION	Zee Network	2016
Times Now	Times of India Group	2006
Republic TV	ARG Outlier Media	2017

Source: Compiled by author.

one of India's most controversial news anchors) (see Table 4.1). Given that these are private networks and driven by market forces, they do not appear to be concerned to cater to an international news market. Instead, the international dimension of commercial news channels resides primarily in their reach to the global diasporic audience, who are perhaps more interested in the coverage of India itself rather than broader international affairs.

These private players—often in conjunction with transnational corporations—have recognized that combining news with show business and advertising can bring them financial gains. While television news outlets have proliferated in the liberalized and privatized economy, the competition for audiences and, crucially, advertising revenue, has intensified. The growing commercialization of television news has forced broadcast journalists and television producers to recognize the need to make news entertaining. They borrow and adapt ideas from entertainment and adopt an informal style with an emphasis on personalities, storytelling, and spectacle (Thussu 2007; Mehta 2008; Bhusan 2013). As a recent study notes: 'the multitude of news outlets and of delivery platforms have come to exert increasing pressure to be the first—often accompanied by compromises in not only the diversity of original sources, but also the ethics and quality of news offerings' (Parthasarathi and Srinivas 2012: 141).

As cross-media ownership rules are relaxed, there is greater trend towards concentration of media power: non-media groups have invested heavily in television and telecommunication. New 'media conglomerates', with a presence across various segments of the media and entertainment world, draw their inspiration from the US model

(Bhattacharjee et al. 2016). One prominent example is Reliance, one of India's largest conglomerates, which since 2013 has owned Network 18, the company that also operates CNN-IBN. As in the United States, where such moves have been reinforced by the takeover of news networks by huge media corporations whose primary interest is in the entertainment business, in India too, media conglomerates who make profits in the entertainment industry also have investments in news networks. Such ownership structures can be reflected in the type of stories—about celebrities from the world of entertainment, for example—that receive prominence on news (Thussu 2007).

NEWS AS 'BOLLYWOODIZED' INFOTAINMENT

In a fiercely competitive and crowded media market, such as the one in India, news networks are under constant pressure to raise their TRPs (television rating points) and acquire new programming to ensure a regular stream of advertising revenue. There is a tendency to make news entertaining, which in the context of India means drawing on Bollywood or Bollywoodized content (Thussu 2007; Nayar 2009). Such infotainment fare is now a common practice on news networks, where a flashier and visually dynamic presentation is routinized and debates reduced to shouting matches. Parthasarathi and Srinivas note 'strong tendencies toward sameness in the themes and emphasis of news, even in vernacular languages—coupled with a near uniform preference for sensational treatment' (2012: 142). An informal, entertaining schedule is created to increase the audience base across the channels. Ratings and revenue-delivering programmes—sports, entertainment, and lifestyle—have increased, while sober news and analysis have shown a corresponding decline. The popularization of celebrity-driven and sensationalist news may have made it a more marketable commodity, but this has also debased public discourse, increasingly aiming at the lowest common denominator. With a few honourable exceptions, much of television news has almost negligible reporting on international affairs, as they rarely translate into ratings or interest advertisers, on whose support the edifice of commercial television news is ultimately based.

If excessive marketization has contributed to privileging sport and celebrity spectacle in the news, the shift from bureaucrats to marketing executives has also influenced the politics of television news. News is increasingly shrill, bipartisan, and noisy. Scholars have argued that contemporary trends in the Indian media landscape have significant and deeply negative implications for the quality of journalism (Chadha 2017; Jain 2015; Rao 2009). During Doordarshan's monopoly of broadcast journalism, news on television was considered little more than the government's view of the day's events, with only primary definers of news—mostly politicians and other elite groups—dominating the discourse. In terms of presentation and style, the news was bland and bureaucratic: audience interest did not matter, as there was no competition with private television.

NEWS FOR DIASPORA

Since the 1990s, a new kind of migration from India—of the professional middle classes—has brought with it Indian media to the rest of the world. The opening up of the media sphere in India, part of India's gradual integration in global neoliberal capitalism, has in return given a boost to Indians abroad. Digitization and the growing availability of satellite and cable television, as well as online delivery mechanisms, have ensured that Indian media content—films, sports, entertainment, and news—is regularly consumed among the diaspora. Indian television has been active in selling the global Indian to Indian audiences, and the glitz and glamour of Bollywood to the famed NRIs (non-resident Indians). Members of the Indian diaspora, scattered around the globe, have excelled in many spheres of life and enriched the cultural, economic, and intellectual experience of countries like the US and Britain. They have also made a significant contribution to India's emergence as an economic and cultural power. The net worth of the Indian diaspora is estimated to be $300 billion and their annual contribution to the Indian economy is valued at up to $10 billion (Kapur 2010; Thussu 2013). With growing professional migration becoming a reality, Indian news channels and news portals—in English and other Indian languages—provide information and analysis to help Indians abroad keep abreast of developments in the home country.

In a globalized and interconnected world, depending on their economic and political influence within the centres of global power, diasporas can be a vital strategic instrument and channel of communication to further foreign policy goals and gains. Varadarajan (2010) has argued that diasporic relationships reflect globalized neo-liberal economics as well as the changing notions of territoriality. She conceptualizes this as the 'domestic abroad', suggesting that 'the production of the domestic abroad rests on the constitution of diasporas as subjects of an expanded, territorially diffused nation' (Varadarajan 2010: 6). This diffused community has emerged in recent years as a vocal and valuable voice in the global arena. Its most articulate and effective manifestation is the growing presence of members of the Indian diaspora in Ivy League universities, international media, and multilateral organizations, as well as in transnational corporations.

Communication of the Indian presence among the leading US-based journalistic outlets has been facilitated by the fact that many Indians have reached top positions in international media organizations: prominent examples include Bobby Ghosh, who had the distinction of being the first non-American to be chosen as editor of *Time* International; Fareed Zakaria, editor-at-large of *Time* and a leading CNN commentator; Tunku Varadarajan, who has held various senior positions as editor of *Newsweek International*; Raju Nerisetti who headed digital operations at *Wall Street Journal* and was formerly managing editor of the *Washington Post*, and Rajiv Chandrasekaran, who was the national editor of the same newspaper; Nikhil Deogun, who was managing editor at CNBC; and Jimmy Soni, managing editor of *Huffington Post*. In London too, within the mainstream British media, Krishnan Guru-murthy at Channel 4 News, Nisha Pillai of the BBC World News, and the *Guardian* columnist Aditya Chakraborty are examples of the Indian presence; while in 2013 Amol Rajan became the first Indian-origin editor of a British national newspaper, the *Independent* (Thussu 2013). As Tharoor has noted, the diaspora's active presence on social media, debating and discussing India-related issues, wields 'a disproportionate influence on international perceptions of India' (2012: 307).

Another major constituency for Indian news is the Indian corporates: more than 700 Indian companies were operating in Britain in 2012, with such blue-chip corporations as Tata—which owns the luxury brands British Jaguar and Land Rover, as well as key industrial companies such as steel—becoming the biggest private sector employer in the country. A new market of news is constituted by the growing presence of Indian students in universities in the US and UK: India is the second largest source of overseas students in the US-UK higher education sector, after China.

The instantaneous and 24/7 availability of news from India provides the Indian diaspora with access to the latest information from India. The growth of online content emanating from India, particularly relevant for the younger generation of these communities, is reformulating the sense of India among this demographic. As Kapur suggests, 'given India's demographics and those of industrialized countries, international migration from India will continue to grow, as will the diaspora's reshaping of both India and its destination countries' (2010: 15).

INDIAN TELEVISION NEWS IN THE GLOBAL MEDIA SPHERE

The growing profile of India on the global scene has been helped by the increasing visibility of its cultural and creative industries, its diaspora, and its media operating in a vibrant and expanding media sphere in one of the world's fastest-growing economies (despite the global economic downturn, in 2016, India still posted an economic growth of more than 7 per cent). Given the size and scale of the Indian media industry and the globalization of Indian businesses, the Indian version of news potentially has an audience base beyond the diasporic one.

Unlike in the Western world, the media and cultural industries in India are growing rapidly: in 2016, the Indian entertainment and media industry was worth $29 billion, with a steady annual growth rate. International investment is increasing in India's media sector, as cross-media ownership rules are relaxed (Kohli-Khandekar 2013; Punathambekar 2013; FICCI-KPMG 2017). At the same time, Indian media companies are also investing outside national territories. However, India's communication of its developments to a general global audience remains limited, given the US-UK domination of international news and a woeful lack of visibility of Indian news media on the broadcasting scene. This is ironic for a nation with a highly developed model of journalism and the increasing presence of Indian-born or Indian-origin journalists leading global news outlets, as mentioned above. Unlike many other developing countries, India has a long tradition of politically engaged journalism with roots in the anti-colonial nationalist movement. An intellectual engagement with the wider world is a rich legacy of Indian journalism. Indian democracy has been underpinned by a journalism which has by and large delivered its fourth estate function.

India is also one of the world's largest English-language news markets, as many of its news channels broadcast in English (Athique 2012). As noted earlier, some of these channels—especially those broadcasting in English—have a global reach and ambition. Indian news operators are also or have been in partnerships with Western news organizations such as CNN-IBN, and the NDTV Group had strategic ties with NBC, while Times Now ran a joint news operation with Reuters between 2006 and 2008. The growth of English-language journalism in India could open up possibilities for journalistic opportunities offered by the globalization of Indian media industries. According to the Registrar of Newspapers of India, in 2016, India had more than 1,406 English-language newspapers, employing journalists who could operate in a global media sphere.

Paradoxically, Indian journalism and media in general are losing interest in the wider world at a time when Indian industry is increasingly globalizing and international engagement with India is growing across the globe. As for news networks, NDTV 24×7 is the most widely watched internationally, while its domestic audience—like other English-language networks—is rather small, though influential. The absence of Doordarshan in the global media sphere can be ascribed to bureaucratic apathy and inefficiency. For private news networks, the need for global expansion is limited since, in market terms, news has a relatively small audience and therefore meagre advertising revenue.

However, the Indian government has belatedly woken up to promoting its external broadcasting. An eight-member committee headed by Sam Pitroda, former advisor to the prime minister of India on public information infrastructure and innovation, recommended that Prasar Bharati, India's public-sector broadcaster, should have a 'global outreach' (Prasar Bharati 2014). Its vision was ambitious:

Create a world-class broadcasting service benchmarked with the best in the world using next-generation opportunities, technologies, business models and strategies. The platform should be designed for new media first and then extended to conventional TV. Outline an effective content strategy for Prasar Bharati's global platforms (TV and Radio) focused on projecting the national view rather than the narrow official viewpoint. (Bharati 2014: 15)

Recommending professional and financial autonomy, with the latest technological support, the committee suggested that such internationalization would contribute to India's soft power. The objective of this 'global outreach strategy' should be to create a strong international presence, using all possible platforms and content 'to portray the story of emerging India and its vibrant democracy to the world: its cultural diplomacy and soft power and to influence opinion about India. Uniquely Indian themes such as yoga, ayurveda, or Bollywood are obvious areas, but information about Indian business successes and the richness and diversity of the country needs prominence.'

According to India's Ministry of External Affairs estimates, in 2016, DD (Doordarshan) News was reaching just 36 overseas markets, down from over 100. Where it was available, the audience was extremely small and, as a free-to-air channel, it received very meagre advertising revenue. There have been suggestions to seek reciprocal landing rights in different markets; so, for example, if France 24 is available in India, DD News should be given access in France. Another suggestion was to have direct deals with leading international hotel chains, where executives and elites consume international news. One other possibility was to use *Antrix*, the commercial arm of the government-run Indian Space Research Organization, to negotiate with satellite providers for whom they are important customers and to seek access to global markets on a reciprocal basis. It may also use existing distribution networks that work with private Indian operators such as NDTV 24×7 or even global networks like Star, to explore platform sharing (Prasar Bharati 2014).

INDIAN NEWS ONLINE

One potential area for growth is online news. The global presence of Indian news media is likely to expand with the convergence of communications technologies and content via the internet. As an industry report on India notes, the number of internet users is expected to cross 900 million by 2021, increasingly driven by wireless connections (FICCI-KPMG 2017). The most explosive growth is in mobile communication, as India is already one of the planet's biggest mobile phone markets. However, internet penetration remains low: as of 2017, nearly 400 million Indians had internet access, a penetration rate of just below 40 per cent of India's 1.2 billion population. There is no doubt that, with the growth of mobile internet making 3G phones affordable and 4G accessible, this will accelerate. As elsewhere, young people in India are the biggest consumers as well as producers of mobile digital content and of social media—India had 300 million social media users in 2016 (FICCI-KPMG 2017).

What makes the case of India particularly noteworthy is the scale and scope of the potential change: though an ancient civilization, India is a very young nation, with more than 70 per cent of Indians being below the age of 35. It is interesting to speculate what kind of content will be circulating on the electronic superhighways as more and more Indians are able to use the internet. As their connectivity grows, a sizeable segment of young Indians will increasingly be going online, producing, distributing, and consuming media. Given their proficiency in English, the dominant language of global commerce and communication, coupled with the growth of English-language media in India and the globalization of Indian media industries, they are likely to be more visible in the international media sphere. Such online English-language news portals as the *Wire* and *Scroll.in* have already created a niche for a global audience (Chaudhry 2016; Sen and Nielsen 2016). The expert committee has proposed setting up Prasar Bharati Connect, which would be tasked with managing the Doordarshan websites 'to make them more appealing, interactive, and engaging, and also integrate them with the existing social media channels' (Prasar Bharati 2014: 33).

AN INDEPENDENT VOICE?

Will a government-supported news outlet morph into an alternative voice in the international news sphere, or will it be reduced to New Delhi's propaganda channel? Will it complement or counter Western news and information hegemony? With the emergence of new geopolitical groupings such as BRICS (Brazil, Russia, India, China, and South Africa)—coinciding with cracks within the neoliberal model of US-led capitalism—there are possibilities of strengthening a global news agenda not shaped by the West in which India can play a significant role. Unlike China, Indian journalism has a long history of professionalism, operating within the infrastructure—however imperfect—of the world's largest democracy. The digital revolution in communication currently under way in India—which has the world's largest 'open' internet—offers many opportunities to circulate Indian ideas globally. Would the presence of Indian news on the international scene provide a different perspective? Two areas where this difference can be marked are how Indian news media could contribute to liberal pluralism. Unlike in the West, where multiculturalism is an imposed 'official' policy, and not always an acceptable social and cultural position, India is a multicultural, multi-faith, and multilingual country, despite recent attempts of Hindu right-wing groups to undermine this rich legacy. Every major religious festival is celebrated there—both officially and socially: different languages, dialects, and accents coexist. The composite culture which India embodies has given its media a degree of plurality not found in many other countries.

The other area where a global Indian news presence could make a meaningful difference is in the field of development communication: it was the first country to use television for education through its 1970s Satellite Instructional Television Experiment (SITE) programme. Today, despite the massive expansion of television, the educational aspects of the news media have been mostly ignored, although India remains home to the world's largest number of illiterate people: on all major indices of social progress, it ranks abysmally low. India and Indian media therefore have a moral and material imperative to be at the forefront of shaping discourse about how to deploy media and communication tools for poverty alleviation programmes at home and internationally.

Indian journalists could learn from what their giant eastern neighbour has achieved in reducing—almost eliminating—poverty. According to the World Bank's 2017 *Atlas of Sustainable Development Goals*, in 1990 China had 756 million citizens living in extreme poverty (at less than $2 a day), while India had less than half that number, at 338 million; by 2013, barely 25 million Chinese lived in extreme poverty, while the corresponding figure for India was as many as 218 million. In other words, in just over two decades, the much-maligned one-party state of China was able to raise more than 700 million people out of poverty while democratic India only managed 120 million in the same period (World Bank 2017). Yet, the coverage of China in the Indian media remains very limited, generally negative, and arguably influenced by Western perspectives. A recent study observes: 'It is also worth noting that since the European and American news media are major sources for Indian English newspapers that serve the political elites, the China-related media agenda in India is always consistent with that of the Western media, for example, the constant criticism of Chinese nationalist emotion' (Ji et al. 2016: 238). The coverage of India within Chinese media is equally problematic, where, in official discourses, Indian democracy is deemed as 'dysfunctional'. Li Xin, managing editor of *Caixin*, China's leading financial magazine, has written: 'Despite its size and proximity, India is a gigantic blind spot in China's foreign policy. On the rare occasions when India comes to mind, it is usually for its association with other, apparently more pressing countries— the United States, Pakistan, or Tibet' (Li 2013).

Indian journalism evolved within the context of a fight for democracy in the tradition of anti-colonialism, represented by leaders like Mahatma Gandhi (the iconic leader of India's independence movement, who edited for most of his political life the weekly newspaper *Young India*, later renamed *Harijan*). After independence, an anti-imperialist ideology—sometimes more as rhetoric than reality—continued to define mainstream media under Nehruvian socialism. Making use of this legacy of articulating the voice of the global South, India can make a real contribution to international debates. It could be an important source of distinctive perspectives in global forums like UNESCO, the International Telecommunication Union, and the World Intellectual Property Organization on such diverse and contested issues as multiculturalism, intellectual property rights in the digital environment, and the safeguarding of media plurality. Apart from the globalization of Indian news media, the growing Indian presence within the international non-governmental sector, multilateral bureaucracies, and the development communication field could be harnessed to this end (Thussu 2013).

The issues that confront the Indian situation—about governance, sustainable development, pervasive poverty—have striking resonances in many other countries in the global South (Thomas 2010). Despite India's integration with the US-led neoliberal economic system, there is a deeply entrenched tradition of argumentation and critical conversation in the Indian body politic and in its intellectual life, reflected also in its journalistic discourses (Sen 2005; Rajagopal 2009). As Indian journalism globalizes, will this critical mass contribute to providing an alternative voice on global issues or will India act as a surrogate for the US-inspired infotainment?

REFERENCES

Athique, Adrian (2012). *Indian Media*. Cambridge: Polity.

Bhattacharjee, Anuradha, Liwei Wang, and Tapasya Banerjee (2016). 'India'. In *Who Owns the World's Media? Media Concentration and Ownership*, ed. Eli Noam, pp. 772–90. New York: Oxford University Press.

Bhusan, Bharat (2013). 'News in Monochrome: Journalism in India'. *Index on Censorship*, 42(36): 37–42.

Boyd-Barrett, Oliver (2014). *Media Imperialism*. London: Sage.

Boyd-Barrett, Oliver and Daya Kishan Thussu (1992). *Contraflow in Global News: International and Regional News Exchange Mechanisms*. London: John Libbey, in association with UNESCO.

Chadha, Kalyani (2017). 'The Indian News Media Industry: Structural Trends and Journalistic Implications'. *Global Media and Communication*, 13(2). doi: 10.1177/1742766517704674.

Chaudhry, Lakshmi (2016). 'Can the Digital Revolution Save Indian Journalism?' *Columbia Journalism Review*, Fall/Winter. Retrieved from https://www.cjr.org/special_report/india_digital_revolution_startups_scoopwhop_wire_times.php (accessed on 5 August 2017).

Cushion, Stephen and Richard Sambrook (eds) (2016). *The Future of 24-Hour News: New Directions, New Challenges*. New York: Peter Lang.

FICCI-KPMG (2017). *Media for the Masses: The Promise Unfolds— FICCI/KPMG Indian Media and Entertainment Industry Report 2017*. Mumbai: Federation of Indian Chambers of Commerce and Industry/ KPMG India.

Figenschou, Tine Ustad (2014). *Al Jazeera and the Global Media Landscape: The South Is Talking Back*. New York: Routledge.

Hallin, Daniel and Paolo Mancini (2004). *Comparing Media Systems: Three Models of Media and Politics*. Cambridge: Cambridge University Press.

Jain, Savyasaachi (2015). 'India: Multiple Media Explosion'. In *Mapping BRICS Media*, eds Kaarle Nordenstreng and Daya Kishan Thussu, pp. 145–65. London: Routledge.

Ji, Deqiang, Zhengrong Hu, and Yousaf Muhammad (2016). 'Neighbouring Competitor? Indian Image in Chinese Media'. *Global Media and China*, 1(3): 234–50.

Kapur, Davesh (2010). *Diaspora, Development, and Democracy: The Domestic Impact of International Migration from India*. Princeton: Princeton University Press.

Kohli-Khandekar, Vanita (2013). *The Indian Media Business*, 4th edn. New Delhi: Sage.

Li, Xin (2013). 'India through Chinese Eyes'. *World Policy Journal*, Winter. Retrieved from http://www.worldpolicy.org/journal/winter2013/india-through-chinese-eyes (accessed on 5 August 2017).

Mehta, Nalin (2008). *India on Television: How Satellite News Channels Have Changed the Way We Think and Act*. New Delhi: HarperCollins.

Nayar, Pramod (2009). *Seeing Stars: Spectacle, Society and Celebrity Culture*. New Delhi: Sage.

Parthasarathi, Vibodh and Alam Srinivas (2012). *Mapping Digital Media: India*. A Report by the Open Society Foundations. London: Open Society Foundation. Retrieved from https://www.opensocietyfoundations.org/sites/default/files/mapping-digital media-india-20130326.pdf (accessed on 4 August 2017).

Prasar Bharati (2014). *Report of the Expert Committee on Prasar Bharati*. New Delhi: Government of India. Retrieved from http://mib.nic.in/sites/default/files/Sam_Pitroda_Expert_Committee_on_PrasarBharati_January_2014_-Vol_1.pdf (accessed on 6 August 2017).

Punathambekar, Aswin (2013). *From Bombay to Bollywood: The Making of a Global Media Industry*. New York: New York University Press.

Rajagopal, Arvind (ed.) (2009). *The Indian Public Sphere: Readings in Media History*. New York: Oxford University Press.

Rao, Shakuntala (2009). 'Glocalization of Indian Journalism'. *Journalism Studies*, 10(4): 474–88.

Sen, Amartya (2005). *The Argumentative Indian*. London: Penguin.

Sen, Arijit and Rasmus Nielsen (2016). *Digital Journalism Startups in India*. Oxford: Reuters Institute for the Study of Journalism, May. Retrieved from https://reutersinstitute.politics.ox.ac.uk/sites/default/files/Digital%20Journalim%20Start-ups%20in%20India_0.pdf (accessed on 4 August 2017).

Sinha-Palit, Parama (2017). *Analysing China's Soft Power Strategy and Comparative Indian Initiatives*. New Delhi: Sage.

Siwek, Stephen (2016). *Copyright Industries in the U.S. Economy: The 2016 Report*. Incorporated, prepared for the International Intellectual Property Alliance, November. Retrieved from https://iipa.org/files/uploads/2018/01/2016CpyrtRptFull-1.pdf.

Tharoor, Shashi (2012). *Pax Indica: India and the World of the Twenty-first Century*. New Delhi: Penguin.

Thomas, Pradip (2010). *The Political Economy of Communications in India: The Good, the Bad and the Ugly*. New Delhi: Sage.

Thussu, Daya Kishan (2007). *News as Entertainment: The Rise of Global Infotainment*. London: Sage.

——— (2013). *Communicating India's Soft Power: Buddha to Bollywood*. New York: Palgrave Macmillan.

——— (2018). *International Communication: Continuity and Change*, 3rd edn. New York: Bloomsbury Academic.

Thussu, Daya Kishan, Hugo de-Burgh, and Anbin Shi (eds) (2018). *China's Media Go Global*. London: Routledge.

Tunstall, Jeremy (1977). *The Media Are American: Anglo-American Media in the World*. London: Constable.

Varadarajan, Latha (2010). *The Domestic Abroad: Diasporas in International Relations*. New York: Oxford University Press.

World Bank (2017). *Atlas of Sustainable Development Goals 2017*. Washington: World Bank.

CHAPTER FIVE

An Incomplete Journalism *Parivar*

The Story of India's Missing News Magazine Industry

RADHIKA PARAMESWARAN,
ROSHNI SUSANA VERGHESE, AND
SUNITHA CHITRAPU

· ·

A growing body of scholarship in journalism and media studies has documented the evolving conditions of Indian newspaper and television journalism over the last three decades (since the onset of economic liberalization in India), but English-language Indian news magazines, which have ebbed and flowed alongside these more pervasive media, have somehow fallen through the cracks of academic scrutiny.[1] Exploring relatively neglected terrain in a bustling and fluid Indian mediascape, this chapter plots the collective itinerary of English-language news magazines—from a jet-plane view *and* from a chronological perspective—with a focus on post-independence India. Rather than delving deep into the content of specific magazines, this chapter forages for and culls together information from a wide variety of sources to, instead, selectively mark key milestones and major turning points in the unfinished journey of a near-invisible industry in academic research.

But we first offer a very brief detour into the colonial history of magazines in India. While the earliest magazines produced in colonial India towards the end of the eighteenth century were British magazines (for example, the *Oriental Magazine* or *Calcutta Amusement*), Kasbekar (2006: 118–19) traces the origins of Indian magazines, those that are edited and published by Indians within India, to Bengali literary publications of the early 1900s that featured a blend of book excerpts, poetry, plays, serialized fiction, and essays. Although quite different from today's Indian news magazines, such early-twentieth-century political journals and periodicals as *Modern Indian Review*, *Indian Social Reformer*, and *Hindustan Review*, all edited and published by progressive male editors who challenged colonial rule and advocated for changes in Indian society, targeted their English-language content to a pan-Indian educated middle class, thus foreshadowing the national audiences or imagined communities of contemporary news magazines in India (Guha 1999). The historical antecedents of Indian news magazines, like their newspaper counterparts, can be traced to the role they played in mobilizing support for independence from British rule and in catalysing social movements that sought to reform gross inequities arising from caste, class, and gender hierarchies. As English-language magazines have emerged, survived, or collapsed over the years since India achieved independence in 1947, the destiny of this segment of news media has been shaped by economic, social, and technological developments and, most importantly, by the arrival and rapid spread of television.

This chapter notes at the outset that mainstream commercial Indian English-language news magazines cater to a very small segment of the Indian reading public, but the educated and largely urban middle-class readership of these magazines exercises considerable influence in national and global business, culture, and politics. Vernacular-language Indian media whose spheres of influence continue to grow have accounted for the greatest increase in readership in recent years.

According to the Indian Readership Survey (IRS) from 2011, the total readership of all publications in Indian languages and English amounted to 347.8 million, with Hindi publications garnering 53 per cent and English publications 16.8 per cent of this readership. A previous survey from 2006 reported that the top 10 most read daily newspapers in India were all vernacular-language publications (Ram 2011: 8–9). Simultaneously, however, English continues to be pervasive in India, and a new generation of upwardly mobile young Indians, who are literate in vernacular languages, often aspire to gain fluency in written and spoken English so they can avail of employment opportunities that can potentially lead to professional-managerial careers (Joseph 2011). English-language media, including news magazines, benefit from the aspirational prestige and status accorded to English as a coveted form of cultural capital in postcolonial India.

EMERGENCE AND MATURATION OF NEWS MAGAZINES

English-language news magazines became voices to be reckoned with—both in terms of the number of magazines and the roles they played—during the late 1970s, in the aftermath of the Emergency, a two-year period during which Prime Minister Indira Gandhi muzzled opposing political voices, stifled freedom of expression, imposed censorship, bartered government advertising for newspapers' political support, and forced hundreds of poor Indians to submit to sterilization procedures (under the guise of population reduction). Robin Jeffrey (2000: 38) describes the impact of the Emergency on Indian citizens:

> On the night of 25/26 June 1975, Mrs. Gandhi proclaimed an emergency, police shut off the power to New Delhi's street of newspapers, and by the time India awoke on the morning of 26 June, authoritarian rule and censorship had been imposed that were to last for nineteen months.... the censorship of the emergency produced boring newspapers and falling circulations. Printing, publishing and newspapers were never more depressed or depressing. Yet, inside the bottle into which Mrs. Gandhi had jammed a cork in 1975, immense curiosity built up. Once she was defeated in the 1977 elections, tens of millions of people searched eagerly for news of what had happened around them in the previous nineteen months.

Looking back on the tumultuous Emergency days, the editor of *India Today* magazine Aroon Purie (2015) recalls his magazine's confrontational relationship with the Indira Gandhi regime:

> During the Emergency, I was called into the South Block office of Mohammed Yunus, Special Envoy to the Prime Minister and a Gandhi family retainer, and threatened that if we didn't fall in line he would crush us like he had crushed the famous lawyer Nani Palkhiwala, who, according to him, had turned against Indira Gandhi. Later, we were called 'anti-national' by Mrs. Gandhi herself.

Borrowing from Jeffrey's characterization of the growth in newspapers since the mid-1970s as a 'revolution', Kasbekar (2006: 121–2) notes that a similar 'magazine revolution' ensued in the 1970s with the launch of the English version of *India Today* in 1975, followed by *Sunday* magazine in 1976 (the first weekly political news magazine); the revitalization of the much older *Illustrated Weekly of India*; and the sprouting of other niche sectors of the magazine industry, including film, women's, and sports magazines. A nostalgic story on *India Today*'s early beginnings as a pioneer of India's magazine boom describes the post-Emergency days, which precipitated a series of investigative stories with 'hardly a pause', as a hectic period for a small band of reporters who endured 'travel and travails' and 'did multiple-duty from writing to subbing, proof-reading and production' (*India Today* 2014).

Similarly, the now defunct *Sunday* news magazine, founded and edited in 1976 by journalist M. J. Akbar, 'took an uncompromising stand against Emergency and fought press censorship and dictatorship' (Khan 2016). Journalist Salil Tripathi (2014), a former senior correspondent at *India Today*, attributes his interest in a career in reporting to the stories he read in his youth in the *Sunday* magazine:

> For those of us who grew up reading the journalism of the Emergency of 1975 and its aftermath, what Mobashar Jawed Akbar did at *Sunday* magazine was inspiring. Akbar set his reporters free to bring back stories of police brutality, corruption and communal violence across the country, making us feel the anger. Our generation can trace some of our early inspiration to such stirring journalism.

It is a testimony to *Sunday* magazine's reputation and 'nationwide influence' that almost 20 years after its demise, there was still speculation and mourning about what caused its mysterious and unfortunate closure (Mitra 2015).

We will return later to other mainstream news magazines, but now dwell on the *Illustrated Weekly of India* (1880–1993), a long-lasting and unique pictorial magazine that enjoyed a wide readership in the 1970s and 1980s, covering news and current events alongside 'contending points of view on every conceivable subject: politics, economics, religion, and the arts' (A. Singh 2006). It is striking that this magazine has thus far escaped the attention of media scholars and historians. A publication of the Times group, the *Illustrated Weekly* rose to prominence under the editorship of its well-known second Indian editor, Khushwant Singh. During Singh's tenure as editor, the magazine's circulation went from 60,000 to almost 400,000, and, by the 1980s, it had earned a reputation for its salty and irreverent mix of politics, opinion columns and essays, and riveting pictures (*Economist* 2014). Although Singh did not join other editors and journalists in opposing Indira Gandhi, he ultimately took issue with her decision to storm the Amritsar Golden Temple in 1984 and returned the Padma Bhushan award, a high government honour, as a sign of protest (*Economist* 2014). Amardeep Singh (2006) writes that Khushwant Singh, an iconic, larger-than-life figure of Indian journalism, changed the ethos of the magazine, from its fare of respectable, bucolic short stories and insipid news features to a brash journalistic style that broke the 'stranglehold of Anglophilia' and looked to the United States rather than Britain as a cultural reference point: 'As an editor, it was wild, sometimes trashy American culture in and after the 1960s that Khushwant brought into the pages of *The Illustrated Weekly*: rock "n" roll, the Vietnam war protests, and the counter-culture (including the significant component of barefoot, Enlightenment-seeking hippies who ended up in India)'. Amardeep Singh notes that the pages of the magazine reflected Khushwant Singh's unwavering commitment to secularism and his mission of poking fun at middle-class India's repressed and hypocritical attitudes to sex.

The only academic survey we located on English-speaking Indian magazine readers discovered that *Illustrated Weekly* was the top favourite of all magazines (including film and women's magazines) for both male and female readers in Delhi in 1980–1, followed by *India Today* (4th place), *Time* (7th place), and *Newsweek* (11th place) in that order (Johnson 1981). Supplementing readers' daily diet of newspapers, this weekly magazine's covers, photographs, cartoons, and drawings, and its many full-page advertisements carried a visual culture of still images and photojournalism into the Indian public sphere *and* into the quotidian spaces of middle-class homes across India, preceding the full frontal assault of television's immediate and incessant flow of images. The *India Today* magazine soon emulated the *Illustrated Weekly's* lead on the visual news front by investing in skilled staff photojournalists in the 1980s:

> Raghu Rai, India's best known photographer, joined the staff as picture editor and has ever since been embroiled in a running battle with the writers over visual space ('windows versus the brickwork of text'), which in his case invariably meant five columns for pictures and the remaining one column for text. The talented Bhawan Singh followed suit to join him and the durable Pramod Pushkarna to make a potent team of lensmen. (*India Today* 2014)

The growth in the size of the Indian middle classes and their consuming aspirations, urbanization, improvements in literacy rates, advancements in printing technology, and the coming of age of Indian advertising fuelled the boom in the magazine sector during the 1970s and 1980s (Kasbekar 2006). Following the launch of *India Today* and *Sunday* magazines in the mid-1970s, other prominent news magazines followed in their wake. The founding of the *Week* in 1982 and *Frontline* in 1984 represented the growth in general-interest news magazines, and the births of *Business India* in 1978 and *Businessworld* in 1981 anticipated the capitalist boom in the business and financial sectors that would take place in a very different India of the 1990s and beyond, a 'New India' that made it to the cover of a 2006 issue of *Newsweek* magazine disguised in the avatar of Indian American celebrity chef Padma Lakshmi standing next to the headline, 'Asia's Other Powerhouse Steps Out'. When the *Illustrated Weekly* departed from the Indian news magazine world in 1993, it left behind print siblings that not only had to compete with one another, but with a large extended family of noisy screen cousins, who thrived without eating newsprint and walked, talked, and moved all day.

FAST-FORWARD TO THE NEW INDIA: NEWS MAGAZINES IN AN ALTERED MEDIA ENVIRONMENT

The Indian media economy witnessed a major and ongoing transformation, along with the services and manufacturing economies, starting in the early 1990s when the central government launched reforms to deregulate and dismantle state control, promote a free-market consumer economy, and facilitate the entry of multinationals. As Rao (2009: 478) notes in her article on the glocalization of journalism in India, television registered the most dramatic and visible changes in post-liberalized India: 'Foreign channels like CNNI and BBC World, and domestic channels like Zee TV, NDTV, and Sun TV, suddenly and explosively increased the demand for cable. Before 1991, Indian viewers had received only two channels but, by 2007, they were receiving more than 90 channels.' Accelerating an earlier trend from the 1980s, and counter to the economic woes of print media in the United States and elsewhere in the West, the readership of daily newspapers in India, especially vernacular dailies, grew throughout the last two decades, and these dailies continue to maintain their lead position.

What do we know about the contemporary conditions of English-language news magazines in India? The magazine industry as a whole has faced a haemorrhaging of readership that began in the late 1990s and has continued throughout the 2000s, but general-interest news magazines have suffered the most serious declines ('Indian Magazine Market Overview' 2010). Losing the readership battle to daily newspapers in 2002, magazines 'lost 22 per cent of their reach since 1999 when taking account the population growth over these years' with a 25 percentage average decline for general interest, film/entertainment, and sports magazines (*Hoot* 2002). With the exception of niche magazines such as *Femina Girl*, most magazines saw a drop in readership in 2010 with *Frontline* showing the sharpest drop (20.8 per cent) among news magazines ('Indian Magazine Market Overview' 2010). The IRS data of 2012, for example, showed that the average issue readership of 8 out of the top 10 magazines had declined with *India Today*, the only English-language news magazine to make it to the top 10 list, losing 48,000 readers in the fourth quarter of 2012 (Bansal 2013). General-interest news magazines have struggled to stay afloat due to the following reasons: stiff competition from more nimble daily newspapers, which have produced localized editions at low prices to penetrate small markets; lack of steady and lucrative government advertising; difficulties with distribution (newspapers have filled up vendors' capacities); and an associated drop in advertising revenues (Bansal 2013). Although magazines draw about 70 per cent of their revenue from advertising alone, advertising spending in magazines was going down even as overall advertising spending in print media was growing at a healthy 20–25 per cent (Shine.com 2011). In addition, the rapid proliferation of television, which is not impeded by literacy barriers, and the spread of the internet along with mobile devices which facilitate free access to news content, have encroached on potential magazine readership ('Indian Magazine Market Overview' 2010; Sen 2017), particularly among urban middle-class youth, who are turning to a wide range of online news sources, including those from the UK and the US. Despite the rather gloomy scenario, the business news sector of the news magazine industry has fared well along with growth in other niche areas, including auto, travel, lifestyle, and education. According to the IRS report of 2010, business magazines—*Business Today, Outlook Business, Businessworld,* and *Outlook Money*—saw gains in readership in 2009 with *Business India* maintaining the same levels as the previous year (Shine.com 2011). Yet, these niche news magazines, which cater to an urban upper-income segment of readers, are not altogether immune from the competitive pressures of financial performance. When the revenue from *Businessworld* started dwindling in 2013, the conglomerate ABP Group sold it to exchange4media, and several journalists, including the editor, quit the magazine a year later, citing management interference and a lack of respect for journalists' autonomy (Mehra 2014).

Indian magazine stalwarts from the old India, *India Today,* the *Week,* and *Frontline,* are now joined by other prominent news magazines, both born and reinvented in the new India—*Outlook* (started in 1995), *Tehelka* (revamped in 2007 in magazine form), *Open* (started in 2009), and *Caravan* (restarted in 2010 after a long hiatus). According to the 2014 IRS data on English-language Indian news magazines, *India Today* continues to lead the pack as it did in the 1970s and 1980s with *Outlook* taking a rather distant second place, followed by the *Week, Business India, Businessworld,* and *Frontline* in descending order (see Table 5.1). Such data on readership, however,

Table 5.1 Information on English-Language News Magazines

	Name of Publication	Year of First Issue	Frequencies of Issues	Annual Subscription Price (in Rupees)	IRS 2014 Readership ('000s)
1	Business India	1978	26 issues	Rs 1,045 print and digital	142
2	Business World	1981	26 issues	Rs 1,999 print/ Rs 299 digital/ Rs 2,298 print and digital	137
3	Frontline	1984	26 issues	Rs 1,250 print and digital	101
4	Illustrated Weekly of India	1880–1993	—	—	Discontinued
5	India Today	1975	52 issues	Rs 2,340 print/ Rs 2,933 print and digital	1,634
6	Open	2009	51 issues	Rs 1,748 print and digital	N/A
7	Outlook	1995	51 issues	Rs 1,799 print and digital	425
8	Tehelka	2007	51 issues	Rs 649 print	N/A
9	Caravan	2010	12 issues	Rs 950 print/ Rs 1,575 print and digital	N/A
10	Week	1982	52 issues	Rs 1,000 print/ Rs 1,575 print and digital	270
11	Forbes India	2008	27 issues	Rs 1,499 print/ Rs 1,599 digital/ Rs 2,999 print and digital	N/A
12	Time Asia	N/A	54 issues	Rs 3,672 print and digital/ Rs 3,024 digital	212

Source: Compiled by the authors.
Notes:*N/A = Not available.
**These prices reflect information provided on the official magazine web pages as of May 2017.

has to be approached with caution due to the controversies and concerns surrounding the Media Research Users Council's methodology in conducting the IRS, amidst the challenges of accounting for the significant changes and fluctuations in the demographics and psychographics of Indian media audiences (Gupta 2015). One prominent publisher of news magazines also criticized the IRS for equating cheaply priced newspapers with more expensive magazines and for ignoring the costs that magazines routinely incur to improve paper and print quality (Saha 2013).

Not surprisingly, as a consequence of these anaemic readership trends, the Indian magazine industry has a small share (about 7 per cent) of total media advertising revenues ('Indian Magazine Market Overview' 2010), and lifestyle and business magazines, not current affairs or news magazines, are predicted to benefit from any future growth in magazine advertising (Choudhary and Shukla 2013). Seeking to preserve and increase advertising revenue for the magazine industry, the Association of Indian Magazines, a lobby group for magazine publishers, preaches the value of magazine advertising as a powerful way to reach niche audiences. The association partnered with exchange4media to organize the 2016 Magzimise Awards event, which recognized and rewarded the most creative magazine advertising, and three prominent English-language news magazines—*India Today*, *Outlook*, and the *Week*—were among the major co-partners of the event.

Our inventory of advertisements in a convenience sample of print versions of general news magazines from 2017, shows that higher education ads for private universities and institutes dominate this space, followed by a mix of ads for upscale hospitals, financial services, and luxury consumer commodities, although not necessarily in that order. Indexing the neoliberal privatization of higher education in the New India, the preponderance of higher education ads could suggest that these magazines are reaching a group of upwardly mobile youth and their parents (who help them make decisions) and young readers, who read news magazines for various competitive exams, including screening tests for jobs in government and the banking sector, which test them on their knowledge of current affairs. Of all the news magazines we surveyed, *Frontline* carried the least advertising content, with ads typically occupying the inside covers and back cover. Ads for banks and financial services, home fixtures and appliances, men's personal care products, luxury hotels, and upscale designer apparel and watches litter the pages of business news magazines (*Business India*, *Businessworld*, and *Forbes India*).

Reflecting privatized commercial media ownership patterns in other capitalist democratic nations, these magazines represent only one business interest among a host of other interests for the conglomerates that own them. *India Today* is published by Living Media Limited (with a 27.5 per cent stake from the Aditya Birla Group), which has an expansive financial portfolio that includes investments in other print media, television, radio, online shopping, education, and music. The Raheja Group, which produces *Outlook*, has print subsidiaries *Outlook Money*, *Outlook Business*, *Outlook Traveller*, and ownership in cement, automotive, and industrial batteries, financial services, food, beauty, real estate, and petrochemicals. Newcomer *Open* magazine is a part of the RP-Sanjiv Goenka Group's Open Media Network, and this corporation has its fingers in music and food retail, power and natural resources, infrastructure building, and education. *Frontline*, owned by the well-established Hindu Group; the *Week*, owned by Malayala Manorama; and *Caravan*, operated by the Delhi Press Group, belong to companies with a narrower range of interests focused primarily in media ventures. While there needs to be more systematic and longitudinal research on the overarching political orientation of these news magazines, our impressionistic and anecdotal observations and informal conversations with Indian journalists indicate that *India Today* tends to veer towards right of centre positions whereas *Outlook*, the *Week, Caravan*, and *Tehelka* lean in the direction of left of centre positions during this current era of a BJP-led central government. *Frontline*, the most sober and progressive of these magazines, tends to adopt left positions that are consistently critical of the government and other elites for not serving marginalized groups.

Continuing its deregulation agenda, in 2008, the Indian central government 'unveiled a set of guidelines to allow Indian editions of foreign news and current affairs magazines 26 per cent FDI as long as all key executives and editorial staff are Indian', and, in 2009, this mode of opening up ownership in the news economic arena was followed by the concession of 'customs duty exemption on newsprint for the newspaper and magazine publishing industry' to offset the spiralling costs of this essential publishing commodity ('Indian Magazine Market Overview' 2010). Taking advantage of these economic reforms and eager to tap into a large emerging market, *Fortune* and *Forbes*, along with a host of other niche magazines—*Cosmopolitan*, *Vogue*, *Maxim*, and *Good Housekeeping*—decided to launch Indian editions in 2008 and 2010 respectively. *Time* magazine currently distributes its *Time Asia* edition in India and, in 2016, IBT Private Media Limited, the parent company of *Newsweek* magazine (which closed in 2012 and reopened in 2014) announced plans to produce an Indian edition with a news team located in Bangalore (Sterne 2016), but that edition has not yet materialized. *Time Asia* lags well behind major Indian news magazines for readership, and it is not likely that Indian editions of foreign general-interest news magazines can overtake the popularity of Indian magazines in the current affairs arena. Rohn (2010: 213–51) outlines the challenges that English-language magazines from the UK and the US face in India, even though language barriers may not be an obstacle as they are in China or Japan: audience tastes for local content, particularly in politics, sports, and popular culture; fierce competition for the attention of the upper-income English-speaking educated Indian reader; inadequate and heterogeneous distribution networks; and pressures of generating local advertising content. Signalling the high mortality rates of some Western magazines in India, *Outlook* magazine decided in 2013 that it would no longer produce the Indian editions of *Marie Clare, People*, and *Geo* due to dwindling ad revenue in the high-end lifestyle magazine niche area (Polanki 2014).

Capitalizing on the steady growth in internet access and use in India, both Indian and foreign editions of news magazines that we scrutinize in this chapter produce print *and* digital versions of their publications. Although India lags behind many other industrialized nations in internet availability and use, it also has the world's second largest market of online users with over 462 million internet users; 26 per cent of the Indian population accessed the internet in 2010, up from 7.5 per cent in 2010 (Statista.com 2017). Internet penetration, according to one report, is 60 per cent among the largely urban markets that English-language magazines target, and e-mail use, social networking, and online shopping—indicators of professional occupations, education levels, and purchasing power—are becoming pervasive in urban middle-class India, while entertainment in the form of 'video and audio content is driving Internet consumption in the rural counterpart of the country' (Chopra 2017). Our cursory browsing of Indian news magazines' websites reveals that these digital versions typically showcase a combination of what is included in the print issues as well as shorter, more current news updates on domestic and global politics, sports, and entertainment.

Short of a full-fledged and systematic comparison of each magazine's print and digital versions, it was not easy to ascertain the precise differences between print and digital versions of news magazines. We did find some variation in access to and availability of free content across these news magazines' websites. For example, *Outlook* grants all visitors access to their archives and content in their current issue for free, while the *Week* and *India Today* make it easier for subscribers to gain access to their complete set of archives. Unlike news magazines in the United States, however, these magazines do not seem to frequently block or restrict non-subscribers from accessing certain articles from current or past issues, nor do they seem to provide limited access to a certain number of stories. One business journalist, Saritha Rai of Bloomberg India, whom the first author interviewed in the city of Bangalore, observed that most Indian news magazines offer a significant portion of their online content for free. Rather than grant greater or full access to content to their digital and print subscribers, Indian news magazines appear to be using digital subscriptions to enable convenience of access and usage. With digital subscriptions, multiple members within a household or organization can share one membership while accessing content on various devices like iPads, Kindles, mobile phones, desktops, and laptop computers. Digital subscriptions facilitate portable and user-friendly access to content in addition to allowing multiple readers to share a membership. Expressing concerns for the long-term sustainability of the news magazine genre, Indrani Sen, a veteran media and marketing agency professional, observes that Indian magazines 'have started exploring and distributing their content on the web and mobile platforms, but their efforts need to be stepped up through innovative marketing strategies and tie-ups' (Sen 2017).

How have some older news magazines reinvented themselves for the current climate of increased competition and a growing youth population? *India Today* recently announced a major relaunch of its 41-year-old magazine with a focus on curated news pertaining to India's diverse states and high-quality writing, infographics, edgy design, and content from other media platforms to reflect the tastes of younger Indian readers, predicted to be the world's largest youth population by 2050. As the long-standing editor-in-chief, Aroon Purie, put it, 'In keeping with the changing times, *India Today* magazine has now been reimagined to enhance not only its core values of clarity, credibility and relevance, but also provide readers with a dazzling variety of finely curated information and features' (Bestmediainfo. com 2017). *Frontline* magazine, which was edited by N. Ram, a leading journalist and public intellectual for over two decades until he stepped down in 2011, also announced that it would add content to attract younger readers. News editor R. Vijayasankar came to his position as *Frontline*'s editor after a reporting career at the *Indian Express* and the *Hindu* and with a publication portfolio that included books on the Dravidian movement, Latin American politics, and identity politics in Tamil Nadu. Vice-President Ansari released the newly revamped *Frontline* in 2012 at an event which also featured a panel discussion on sovereignty, socialism, and democracy in India. Announcing the magazine's ongoing renovation plans at this event, Vijayasankar first explained the reputation *Frontline* had developed over the years for resisting neoliberal narratives of 'shining India' where all Indian citizens could achieve prosperity: 'The magazine has been unwavering in its focus on the lives of the marginalized, deprived and downtrodden sections of the people of India. In the post-liberalisation era, the magazine has been consistent in its objective assessment and critical evaluation of India's growth story' (*Hindu* 2012). Vijayasankar then reassured the audience that *Frontline* would not stray from its original vision to produce analytical long-form stories on politics and economic policies, but that new columns and design features would be added to appeal to the younger generation.

In the meantime, as the old news magazine guard has struggled to ensure longevity, newer kids on the media block have sought to carve out their own spaces and brand identities. *Outlook*, founded in 1995 by former editor-in-chief Vinod Mehta, who ran the magazine until 2015 when he passed away, soon became a formidable competitor for *India Today*. Preceding his stint at *Outlook* magazine, Vinod Mehta had founded the following news publications: *Sunday Observer, Indian Post, Pioneer,* and the *Independent.* A frugal and down-to-earth editor with a passion for spare writing, Mehta, who often appeared on television news talk shows and debates, was known for his 'fearless and irreverent' opinions on the 'shenanigans of politicians' (Associated Press 2015). Another recent addition to the magazine parivar, *Caravan,* which was founded originally in 1939 and shut down in 1988, was revived again in 2009 by the Nath family's Delhi Press Group with a completely new format and a fresh editorial agenda. One among 36 other magazines (for example, *Women's Era* and *Champak*) owned by the Delhi Press Group, *Caravan,* the brainchild of owner-editor Anant Nath, who studied at Columbia University, New York, was conceived as a hybrid magazine of politics, culture, and art that would bring together elements of the long-form narrative styles of the *New Yorker,* the *Atlantic,* and *Mother Jones* (Bansal 2013). By putting his unique editorial imprint on the *Caravan,* Anant Nath wanted to stake out his own space in Indian journalism, separate from his father Paresh Nath, a hands-on editor of more than 30 magazine titles owned by the family company (Bansal 2013). Supporting his son's venture, the elder Nath praised the work ethic of his son's reporting team and also spoke highly of *Caravan's* editorial ethics, which banned alcohol, cigarette, and *pan masala* advertising at any cost and shunned industrial and political connections or financing that might cast a shadow on the magazine's integrity (Saha 2013). *Open* magazine, launched in 2009 and aimed at the 'global-minded resident Indian reader', claims that its 'clutter free, vibrant design and superior visual content' supports the best of narrative journalism in India. This magazine boldly proclaims its mission to acquire a 'loyal following outside India'—a 'commanding geographical sweep'—by leveraging its online version.[2] The magazine consistently features three sections: the first one called 'Openings' offers a curated selection of short news updates, a middle/second section features longer analytical articles, and a final third section called 'Salon' carries news and views on art, books, food, cinema, and theatre.

Among the most aggressive renovated arrivals to the magazine industry, *Tehelka* (an Urdu word which means 'tumult' or 'sensation') went through multiple avatars before it joined the genre of the weekly news magazine. Founded as an investigative news website in 2000,

Tarun Tejpal's publication *Tehelka* rose to prominence for its sting operations on match fixing and breaches of ethics in cricket and on high-level government corruption in the awarding of defence contracts (Risam 2011). Shut down after a three-year government campaign that targeted the magazine for tax evasion, *Tehelka* resurfaced in 2003 as a weekly tabloid newspaper. In 2004, *Tehelka* added a revamped news portal and then, in 2007, the publication changed genres and became a weekly magazine with a commitment to 'constructive crusading journalism' and a mission to bring back into 'hard focus public interest and an appetite to question'.[3] The magazine's website explains its conversion to the new format: 'This follows repeated demand by readers to switch to a magazine format, since the contents of *Tehelka* are seen to have much more shelf value and depth than a newspaper. This format with its easy size allows for longevity and high pass-along readership.' This progressive magazine got embroiled in intense controversy in 2014 when editor Tarun Tejpal, a journalist, novelist, and public intellectual, resigned after a young female colleague filed sexual assault and rape charges against him. Having lost several staff journalists and advertising revenue after Tejpal's precipitous fall from grace, *Tehelka* has since then struggled to retrieve its original foothold (Balachandran 2015).

CONCLUSION: FROM THE JET PLANE TO THE RUNWAY ...
AND A WALKING TOUR

This chapter has offered an uneven and incomplete airborne, jet-plane view of English-language news magazines in India, a long-standing member of the Indian journalism parivar that has been conspicuously missing from scholarship. We hope that our chapter's selective survey of overlooked terrain stimulates more intimate historical, social-scientific, and cultural studies scholarly research that descends to the runway and takes readers on a guided walking tour of a fascinating media industry. Explaining the omission of magazines from his now canonical book on Indian newspapers, Robin Jeffrey (2000: xii) predicted that magazines would struggle to survive in the face of television's unstoppable march across India. Almost two decades later, one prominent magazine publisher acknowledges Jeffrey's prediction, but also argues that magazines, which feed readers' motivated and discerning appetite for specific types of content, will not disappear anytime soon from the Indian mediascape (Saha 2013). Dying, morphing, and adjusting to economic and technological challenges and readers' changing tastes and practices, news magazines in India, as this chapter demonstrates, provide spaces for sustained and deep analysis of news events, dissent against state and corporate power, experimentation with long-form narrative styles and visual storytelling, the incubation of high-quality journalism, and the cultivation of a new generation of journalists. The pages of these magazines in print and in their online incarnations await future scholarship from such diverse approaches as political economy, history, content and textual analysis, and reception and audience studies.

NOTES

1. The word *parivar* employed in the title means 'family' in the Hindi language.
2. See http://www.openthemagazine.com/.
3. See http://tehelka.com/.

REFERENCES

Associated Press (2015). 'Vinod Mehta, Editor of India's Outlook Magazine Dies at 73'. *San Diego Union-Tribune*, 8 March. Retrieved from http://www.sandiegouniontribune.com/sdut-vinod-mehta-editor-of-indian-magazine-outlook-2015mar08-story.html (accessed on 12 August 2018).

Balachandran, Manu (2015). 'How Tehelka Is Attempting to Remake Itself after Tarun Tejpal'. *Scroll.in*, 3 January. Retrieved from https://scroll.in/article/698326/how-tehelka-is-attempting-to-remake-itself-after-tarun-tejpal (accessed on 12 August 2018).

Bansal, Shuchi (2013). 'As Magazines Dwindle, Delhi Press Seeks to Add More'. *LiveMint*, 25 April. Retrieved from http://www.livemint.com/Consumer/78YQTesQtr28UUC18SQI9J/As-magazines-dwindle-Delhi-Press-seeks-to-add-more.html (accessed on 12 August 2018).

Bestmediainfo.com (2017). 'India Today Transforms for India Today', 27 January. Retrieved from http://bestmediainfo.com/2017/01/india-today-transforms-for-india-today/

Chopra, Arushi (2017). 'Number of Internet Users in India Could Cross 450 Million by June: Report'. *LiveMint*, 2 March. Retrieved from http://www.livemint.com/Industry/QWzIOYEsfQJknXhC3HiuVI/Number-of-Internet-users-in-India-could-cross-450-million-by.html (accessed on 12 August 2018).

Choudhary, Vidhi and Tarun Shukla (2013). 'Outlook to Stop Publishing *People*, *Geo*, *Marie Claire* in India'. *LiveMint*, 26 July. Retrieved from http://www.livemint.com/Companies/hEWlSTz2UrduDan81NaF6N/Outlook-to-stop-publishing-People-Geo-Marie-Claire-in-Indi.html (accessed on 12 August 2018).

Economist (2014). 'Khushwant Singh: India's Gadfly', 5 April. Retrieved from http://www.economist.com/news/obituary/21600081-khushwant-singh-indias-pre-eminent-gadfly-died-march-20th-aged-99-indias-gadfly (accessed on 12 August 2018).

Guha, Ramachandra (1999). 'The Independent Journal of Opinion'. *Seminar*. Retrieved from http://www.india-seminar.com/1999/481/481%20guha.htm (accessed on 18 August 2018).

Gupta, Devesh (2015). 'A Matter of Measure'. *Afaqs*, 11 February. Retrieved from http://www.afaqs.com/news/story/43247_ABC-vs-IRS (accessed on 12 August 2018).

Hindu (2012). 'Ansari to Relaunch *Frontline*', 19 September. Retrieved from http://www.thehindu.com/news/national/ansari-to-relaunch-frontline/article3912107.ece (accessed on 12 August 2018).

Hoot (2002). 'Newspaper Readership Up, Magazine Reading Down in India', 2 September. Retrieved from http://www.thehoot.org/story_popup/newspaper-readership-up-magazine-reading-down-in-india-441 (accessed on 12 August 2018).

India Today (2014). 'India Today: The Inside Story', 28 January. Retrieved from http://indiatoday.intoday.in/story/india-today-looks-back-at-its-origins-evolution-and-the-people-behind-its-success/1/354812.html (accessed on 12 August 2018).

'Indian Magazine Market Overview' (2010). Arcgate (blog). Retrieved from http://arcgate.com/blog/indian-magazine-market-overview (accessed on 12 June 2017).

IRS (Indian Readership Survey) (2014). *Indian Readership Survey*. Retrieved from http://www.mruc.net/sites/default/files/IRS%202014%20Topline%20Findings_0.pdf (accessed on 12 August 2018).

Jeffrey, Robin (2000). *India's Newspaper Revolution: Capitalism, Technology and the Indian-Language Press, 1977–1997*. London: Palgrave Macmillan.

Johnson, Lynda D. (1981). 'Magazine Use of Middle-Class English-Speaking Indians in New Delhi, India'. Presentation at Annual Meeting of the Association for Education in Journalism, Lansing, MI.

Joseph, Manu (2011). 'India Faces a Linguistic Truth: English Spoken Here'. *New York Times*, 16 February. Retrieved from http://www.nytimes.com/2011/02/17/world/asia/17iht-letter17.html (accessed on 12 August 2018).

Kasbekar, Asha (2006). *Pop Culture India! Media, Arts and Lifestyle.* California: ABC Clio.

Khan, Zafarul-Islam (2016). 'The Man Who Lost His Shadow'. *Milli Gazette*, 2 August. Retrieved from http://www.milligazette.com/news/14558-the-man-who-lost-his-shadow (accessed on 12 August 2018).

Mehra, Pranati B. (2014). 'Crisis Strikes Businessworld'. *Hoot*, 17 December. Retrieved from http://www.thehoot.org/media-watch/media-business/crisis-strikes-businessworld-7958 (accessed on 12 August 2018).

Mitra, Dola (2015). 'Babudom on a Sunday'. *Outlook India*, 2 November. Retrieved from http://www.outlookindia.com/magazine/story/babudom-on-a-sunday/295679 (accessed on 12 August 2018).

Polanki, Pallavi (2014). 'How Shut Down of Marie Claire Shows Lack of Readers for Lifestyle Magazines'. *Firstpost*, 20 December. Retrieved from http://www.firstpost.com/business/how-shut-down-of-marie-claire-shows-lack-of-readers-for-lifestyle-magazines-991035.html (accessed on 12 August 2018).

Purie, Aroon (2015). 'Letter from the Editor-in-Chief'. *Indian Express*, 9 December. Retrieved from http://indiatoday.intoday.in/story/india-today-40th-anniversary-from-the-editor-in-chief-aroon-purie/1/542979.html (accessed on 12 August 2018).

Ram, N. (2011). 'The Changing Role of the News Media in Contemporary India'. Presentation at Indian History Congress, 72nd Session, Punjabi University, Patiala. Retrieved from https://pdfs.semanticscholar.org/9b3a/f690a7c3186fca407e38c6a198677afaa5f3.pdf (accessed on 18 June 2017).

Rao, Shakuntala (2009). 'Glocalization of Indian Journalism'. *Journalism Studies*, 10(4): 474–88. doi: 10.1080/14616700802618563.

Risam, Roopika (2011). 'Tehelka Magazine (India)'. In *Encyclopedia of Social Movement Media*, ed. John Downing, pp. 521–2. Thousand Oaks, CA: Sage.

Rohn, Ulrike (2010). 'Western Magazines in China, India and Japan'. In *Cultural Barriers to the Success of Foreign Media Content: Western Media in China, India and Japan*, ed. Ulrike Rohn, pp. 213–43. New York: Peter Lang.

Saha, Ananya (2013). 'Times Aren't Good, but Print Media Should Not Give Up: Paresh Nath, Delhi Press'. MXMIndia.com, 23 April. Retrieved from http://www.mxmindia.com/2013/04/times-arent-good-but-print-media-should-not-give-up-paresh-nath-delhi-press/ (accessed on 12 August 2018).

Sen, Indrani (2017). 'Indian Magazine Industry Needs to Look beyond Print'. MxmIndia.com, 6 March. Retrieved from http://www.mxmindia.com/2017/03/indian-magazine-industry-needs-to-look-beyond-print/ (accessed on 12 August 2018).

Sengupta, Somini (2014). 'Khushwant Singh, Provocative Indian Journalist, Dies at 99'. *New York Times*, 20 March. Retrieved from https://www.nytimes.com/2014/03/21/world/asia/khushwant-singh-provocative-indian-journalist-dies-at-99.html?_r=0 (accessed on 12 August 2018).

Shine.com (2011). 'Magazine Readership in India Continues to Follow Decline Trend', 5 October. Retrieved from http://info.shine.com/article/magazine-readership-in-india-continues-to-follow-the-decline-trend/6187.html (accessed on 12 August 2018).

Singh, Amardeep (2006). 'Khushwant Singh's Journalism: The Illustrated Weekly of India'. Lehigh.edu (blog). Retrieved from http://www.lehigh.edu/~amsp/2006/08/khushwant-singhs-journalism.html (accessed on 12 August 2018).

Statista.com (2017). 'Percentage of Population Using the Internet in India from 2000 to 2015'. Retrieved from https://www.statista.com/statistics/255135/internet-penetration-in-india/ (accessed on 12 August 2018).

Sterne, Peter (2016). 'Newsweek Plans Indian Edition'. *Politico*, 7 July. Retrieved from http://www.politico.com/media/story/2016/07/newsweek-plans-indian-edition-004648 (accessed on 12 August 2018).

Tripathi, Salil (2014). 'M.J. Akbar and His Politics'. *LiveMint*, 26 March. Retrieved from http://www.livemint.com/Opinion/rydxuMOAYUmrFpTy8L2UIM/MJ-Akbar-and-his-politics.html (accessed on 12 August 2018).

PART TWO

Social Media and e-Journalism

· ·

CHAPTER SIX

Internet Vernacularization, Mobilization, and Journalism

TABEREZ AHMED NEYAZI

· ·

Two conspicuous transformations have been noticed in the internet ecosystem in India:[1] (*a*) massive growth in contents on the web in Indian vernacular languages; (*b*) and increasing numbers of citizens, in both urban and rural areas, accessing the internet in the vernacular languages. These transformations, which I term 'internet vernacularization', have received little or no attention from scholars, but have been the subject of many news stories. The growing number of Indian-language internet users has been reported in a study by KPMG (2017). There are now more internet users in vernacular languages in India than in the English language. From 42 million Indian-language internet users in 2011, the number has grown to an estimated 234 million in 2016, a compound annual growth rate of 41 per cent. This massive growth of internet users in Indian languages is higher than that of English-language internet users, which has grown from

68 million in 2011 to 175 million in 2016 (KPMG 2017). Earlier, people were discouraged from using the internet even when it was available as the content was mainly in English, and incomprehensible to a majority of people. With an increasing amount of web content available in various Indian languages, the vast majority of people speaking vernacular languages are accessing the net in their own languages. The diversification in the profiles of internet users along with internet vernacularization has begun to influence society, economy, and politics.

This trend of internet vernacularization in India is in line with the global trend of decentralization and de-Americanization of the world-wide web, along with the rise of the global South in terms of the number of web users, as noted in the study by Wu and Taneja (2016). However, the process of internet vernacularization is more nuanced and complex, as many English-language users are also accessing the content in the vernacular languages, leading to the emergence of fertile interactions between elites and the vernacular masses and the sharing of information between one level and the other. The continued existence of the digital divide, in which a large number of people are not yet connected with the internet, leads one to question if internet vernacularization is leading to meaningful transformation at the grassroots level.[2] The idea of the 'digital divide' assumes two separate realms for the connected and the disconnected, ignoring the possibilities of interactions between these two realms. I argue that there are instead increasing interactions between online and offline publics through various channels of mediators. In this chapter, I analyse the factors propelling internet vernacularization and its implications for political mobilization and journalism. I first outline the relationship between the internet and mobilization, and then discuss the evolution of the internet in India, looking at the transformation in the user base over the years. I then analyse the factors responsible for internet vernacularization and conclude with an analysis of mobilization enabled through internet vernacularization and how it is affecting journalism.

INTERNET AND MOBILIZATION

Mobilization is considered a precondition before citizens can participate in any civic and political activities. Several studies have demonstrated the role of information in creating more mobilized and active citizens (Verba et al. 1995). Traditionally, face-to-face contact has been seen as an important factor leading to participation in political activities (Klandermans and Oegema 1987; Verba et al. 1995). After the arrival of the internet, scholars questioned whether the internet or online contact led to mobilization. Although there is no agreement among scholars, several studies have demonstrated the positive impact of the internet for democratic politics, which has allowed citizens to critically monitor the government's actions (Chadwick 2006; Hindman 2008; Howard 2005, 2010; Loader and Mercea 2012; Mossberger et al. 2007). The rise of the internet and social media has also facilitated self-mobilization (Lee 2015) and a growing trend of internet-based activism (Velasquez and LaRose 2015). The increasing use of the internet among civil society groups for political mobilization, which in turn is replacing traditional forms of face-to-face recruitment and mobilization, has been reported in various studies (Hooghe et al. 2010). The 'continuous connectivity' of the internet has certainly decreased the cost and time of reaching out to potential supporters for a cause (Semetko and Scammell 2012: 2).

To what extent is internet-based mobilization promoting democracy? Referring to representative democracy, in which only citizens have voting rights and ordinary citizens feel marginalized, creating 'passivity and cynicism', Benjamin Barber (1984) called for strong democracy. In a strong democracy citizens can participate in the democratic process without any 'intermediary of expertise'. In other words, 'strong democracy requires unmediated self-government by an engaged citizenry' (Barber 1984: 261). Barber saw potential in technology for creating direct participation for citizens in democratic discourse.

India has been facing a paradoxical situation, in which political information is available online, but the information has been inaccessible to the average citizen. When information is inaccessible, either because it is intangible to the common vernacular world or not available in local languages, citizens require intermediaries to meaningfully participate in the democratic process. The inaccessibility of information for common citizens has resulted in the failures of many government programmes and policies that have been captured by more informed citizens. This phenomenon has also been known as 'elite capture'. Information on the web is now more diffused, reaching both elites and the vernacular masses, leading to a bridging of the gap between those who had a monopoly over information and those who were unable to access that information. Although the phenomenon of elite capture has not completely disappeared, particularly in rural areas, internet vernacularization has made it difficult for elites to claim exclusive monopoly over information. By making the information available in Indian vernacular languages and creating digital literacy, the vast majority of the masses outside of elite English circles can access and process the information in their own languages. This accessibility has also allowed citizens to self-evaluate the government's programmes and policies and share their daily life experiences with one another and the outside world, without needing to depend on intermediaries.

By including the vast majority of the population, internet vernacularization will enhance democratic participation and promote pluralistic viewpoints and discourses necessary for democracy. Yet, the virtue of inclusion could be negated by certain features of the internet—that is, speed and instant communication. Democracy requires deliberation and deliberation requires contemplation, reflection, and reconsideration. Instant communication is often informed by ill-conceived and inchoate ideas, which is antithetical to democracy which requires patience. Let us first discuss how internet vernacularization has evolved in India and the factors propelling it, before discussing its role in mobilization.

EVOLUTION OF INTERNET VERNACULARIZATION

The English language dominated internet content for a very long time in India, which, in addition to unavailable internet connections, kept a large number of non-English-speaking Indians from accessing the internet. Since the number of English speakers is only about 10 per cent of the total population, non-availability of Indian-language content resulted in a very slow growth in the number of internet users in India.[3] Since the launch of publicly available internet services in 1995, it took almost 25 years for the internet to reach the first 100 million users in 2011. The pace of growth has accelerated rapidly since 2010,

Table 6.1   Number of Internet Users in India, 2000 to 2016

Years	No. of Internet Users (in Millions)
2016	462.1
2015	354.1
2010	92.3
2005	27.3
2000	5.55

Source: Internet Live Stats, 'Internet Usage and Social Media
Statistics', 2017. Retrieved from http://www.internetlivestats.com/.

with over 300 million internet users within a short of span of six years,
as shown in Table 6.1. Although this growth remains biased towards
urban areas in which nearly 70 per cent of internet users are located,
penetration in rural areas is growing steadily. According to the latest
available data on internet users' geographical locations, rural India
accounted for 186 million internet users, while urban India had
295 million internet users at the end of December 2017 (IAMAI and
KANTAR IMRB 2018). With the number of internet users reaching
saturation point in urban areas with nearly 65 per cent penetration,
the growth potential lies in rural areas. The ever-increasing number of
internet users and their potential to influence non-users has prompted
business and government, political parties and civil society groups,
to incorporate the internet and social media as primary vehicles of
communication in their campaign strategies.

Diversification of Internet Users

There has been growing diversification of internet users since the
internet was introduced in India. Yet, the process of diversification
has been quite slow, which is also the case with other media types
such as newspapers and television. The profile of the first 100 million
internet users was predominantly English-speaking middle classes
mainly concentrated in metropolitan cities (Shah et al. 2015). The
diversification in the internet users' base began to take place only
after 2010 with government initiatives such as connecting the gram
panchayats in large villages to the internet along with commercial and
educational interests.

When we compare the growth trajectory of legacy media, such as the press and television in India, with the internet, we notice a similar trend of diversification in the audience base after the initial concentration. Soon after independence, English-language newspapers dominated the media landscape, and it took nearly three decades, until 1979, for Indian-language newspapers to surpass the English-language newspapers in terms of circulation. The massive increase in Indian-language newspaper circulation in the 1980s was accompanied by a parallel trend of increasing mobilization of the masses in India (Neyazi 2011, 2018). Similarly, looking at the history of the growth of television, we notice that the initial decades of the expansion of private television since 1990 were mostly dominated by programmes in the English language, and catered mainly to the urban middle class. From the late 1990s and early 2000s, content on Indian television began to diversify with the growth of Indian-language programming on private television. There has been a massive growth in the number of Indian-language news channels since the early 2000s, which has redefined the media landscape in India. This transformation in the profile of press and broadcast media has affected the process of political communication and helped mobilize those who were earlier difficult to reach. The growth in internet users, which has begun to be more diffused and diversified, is imbued with potential that could mobilize large number of people because of increasing interactions between online and offline worlds.

Causes of Internet Vernacularization

There are a number of factors that have propelled the massive growth in internet users, including availability of internet content in Indian vernacular languages, the growth of cheap smartphones with Indian vernacular language keyboards, and the availability of internet access in rural areas. The most important initiative for the growth of the internet in rural India was launched in 2011 by the Manmohan Singh–led United Progressive Alliance (UPA) government, which aimed at connecting all 2.5 lakh (250,000) gram panchayats of India with broadband connectivity by 2013. This policy was based on two important recommendations: the first recommendation came from the then advisor to the prime minister, Sam Pitroda, which was released in the form of a white paper titled 'Broadband to Panchayats' (Office of the Adviser 2010). The second was a report of recommendations on the state of broadband in India released by the Telecom Regulatory Authority of India in December 2010. For the purposes of connecting villages to the internet, the National Optical Fibre Network project was launched in October 2011 to ensure that the government is able to deliver e-services in the areas of education, health, entertainment, commerce, and governance to all its citizens.[4] The project required nearly 500,000 kilometres of optic fibre to be laid across the country in three years at an estimated cost of $4 billion (see Srinivasan and Ilavarasan 2015).[5] This effort to connect all villages proved an important initiative, which received renewed interest under the Bharatiya Janata Party (BJP) government led by Prime Minister Narendra Modi. The National Optical Fibre Network project has been rechristened as BharatNet, and a new deadline to complete the roll-out of broadband was set for December 2016, which has now been deferred to March 2019 (see Bhargava 2017).[6]

Prime Minister Modi's government has been making concerted efforts to create a digital infrastructure to provide services to citizens and create digital literacy. Under the umbrella of the Digital India programme, the central government has initiated the Pradhan Mantri Gramin Digital Saksharta Abhiyan (Prime Minister's Rural Digital Literacy Campaign), which aims to empower rural citizens through digital literacy and train 60 million people in rural areas by 2019 (PMGDSA official website). Digital literacy is an important component for semi-literate citizens to be able to use the e-services and e-applications offered by the government. One of the factors affecting digital literacy is the absence of support of digital content in local vernacular languages. This handicap has now been overcome with increasing content available in local languages as well as the availability of devices configured with Indian languages. In order to enhance the adoption of internet among the novice and semi-literate population, it is imperative that more content in vernacular languages is developed. India has hundreds of vernacular languages, with 22 officially recognized languages, and about 122 spoken by substantial numbers, according to the 2001 census.[7]

Google launched the Indian Language Internet Alliance (ILIA) in 2014, which promotes Indian languages on the web; this facilitated the massive growth of internet users in India. Most of the prominent media companies with a strong presence in the Indian-language media market have partnered with Google's initiative, including ABP News, the Amarujala Group, Bhaskar Group, Jagran Prakashan Ltd, Network 18, NDTV India, and others. According to Google, they currently have 30 partners in ILIA. This Google initiative is currently confined to promoting only Hindi-language content on the web, with little attempt to diversify to other Indian languages. Google launched www.Hindiweb.com in order to provide users a single platform where they could access content from various media groups. Although the initiative is helping to grow the vernacular content on the web, the downside may be that it may disadvantage many of the Indian vernacular-language media groups if, instead of visiting the respective news media website, users are diverted to Google, where they will get all their required information. Vernacular-language media groups that have a strong presence in small towns and rural areas and that invest their resources in getting such localized content, need to ensure that Google is not going to monetize information through their voluntary participation. A number of cases have already been reported from Europe in which local media companies registered their concerns about alleged unfair practices by Google on sharing advertising revenues generated by using local media content (Rajawat 2014). For example, in October 2014, Spain introduced a law that required online aggregators such as Google to pay a non-waivable copyright fee for screening content created by newspapers and publishers (Majó-Vázquez et al. 2017). The relationship of platform companies with news organizations is increasingly driven by tension and the news media's fear of an asymmetrical relationship (Nielsen and Ganter 2017).

Yet another challenge for the Google initiative is to promote other Indian languages through ILIA. Hindi no doubt is spoken by the vast majority of the people in India and offers market potential, but other Indian languages cannot be ignored. At the launch event of www. Hindiweb.com in November 2014, Google indicated that it would add other Indian languages in the coming months (Parab 2014). But it took almost three years to include just two other Indian languages— Bengali (October 2017) and Tamil (February 2018). This delay in adding languages other than Hindi in Google's ILIA also raises the question if global private companies are aligning their market interest with the local government's interest; the current BJP-led government is making aggressive attempts to promote Hindi.

Content Creators

Despite the lack of concerted effort by a large private entity, such as Google, or the central government (the current government is focusing more on promoting Hindi), online content in other Indian vernacular languages has been growing rapidly for four important reasons. First, the new smartphones launched in the Indian market are enabled for Indian languages, which was not previously the case. The Indian government issued the order that mobile phones sold in Indian markets from 1 July 2017 onwards must be enabled for Indian languages (Press Trust of India 2016). However, this mandate to integrate Indian-language support in the mobile handsets has been extended twice; from 1 October 2017 to a new deadline of 23 February 2018 (Ministry of Electronics and Information Technology, official website). This mandate implies that all mobile phones have to provide text-reading facilities in all 22 official Indian languages on their devices. Message-typing facility is available in English, Hindi, and one regional language as per the preference of the user, which is facilitating the adoption of mobile internet among the semi-literate population. With the availability of cheap smartphones at a cost of around 1,000 rupees (equivalent to $17), the pace of adoption may accelerate in the near future. Second, both the big and small market players see potential in specific language markets, and are tailoring their content to capture specific markets. While the online regional news and entertainment market has grown rapidly, the pace of growth is slow in other sectors, including e-commerce. Only in January 2017 did Amazon India add three Indian languages—Kannada, Tamil, and Telugu—besides English and Hindi to provide customer support. Third, state governments are promoting their own languages in their respective states, and resisting the efforts by the central government to impose Hindi. For example, the Karnataka state government headed by the opposition Congress party has issued an order to take down all Hindi signboards in metro railway stations.[8] Finally, two important social networking sites now have a significant presence in

Indian languages: Facebook is available in 11 Indian languages, and Twitter in 6 Indian languages. Yahoo has now extended e-mail services in 8 Indian languages—Hindi, Gujarati, Bengali, Tamil, Telugu, Kannada, Marathi, and Malayalam, while Gmail provides support to 9 Indian languages.

The online content in Indian languages initially created by the government was in the form of delivering services to citizens, ranging from e-governance to e-agriculture. The next big boost came from private entities, including social networking sites that wanted to promote their businesses online, and needed to make information available in various Indian languages. The simultaneous interplay of these factors and efforts has resulted in internet vernacularization. The most important contribution of internet vernacularization is the vast amount of *user-generated online content* available in various Indian languages. This not only offers new opportunities to understand the emerging digital vernacular cultures, but also provides a window to understanding the regional public sphere.

MOBILIZATION IN THE VERNACULAR

When the non-English-speaking, vernacular population begins expressing itself in the online arena, this offers potential for creating a more inclusive online space in which diverse viewpoints and demands are debated and discussed in the vernacular. The KPMG (2017) report highlights the fact that the majority of the internet content available in Indian languages is about news and entertainment. Nearly 60 per cent of Indian-language internet users prefer to consume regional news, while one-third of them consume news on digital platforms exclusively. This preference for online regional news is essentially driven by real-time updates. This is important, as several studies in the Western context have demonstrated that people who consume more news are more likely to be politically active and engaged (Eveland et al. 2005; Norris 2000).

As a result of internet vernacularization, the potential for mobilization is even greater with 'contextual hybridity' in information flow: in other words, a number of messages first emerging in a particular medium get remediated through another medium, thus reaching beyond their primary audience. For example, a message originating in an online platform is often picked up by traditional media, such as newspaper and television, gets discussed and debated by civil society groups and lawmakers, leading in turn to wider public debate. In such cases, many people who are not consumers of new media do get informed about happenings in the online world. Even when the number of internet users was small, the internet was used effectively in mobilization strategies by various political actors. It was civil society groups in India which first realized the potential of mobilization through the strategic use of the internet. The 2011 anti-corruption movement led by Anna Hazare began by launching its campaign on online platforms such as Facebook and Twitter, alongside targeted e-mails sent to potential supporters. These online strategies were in addition to their robust campaigns using mobile phones for sending mass SMS messages on regular cell phones to their potential supporters. Since then, a number of other civil society groups have incorporated the internet in their campaign strategies. With the increasing number of internet users using the net in local vernacular languages, the potential to use digital platforms for mobilization is even greater. The 2014 Indian national election saw the effective use of embryonic vernacular digital platforms by BJP's prime ministerial candidate, Narendra Modi. All his tweets were immediately translated into all 22 official languages and shared widely by his campaign team. Similarly, mobile SMS messages were sent in Indian languages as per the preferences of users. While there is no direct evidence of the impact of these strategies in influencing voters, we cannot discount the role of contacting voters in their own languages as a better strategy than connecting with them in the English language.

All these instances of political mobilization using digital media reflect the top-down approach to mobilizing citizens, in which media elites advance their own self-defined agenda to gain political mileage instead of fostering citizen participation through grassroots mobilization. Internet vernacularization could thus prove to be paradoxical in nature: on the one hand, it allows citizens to participate in ongoing public debates without needing to depend on external actors, and promotes self-mobilization. On the other hand, it allows political elites to further their self-interest instead of empowering citizens.

Internet Vernacularization and Propaganda

Although internet vernacularization has great potential for mobilization, we cannot ignore the challenges and potential dangers. While citizens are able to receive and process online information without any intermediary of expertise, since the content is available in their own languages, internet vernacularization can also allow false propaganda to flourish and promote a disinformation economy. There are already many cases of fake news being spread through online platforms globally. In the context of India, WhatsApp, purchased by Facebook in February 2014 for $19 billion, has emerged as an important platform to spread rumours and false information, leading to conflicts between religious groups. India has a growing number of WhatsApp users, which currently stands at over 200 million. In contrast to Western countries, most new users in India are often introduced to the internet through WhatsApp. The growing popularity of WhatsApp is said to be driven by its features of anonymity and end-to-end encryption of messages, which supposedly protect one's privacy.

Doctored images and videos, often emerging on the internet, get shared widely through WhatsApp and mobile phones. While there are several small and localized incidents in which WhatsApp has been used to spread rumours and serve politically motivated agendas, there are also instances of major killings. The 2013 Muzaffarnagar riots in the Indian state of Uttar Pradesh are one example where old images and rumours were circulated through WhatsApp, resulting in the killing of 40 Hindus and Muslims; several Muslim women were raped and nearly 40,000 Muslims were evicted from the town, taking shelter in refugee camps in nearby villages (Allana 2017). In yet another example, a rumour about a child kidnapper, spread through WhatsApp, led to the lynching of four youths in the state of Jharkhand in May 2017 (Allana 2017).

The use of the internet and mobile phones to mobilize groups and communities against each other will be accentuated with internet vernacularization, as the process will bring substantial numbers of people from rural areas and small towns into the digital space. India's multiple languages and the circulation of propaganda messaged through micro groups over mobile phones and WhatsApp make it difficult to combat deliberate digital propaganda. While creating the digital literacy to develop more informed and educated internet users is on the government's agenda, placing a check on the disinformation economy is no easy task. A growing number of cases of fake news and online propaganda have been found in Western developed democracies, designed to influence public opinion and voting behaviour in elections such as the US elections in 2016, and in referendums such as that held in Britain in the same year (Semetko and Tworzecki 2017). The occurrence of such instances in advanced, developed countries that have achieved universal literacy in turn demonstrates that even educated people are prone to manipulative propaganda orchestrated online. These instances serve as portents for the tenuous situation in developing countries, including India, where universal literacy is not yet fully realized and that have a weak social fabric with instances of ethnic conflict.

Internet Vernacularization and Journalism

It is in this context of the rise of online propaganda involving various actors that one should consider the implications of internet vernacularization for journalism. Newsrooms tracking events online may fall into the trap of such propaganda, as seen from past experience. There is now growing concern globally, since various actors are trying to influence public opinion through online propaganda while simultaneously aiming to influence mainstream media. Such fears have also led some news organizations to adopt a cautionary approach and set up institutional mechanisms to detect real news from fake propaganda.[9] The BBC, in particular, has set up a fake news detection team to ensure that such propaganda is not published on their platforms. Similarly, Facebook, in its effort to fight manipulative propaganda and fake news, has been deleting accounts found to be involved in such activities. Yet, the recent exposure that Facebook overlooked the breach of privacy of nearly 50 million users by Cambridge Analytica, raises questions about the accountability of platform companies to their users (see *Globe and Mail* 2018).

With mushrooming vernacular online content and an overwhelming number of Indians accessing it every day, it is a challenge for social media to ensure that fake content is not circulated through their platforms. With India having many languages, it would be difficult for social media groups to monitor and filter contentious content, though attempts have been made by organizations such as Facebook (TNN 2017). Since internet programming in Indian languages is still in an embryonic stage, companies detecting fake news and trolls have to depend on humans who can better understand the meanings of words and the context. At the same time, there are limited attempts by Indian news media organizations to institute fact-checking mechanisms. Even well-established news organizations known for quality journalism are falling prey to fake news.[10] This is more disturbing, since a story published in a quality news outlet is more likely to be trusted and widely shared as compared to blogs or little-known online sources. Internet vernacularization is placing additional responsibilities and growing challenges before Indian news outlets with respect to the safeguarding of quality journalism through apposite editorial supervision. In the 24/7 news cycle, where each news organization tries to be the first to break the story, one can expect to see the circulation of more doctored images and compromising on journalistic norms. This is because with dwindling revenues and declining profits, it is unlikely that Indian news outlets are going to spend additional resources on setting up fact-checking mechanisms.

* * *

Internet vernacularization is leading to far greater mobilization as compared to the mobilization that occurred after the rise of Indian-language newspapers and news channels. Internet technology by its very nature is far more diffused, and can easily be personalized and customized according to the needs of the audience. In the ever-changing media environment, personal and social networks along with the proliferation of vernacular internet content will affect the competing ideas of articulating one's demands in the public arena, allowing disparate publics to come together in a web of networks and make their interventions in the ongoing public debates. In addition to the increase in digital media outlets, the sphere of democratic interactions has not only deepened into regional and local levels, but has also expanded to the global level. The growing availability of user-generated content online in the vernacular languages could be an important window to understand the agendas and issues in the regional public sphere, while simultaneously connecting these to the global public sphere. The rise of digital vernacular communication in India is going to change the ways in which political parties and civil society groups use the platforms to mobilize citizens, localizing and customizing initiatives in the first instance.

Yet, we cannot ignore the potential downside of the process of internet vernacularization and the use of digital networks by political elites to advance their self-interest and political agendas. There are already attempts by various actors to manipulate public opinion and create political polarization by unleashing targeted propaganda through digital media, as noted earlier. These attempts already have precarious effects, leading to conflicts and killings of citizens. While the use of online propaganda has accentuated with more diverse publics being brought to online platforms, such propaganda does not go uncontested. There are many civil society and advocacy groups and journalists simultaneously exposing and busting such propaganda (see Perera 2017). These contestations among various actors to wield political power and control public opinion are not going to be resolved with internet vernacularization, but are going to get more pronounced.

NOTES

1. This chapter is a revised version of the paper presented at the 68th Annual International Communication Association Conference, Prague, 24–8 May 2018. Another version of this chapter was presented at the Reuters Institute of Journalism, University of Oxford, 27 March 2018. I am grateful to the participants for their comments, particularly to Rasmus Nielsen, Lucas Graves, and Sílvia Majó-Vázquez.
2. For a critical analysis of the concept of digital divide with a case study from various countries, please see Ragnedda and Muschert (2013).
3. There is no agreement about the number of English speakers in India and the estimate varies from 7 to 15 per cent. This disagreement about the number of English speakers has been further fuelled since the *Census of India 2011* did not release the list of people speaking English as their second language.
4. The plan to deliver e-services to all citizens began in 2006 with the National e-Governance Plan, which resulted in the creation of various

forms of internet infrastructures in the states, including the State Wide Access Network. Despite many efforts, India lacked a specific policy initiative for the development of broadband infrastructure and its uptake by businesses, which resulted in the slow progress of broadband connectivity in the country. For details see Jayakar and Liu (2014).

5. The initial deadline to roll out the fibre optic was fixed for December 2013, which was deferred to September 2015 by the then UPA government.

6. The deadline for the roll-out has been strategically fixed for March 2019, just before the next general election is due. The deadline is likely to be deferred further when the next general election approaches.

7. While 60 Indian languages have more than 100,000 speakers, 122 Indian languages have more than 10,000 native speakers.

8. The order was issued by the Karnataka chief minister in response to the recent attempts by the BJP-led central government to foist Hindi on the southern states, which has met with opposition. In the letter written to the central government, the Karnataka chief minister advised that 'it will be better to follow a persuasive approach rather than a mandatory approach in the matter of the use of Hindi' (Gopal 2017).

9. While newsrooms have long employed fact checkers to verify stories before they are broadcast or printed, more stringent political fact checking mechanisms and new kinds of journalistic practices are now emerging to make public figures more accountable, particularly in the context of the US. For details see Graves (2016).

10. After a tragic incident of stampeding in a Mumbai metro station on 29 September 2017, in which 22 died, people rushed to the scene to help the victims. A picture emerged that showed a man standing close to some injured women, which led to the publication of a story in the *Hindu*, an English newspaper known for quality journalism, claiming that the man was attempting to molest women who were fighting for their lives. After the falsity of the image was exposed, the *Hindu* tendered an apology and withdrew the story from its online platforms. See *Hindu* (2017).

REFERENCES

Allana, Alia (2017). 'WhatsApp, Crowds and Power in India'. *New York Times*, 21 June. Retrieved from https://www.nytimes.com/2017/06/21/opinion/whatsapp-crowds-and-power-in-india.html?mwrsm=Facebook (accessed on 12 August 2018).

Barber, Benjamin (1984). *Strong Democracy: Participatory Politics for a New Age*. Berkeley: University of California Press.

Bhargava, Yuthika (2017). 'BharatNet Deadline Pushed to March 2019'. *Hindu*, 19 July. Retrieved from http://www.thehindu.com/business/bharatnet-deadline-pushed-to-march-2019/article19309467.ece (accessed on 12 August 2018).

Business Standard (2016). 'Hindi Internet Users Estimated at 60 Million in India: Survey', 4 February. Retrieved from http://www.business-standard.com/article/current-affairs/hindi-internet-users-estimated-at-60-million-in-india-survey-116020400922_1.html (accessed on 12 August 2018).

Chadwick, Andrew (2006). *Internet Politics: States, Citizens, and New Communication Technologies*. New York: Oxford University Press.

Eveland Jr, William P., Andrew F. Hayes, Dhavan V. Shah, and Nojin Kwak (2005). 'Understanding the Relationship between Communication and Political Knowledge: A Model Comparison Approach Using Panel Data'. *Political Communication*, 22(4): 423–46.

Globe and Mail (2018). 'What Is Cambridge Analytica, and What Did It Do? A Guide to the Facebook Scandal and Its Political Fallout', 19 March. Retrieved from https://www.theglobeandmail.com/world/article-what-is-cambridge-analytica-and-what-did-it-do-a-guide/?utm_medium=Referrer:+Social+Network+/+Media&utm_campaign=Shared+Web+Article+Links.

Gopal, Vikram (2017). 'Hindi to Be Dropped from Metro Signboards: Karnataka Chief Minister Siddaramaiah Tells Govt'. *Hindustan Times*, 28 July. Retrieved from http://www.hindustantimes.com/karnataka/hindi-will-be-removed-from-metro-signboards-karnataka-cm-siddaramaiah-tells-govt/story-XnTKW8ct0yCJCsxGRYTFxJ.html (accessed on 12 August 2018).

Graves, Lucas (2016). *Deciding What's True: The Rise of Political Fact-Checking in American Journalism*. New York: Columbia University Press.

Hindman, Mathew (2008). *The Myth of Digital Democracy*. Princeton: Princeton University Press.

Hindu (2017). 'Apology', 4 October. Retrieved from http://www.thehindu.com/news/cities/mumbai/apology/article19779566.ece (accessed on 12 August 2018).

Hooghe, Marc, Sara Vissers, Dietlind Stolle, and Valérie-Anne Mahéo (2010). 'The Potential of Internet Mobilization: An Experimental Study on the Effect of Internet and Face-to-Face Mobilization Efforts'. *Political Communication*, 27(4): 406–31.

Howard, Philip N. (2005). *New Media Campaigns and the Managed Citizen*. Cambridge: Cambridge University Press.

——— (2010). *The Digital Origins of Dictatorship and Democracy: Information Technology and Political Islam*. New York: Oxford University Press.

IAMAI and KANTAR IMRB (2018). *Internet in India—2017: A Report.* New Delhi: IAMAI and KANTAR IMRB. Summary of the report retrieved from http://www.iamai.in/media/details/4990.

Jain, Nimisha and Kanika Sanghi (2016). 'The Rising Connected Consumers in Rural India'. *BGC Perspective.* Retrieved from https://www.bcgperspectives.com/content/articles/globalization-customer-insight-rising-connected-consumer-rural-india/#chapter1 (accessed on 12 August 2018).

Jayakar, Krishna and Chun Liu (2014). 'The Race between the Dragon and the Elephant: Comparing China and India's National Broadband Plans'. *Media International Australia*, 151(1): 180–90.

Klandermans, Bert and Dirk Oegema (1987). 'Potentials, Networks, Motivations, and Barriers: Steps towards Participation in Social Movements'. *American Sociological Review*, 52: 519–31.

KPMG (2017). *Indian Languages: Defining India's Internet.* New Delhi: KPMG and Google.

Lee, Francis L. F. (2015). 'Internet, Citizen Self-Mobilisation, and Social Movement Organisations in Environmental Collective Action Campaigns: Two Hong Kong Cases'. *Environmental Politics*, 24(2): 308–25.

Loader, Brian D., and Dan Mercea (eds) (2012). *Social Media and Democracy: Innovations in Participatory Politics.* London: Routledge.

Majó-Vázquez, Sílvia, Ana S. Cardenal, and Sandra González-Bailón (2017). 'Digital News Consumption and Copyright Intervention: Evidence from Spain before and after the 2015 "Link Tax"'. *Journal of Computer-Mediated Communication*, 22(5): 284–301.

Ministry of Electronics and Information Technology (2018). 'Extension in Date of Implementation of Indian Language Support for Mobile Phones'. Retrieved from http://meity.gov.in/writereaddata/files/Extension%20in%20date%20of%20implementation%20of%20IS%2016333%20%28Part%203%292016-%20Indian%20Language%20Support%20for%20Mobile%20Phones%20dated%2017.01.2018.pdf.

Mossberger, Karen, Caroline J. Tolbert, and Ramona S. McNeal (2007). *Digital Citizenship: The Internet, Society and Participation.* Cambridge: MIT Press.

Neyazi, Taberez A. (2011). 'Politics after Vernacularisation: Hindi Media and Indian Democracy'. *Economic and Political Weekly*, 46(10): 75–82.

——— (2018). *Political Communication and Mobilisation: The Hindi Media in India.* New Delhi: Cambridge University Press.

Nielsen, Rasmus K. and Sarah Anne Ganter (2017). 'Dealing with Digital Intermediaries: A Case Study of the Relations between Publishers and Platforms'. *New Media & Society*, online first 1461444817701318.

Norris, Pippa (2000). *A Virtuous Circle: Political Communications in Postindustrial Societies*. Cambridge: Cambridge University Press.

Office of the Adviser (2010). 'Broadband to Panchayats: Empowering Panchayats and Rural India by Democratising Information through Broadband'. Retrieved from http://initiatives.sampitroda.com/iii/images/stories/innovation/Whitepaper_BB_to_Panchayat.pdf (accessed on 12 August 2018).

Parab, Pranay (2014). 'Google's India Language Internet Alliance Aims to Get 50 Crore People Online'. NDTV, 3 November. Retrieved from http://gadgets.ndtv.com/internet/news/googles-indian-language-internet-alliance-aims-to-get-50-crore-people-online-615543 (accessed on 12 August 2018).

Perera, Ayeshea (2017). 'The People Trying to Fight Fake News in India'. BBC, 24 July. Retrieved from http://www.bbc.com/news/world-asia-india-40657074?utm_content=buffer5f1c4&utm_medium=social&utm_source=facebook.com&utm_campaign=buffer (accessed on 12 August 2018).

Press Trust of India (2016). 'Government Mandates Indian Language Support in Phones from July 2017'. *Indian Express*, 28 October. Retrieved from http://indianexpress.com/article/technology/mobile-tabs/govt-mandates-indian-language-support-in-phones-from-july-2017-3726977/ (accessed on 12 August 2018).

Ragnedda, Massimo and Glenn W. Muschert, eds (2013). *The Digital Divide: The Internet and Social Inequality in International Perspective*. London: Routledge.

Rajawat, K. Yatish (2014). 'Google Will Destroy Local Newspapers with Indian Language Internet Alliance'. *FirstPost*. Retrieved from http://www.firstpost.com/business/google-will-destroy-local-newspapers-with-indian-language-internet-alliance-1995349.html (accessed on 27 June 2017).

Semetko, Holli A. and Margaret Scammell (2012). 'The Expanding Field of Political Communication in the Era of Continuous Connectivity'. In *The Sage Handbook of Political Communication*, eds Holli A. Semetko and Margaret Scammell, pp. 1–5. London and New Delhi: Sage.

Semetko, Holli A. and Hubert Tworzecki (2017). 'Campaign Strategies, Media and Voters: The Fourth Era of Political Communication'. In *The Routledge Handbook of Public Opinion and Voting Behaviour*, eds Justin Fisher, Edward Fieldhouse, Mark N. Franklin, Rachel Gibson, Christopher Wlezien, and Marta Cantijoch, pp. 293–304. London: Routledge.

Shah, Alpesh, Nimisha Jain, and Shweta Bajpai (2015). *India@Digital Bharat: Creating a $200 Billion Internet Economy*. New Delhi: Boston Consulting Group and Internet and Mobile Association of India.

Srinivasan, Nalini and Vigneswara Ilavarasan (2015). 'White Elephant or a Game Changer? An Analysis of National Optical Fibre Network of India'. *Economic and Political Weekly*, 50(42): 59–66.

TNN (2017). 'Firms Hire Locals to Tackle Regional Trolls'. *Times of India*, 22 August. Retrieved from https://timesofindia.indiatimes.com/city/lucknow/firms-hire-locals-to-tackle-regional-trolls/articleshow/60169063.cms (accessed on 12 August 2018).

TRAI (Telecom Regulatory Authority of India) (2010). *Recommendations on National Broadband Plan*. Retrieved from http://www.trai.gov.in/sites/default/files/53.pdf (accessed on 11 September 2018).

Velasquez, Alcides and Robert LaRose (2015). 'Social Media for Social Change: Social Media Political Efficacy and Activism in Student Activist Groups'. *Journal of Broadcasting and Electronic Media*, 59(3): 456–74.

Verba, S., Kay Lehman Schlozman, and Henry E. Brady (1995). *Voice and Equality: Civic Voluntarism in American Politics*. Cambridge, MA: Harvard University Press.

Wu, Angela Xiao and Harsh Taneja (2016). 'Reimagining Internet Geographies: A User-centric Ethnological Mapping of the World Wide Web'. *Journal of Computer-Mediated Communication*, 21(3): 230–46.

CHAPTER SEVEN

The Media Are Biased

Exploring Online Right-Wing Responses
to Mainstream News in India

KALYANI CHADHA AND PRASHANTH BHAT

. . . .

India's national election of 2014 was significant for bringing to power the Hindu nationalist BJP in a decisive victory that ended decades of coalition rule in the country. From a media standpoint, this election was also notable for the extensive coverage given to the successful party and its leader Narendra Modi. According to an analysis conducted by the non-partisan CMS Media Lab, Mr Modi and the BJP got close to 40 per cent of all prime-time television coverage in the run-up to the election, significantly more than any other politician or political group (CMS Media Lab 2014: 1). Some media observers even commented on what they perceived to be the overt support of Mr Modi by sections of the national media (Guha Thakurta 2014).

But despite the recent favourable coverage, members of the Indian political right as represented by the BJP and its ideological allies[1] have long taken the position that the country's so-called 'left-liberal' and 'pseudo-secular', mainstream media—particularly the national press which plays a crucial agenda-setting role—is opposed to the right (Sonwalkar 2006). The tensions between the political right and mainstream Indian media can be traced back to the late 1980s, when the BJP, acting in concert with other Hindu nationalist groups, launched the Hindutva or 'Hinduness', campaign, an ideological effort aimed at redefining India as a 'Hindu' nation (Davis 2005). Integral to the campaign was the proposed construction of a temple in the northern city of Ayodhya, at a spot which devout Hindus identified as the birthplace of their god, Rama. As this spot was occupied by a fifteenth-century mosque, the demand for a temple resulted in a dispute, which eventually culminated in the destruction of the mosque by so-called 'volunteers' from Hindu nationalist organizations in December 1992 (Guha 2012). This was followed by violent riots in several north Indian cities. Not surprisingly, these events, which marked a watershed in the Hindu nationalist movement, generated considerable media coverage. Interestingly, although some commentators criticized the 'general culpability of the Indian media in adopting a celebratory attitude towards the Hindu Right's Ram Janmabhumi movement' (Ram 2012: 20), right-wing groups argued that national media outlets which were intent on 'minority appeasement' were biased against the majority and its authentic claims (Prasad 2002). While right-wing outrage against mainstream national media continued to simmer, it surfaced on a country-wide scale in 1999, in response to what the BJP and others perceived to be a one-sided media coverage of the murder of an Australian missionary and his two young sons by activists of the Bajrang Dal, a Hindu activist organization. As one commentator put it:

> The beating up of conversion-resisting tribals; desecrations of Hindu idols; a forced exodus of non-Christians ... None of which items were/ are investigated or debated or published by the 'mainstream' media. Instead, there's only more of the uneven coverage: Inconvenient details are systematically ignored; there is no retraction of bogus 'news'; and there's the hard sell of an angelic Christendom suffering under a barbaric Hindutva. At the editorial level, this kind of consensus can only be an engineered one. (Bhosle 1999)

Similarly, in 2001, a sting operation conducted by the news weekly *Tehelka*, showing the BJP president Mr Bangaru Laxman accepting a bribe from a fake arms dealer in return for awarding him a defense contract, riled both BJP leaders and members of Hindu nationalist organizations who condemned mainstream media coverage as a political hit job by a partisan media (Chaudhury 2002). However, the perception of a 'left-liberal media bias' among right-wing circles was perhaps most effectively reinforced by mainstream media coverage of the riots that took place in Gujarat in 2002, a state governed at the time by India's current prime minister, Narendra Modi. These riots in which about a thousand people, mostly Muslim, were killed, constituted the first large-scale communal[2] riots following the launch of 24-hour television news channels in the country, and for the first time in Indian history, violence was carried 'live', on television. In the coverage that ensued, the national press actively questioned the state government's failure to contain the riots, and some suggested that the Modi administration had in fact been complicit in the violence (Ram 2012) and even sought his apology (News18.com 2013). Predictably, such coverage invited charges of biased reporting from the BJP and other right-wing groups who accused the national media, notably the English-language press, of 'distorting' the issue and 'demonizing Hindu organizations and their supporters' (Hinduism Today 2002). Right-wing activists were notably incensed by editorials that called on Narendra Modi to apologize for his government's failures, arguing that such demands were not only unfair given that non-BJP chief ministers were never asked to apologize for communal clashes in their states, but also revealed the national media's deep-seated anti-BJP/anti-Hindu stance. As they put it, 'they [media] only listen to Muslims and ignore Hindus' (Patel et al. 2002).

In 2012, Modi was finally cleared of involvement in the 2002 riots by the Supreme Court of India. His acquittal gave further credence to the perception of liberal media bias among BJP supporters and right-wing activists, who asserted that the highest court's judgment showed that the mainstream press had been unfair to Modi all along. Commenting on the impact of the coverage, conservative commentator Minhaz Merchant stated: 'Some columnists were so obsessively and often viciously anti-Modi that they achieved three unintended objectives: one, they eroded their own credibility; two they generated unexpected support for Modi among readers who felt he was being unfairly maligned; and three, they caused widespread revulsion in the public for mainstream media' (Merchant 2015).

Indeed, a pervasive feeling within right-wing circles seemed to be that 'an entire constellation of powers with a negative intent', with a 'galaxy of sepoys, especially in media and academia', was 'arrayed against them' (Srinivasan 2016). But unlike media scholars and observers who have criticized the increasingly 'commercialized and corporatized' nature of the Indian news media (Rao and Mudgal 2015) which has resulted in negative implications for journalism, including growing sensationalism (Thussu 2007), a failure to focus on substantive issues (Mudgal 2011), as well as the growing influence of political and business interests over news (Chadha and Koliska 2016), what sets the right-wing's attack on mainstream media apart is its emphasis on what it considers the 'anti-Hindu bias' of the latter.

And although this sense of grievance is by no means new, it found an especially potent avenue for expression due to changes in India's technological landscape (Vaidya 2016). Thus, whereas until this point, the Hindu right had mainly sought to counter what they perceived to be the anti-Hindu and anti-BJP tenor of mainstream media narratives through publications such as the pro-BJP paper the *Pioneer*, or the RSS mouthpiece the *Organizer*, they could now take advantage of the tremendous surge in internet use in India as well as the growth of online media platforms. Indeed, just as the medium of state television— through its broadcasting of the Hindu epic the *Ramayana*—contributed to the rise of Hindutva-related ideologies in the 1980s (Rajagopal 2001), the combination of enhanced connectivity and new virtual spaces enabled right-wing intellectuals and activists to establish a variety of websites and news and commentary portals that are characterized by an oppositional stance vis-à-vis mainstream media.

The earliest and initially most influential exemplar of such websites was NitiCentral.com. Established in August 2012 'to challenge the mainstream media by providing an alternate, Right of Center, perspective', this site was shut down in 2015. Since then, the task of opposing mainstream news narratives has been taken on by other right-leaning news and commentary websites. In this chapter, we explore the discourse of Swarajyamag.com, OpIndia.com, and Indiafacts.org—three right-wing online news portals that are exemplars of the varied types of sites that have gained a growing following among the so-called 'Internet Hindus', and that contain 'a new kind of ideology-centric journalism' (Khan 2015) aimed at challenging and countering mainstream news accounts. In doing so, we aim to provide empirical insight into a crucial component of the country's emergent conservative counter-sphere, which offers an institutionalized 'communicative environment' for right-wing thinkers (Schmidt 2008). We begin by offering a brief description of these sites, followed by a discussion of their media-related discourse, and conclude by reflecting on their role in the emergence of an increasingly visible conservative Hindu counter-sphere that appears to be inspired by the 'conservative counter-sphere' in the United States (Major 2012).

Defining itself as the 'big tent for right of center discourse', *Swarajya* (meaning freedom) states that it believes in 'celebrating and promoting India's cultural heritage', 'secularism which does not pander', and supporting the 'integrity of India'. The news portal which was launched in September 2014 evolved out of a print weekly founded in 1956, which promoted quintessentially conservative values such as individual liberty, limited government, and free-market economics that represented a stark contrast to the socialist ethos that characterized India at the time. While the magazine shut down following the death of its founders in 1980, the owners of a right-wing website, www.centreright.in, purchased the rights to its name and relaunched it as an online news portal in 2014.[3] Despite its relatively recent provenance, Swarajyamag.com currently enjoys the most traffic among similar right-wing news portals in India, with an estimated 751,136 unique visitors every month. It also has 496,007 'likes' on Facebook and over 42,000 followers on Twitter as of June 2017.

But while the portal bills itself as 'an independent voice', its content—which is provided by a combination of professional staff and independent contributors—makes its political affiliation and ideology unambiguous. Articles with headlines such as 'Why They (Left-Liberals) Don't Want Modi to Succeed', and 'Radical Islamists Are Now Looking to Destroy Tamil Nadu's Dargahs',[4] give away the site's ideological moorings (see also www.Swarajyamag.com 2015). Not only does its executive editorial board include several well-known right-wing intellectuals, but many prominent members of the BJP and the Modi government also contribute to the website, which contains articles on topics such as 'countering media propaganda against Modi' and 'mainstream media's liberal bias'. Like Swarajyamag.com, OpIndia.com was launched in December 2014 by a right-leaning academic, and focuses exclusively on criticism of so-called 'liberal media'. The site highlights what it perceives to be biased reporting by both national and international English-language press, both of which it deems anti-Hindu and anti-India. Stating that 'In India, politics and journalism attract some of the worst brains, thanks to the system that has evolved over time', OpIndia.com represents itself as 'an attempt to break free of this system' by supporting 'libertarian politics and journalism that is free from the burden of liberal bias and political correctness'. The website has 522,460 monthly visitors and is regularly followed by over 41,000 readers on Twitter and 108,000 people on Facebook. In addition to articles and rebuttals to the content published in mainstream news outlets, OpIndia.com also invites its readers to contribute articles and opinion pieces.

With a self-proclaimed aim of countering the so-called propaganda against Hinduism, a group of Indologists started Indiafacts.org, a website dedicated to the discussion of Hindu philosophy, politics, and media-related topics. The site is less popular than both *Swarajya* and OpIndia, but, like them, caters to right-wing audiences. Containing the tagline 'Truth be told', the site 'aims to provide a counter to the mainstream media narrative about India', writings by right-leaning historians, academics, and commentators on topics such as the 'distortion and appropriation of Indian identity', the growing threat posed by radical Islam and evangelical Christianity, as well as religiously motivated attacks on Hindus in India and abroad, enumerated through its monthly Hindu Persecution digest.

ANALYSING ONLINE RIGHT-WING MEDIA-RELATED DISCOURSE

Mirroring conservative commentary in the United States with its attacks on the so-called 'liberal' and 'elite' media, the general contention of the right-wing online outlets that we examined vis-à-vis national media outlets is that the latter are dominated by 'left-liberal' journalists who are inclined to 'distort, inflame and promote a line of propaganda' (Mukherji 2015). According to these sites, claims to independence notwithstanding, the national press are actually closely allied with political parties such as the Aam Aadmi Party (AAP), which emerged in the wake of the anti-corruption movement of 2012, and the erstwhile ruling Congress. As one commentator reflecting on media coverage of the parliamentary elections in Delhi of May 2014 and the victory of the AAP leader put it:

> I have always had a sense at the back of my mind that the MSM brigade is too deeply invested in the Kejriwal phenomenon and would try to reinvent him at some point of time. The present Delhi election became a God-sent opportunity for almost the entire media universe.... TV studios were virtually converted into AAP campaign offices for the last one month wherein 2–3 supposedly 'neutral' commentators of the likes of Aarti Jeraths, Dibangs and Manini Chatterjees would sit and pontificate on the virtues of AAP even while deriding the ruling party. (Patil 2015a)

Another noted that 'there is a concerted effort on the part of the Congress to project the current NDA government as UPA-3, and the media is playing by its script' (Dasgupta 2015). Indeed, writers on these sites regularly made the claim that mainstream news outlets had to all intents and purposes been co-opted by the political establishment as represented by the Congress party and that they tailored their coverage accordingly. Reflecting this position, a piece on OpIndia.com stated:

> If not for anything else, the ten year UPA rule provided innumerable opportunities to journalists to permanently establish their credentials. There were so many flabbergasting stories of misuse of power and corruption coming out from Delhi, that our journalists should have been fretting over the agony of choice. But none of the so called top journalists broke the 2G scam, Coalgate, Adarsh, CWG scam or any of the countless gifts from UPA. The corruption was instead uncovered by NGOs, individual MPs, private citizens and the CAG. Even more criminal was the lack of proper investigative follow-ups to these breaking stories.... Such lack of curiosity would have been mysterious if not for the timely release of the Radia tapes which did a splendid job of encapsulating how compromised and beholden the Indian media is to those very powers it is supposed to keep a watch on. (OpIndia.com 2015)

In addition to characterizing mainstream media outlets as corrupt—sometimes referring to them as 'presstitutes'—right-wing news outlets also routinely deride 'left-liberal' journalists for their dissemination of an 'anti-Indian narrative', particularly through their coverage of Kashmir. Thus, in contrast to media observers who have criticized Indian media coverage as 'overwhelmingly in favor of the Indian government and armed forces' (Khalid 2016), writers on the sites we analysed routinely make the case that mainstream media in fact provide support to the separatist cause through coverage that emphasizes the 'killing of innocent Kashmiris', while ignoring the deaths of security personnel as well as the 'ethnic cleansing' of Kashmiri Hindus from the state (Simha 2016) and advocating for talks with both Kashmiri leaders as well as Pakistan (R. Sharma 2016; Simha 2016). In fact, one writer for Indiafacts.org went so far as to state that 'on the Kashmir issue, even the Pakistani media does not attack India as much as left liberal journalists' (Simha 2016), while a *Swarajya* commentator held the media responsible for weakening the position of the Indian government (Jagannathan 2017).

Another popular and widely circulated line of critique in the discursive attack mounted by right-wing news and commentary sites vis-à-vis mainstream news outlets is that the latter are deeply 'biased' against Hindus and Hinduism. This bias, they contend, is evident in the mainstream press's 'negative' coverage of Hindu faith and culture wherein elite journalists and media commentators are quick to deride Hinduism and represent its believers as 'regressive', while avoiding any criticism of minority faiths (Manini 2015). Underscoring this point, an editorial on OpIndia.com asserted that 'We find that in the news media, including that of India itself, anti-Hindu attitudes are common. Hindus are spoken of in negative way that is not done relative to religious groups whose behavior has been more violent, exclusive or oppressive. Anti-Hindu statements appear to be acceptable to everyone and no one questions them very much' (IndiaFacts.com 2015).

Some contributors go so far as to assert that even though they make up the majority of India's population, Hindus are representationally challenged by the 'biased' national media. In this vein a right-wing commentator wrote:

> Christianity, Islam and Judaism have numerous news stations, media outlets, and media analysts both in countries where they are in a majority and in those where they are minorities. Unfortunately, Hindus do not have much comparable in the mass media, even in Bharat,[5] which

puts them at a severe disadvantage in this information era.... Bharat's media is dominated by leftist groups, including well known members of Bharat's communist parties, who have formed an extensive network with anti-Hindu groups. (Frawley 2016)

Moreover, contributors on these sites also claim that mainstream news media outlets espouse a type of 'pseudo-secularism' that favours the rights of minorities and is inimical to the Hindu majority. In this context, one commentator wrote: 'India's media portrays Hindus as a privileged majority, as if the laws benefitted them unfairly. It promotes anti-Hindu attitudes, and encourages government and judicial interference in Hindu affairs. And when Hindus complain about the brazen discrimination against them, the media accuses Hindus of being intolerant' (Frawley 2016).

Apart from disseminating what one Indiafacts writer terms the 'chronic hate Hindu narrative' (Manini 2015), writers on these sites frequently argue that national media outlets display active 'partisanship' in their 'favourable' treatment of minorities, exemplified in their reluctance to use the term 'Islamic' terror and their attempts to 'humanize Muslim terrorists' (Sarkar 2014) while displaying little hesitation in condemning Hindu nationalist organizations as 'extremist', or even 'fascist', with a view to discrediting them (Frawley 2015). Indeed, this trend, many right-wing commentators asserted, was evident in the writings of many 'leftist' mainstream news columnists who 'portrayed Yakub Memon one of the masterminds in the 1993 Islamic terror attack on Mumbai as innocent' and questioned the decision to execute him (OpIndia.com 2016). Writers also frequently emphasize that the national media has been deliberately 'apathetic' to the religious persecution of Hindus worldwide. Emphasizing this point, a *Swarajya* contributor wrote:

> Indian media has done a 'commendable' job in covering international events, be it Arab spring, Tahrir square, Gaza conflicts to beatification of saints at Vatican. The only blind spot has been the plight, or rather the disappearance, of Hindus worldwide, including in India's own backyard. This is quite inexplicable given that other events in these regions, elections and terror attacks in Pakistan, have been generously covered.... The apathy of Indian media about Hindu victims of persecution has not been induced by the lack of resources. (Sarkar 2014)

Others accuse the 'liberal' mainstream press of failing to acknowledge what they perceive to be the growing threat to the Hindu community posed by other religions. In this regard, a *Swarajya* writer claimed: 'Newspapers have not, over the decades, ever used the phrase "onslaught of Christianity", which is actually a more accurate description of what is happening through the proselytization efforts of aggressive evangelical missionaries funded by the West' (Venkataraman 2015).

In a similar vein, another contributor lamented the failure of 'secular media' to recognize the phenomenon of 'love jihad', whereby Hindu women were being persuaded to marry Muslim men and convert to Islam (Kapoor 2014). Meanwhile, many other commentators deplored the national media's failure to highlight what they termed 'religious' demographic changes in India (Dikgaj et al. 2016; Bajaj 2016). Reflecting this view, a commentator on OpIndia.com noted:

> In India, see how the demography of the country is being systematically changed. North East India, Kerala, Tamil Nadu, Andhra Pradesh, Telangana & many tribal & rural areas are falling to massive, systematic, and organized Christian conversations supported by fake NGOs and evangelical missionaries' networks. States like Kashmir, West Bengal, Bihar, UP, and many other parts of India are radically Islamized.... This is further supported by complete silence from our 'secular' media. (IntolerantIndian 2016)

However, perhaps the most persistent and recurring critiques directed at the mainstream press in the articles that we examined, was that these outlets engage in 'selective outrage', resulting in 'hysteria over majoritarian communalism/intolerance and a blind eye towards or muted criticism of minority communalism/intolerance' (Seetha 2015). This, numerous writers have argued, results in biased coverage, whereby acts of violence committed by Hindus against other communities receive 'disproportionate' media attention whereas attacks targeting Hindus evoke little response from national media outlets. As evidence, commentators offered examples of cases that in their view revealed the media's so-called 'double-standards'. One such issue was coverage of the 2016 unrest in West Bengal. Discussing the incident, a *Swarajya* journalist argued that mainstream accounts which sought to explain the mob's violence as a response to a Hindu leader's allegedly inflammatory remarks not only misrepresented the situation, but also downplayed the incident because the mob belonged to a minority community. Condemning mainstream coverage, she said, 'In Malda, the administration continues to enable the rioters with soft-action and political posturing to deflect blame. Many sections of the media continue to aid and abet this. For instance, a senior journalist, who failed in his duty to report, accused others of fanning communal flames when they carried the story. The underlying message was to downplay the events' (Barooah 2016).

Another example of the so-called anti-Hindu bias cited by *Swarajya* writers was the murder of a Hindu boy by three Muslim youths, in what the website identified as a religiously motivated attack. Reacting to the incident, a commentator wrote:

> Indian media had extensively covered the murder of a Muslim techie by Hindu goons in Pune but barely mentioned brutal killings of an RSS[6] pracharak in Kerala and a BJP secretary in Tamil Nadu or the rape of a 9 year-old Hindu girl by a Muslim. Your life is worth an awful lot if you happen to be a Muslim, and you are a victim of violence at the hands of Hindus—like it happened in Dadri[7].... When one Mohammad Ikhlaq died in a hate crime at the hands of a few Hindus, a whole nation was declared intolerant but when Sawan Rathod was brutally, cruelly murdered because he was a Hindu, it is made out to be just a 'law and order' crime! If you are just a poor, uneducated Hindu kid of 16, burnt alive by Muslims, your life is not worth the amount of petrol used to turn you into a human torch! (Vaidya 2016)

More recently, right-wing news sites mounted a similar attack on mainstream news media for their coverage of recent riots in West Bengal, on the grounds that they ignored violence by Muslims (Ghosh 2017; Jagannathan 2017). In this context, a writer for OpIndia claimed:

> It is clear that Hindu lives don't matter to the 'secular-liberal' media. Not a word for the man who was killed. Contrast that to copious tears they shed when a victim is Muslim.... In sifting through all the reports about the subsequent violence, I am yet to come across one intellectual taking issue with the fact that the West Bengal police is

taking action against the victim (a minor no less!) instead of going out and containing the rioters.... Instead, I have seen media reporting on the original FB post calling it anything from 'objectionable' to 'blasphemous' ... neither can I find anyone willing to meet with the family of Kartik Ghosh and report on the tragedy they have faced. It is as if Kartik Ghosh's life was less real. No one wants to ask who is responsible for the loss of Kartik Ghosh's life. Meanwhile, the death of Junaid Khan is being blamed collectively on the 1 billion Hindus of this country. (Ghosh 2017)

The perception of Hindu victimization—reflected in coverage that is believed to favour minorities while ignoring threats to the majority—thus constitutes an important component of media-related discourse on these sites, where arguably, it serves to consolidate a sense of collective identity among disaffected sections of India's dominant faith group.

NEGATIVE COVERAGE OF THE BJP GOVERNMENT AND ITS LEADER

In addition to stories highlighting media neglect of Hindu concerns, another significant focus of stories on right-wing news portals centred on what contributors identified as the national media's 'biased' coverage of the ruling BJP government and its leader, Prime Minister Narendra Modi. Contributors to these sites routinely claim that the Congress party, which had dominated India for most of its post-independence history, had co-opted a large section of the national media to vilify Modi and his supporters. As one writer put it, 'The English-language media is the vehicle through which double standards in India are propagated. The simple reality is the English press is out to get Modi at every opportunity' (Bhalla 2015).

For instance, on the Swarajyamag.com site, numerous articles argued—often using virtually identical language—that the national press's claims to independence notwithstanding, it was backed by 'big corporates' as well as 'left-liberal parties such as the Congress'. In the words of a *Swarajya* writer, 'The fascism emerging from India's newsrooms is backed by big businesses and the nation's dynasty. Corporates and dynastic centers of power pose a threat to democracies in every country. Indian media houses are ideologically configured' (Ahmad 2015).

This, they asserted, resulted in unfairly partisan and negative coverage of the present government and its policies. Commenting on this, a contributor to OpIndia.com stated:

> There are numerous other examples of political ownership and connections in media. This insidious and incestuous relationship exists with the main objective of distorting public opinion and manipulating issues to suit the agenda of a political party. Since it is done under the guise of neutrality, there is a large element of deceit inbuilt into this kind of mechanism of providing news. (Bhandari 2015)

Writers also asserted that the long-standing relationship between national journalists (including those employed by the public broadcaster Doordarshan) and the Congress party 'which was the source of all favors' (Patil 2015b) led the national media to disseminate 'negative' stories aimed at downplaying the BJP government's successes and portraying the BJP as no different from the Congress government that it succeeded (Dasgupta 2015). Elaborating on this, an Indiafacts writer commented:

> There is no shortage of good stories coming out of India. Of course if you are outside the country you will hear absolutely nothing of this for the simple reason that this will show Prime Minister Narendra Modi in good light…. Let's face it, no matter what Modi does, no matter what he achieves, no matter how he transforms this nation, senior editors, (pseudo) intellectuals, (pseudo) seculars, (pseudo) liberals, writers, artists and (un) Civil Society will continue to attack him 24×7. (Rajguru 2016)

Similarly, a *Swarajya* journalist opined, 'The Modi government has significant achievements under its belt, especially on the economic front. And yet, barring the business press, the impression conveyed by most publications and news channels is that of a clueless government, which is efficient only in pursuing a communal agenda' (Seetha 2015).

Similarly, a commentator on OpIndia.com attacked the English-language press for not giving the Modi government credit for various policy initiatives and instead presenting them as 'repackaged' versions of earlier programmes. As he put it:

> Some are claiming that the 'National Girl Child Day' of UPA was renamed to 'Beti Bachao Beti Padhao' program of the NDA. This is even more specious comparison than the insurance schemes—to compare the celebration of a day to a mass campaign program like Beti Bachao Beti Padhao! However, this is not result of some lack of understanding. There is a clear agenda. To make these lazy accusations multiple times so that people start believing that they are true. An influential part of the media is complicit in fanning this narrative. (Kumar 2017)

Aside from their general resentment at what they deemed to be the national media's unjustifiably negative stance towards India's right-wing government, writers also voiced outrage at the fact that not only did mainstream media outlets dismiss popular initiatives like Yoga Day that were 'enthusiastically received across the country but covered with the same bout of sneering elitism and cynicism that had accompanied earlier events of the Modi government' (Shankar 2015), but, more importantly, failed to give Prime Minister Modi credit for any 'positive' policy changes. In this context, a *Swarajya* contributor wondered

> … whether the elimination of the idea of corruption which had become synonymous with governance under the UPA, the time bound electrification of all of India's villages, unprecedented focus on agriculture through crop insurance, Direct Benefit Transfer (DBT) preventing subsidy leakages and the planned massive infrastructure and development from road to rail occurred in some other continent. Reading or viewing exclusively that form of old media which elevates (often spurious) news of 'Hindu(tva)' intolerance as front page headlines, while often almost censoring the tectonic developmental initiatives, does provide such an impression though. (Basu 2016)

Emphasizing that the national media were only interested in 'sensationalizing' and 'distorting' news (Saraswat 2017; Vaidya 2017), several right-wing commentators protested that mainstream media routinely attacked Hindu organizations, often 'fabricating' stories that made them appear in a negative light (Neelankandan 2015). Emphasizing this point, an Indiafacts contributor asserted, 'The media is clearly being used against the RSS and affiliated Hindu organizations. Rather than being the fourth estate of civil society, India's media is more like a bludgeon. It decides what is relevant to its pre-scripted scenario and cherrypicks information to fit into its pre-ordained script. This propaganda is then disseminated and imposed upon the public' (Parker 2015).

Meanwhile, other writers emphasized that although the prime minister had done nothing that threatened secular values, he was nevertheless painted as an 'extremist' (Basu 2016; K. Sharma 2016). Underlining this point, a staffer for the website wrote, 'The end of this year will mark the halfway point of the Modi government. The Prime Minister has not said or done anything so far that has threatened to disrupt communal harmony. While it is entirely acceptable to criticize the Prime Minister in a democracy, such media criticism has to be grounded in fact rather than bias' (Basu 2016; K. Sharma 2016).

However, right wing contributors' greatest ire was reserved for what they termed the creation of a 'false narrative' of rising intolerance and Muslim persecution by the mainstream media (Vidyasagar 2015; Vyas 2015; Rajguru 2017). In this vein, a writer on the OpIndia site commented:

> If you read and watch Indian media, and more importantly believe all the things they say, you certainly think that since 2014, India has been a different place altogether. Suddenly, Indian people have become intolerant. Majoritarian rule has dawned so religious minorities (especially Muslims) are horrified. Fringe elements on the right have been empowered by this 'sympathizing' government and they started pursuing their agenda brazenly.... (LiberalRight 2017)

Meanwhile, writers also expressed anger at what they considered to be the national press's tendency to hold Mr Modi personally responsible for this development. Underscoring this observation, *Swarajya*'s editorial director said, 'It is important to keep in-built biases in mind when discussing the heavily lopsided coverage of "growing intolerance" in the country, a phrase invented to nail all the blame for it at Narendra Modi's door. It is worthwhile remembering that for 55 of the 68 years since Independence, it is the Congress party that has been in power' (Jagannathan 2015b).

Indeed, many writers contended that the mainstream media not only 'manufactured' controversies related to cow vigilantism or lynchings, but also that they chose to cover violence only when victims were members of marginalized groups. As one writer on OpIndia put it, 'It has been more than 3 nauseating months since media started running a vicious Rising Intolerance campaign based on cherry picked incidents to paint Hindu/upper caste as intolerant lot and blame NDA government for this. Dadri incident became the face of the campaign and Kalburgi/Pansare/Dabholkar murders played the supporting roles' (Shaitaan Khopdi 2015).

Similarly, another commentator on Swarajya.com wrote:

> What is also undeniable is that the outrage against lynching or mob violence is highly selective, to put it kindly. The same liberals standing with #NotInMyName placards have been silent on the murders of Rashtriya Swayamsevak Sangh (RSS) workers in Kerala.... You can't blame the Khattar government in Haryana for Junaid's murder and remain conspicuously silent over Pinarayi Vijayan's lawless Kerala. For the same reason, it is perfectly legitimate to question the media's silence on the appalling situation under the previous, Congress-led government at the centre. (Didolkar 2017)

While yet another commented:

> This Intolerance debate sprung from the Dadri incident, where a Muslim man was killed by Hindu men of his own village, for allegedly slaughtering and eating cow meat. This act is despicable and requires condemnation. But, bracketing the whole of Hindus, 800 million of them, for the crime done by 50 Hindus, does it sounds sane? Not to mention, the Moodbidri incident, where a Hindu man was killed by Muslim Men, for preventing cow slaughter, can we extend the bracket there too? If whole of Hindus should be ashamed and declared Intolerant for the crime of a very few Hindus, can we extend the same to other religions? (Manithan 2015)

In fact, many writers contended that the so-called 'intolerance' issue was a 'hoax' (Vyas 2015), propagated by the mainstream media (Bijapurkar 2017; Saraswat 2017).

CONSERVATIVE ALTERNATIVES TO MAINSTREAM NATIONAL MEDIA

In response to such perceived misrepresentations of right-wing positions by mainstream media, many contributors to these sites emphasized the necessity of creating alternatives for the expression of right-wing ideas and voices (Manini 2015; Ghosh 2017). In this vein, in an article titled 'Why the BJP Needs Its Own Fox News', a right-wing activist stated:

> The Indian media like other left-liberal institutions has gone unchallenged for a long time. Starting with the state-owned media, the channels have promoted leftist and now far-left oriented narratives stifling any other alternative viewpoints. Today we are in a situation where the 'Right' seems to have a space only on social media or big tents like this publication. It's important that mainstream media, especially English news channels also create viable space for the right…. What the Right and the BJP need is a proper 'Right of Center' mainstream English news channel like Fox News. (Sethumadhavrao 2016)

While the editorial director of *Swarajya*'s editorial team wrote, 'Social media may currently be dominated by right-wing voices, but this is largely because these voices were—and still are—stifled in old media. One should not be surprised if anonymous voices on Twitter are often the same newsroom guys whose views are blackballed by authoritarian editors with their monochromatic views on issues' (Jagannathan 2015a).

Consequently, many writers argued that it was imperative for Indian conservatives to 'engage' with the wider Indian public via the development of conservative media sources (Prasanna 2014). Not surprisingly, writers exhorted right-wing intellectuals, journalists, and activists to reach out to ordinary citizens who are 'fatigued and jaded' by mainstream media and have 'little time or sympathy for the kind of fraud that masquerades as political discourse in the country, especially in the English language press and media', on the grounds that they were likely to be receptive to alternative sources of information (Ramnath 2015). Such outreach, they argued, not only includes presenting right-wing perspectives on traditional media outlets whenever possible, but the active institutionalization of alternative spaces where conservatives can develop counter-narratives and discursively contest the dominant media news frames and discourse. As one writer put it,

> Thanks to the advent of social media, we are now seeing more active participation from the masses in the electoral process, more informed conversation on issues which matter to the public, a challenge and a counterpoint to the narrative of the old media.... But the while those who are of a right-of-center persuasion have made a dent in the outer circle of power (electoral politics), they lack the knowhow to penetrate the inner circles of power.... India's right-wing, which is a very large umbrella, needs to add institutionalized intellectual heft *online* to build on its current popular appeal among the masses. (Abhishek 2016)

* * *

Arguably, right-wing sites such as Swarajya.com, Indiafacts.org, and OpIndia.com are crucial building blocks of this effort to establish a right-wing ecosystem. Consequently, even though some scholars dismiss the emergence of right-wing online discourse as characterized by 'rage, profanity and bigotry' (Kesavan 2015), we suggest that these sites are coming to constitute a parallel discursive arena where conservative activists are not only able to articulate their core principles, but can also define their own identity, highlight perceived misrepresentations, and develop oppositional discourses challenging what they consider to be a biased mainstream media narrative. And although such activities have generally been associated with subaltern groups, who have developed such arenas in response to the politics of stratified societies whose deliberative practices tend to exclude marginalized groups (Fraser 1990), these tactics have increasingly been appropriated by conservative groups who are not discernibly subordinate, but nevertheless define themselves as such. Major (2012) makes this observation with regard to the conservative movement in the United States, and we similarly make the case that while there is little to suggest that members of the Hindu right are subject to social and political marginalization, they nevertheless perceive themselves as excluded from the public discourse. Right-wing news and commentary sites thus offer them the opportunity to 'mimic', in the words of Major, the actions of subaltern groups and, in doing so, contribute to the establishment of a Hindu 'counter-sphere'—a discursive alternative to the mainstream public sphere that serves to articulate a rhetorical assault against mainstream news media. And although the impact of these sites is currently largely limited to an urban, English-speaking elite, this situation is likely to change with the rapid increase in the number of internet users. In other words, the emergence of this counter-sphere potentially has significant implications, and further research is required to examine how this development affects both the workings of the mainstream press as well as audience perceptions of media bias in the Indian context.

NOTES

1. These include a variety of Hindu nationalist organizations, such as the Rashtriya Swayamsevak Sangh, the Bajrang Dal, and the Vishwa Hindu Parishad.
2. Communal riots in the Indian context refer to clashes between the Hindu and Muslim communities.
3. The website also has a monthly print magazine.
4. Dargahs are Sufi shrines.
5. The term 'Bharat' is used in classical Sanskrit texts to refer to India.
6. The Rashtriya Swayamsevak Sangh (RSS) is India's leading Hindu nationalist organization, and the term *pracharak* refers to the organization's workers.
7. Referring to a case where a Muslim was lynched by a Hindu mob.

REFERENCES

Abhishek, P. (2016). 'The Right Must Carve Out Its Own Intellectual Space'. *Swarajya*, 22 February. Retrieved from http://swarajyamag.com/politics/the-right-must-carve-out-its-own-intellectual-space (accessed on 15 August 2018).

Ahmad, T. (2015). 'The Rise of Fascism from India's TV Studios'. *Swarajya*, 2 November. Retrieved from http://swarajyamag.com/politics/the-rise-of-fascism-from-indias-tv-studios (accessed on 15 August 2018).

Bajaj, J. K. (2016). 'The Continuing Decline of Hindus in Kerala'. Swarajya.com, 25 April. Retrieved from https://swarajyamag.com/politics/the-continuing-decline-of-hindus-in-kerala (accessed in June 2016).

Barooah, S. (2016). 'Cologne and Malda: A Tale of Two Cities and Dysfunctional Enablers'. *Swarajya*, 16 January. Retrieved from http://

swarajyamag.com/politics/cologne-and-malda-a-tale-of-two-cities-and-dysfunctional-enablers (accessed in March 2016).

Basu, S. (2016). 'PM Modi Is Failing the Hindus. Will He Stand Up Please?' *Swarajya*, 8 March. Retrieved from http://swarajyamag.com/politics/pm-modi-is-failing-the-hindus-will-he-stand-up (accessed on 15 August 2018).

Bhalla, S. (2015). 'No Proof Required: Confessions of a Self-Styled Liberal'. *Indian Express*, 17 October. Retrieved from http://indianexpress.com/article/opinion/columns/no-proof-required-confessions-of-a-self-styled-liberal/ (accessed on 15 August 2018).

Bhandari, S. (2015). 'Why I Lost Faith in Indian Media and Indian Journalism'. Opindia.com, 21 December. Retrieved from http://myvoice.opindia.com/2015/12/why-i-lost-faith-in-indian-media-and-indian-journalism/ (accessed in March 2016).

Bhosle, V. (1999). 'Old Habits Die Hard'. Rediff.com, 1 April. Retrieved from http://www.rediff.com/news/1999/apr/01varsha.htm (accessed on 15 August 2018).

Bijapurkar, H. (2017). 'After "Church Attacks" and "Growing Intolerance", Usual Suspects Declare "Lynchings" as New Narrative'. OpIndia.com, 26 June. Retrieved from http://www.opindia.com/2017/06/after-church-attacks-and-growing-intolerance-usual-suspects-declare-lynchings-as-new-narrative/ (accessed in July 2017).

Chadha, C. and M. Koliska (2016). 'Playing by a Different Set of Rules: Journalistic Values in India's Regional Television Newsrooms'. *Journalism Practice*, 10(5): 608–25.

Chaudhury, S. (2002). 'Offence, the Best Form of Defence? Vicious and Vindictive Response of the Political Establishment'. *Manushi*, 128: 5–9.

CMS Media Lab (2014). 'It Is Modi Driven Television Coverage—2014 Poll Campaign'. Retrieved from www.cmsindia.org/2014-Lok-Sabha-Election-media-coverage.docx (accessed on 15 August 2018).

Dasgupta, S. (2015). 'Media Dancing to Congress's Tunes'. *Swarajya*, 28 June. Retrieved from http://swarajyamag.com/politics/media-dancing-to-congresss-tunes (accessed on 15 August 2018).

Davis, R. H. (2005). 'The Cultural Background of Hindutva'. In *India Briefing: Takeoff at Last?* eds A. Ayres and P. Oldenburg, pp. 107–40. Armonk, NY: M. E. Sharpe.

Didolkar, M. (2017). 'Manufacturing "Lynchistan": In the Name of Media?' *Swarajya*, 29 June. Retrieved from https://swarajyamag.com/ideas/manufacturing-lynchistan-in-the-name-of-media (accessed in July 2017).

Dikgaj, S., S. Sarkar, and Aparna (2016). 'Why Are the Tribal Regions of Central India Being Rapidly Christianized?' Indiafacts.org, 10 March.

Retrieved from http://indiafacts.org/tribal-regions-central-india-rapidly-christianized/ (accessed in May 2016).

Fraser, N. (1990). 'Rethinking the Public Sphere: A Contribution to the Critique of Actually Existing Democracy'. *Social Text*, 25/26: 56–80.

Frawley, D. (2015). 'Hypocrisy of the Indian Left: Anti Hindu and against Fascist Modi'. *DailyO*, 15 October. Retrieved from http://www.dailyo.in/politics/modi-left-bjp-rss-indian-left-religious-intolerance-cow-slaughter-radicalism/story/1/6790.html (accessed on 15 August 2018).

——— (2016). 'The Need for a Strong Hindu Voice'. *Hindu Post*, 3 March. Retrieved from http://www.hindupost.in/media/the-need-for-a-strong-hindu-voice/ (accessed on 15 August 2018).

Ghosh, S. (2017). 'Dear Bengali Hindus, Liberal-Secular Establishment Doesn't Care If You Die, but Do You?' http://www.opindia.com/2017/07/dear-bengali-hindus-liberal-secular-establishment-doesnt-care-if-you-die-but-do-you/ (accessed on 15 August 2018).

Guha, R. (2012). *Patriots and Partisans*. New Delhi: Allen Lane.

Guha Thakurta, P. (2014). 'Mass Media and the Modi Wave'. *Himal Asia*, 30 June. Retrieved from http://himalmag.com/media-modi-elections/ (accessed on 15 August 2018).

Hinduism Today (2002). 'Hindu Vivek Kendra Blasts Editor's Guild Report on Gujarat'. Retrieved from http://www.hinduismtoday.com/blogs-news/hindu-press-international/hindu-vivek-kendra-blasts-editors-guild-report-on-gujarat/2447.html (accessed on 15 August 2018).

Indiafacts.org (2015). 'Misrepresentations of Hinduism in the Media'. Retrieved from http://indiafacts.org/misrepresentations-hinduism-media/ (accessed on 15 August 2018).

IntolerantIndian (2016). 'The Need to Stand Up to Religious Demographic Change'. http://myvoice.opindia.com/2016/01/the-need-to-stand-up-to-religious-demographic-change/ (accessed on 15 August 2018).

Jagannathan, R. (2015a). 'Old Media Simply Does Not Get It: A Twitter Handle Does Not Make You Media Savvy'. *Swarajya*, 9 December. Retrieved from http://swarajyamag.com/politics/old-media-simply-does-not-get-it-a-twitter-handle-does-not-make-you-social-media-savvy (accessed on 15 August 2018).

——— (2015b). 'The Media Is Now a Player'. *Swarajya*, 30 December. Retrieved from https://swarajyamag.com/magazine/the-media-is-now-a-player (accessed in March 2016).

——— (2017). 'Mamata Bannerjee's Appeasement Politics Leads to Predictable Slide into Mob Violence'. *Swarajya*, 5 July. Retrieved from https://swarajyamag.com/politics/mamata-banerjees-appeasement-politics-leads-to-predictable-slide-into-mob-violence (accessed on 15 August 2018).

136   *Kalyani Chadha and Prashanth Bhat*

Kapoor, R. S. (2014). 'Intellectuals Refuse to See Love Jihad'. Indiafacts.org, 2 September. Retrieved from http://indiafacts.org/medias-chronic-hate-hindu-narrative-thrives/ (accessed in April 2016).

Kesavan, M. (2015). 'Five Types of Right-Wing Commentary in India'. NDTV, 26 September. Retrieved from http://www.ndtv.com/opinion/five-types-of-right-wing-commentary-in-contemporary-india-1223252 (accessed on 15 August 2018).

Khalid, W. (2016). 'Media'. http://reutersinstitute.politics.ox.ac.uk/publication/media-propaganda-and-kashmir-dispute-case-study-kashmir-floods (accessed on 15 August 2018).

Khan, S. A. (2015). 'The Rise and Rise of Online Hindutva'. *Hoot*, 13 July. Retrieved from http://www.thehoot.org/media-watch/digital-media/the-rise-and-rise-of-online-hindutva-8759 (accessed on 15 August 2018).

Kumar, S. S. (2017). 'A Fact-Check on "NDA Govt Schemes Are Just Copies of UPA Schemes" Claim'. OpIndia.com, 14 June. Retrieved from http://www.opindia.com/2017/06/a-fact-check-on-nda-govt-schemes-are-just-copies-of-upa-schemes-claim/ (accessed in July 2017).

LiberalRight (2017). 'A Different India Painted by Indian Media Post 2014'. OpIndia.com, 20 April. Retrieved from http://myvoice.opindia.com/2017/04/a-different-india-painted-by-indian-media-post-2014/ (accessed in May 2017).

Major, M. (2012). 'Objective but Not Impartial: Human Events, Barry Goldwater and the Development of the "Liberal Media" in the Conservative Counter-Sphere'. *New Political Science*, 34(4): 455–68.

Manini (2015). 'Media's Chronic Hate-Hindu Narrative Thrives'. Indiafacts. org, 25 March. Retrieved from http://indiafacts.org/medias-chronic-hate-hindu-narrative-thrives/ (accessed, March 2016).

Manithan (2015). 'Respected Intolerance Brigade, Can You Please Be More Specific about Who Is Intolerant in India?' OpIndia.com, 22 November. Retrieved from http://myvoice.opindia.com/2015/11/respected-intoler-ance-brigade-can-you-please-be-more-specific-about-who-is-intolerant-in-india/ (accessed in January 2016).

Merchant, M. (2015). 'Why India No Longer Trusts Anti-Modi Media'. *DailyO*, 27 November. Retrieved from http://www.dailyo.in/politics/modi-government-indian-media-hindu-taliban-sonia-gandhi-congress-bjp-upa/story/1/7638.html (accessed on 15 August 2018).

Mudgal, V. (2011). 'Rural Coverage in the Hindi and English Dailies'. *Economic and Political Weekly*, 46(35): 92–7.

Mukherji, A. (2015). 'RSS Is on a Roll: Number of Shakhas up 61% in 5 Years'. *Times of India*, 16 August. Retrieved from http://timesofindia.indiatimes.

com/india/RSS-is-on-a-roll-Number-of-shakhas-up-61-in-5-years/ articleshow/48498034.cms (accessed on 15 August 2018).

Neelankandan, A. (2015). 'Leftist Media Slanders RSS'. *Swarajya*, 16 January. Retrieved from http://swarajyamag.com/culture/leftist-media-slanders-rss-bjp-to-uphold-freedom-of-libel (accessed on 15 August 2018).

News18.com (2013). 'Media Bias Theory against Modi Is a Myth: Sagarika Ghose'. 10 July. Retrieved from http://www.news18.com/news/india/media-bias-theory-against-modi-is-a-myth-sagarika-ghose-622707.html (accessed on 15 August 2018).

OpIndia.com (2015). 'Kim Kardashians of the Indian Media'. 28 January. Retrieved from http://www.opindia.com/2015/01/kim-kardashians-of-the-indian-media/ (accessed on 15 August 2018).

——— (2016). 'Thousands Attend Funerals of SIMI Terrorists Killed in Police Encounter'. 2 November. Retrieved from http://www.opindia.com/2016/11/thousands-attend-funerals-of-simi-terrorists-killed-in-police-encounter/ (accessed on 15 August 2018).

Parker, B. (2015). 'Time to Hold India's Media Accountable'. Indiafacts.org, 17 April. Retrieved from http://indiafacts.org/time-to-hold-indias-media-legally-accountable/ (accessed in February 2016).

Patel, A., D. Padagaonkar, and B. G. Verghese (2002). 'Ordeal by Fire in the Killing Fields of Gujarat: Report, Editors Guild Fact Finding Mission, New Delhi, 3 May'. Retrieved from http://www.sabrang.com/gujarat/statement/report.htm (accessed on 15 August 2018).

Patil, P. (2015a). 'The Mirage of Delhi'. *Swarajya*, 8 February. Retrieved from https://swarajyamag.com/politics/the-mirage-of-delhi (accessed on 15 August 2018).

——— (2015b). 'Constructing the Narrative of an Intolerant India'. *Swarajya*, 27 October. Retrieved from http://swarajyamag.com/politics/constructing-the-narrative-of-an-intolerant-india (accessed on 15 August 2018).

Prasad, M. (2002). 'They Didn't Even Know, and They Were Punished'. *Manushi*, June. Retrieved from http://indiatogether.org/manushi/issue129/prasad.htm (accessed on 15 August 2018).

Prasanna (2014). 'The India Ideas Conclave—Towards an Enduring Intellectual Infrastructure'. *Swarajya*, 22 December. Retrieved from http://swarajyamag.com/india-ideas-conclave-2014/the-india-ideas-conclave-towards-an-enduring-intellectual-infrastructure (accessed on 15 August 2018).

Rajagopal, A. (2001). *Politics after Television: Hindu Nationalism and the Reshaping of the Public in India*. Cambridge: Cambridge University Press.

Rajguru, S. (2016). 'Modi Haters Will Outrage and Fume until 2019 No Matter What'. Indiafacts.org, 2 February. Retrieved from http://indiafacts.

org/modi-haters-will-outrage-and-fume-till-2019-no-matter-what/ (accessed in May 2016).

Ram, N. (2012). 'Sharing the Best and the Worst: The Indian News Media in a Global Context'. *Hindu*, 6 October. Retrieved from https://www.thehindu.com/news/resources/Sharing-the-Best-and-the-Worst-The-Indian-news-media-in-a-global-context/article12548857.ece (accessed in May 2016).

Ramnath, D. (2015). 'A Belated Response to Kafila's Hindutva Media—An Online Upheaval'. *Swarajya*, 13 August. Retrieved from http://swarajyamag.com/columns/a-belated-response-to-kafilas-hindutva-media-an-online-upheaval-2 (accessed in March 2016).

Rao, S. and V. Mudgal (2015). 'Democracy, Civil Society and Journalism in India'. *Journalism Studies*, 16(5): 615–23.

Saraswat, V. (2017). 'Dear Media, What Was That about Post-truth Again?' *Swarajya*, 3 July. Retrieved from https://swarajyamag.com/ideas/dear-media-what-was-that-about-post-truth-again (accessed on 15 August 2018).

Sarkar, S. (2014). 'Discrimination against Hindus in Indian Public Discourse'. *Swarajya*, 30 December. Retrieved from http://swarajyamag.com/politics/discrimination-against-hindus-in-indian-public-discourse (accessed on 15 August 2018).

Schmidt, V. (2008). 'Discursive Institutionalism: The Explanatory Power of Ideas and Discourse'. *Annual Review of Political Science*, 11: 303–26.

Seetha (2015). 'What about "Whataboutery"?' *Swarajya*, 30 December. Retrieved from http://swarajyamag.com/magazine/what-about-whataboutery (accessed on 15 August 2018).

Sethumadhavrao, N. (2016). 'Why the BJP Needs Its Own Fox News'. *Swarajya*, 20 February. Retrieved from http://swarajyamag.com/ideas/why-the-bjp-needs-its-own-fox-news (accessed on 15 August 2018).

Shaitaan Khopdi (2015). 'How the Common Man Wielded Its Power and Turned the Tables on the Intolerance Debate'. OpIndia.com, 24 December. Retrieved from http://myvoice.opindia.com/2015/12/how-the-common-man-wielded-its-power-and-turned-tables-on-intolerance-debate/ (accessed in March 2016).

Shankar, P. (2015). 'Government Needs to Be Supported on JNU'. *Swarajya*, 18 February. Retrieved from http://swarajyamag.com/politics/government-needs-to-be-supported-on-jnu (accessed on 15 August 2018).

Sharma, K. (2016). 'Debunking the Western Media's Anti Modi Propaganda'. *Swarajya*, 29 February. Retrieved from http://swarajyamag.com/politics/debunking-the-western-medias-anti-modi-propaganda (accessed on 15 August 2018).

Sharma, R. (2016). 'Indian Media Should Focus on Pak Crimes and Pandits, Not Separatist Agenda'. *Swarajya*, 2 August. Retrieved from https://swarajyamag.com/politics/jandk-indian-media-should-focus-on-pak-crimes-and-pandits-not-separatist-agenda (accessed on 15 August 2018).

Simha, R. K. (2016). 'How the Media Conspires to Work against India'. Indiafacts.org, 2 August. Retrieved from http://indiafacts.org/media-conspires-work-india/ (accessed on 15 August 2018).

Sonwalkar, P. (2006). 'Shooting the Messenger: Political Violence, Gujarat 2002 and the Indian News Media'. In *Conflict, Terrorism and the Media in Asia*, ed. B. Cole, pp. 82–97. London: Routledge.

Srinivasan, R. (2016). 'Putting the Mainstream Media on Notice: The Time for "Good" Dissent and "Bad" Dissent Is Over'. *Swarajya*, 7 November. Retrieved from https://swarajyamag.com/politics/putting-the-mainstream-media-on-notice-the-time-for-good-dissent-and-bad-dissent-is-over (accessed in December 2016).

Thussu, D. K. (2007). *News as Entertainment: The Rise of Global Infotainment*. London: Sage.

Vaidya, S. (2016). 'Why a Rohith Vemula Suicide Is Big News, but a Sawan Murder Is Just a Item'. *Swarajya*, 23 January. Retrieved from http://swarajyamag.com/politics/why-a-rohith-vemula-suicide-is-big-news-but-a-sawan-murder-is-just-a-item (accessed on 12 August 2018).

——— (2017). 'World Press Freedom Day: Why Indian Media Still Does Not Get It'. *Swarajya*, 3 May. Retrieved from https://swarajyamag.com/media/world-press-freedom-day-indian-mainstream-media-still-doesnt-get-it (accessed on 15 August 2018).

Venkataraman, S. (2015). 'Ravana, Hinduism and the Indian Left'. *Swarajya*, 19 November. Retrieved from http://swarajyamag.com/culture/ravana-tolerance-and-the-indian-left (accessed on 15 August 2018).

Vidyasagar, M. (2015). 'India's Civil War'. *Swarajya*, 30 May. Retrieved from http://swarajyamag.com/politics/indias-civil-war (accessed on 15 August 2018).

Vyas, K. (2015). 'Rising Hoax of Intolerance in India'. OpIndia.com, 5 December. Retrieved from http://myvoice.opindia.com/2015/12/rising-hoax-of-intolerance-in-india/ (accessed in March 2016).

CHAPTER EIGHT

'Tweet First, Work on the Story Later'

Role of Social Media in Indian Journalism

SMEETA MISHRA

. . . .

It all started when students from opposing political groups clashed in a college in New Delhi on 22 February 2017. They were fighting over an invite sent to a student to speak at a seminar titled 'The Culture of Protests', scheduled to be held at Ramjas College, Delhi University. The invited speaker was Umar Khalid, a student of Jawaharlal Nehru University in New Delhi, who had been arrested briefly in the year 2016 under controversial circumstances and charged with sedition (Soofi 2017). The clashing factions involved members and supporters of the left-wing All India Students Association and the right-wing Akhil Bharatiya Vidyarthi Parishad (ABVP) (PTI 2017).

Reacting to the violence at Ramjas College, Gurmehar Kaur, whose father was killed in the Kargil War between India and

Pakistan in the year 1999, posted a photo of herself on Facebook holding a placard which said: 'I am a student from Delhi University. I am not afraid of ABVP. I am not alone. Every student of India is with me. #StudentsAgainstABVP' (PTI 2017). Kaur's campaign went viral on social media, drawing both support and criticism from people belonging to different ends of the political spectrum. However, it was another Facebook post by her and the message on that placard that provoked country-wide reactions. The message on that placard read 'Pakistan did not kill my father. War did!' (News18.com 2017).

Amongst other reporters covering both the violent protests at Ramjas College, and the social media reactions to Gurmehar Kaur's Facebook posts, was Jaideep Deo Singh, a reporter with the *Hindu* newspaper in New Delhi. He said:

> The main story that day was the violent clash between two student factions and people getting beaten up. The issue was about the freedom of expression. That issue was sidelined because of what social media can create. Gurmehar Kaur was merely reacting to the events. But the way events unfolded online, the main story soon became about her and her message and an entire country reacting to it on various platforms. (Jaideep Deo Singh, personal communication, 7 April 2017)

The issue gained even more publicity on social and traditional media when well-known Indian cricketer Virender Sehwag ridiculed Kaur's message on Pakistan with a tweet saying, 'I didn't score two triple centuries, my bat did,' with Bollywood actor Randeep Hooda cheering him on the remark (News18.com 2017). Even as some people accused Sehwag and Hooda of bullying Kaur, the latter's original message continued to generate memes that took social media by storm. Several politicians from the ruling party also attacked, mocked, and ridiculed Kaur on Twitter for her stand on Pakistan. The Indian media covered the case in great detail.

In the midst of all this, Kaur reported receiving death and rape threats on social media and filed complaints with the local police (Udayakumar 2017). As the controversy grew, Kaur reportedly left New Delhi for her home in Punjab and stopped posting on the events after requesting the media to leave her alone (Udayakumar 2017).

According to the *Hindu* newspaper's Jaideep Deo Singh, the Gurmehar Kaur story represents a classic case of events on social media completely diverting media coverage from the main issue:

> The Gurmehar Kaur story should have just been a snippet on the first day and then disappeared. But she dominated page 1 coverage for a few days. That is how social media has changed journalism in India. This case illustrates how a Facebook campaign by a 20-year student can become a major flashpoint between the ruling party and the opposition parties—all because of the power of social media.

This case clearly shows the power and influence of social media on journalism in India. The chapter will further explore the increasing role of social media in Indian journalism, including tracing its growth in the last decade, analysing the rise of multi-platform delivery among Indian journalists, the popularity of breaking news on Twitter, and the spread of fake news fanned by social media–led journalism. The chapter concludes with analysing the changing nature of social media usage in India, that is, from being restricted to a middle-class phenomenon to a relatively more broad-based one.

INTERNET AND SOCIAL MEDIA USAGE IN INDIA

Referring to social media as 'word of mouth on steroids', Alejandro (2010) argues that journalists are no longer the only gatekeepers of what comprises news:

> The audience now has a say as to what news is important to them and as to what level of engagement they wish to pursue whether watch or listen to it on TV on radio or go online or reply via mobile text or tweet about it or post it on Facebook or upload it on YouTube or if they Digg it on whatever device when they want it and where they want it. (2010: 12)

The fact is that the audience today is no longer passive. Members of the audience want to participate in the media landscape, although which sections of the audience actually get to participate, remains a question.

India had 432 million internet users in December 2016, and the overall internet penetration rate for the country was around

31 per cent during that period, according to the Internet and Mobile Association of India (Chopra 2017). Internet use in India is primarily driven by mobile phones (Sen and Nielsen 2016). In fact, it is a great irony that more Indians have access to a mobile phone than to a toilet, a United Nations report claimed in 2010 (UNU 2010). The number of mobile phone users in India reached a billion in 2016, according to the country's telecom regulator (Rai 2016). India is also the world's second biggest smartphone market in terms of users (*Hindu* 2016).

While the internet penetration rate was close to 60 per cent in urban India, it was approximately 17 per cent in rural areas of the country in the year 2016 (Chopra 2017). Thus, a deep digital divide exists between the rich and the poor, and urban and rural areas (Sen and Nielsen 2016). However, Parthasarathi and Srinivas (2012), who map the digital media environment in India, argue that wide-scale poverty in the country has not resulted in a 'perfect digital divide' since many of the 300 million still below the official poverty line also use digital technology in some form or the other.

Chidanand Rajghatta, *Times of India*'s US-based foreign editor and long-time Washington, D.C., scribe, echoes the same viewpoint. He emphasizes that the digital divide is smaller than the chasm in literacy in India: 'A billion cell phone connections have made so many Indians media consumers now. Even the poorest seem to consume media over cell phones today. It may not be news per se, but some sort of content is being consumed' (Chidanand Rajghatta, personal communication, 27 April 2017). Thus, cheap smartphones are making their way into poor rural households. The Internet and Mobile Association of India estimates that more than 60 per cent of internet users in India are mobile users (Sen and Nielsen 2016). In fact, many among the people who use mobile phones to access the internet are mobile-only users and get 2G and 3G access alone, thus rendering the context of internet usage and social media in India different from that of Western economies (Sen and Nielsen 2016). Although 4G services remain expensive and accessible primarily to the upper social strata, continuing investment in the telecommunication sector, availability of cheap smartphones, lower-ing data tariffs, and so on, are expected to improve internet access for people from lower-income brackets of Indian society who have fluency in local languages and not the English language (Sen and Nielsen 2016).

A report by the Mobile Marketing Association on smartphones and feature phone usage in India in the year 2016–17 claimed that smartphone users in India spent more time on their mobile phones than any other media, and half of that time was spent on social media and messaging apps (MxMIndia.com 2016). Social media platforms have built huge markets in India. As of May 2016, Twitter had more than 41 million monthly active users in India (Statista.com 2016). According to Statista.com, India had 213 million Facebook users as of April 2017, second only to the United States at 219 million users. In March 2016, about 69 million people in India accessed Facebook daily, out of which 64 million accessed the platform through their mobile devices (PTI 2016a).

Surprisingly, even as social media usage increases in India, so does the country's newspaper industry. India has more 82,000 newspapers, and its newspaper industry grew by 8 per cent in 2015 (*Economist* 2016). Vernacular-language newspapers drive growth in the newspaper industry, as evident from the titles present in the list of top 10 newspapers identified by the 2014 Indian Readership Survey: the only English-language newspaper that figures in the top 10 list is *Times of India*, even as *Dainik Jagaran*, a Hindi newspaper, tops the list with 16.6 million readers (*Economist* 2016).

Vernacular-language newspapers are growing as they benefit from rising literacy rates and their focus on local news. Poor internet connectivity in India's heartlands also aids the popularity of newspapers that cost very little to the reader. No wonder print publications account for 43 per cent of all corporate advertising in India, while the corresponding figure for the United States is less than 15 per cent (*Economist* 2016). Apart from print, India also has a large television industry with 857 channels as of 2016 (Government of India 2016). Sixty per cent of all households in India have cable and satellite television (Parthasarathi and Srinivas 2012).

PROTESTS AS INCUBATORS OF SOCIAL MEDIA USAGE IN INDIA

Social media usage became popular in India during the Anna Hazare–led anti-corruption movement in 2011, and the public protests against the Delhi gang rape in 2012 (Belair-Gagnon et al. 2014). These protests served as 'incubators for social media sophistication' in India (Belair-Gagnon et al.: 1071). Rodrigues (2014) describes the use of internet and communication technology among the organizers of the anti-corruption movement led by Anna Hazare and his supporters:

> The IAC [India against Corruption] organisers used their mobile phones to communicate and pick up people, who were dropped off by the police after being picked up from various protest sites. They used mobile phones to spread their messages and warned each other of police action via SMS. They used the social media sites to garner support and spread their messages of upcoming events and protests.

Public protests against the 2012 Delhi gang-rape case also witnessed widespread use of social media both by the people participating in the protests and by journalists (Belair-Gagnon et al. 2014). On 16 December 2012, a 23-year-old physiotherapy intern was raped and tortured by six men after she and her friend boarded a bus in south Delhi. The attackers threw both of them on the roadside, from where they were taken to a hospital. After 13 days, the young woman succumbed to her injuries that 'included severe internal bleeding, the loss of more than 90% of her intestines and brain damage' (Gagnon et al. 2014: 1060). The brutality of the incident and wide coverage by the media led to massive protests across the country. A study on social media usage by Indian and foreign correspondents on the Delhi gang-rape story and related protests in 2012 showed that journalists used social media for gathering 'background information and social discovery, as a Rolodex of potential sources, as an aggregator of updates on rapidly changing events, and as a tool to explore new beats' (Gagnon et al. 2014: 1065). However, such practices 'were managed and rearranged around pre-existing journalistic norms and practices including reputation of sources, balance between social media and non-social media users, time constraints, accountability, and accuracy' (Gagnon et al. 2014: 1071).

In-depth interviews with the reporters showed that the reporters of the English-language press 'used social media primarily in ways that reflected the ideas and interests of the urban middle class, which included members of city-based women's groups, activists, university students and intellectuals' (Belair-Gagnon et al. 2014: 1065). While Twitter helped journalists connect with the urban middle class in India, they emphasized that it could not replace the interviews and interactions on the streets, in neighbourhoods and tea stalls. Despite this, social media has definitely resulted in events being reported faster; it has also helped involve non-resident Indians in discussions about the news in India (Gagnon et al. 2014).

In the last five years, social media usage has spread from being a tool used only by the English-speaking middle classes in metropolitan areas to a tool that is also used by those who speak in local languages and live in India's small towns and adjacent villages. For instance, in January 2017, 'pro-Jallikattu protests' rocked Tamil Nadu, a southern state in India. Jallikattu refers to a popular bull-taming sport in Tamil Nadu. The Supreme Court, which is the apex court in India, banned the sport based on a case filed by animal rights activists group, People for Ethical Treatment of Animals, which claimed that the sport violated the Prevention of Cruelty to Animals Act (PTI 2016b). While protests began with a handful of people, it soon involved thousands as word spread on social media: 'The call for action spread rapidly through social media and WhatsApp. Student unions across India displayed their solidarity with the cause. And Tamilians across the world responded. The diaspora conducted protests in front of the Indian embassies in their respective countries' (Ravishankar and Kumar 2017).

According to journalists who covered the pro-Jallikattu protests, many of the Facebook posts about the protests were written both in Tamil, the local language of the state where the protests happened, and in English. These posts mentioned where people were congregating and others responded with assertions that they would also join the protests. Finally, after days of protests, the Supreme Court ban was overturned by a bill passed in the Tamil Nadu Assembly (Lakshmana and Iyer 2017). Referring to the use of social media in the pro-Jallikattu protests, R. Shafimunna, who has been a part of the Tamil-language press for 30 years, said: 'This time, social media use during protests had moved from New Delhi as its epicentre to semi-urban and rural areas. This time, regional languages were also used to garner support on social media apart from English' (R. Shafimunna, personal communication, 9 April 2017).

Journalists also claim that the nature of protests is changing, taking into account the need to stay in the news, a feat that is extremely difficult to sustain in the age of social media where attention on an issue changes very frequently. For instance, in March 2017, farmers from Tamil Nadu were protesting in New Delhi demanding a meeting with the prime minister, with the goal of getting loan waivers and a drought relief programme. These farmers, who had been staying at Jantar Mantar for almost a month, staged their protests in novel ways to showcase their plight and catch media attention. During the protests, the farmers were photographed putting live mice in their mouth. By engaging in such an act, the farmers were trying to tell the world that they would have to eat mice unless the government helped them out with drought relief programmes. These pictures went viral on social media. Commenting on the protests, Shalini Lobo (2017), a journalist with *India Today*, wrote, 'From demonstrating naked in front of the Prime Minister's Office to putting rats in their mouth, these farmers are finding every possible way to stay in the news and put pressure on the central government.' R. Shafimunna, who also covered the farmers' protests, said, 'These unique visuals were circulated on Facebook, Twitter and WhatsApp. Although the farmers did not know how to create or circulate these visuals on social media, Tamil students in Delhi were helping them out.'

Since what is viral on social media is also covered by traditional media in New Delhi, people find it a more accessible way to make it to national news. 'The English language press in Delhi does not carry regional news unless there's something sensational. But once an issue goes viral on social media, they can no longer ignore it,' Shafimunna explained.

MULTI-SKILLED JOURNALISTS FOR MULTI-PLATFORM DELIVERY

Reporters in India, especially those working in cities and towns, are gradually getting used to multi-platform delivery. For instance, interviews with reporters working at local/city desks of newspapers revealed that they are first asked to tweet their stories on their individual and organizational accounts as the story unfolds, then write it for the website, and finally write a more detailed version for the print edition of the newspaper. Ashok Kalkur, the national editor of the *Hindu* newspaper's New Delhi edition, said: 'A decade ago, we had to just file a print copy. Today, reporters have to file their stories for social media and the website immediately. Nobody waits for the newspaper deadline to file their stories. Everything is immediate. It's fast. Whoever breaks their story first on the web scores' (Ashok Kalkur, personal communication, 6 April 2017).

Television journalists are also beginning to write for the channel's websites. For many years, web reporters alone wrote for the website, but that is rapidly changing. In fact, several news channels are also physically integrating the web desk and the social media desk with the newsroom for better coordination.

Multi-platform delivery has led to changing journalistic routines and processes. For instance, Abdul Mujeeb Faruqui, principal photographer with the Bhopal edition of the *Hindustan Times*, who has spent 22 years in the profession, said that social media has transformed him from a still photographer to a content producer:

> Since social media has become a way of life for us today, I approach an event as a content producer. I first take a call on whether a situation lends itself to a video or to a still photograph with a short story. If I don't think of myself a content producer, I will not be able to keep pace with the young photojournalists and the demands of our profession. (Abdul Mujeeb Faruqui, personal communication, 20 April 2017)

Multi-platform delivery has also helped journalists reach a larger audience. For instance, when one of Faruqui's videos went viral and got two million views, the breadth of the feedback astounded him. 'I could not imagine this kind of feedback was even possible before social media happened,' he said.

But multi-platform delivery has also introduced new challenges. Several journalists said they live with a constant sense of insecurity about their jobs today. A photojournalist with a well-known daily said, 'There were five photojournalists in our team. I am the only one left now. While reporters can take basic photographs, special assignments require special skills. A reporter can only take a photograph as well as I can write a story. Since the day mobile phones came with cameras, it affected the photojournalism profession negatively.'

With the growing role of social media in journalism, getting reporters to be active on social media is a major preoccupation in media organizations today. A former *Times of India* editor said, 'In *Times of India*, unless reporters post a certain number of tweets on Twitter or stories on Facebook, they will be penalized monetarily. Of course, they will not be rewarded if they meet the criteria.' Media organizations have also begun to invest in training reporters and editors in social media usage. 'People from Twitter came down to train us the other day,' said Saahil Menghani, anchor and senior correspondent at CNN News18 (Saahil Menghani, personal communication, 10 April 2017). 'The practice of breaking news on Twitter is becoming commonplace in India, at least at the national level.'

BREAKING NEWS ON TWITTER

Most print and television reporters, especially those working in metros and other Indian cities, usually tweet before they break news on television. Twitter usage is an important feature of newsrooms across television channels. 'The editors and desk chiefs constantly monitor the Twitter handles of news agencies,' said CNN News18's Saahil Menghani. 'Even before a news agency publishes a story, it will tweet about it. We are assigned the story the moment it is tweeted. The agency report, which comes later, is only for confirmation of that news.' Menghani believes Twitter especially complements the nature of television reporting in India. 'Television reporting here is often based on outrage and Twitter helps seal it in 140 characters,' he remarked.

> Apart from tweeting breaking news, I also tweet controversial statements or announcements made by someone I interviewed. In fact, politicians will remind me to tweet and ask me about the number of followers I have. I think we are reaching a stage where those with more followers on Twitter will find it easier to access political figures because of their reach on social media.

Many political stories in India break on Twitter. According to the *Hindu* newspaper's Damini Nath, 'Today we have a chief minister who tweets often. We have to always watch for his tweets and then we scramble to follow up whatever he has tweeted' (Damini Nath, personal communication, 7 April 2017).

In fact, most politicians of the ruling party in Delhi today prefer to make announcements on social media before they talk to the media. Press conferences follow social media announcements. In April 2017, the current prime minister of India, Narendra Modi, had over 28 million followers on his Twitter account. The chief minister of Delhi, Arvind Kejriwal, had 11 million followers, while Sushma Swaraj, the minister of external affairs, had nearly 8 million followers on Twitter. John Parmelee, author of *Politics and the Twitter Revolution*, argues that 'Twitter can set the agenda for what journalists will cover, as evident in the way US President Donald Trump's tweets direct the press to report on specific issues' (Hinsliff 2016). He explains: 'Twitter's basically used by politicians to influence other influencers. It's a very small universe of people, but it's people who can move an agenda' (Hinsliff 2016). He compares it to the process of lobbying, where talking to even a small group of people can make an impact as they are the ones who are involved in the process of legislation.

Tharoor (2016), a member of Parliament from the Congress party and one of the first Indian politicians to use Twitter, points out that in 2009 when he started actively using the platform, it was 'fashionable for Indian politicians to sneer at the use of social media'. However, Indian politicians across party lines and age groups have today embraced social media, especially Twitter, in a big way. Labelling Twitter as the 'interactive Akashvani', Tharoor emphasizes the usefulness of social media for politicians. He argues, 'It [social media] can serve to help set the agenda, because the traditional media— newspapers and television, which do reach most voters—do tap into social media for information about and from politicians. The indirect impact of social media makes it an indispensable communications tool for politicians.'

Considering the popularity of social media among public figures, little wonder that *Times of India*'s Chidanand Rajghatta claims, 'The prime minister, Shahrukh Khan or Trump don't really need the media anymore. They are their own media outlets on social media.'

Social media presence has also become a must for those reporting the news. In fact, during interviews, senior editors have started asking wannabe reporters how many followers they have on Twitter.

While all journalists have a social media presence, names already famous on television or in the print world seem to have the most followers on social media. Nath explains, 'Celebrity journalists like Rajdeep Sardesai or Barkha Dutt often tweet their opinions. People want to know what these people have to say while reporters who are just starting out merely report their stories on Twitter. We tweet facts, not opinion. And, it is strong opinions that catch more attention than objective facts.'

'Veteran members of the bureau are the ones who are most popular on social media,' said Dwaipayan Bose, editor-in-chief of DNA (Daily News and Analysis) publications. 'They took to social media like fish take to water. We are surprised as to how this could happen. We thought they would take a lot of time' (Dwaipayan Bose, personal communication, 8 April 2017). While the celebrity journalists have the maximum number of followers on Twitter, the new generation of journalists who are digital natives are also active on social media. Meanwhile, many who have been in the profession for decades are also learning to use social media to keep their jobs. 'I am a 54-year-old journalist but I had to learn social media to survive,' said Tamil-language journalist Shafimunna. 'After I cover an event, my office has asked me to tweet and post on Facebook. Often, the office people tweet for me. But I also tweet. I have to compete with youngsters or I will be jobless.' Moreover, journalists in Indian newsrooms spend long hours monitoring WhatsApp messages and tweets. For instance, Faruqui gets about 1,500–2,000 WhatsApp messages every day and skims through all of them. He is worried that he will miss something important in the midst of all the noise if he does not go over them. 'News today breaks in WhatsApp groups and Twitter,' he explained. 'You just can't ignore social media or you will lose your job.'

COPING WITH THE ADVERSE EFFECTS OF SOCIAL MEDIA–LED JOURNALISM

Several older journalists reminisced about a time when everyone, old and young, loved reading newspapers. 'But today people below 35 don't really want to *read* news,' said *Hindustan Times*'s Faruqui. 'They want to *glance* at news. They want to *scroll* over news. They want the entire story in two-three sentences. They also want more visuals, powerful visuals within seconds of an event happening. When speed is everything, I use my mobile phone to take pictures so they can be WhatsApp-ed and uploaded within seconds of a breaking news event.'

Thus, an important consequence of social media–led journalism has been the need for speed, which often kills context. While reporters are filing their stories quicker, they are finding it more difficult to provide context. 'You have a maximum of 30 minutes to file a story, especially for the web,' said Damini Nath, a reporter based in New Delhi. 'There's no way you can do justice to an issue in 30 minutes. Moreover, people are happy just reading tweets and they will keep retweeting it but will not read the entire story. All people want today is a nugget of information, not the context.' Like Nath, several journalists are also concerned that on social media platforms such as Twitter, there is a danger of exaggerating information when you are saying it in 140 characters. 'Twitter is a great medium to outrage people,' Nath said. 'Anything can blow out of proportion on social media.'

Social media has made it important for news media to disseminate information in real time and continue giving out bits of information even as the story is being investigated, sometimes leading to the spread of half-baked stories (Alejandro 2010). In the Indian context, lack of a deep-rooted journalistic culture of verification, combined with a frenzy for TRPs and social media shares and a desperate search for the next viral story has affected the authenticity and accuracy of news in the subcontinent (Sreekumar 2016).

Facebook-owned instant messaging app, WhatsApp, which is used by 160 million Indians, has become a hotbed for fake news in India (Dixit 2017). At times, news media pick up stories that go viral on WhatsApp, without thorough and adequate verification (Dixit 2017). Since the instant messaging app is encrypted end-to-end with no API, algorithm, or trending topics, it's extremely difficult to track the spread of messages on WhatsApp (Dixit 2017). While most journalists remain wary of information they find on social media, the pressure to be the first with the news leads to mistakes, and also renders them more vulnerable to legal controversies. Bhuyan (2017) argues that external watchdogs need to keep news media organizations accountable: 'But this accountability can only be extended to—and demanded of—formal news organisations. None of these rules apply to the explosion of dispersed sources of news and information that we now have through social media.' Commenting on the trend of citizens breaking news on social media, *Times of India*'s Chidanand Rajghatta points out, 'The key question here is credibility, the lack of filters. Journalism, traditional journalism as we know it, is not perfect. But it has some filtering mechanism, imperfect and open to subversion as it is. But anybody and everybody breaking news on social media implies there are no filters.'

SOCIAL MEDIA: MOVING BEYOND BEING A MIDDLE-CLASS PHENOMENON IN INDIA

All the journalists interviewed for this chapter emphasized that social media, especially Twitter and Facebook, are moving beyond being a mere middle-class phenomenon, and gradually becoming popular among the masses in India. While those who speak the English language continue to dominate social media in India today, people are starting to tweet and post messages on Facebook in local languages. Social media is becoming popular in small towns as well. 'Earlier, it was just the metros and big cities,' said Saahil Menghani, a senior correspondent with CNN News18. 'But India's Hindi heartland is also getting on social media, gradually but surely.' The improvement of internet technology in India and its better afford-ability has only made social media more popular among Indians, and journalists working in traditional media have become more watchful of developments on that front (Rodrigues 2014). 'Five years ago, social media may have been a tool of the middle classes alone,' said Manish Dixit, political editor of the Bhopal edition of a Hindi-language newspaper titled *Dainik Bhaskar*. 'Today, villages located near towns and cities are beginning to get internet access. Internet packages that used to cost Rs 1,000 five years ago today cost Rs 200. As internet access and mobile phones become more affordable, more and more people from underprivileged sections of society will begin to use social media' (Manish Dixit, personal com-munication, 20 April 2017).

Dixit opened a Twitter account a few years ago and has nearly 2,000 followers today. 'Twitter is no longer considered a platform of the savvy and upmarket audience only,' argues Dixit.

> Also, more and more people in India are learning to converse in English, the language that is most commonly used on social media platforms. I have met so many families where the parents don't know English but ensure that their children learn the language because they believe their offspring will fare better in life if they know English. These children are using social media although their parents may not do so.

Thus, slowly but surely, social media platforms are gradually transforming from being tools exclusively in the hands of well-heeled, English-speaking, middle-class Indians living in cities to also being used by speakers of vernacular languages living in India's urban slums, semi-urban spaces, and small towns.

The Indian media landscape presents opportunities such as rapidly growing internet usage and digital advertising. Since digital advertising is expected to continue to grow by 20–30 per cent a year, both legacy media and digital journalism startups are investing in this opportunity (Sen and Nielsen 2016: 10). However, they also face varied obstacles, including low average revenue per user, and low cost of newspapers and basic TV packages. Sen and Nielsen explain: 'This means that getting Indians to pay for digital news may be even harder than in high-income democracies where the reference price established by print newspapers and pay television is much higher, even in relative terms' (2016: 10).

The digital arena of India's media landscape includes both for-profit and not-for-profit content-based startups, on the one hand, and news aggregators, on the other (Sen and Nielsen 2016). The revenue model for digital is still evolving. 'Everybody is trying to figure out what that revenue model is,' said Dwaipayan Bose, editor-in-chief of DNA publications. 'I don't think a formula has yet emerged.' Even as media organizations struggle to identify a suitable revenue model for their digital operations, it will take some time for the frenzy of social media usage in journalism to settle and for clear patterns to emerge—patterns that are expected to incorporate established routines and values of journalism with the changing nature of news production and dissemination, while the news industry transforms to meet the needs of an ever-interactive audience.

REFERENCES

Alejandro, J. (2010). *Journalism in the Age of Social Media*. Oxford: Reuters Institute for the Study of Journalism, University of Oxford.

Belair-Gagnon, V., S. Mishra, and C. Agur (2014). 'Reconstructing the Indian Public Sphere: Newswork and Social Media in the Delhi Gang Rape Case'. *Journalism*, 15(8): 1059–75.

Bhuyan, A. (2017). 'What the Indian Media Can Learn from the Global War on Fake News'. *Wire*, 21 April. Retrieved from https://thewire.in/126611/fake-news-social-media-2/ (accessed on 17 August 2018).

Chopra, A. (2017). 'Number of Internet Users in India Could Cross 450 Million by June: Report'. *LiveMint*, 2 March. Retrieved from http://www.livemint.com/Industry/QWzIOYEsfQJknXhC3HiuVI/Number-of-Internet-users-in-India-could-cross-450-million-by.html (accessed on 17 August 2018).

Dixit, P. (2017). 'Viral Whatsapp Hoaxes Are India's Own Fake News Crisis'. Buzzfeed.com, 19 January. Retrieved from https://www.buzzfeed.com/pranavdixit/viral-whatsapp-hoaxes-are-indias-own-fake-news-crisis?utm_term=.umZKOkVDb#.pka78qek2 (accessed on 17 August 2018).

Economist (2016). 'Why India's Newspaper Business Is Booming?' 22 February. Retrieved from http://www.economist.com/blogs/economist-explains/2016/02/economist-explains-13 (accessed on 17 August 2018).

Government of India (2016). 'List of Permitted Private Satellite TV Channels as on 31-01-2016'. Ministry of Information and Broadcasting, Government of India. Retrieved from http://cablequest.org/pdfs/i_b/Master_List_of_Permitted_Private_Satellite_TV_Channels_as_on_31.01.2016.pdf (accessed 26 August 2018).

Hindu (2016). 'With 220mn Users, India Is Now World's Second-Biggest Smartphone Market', 3 February. Retrieved from http://www.thehindu.com/news/cities/mumbai/business/with-220mn-users-india-is-now-worlds-secondbiggest-smartphone-market/article8186543.ece (accessed on 17 August 2018).

Hinsliff, G. (2016). 'Trash Talk: How Twitter Is Shaping the New Politics'. *Guardian*, 31 July. Retrieved from https://www.theguardian.com/technology/2016/jul/31/trash-talk-how-twitter-is-shaping-the-new-politics (accessed on 17 August 2018).

Lakshmana, K. V. and A. Iyer (2017). 'Jallikattu Protests: Bill Passed, Hurdles to Sport Removed, Says Tamil Nadu CM'. *Hindustan Times*, 23 January. Retrieved from http://www.hindustantimes.com/india-news/jallikattu-live-police-begin-evicting-protesters-from-marina-beach/story-SmJo5OSBmFH0yIgNsntDOL.html (accessed on 17 August 2018).

Lobo, S. (2017). 'After Nude Protest, Tamil Nadu Farmers Eat Rice off Road'. *India Today*, 11 April. Retrieved from http://indiatoday.intoday.in/story/tamil-nadu-farmers-nude-protest-rice-jantar-mantar/1/926757.html (accessed on 17 August 2018).

MxMIndia.com (2016). 'Indians Spend More Time on Cellphones than TV', 22 December. Retrieved from http://www.mxmindia.com/2016/12/indians-spend-more-time-on-cellphones-than-tv/ (accessed on 17 August 2018).

News18.com (2017). 'Martyr's Daughter in Eye of Political Storm: Facebook Post Triggers Twitter War', 28 February. Retrieved from http://www.news18.com/news/politics/kargil-martyrs-daughter-in-eye-of-political-storm-facebook-post-triggers-twitter-war-1354077.html (accessed on 17 August 2018).

Parthasarathi, V. and A. Srinivas (2012). *Mapping Digital Media: India*. Country Report. London: Open Society Foundations.

PTI (Press Trust of India) (2016a). 'Facebook Userbase Crosses 142 Million in India'. *LiveMint*. http://www.livemint.com/Consumer/tv2ZJPoaI6jldO ZhZKkw4J/Facebook-userbase-crosses-142-million-in-India.html (accessed on 17 August 2018).

——— (2016b). 'PETA: Jallikattu Stay "Partial Victory" for Bulls'. *Hindu*. Retrieved from http://www.thehindu.com/news/national/PETA-Jallikattu-stay-%E2%80%98partial-victory%E2%80%99-for-bulls/article13995899.ece (accessed on 17 August 2018).

——— (2017). '"Not Afraid of ABVP": DU Student Whose Father Died in Kargil War Writes on FB'. *Hindustan Times*. Retrieved from http://www.hindustantimes.com/delhi/kargil-martyr-s-daughter-du-student-starts-i-am-not-afraid-of-abvp-campaign-on-facebook/story-DJabBCr34tCwGI3 CuNH8gP.html (accessed on 17 August 2018).

Rai, S. (2016). 'India Just Crossed 1 Billion Mobile Subscribers Milestone and the Excitement's Just Beginning'. *Forbes*, 6 January. Retrieved from https://www.forbes.com/sites/saritharai/2016/01/06/india-just-crossed-1-billion-mobile-subscribers-milestone-and-the-excitements-just-beginning/#7e1aa24b7db0 (accessed on 17 August 2018).

Ravishankar, S. and A. Kumar (2017). 'Jallikattu Protests: Was the Students' "Movement" in Tamil Nadu Hijacked?' *Hindustan Times*. Retrieved from   http://www.hindustantimes.com/india-news/jallikattu-protests-

was-the-students-movement-in-tamil-nadu-highjacked/story-qbTet83
UwqY3mi62FZgMjM.html (accessed on 17 August 2018).

Rodrigues, U. (2014). 'Social Media's Impact on Journalism: A Study of Media's Coverage of Anti-corruption Protests in India'. *Global Media Journal* (Australian Edition), 8(1).

Sen, A. and R. K. Nielsen (2016). *Digital Journalism Start-Ups in India*. Oxford: Reuters Institute for the Study of Journalism, University of Oxford.

Soofi, M. A. (2017). 'Discover Delhi: Inside Umar Khalid's Hostel Room in JNU'. *Hindustan Times*, 20 May. Retrieved from http://www.hindustantimes. com/delhi-news/discover-delhi-inside-umar-khalid-s-hostel-room-in-jnu/ story-4eXv8zAnWpRJFfCRESFItJ.html (accessed on 17 August 2018).

Sreekumar, S. (2016). 'The Risks of India Ignoring the Global Fake News Debate'. *Wire*, 22 December. https://thewire.in/88717/the-risks-of-india-ignoring-the-global-fake-news-debate/ (accessed on 17 August 2018).

Statista.com (2016). 'Number of Active Twitter Users in Leading Markets as of May 2016'. Retrieved from https://www.statista.com/statistics/242606/ number-of-active-twitter-users-in-selected-countries/ (accessed on 15 April 2017).

Tharoor, S. (2016). 'The Twitter Revolution'. *Outlook*. Retrieved from http:// www.outlookindia.com/magazine/story/the-twitter-revolution/297958 (accessed on 17 August 2018).

Udayakumar, G. K. R. (2017). 'After Gurmehar Kaur Complains of Receiving Death and Rape Threats, Crime Branch to Probe Case'. *India Today*. Retrieved from http://indiatoday.intoday.in/story/gurmehar-kaur-du-lady-shri-ram-delhi-police-crime-branch-ramjas-college/1/893966.html (accessed on 17 August 2018).

UNU (United Nations University) (2010). 'Greater Access to Toilets than Cellphones in India: UN'. Retrieved from https://unu.edu/media-relations/ releases/greater-access-to-cell-phones-than-toilets-in-india.html (accessed on 17 August 2018).

CHAPTER NINE

Indian News Entrepreneurs and Their Digital News Startups

MONICA CHADHA

. . . .

The Indian internet-based industry is vibrant and growing at a lightning pace. Digital advancement has put technology at the fingertips of a large percentage of the population. While 30 per cent of India has internet access, the sheer numbers this translates into puts the country in second place globally—China occupies first place—in terms of the number of people who have internet access (Meeker 2017). Social, political, and economic changes such as lower prices of smartphones, low data charges, increasing disposable income (Bhattacharya 2017), and improved digital infrastructure based on the current central government's 'Digital India' campaign are likely to increase the number of internet users in the coming years. Greater and faster access to the internet as well as a low entry threshold has encouraged the growth of independent news media players in the digital realm. Technological ease and the promise of profits, however, are not the only reasons why this growth has occurred.

The print and broadcast news media industry has come under fire for putting corporate interests before societal benefit, or what Sonwalkar calls the 'Murdochization' of the news (2002: 821). Most prioritize sensational news stories that attract viewership and reject investigative news as well as any content that would upset their advertisers (Rao and Wasserman 2015). Unhappy with the turn taken by mainstream media, several experienced journalists, news media entrepreneurs, and inexperienced citizens alike have launched news startups in the last few years, providing alternatives to Indian citizens (Chaudhry 2016). The majority of these digital outlets are based in metro areas, looking to take advantage of a young reader-ship market that is set to grow by millions (Sen and Nielsen 2016). Mostly privately owned and run by younger Indians, these sites are unafraid to question authority and have been described as 'vibrant' and 'hard-hitting' (Roy 2013: 2). These digital news startups, which have increased in number in the last five years or so, are being held up as positive and promising alternatives to legacy media (Sen and Nielsen 2016; Chaudhry 2016).

There is scepticism, however, about whether these digital news startups will be the future alternatives that audiences may seek over traditional news media (Kohli-Khandekar 2015). This dubiety also extends to whether these sites will introduce or create a sustainable revenue model for news organizations (Kohli-Khandekar 2015). Lack of scholarship on these startups leads to more questions about the sites' purpose, their founders, and whether they have a long-term plan for their news ventures. Journalism practitioners and scholars are interested in studying independent digital news startups of all shapes, forms, and funding because these sites experiment with approaches to storytelling, newsgathering processes, and professional roles (Chadha 2016; Carlson and Usher 2015; Konieczna 2014; Naldi and Picard 2012; Nee 2013). A lot of knowledge related to these ventures and those who founded them, however, has emerged from the United States and Europe. Indian news startups have received some attention (for example, Robinson et al. 2015; Sen and Nielsen 2016). This chapter includes the initial findings of a larger study undertaken in 2016–17 on news startups in India to better understand these new news players.[1]

NEWS MEDIA IN INDIA

Legacy Indian News Media: Not Quite What It Used to Be

After independence in 1947, the Indian press was primarily state owned, and journalists in a newly free India took a critical stance on political issues, but not so much against the government in power as promoting the latter's developmental agenda (Thussu 2005). This history possibly explains what Peterson calls the 'logic of responsibility' felt by the Indian press, dating back to the early days when it was called upon by the Indian government 'to be a partner in India's development' (2015: 677) and adopt the function of 'nation-building' (Thussu 2005: 128). At the same time, the government offered subsidized newsprint and advertising revenue to mostly privately owned newspapers, thus helping develop a 'relatively' autonomous press (Thussu 2005). The 'logic of responsibility' was felt even more by the independent press that competed with state-owned press at a time when India was finding its feet as a new sovereign nation (Peterson 2015).

Following the Indian government's decision to liberalize the country's protectionist economy in the early 1990s and move towards more open markets (Panagariya 2004), the Indian media exploded with several television news channels and digital sites launched within the next few years (Painter 2013). While several of the newspapers were already privately owned, the growth of radio and television channels led to greater corporatization and privatization by international and Indian companies alike. Recent years have seen a consolidation of media power, with a few corporate houses owning most of the news organizations (Rao and Wasserman 2015). These corporate houses have other financial interests that often clash with editorial interests; it is not uncommon for the former to supersede the latter at the cost of public-interest journalism (Saeed 2015). The issue of paid news—selling prime editorial space or television time to the highest bidder—continues to corrode Indian media from the inside. Even though the Press Club of India set up a committee to investigate the matter (Rahman 2010), no significant change or reform has resulted from it.

Indian Journalists: Between a Rock and a Hard Place

Research on journalists working in print and television news media has repeatedly shown reporters' struggles with corporate and political influences that directly affect them and their work. A study of ethical issues facing news journalists in English and vernacular print and television press highlighted the media's propensity for 'tabloidization', image-driven journalism, and paid news to earn revenues (Rao and Johal 2006). The authors also found that reporters thought that newsrooms' methods in undercover operations for investigative stories were unethical, as was the increasing closeness between corporate interests and news editors (Rao and Johal 2006). They felt they were poor watchdogs as their organizations expected them to cover celebrities and city-centred stories rather than social issues and rural news (Rao 2008). A study of online and print journalists also found that traditional news media reporters felt more responsible with regard to their role as information providers for society, compared to those who worked in online news sites (Ramaprasad et al. 2015).

Apart from organizational pressures, journalists also face political and social pressures such as lawsuits from local politicians, violent physical attacks, and online trolling from vigilante mobs (Reporters without Borders 2017). Reporters without Borders states that Indian journalists face lawsuits from local politicians and violent attacks from vigilante groups, leading to self-censorship. Consequently, the organization ranked India 136th out of 180 countries and rated press freedom in the country as 'bad' (Reporters without Borders 2017). Indian media companies also self-censor and regulate to minimize legal troubles, as the country lacks an efficient judiciary and/or an overarching regulatory press body that can swiftly penalize acts of defamation, libel, and violation of privacy (Roy 2013).

To further aggravate matters, the Indian government has taken to punishing reporters and news channels for not toeing the administration line; in 2016, officials banned private news channel NDTV India from the air for 24 hours for broadcasting information that officials deemed sensitive to national security (Ramachandran 2016). Recently, the Central Bureau of India raided the home of the same television company's (NDTV) founder Prannoy Roy and his wife and business partner, Radhika Roy for allegedly causing a loss to a bank

(Barry 2017). Members of the press and legal community, however, protested these raids and claimed it was an effort on the part of the government to silence the news media (*Scroll.in* 2017). Thus, the fourth estate in the world's largest democracy does not quite enjoy the freedom taken for granted by the press in other democracies (Chaudhry 2016).

Digital Native News Sites: Mostly English-Speaking Journalati

There is little information available on the number of independent online news startups in India. Lack of scholarship in the field has resulted in only a basic understanding of the digitally native news market, gleaned from articles in popular media. For example, Chaudhry (2016) provides an overview of digital startups in the *Columbia Journalism Review*; she calls the founders 'legacy refugees', or reporters who started their careers in traditional newspapers and channels but left to start their own ventures. A report by the Reuters Institute studied six startups—a mix of for-profit and not-for-profit ventures that were developing different kinds of content—and found that most were focused on niche audiences and had an English-language focus, but to cast their net wider pursued mobile-first and vernacular content strategies (Sen and Nielsen 2016). These overviews raise more questions about the founders; to learn more about their thinking when starting their news sites, some findings are presented here that are part of a larger ongoing research project on Indian news entrepreneurs.

There is no master list available on the number of digital startups operational in India. Not being multilingual in a country that has 20 major languages (Rao and Wasserman 2015) creates hurdles in tracking all the active, independent news sites. For the purposes of this study, within the constraints of language, time, and finances, interviews were conducted with founders who were based in New Delhi and Mumbai and willing to talk to the researchers. Both these cities are considered news media capitals; New Delhi is the political capital of the country and home to the headquarters of most news media outlets. Mumbai, on the other hand, is the financial and entertainment capital of the country and a significant number of outlets are based here, while almost all have a presence in the city. Semi-structured interviews with founders and editors were conducted at the following websites: (*a*) Janta ka Reporter; (*b*) Youth ki Awaz; (*c*) India Resists; (*d*) IndiaSpend; (*e*) *Scroll.in*; (*f*) the *Quint*; (*g*) Edit Platter; (*h*) NewsLaundry; (*i*) the Daily Pao; and (*j*) ScoopWhoop. Each interview lasted from one hour to one and a half hours. For the discussion presented here, the editors' interviews were excluded from the analysis[2] and only the founders were focused on. Of the founders, seven were male and three were female.

ENTREPRENEURSHIP AND JOURNALISM

Entrepreneurship: A Social Perspective

Entrepreneurship as a field of research involves studying not just 'the *processes* of discovery, evaluation, and exploitation of opportunities', but also 'the set of *individuals* who discover, evaluate, and exploit them (opportunities)' (Shane and Venkataraman 2000: 218). Scholarship in the field, therefore, is usually divided between studies that emphasize either contextual or dispositional conditions on entrepreneurial activities (Sorensen 2007). A growing number of studies, however, have examined the influence of dispositional factors on entrepreneurial processes of founding startups, startup identity, and strategies for growth such as entrepreneurial passion (Cardon et al. 2009), the role of gender in entrepreneurial activities (Minniti and Nardone 2007), prior professional/career experience of entrepreneurs (Roberts et al. 2011), self-efficacy (Chen et al. 1998), founders' social identity (Fauchart and Gruber 2011), and their role identity and its influence on not just founding but also persistence in founding the startup (Hoang and Gimeno 2010).

Founders, however, are not created in a vacuum. People embarking on an entrepreneurial career have occupied prior work roles and/or other social identities that they must transition from into their new work roles (Ashforth 2001). This transition requires individuals to construct a sense of their own identity—who they are—that is consonant with their new role functions and expectations—what they do (Ashforth 2001; Ibarra 1999). These transitions can be micro: movement between two roles held at the same time, such as wife and daughter; and macro: movement between differing roles, such as joining a new firm (Ashforth 2001). Adopting the role of an entrepreneur constitutes a macro transition. How people behave or act in a new professional role is often dependent on how closely they identify with another individual as a social referent for their new behaviours and, by extension, the social group (Ashforth and Mael 1989). Sometimes this feedback is direct and other times, indirect.

Entrepreneurs' new work role adoption is influenced by feedback from the environment around them—people, exemplars, colleagues (Child et al. 2015). This feedback becomes even more important when entrepreneurs start new businesses in emerging industries that lack precedents for what works and what does not work, thus making it difficult for the startup and the industry to gain legitimacy (Aldrich and Fiol 1994). As an entrepreneur, whether one fully embraces the role of being an entrepreneur—what Hoang and Gimeno (2010) refer to as *identity centrality*—can motivate an individual to pursue entrepreneurial activities in the face of initial criticism and strife. On the other hand, not embracing an entrepreneurial identity could lead to abandonment of entrepreneurship and the entrepreneurial venture.

While roles within institutions usually have definite functions and expectations associated with them, adopting the role of an entrepreneur allows an individual to define and design the entrepreneurial role in a manner closest to his/her concept of self (Fauchart and Gruber 2011). These entrepreneurial self-concepts are then reflected in the kind of startups these founders create and promote (Fauchart and Gruber 2011). Additionally, research has shown that activation of a particular role identity within an individual—as entrepreneur or as manager—will likely influence his or her actions and decisions related to the organization (Mathias and Williams 2017).

Journalists as Entrepreneurs

The professional or work identity of a journalist is steeped in an ideology that emphasizes norms, such as objectivity, public service, ethics, immediacy, and legitimacy (Deuze 2005). The business of journalism—the side that deals with advertising revenue and readership numbers—was a separate department within traditional and legacy media that journalists and other editorial staff never dealt with (Sylvie and Witherspoon 2002). The old models, however, have come under fire as digital technologies have disrupted journalistic practices and routines. On the other hand, these technologies have encouraged the growth of entrepreneurial news startups that are challenging traditional journalistic business models, and norms closely associated with the profession (Achtenhagen 2017). More than anything, the startups provide independent media voices and expand the news market, which is crucial for a functional democracy (Hoag 2008).

As discourse around the definition of 'entrepreneurial journalism' is vague (Vos and Singer 2016), the conceptualization of media entrepreneurship put forth by Hoag (2008) is adopted here. She defines it as 'the creation and ownership of an enterprise whose activity adds an independent voice to the media marketplace' (Vos and Singer 2016: 74). This broad conceptualization allows for studying all kinds of media firms, which serves our purpose as startups can be for-profit or not-for profit, big or small, local or a neighbourhood hyperlocal, and cover the federal government or a beach town (Downie and Schudson 2009; Benton 2015). In most instances, news startups fill a void left by mainstream media that no longer covers small towns or local stories of relevance to residents (Downie and Schudson 2009; Carr 2014). In addition, these sites also provide alternatives to those who would like to pursue careers in journalism, but lack of a sustainable revenue plagues these startups as much as it does legacy media (Metzgar et al. 2011).

The founders struggle with navigating the path between their professional identity as journalist and new identity as founder; the lack of role models hinders their role transition to some extent partly because they have no social referent (Chadha 2016). They also struggle with 'formational myopia', where the 'previous knowledge, experience, and practice of entrepreneurs influences their startup of enterprises in the new industries' (Naldi and Picard 2012: 76). In their study of American news media startups, the authors found that prior professional background influenced entrepreneurs' decisions to work on the editorial more than the business strategy. This led to short-sightedness in terms of direction and longevity for the startup, leading to detrimental consequences for the business. Additionally, Harte et al. (2016) found that hyperlocal founders in the UK were entrepreneurial in terms of seeking an opportunity and exploiting it, but their outlook was more civic, to help their community, than economic—to make money and grow the business. The authors also found that the entrepreneurs spent long hours at work and did not get compensated enough, leading to 'self-exploitation' (Harte et al. 2016: 245). Economic uncertainty raises questions about the longevity of a news site and consistency in news reporting. While Harte et al. (2016) mention that revenue is not the motivating factor for these founders to continue working and reporting at their startups, it does raise the question of sustainability—for how long would they continue working under such conditions, self-inflicted as the latter may be, before they throw in the towel.

Regardless, more scholars are calling for journalists—past, present, and future—to take on entrepreneurial roles and create their own jobs (Jarvis 2009). This business-oriented focus has led to concerns that the news media may focus on news that draws in more audiences and revenues versus stories that require people's attention as citizens of an active democracy (Hanitzsch 2007). The Indian mainstream press already suffers from a close nexus between editorial and business interests. In a news startup, often the founders have no choice but to take on the roles of both editor and business manager (Chadha 2016). How does this contradiction play out in digital news startups in India? To address this query and others related to the founders' intentions for starting a news site, respondents were asked to explain the history of the startup, the exemplars they looked to when thinking of the design of their startup, and the work they do on a 'regular' day that reflects the role in which they see themselves as startup creators.

Entrepreneurial Journalism in India

Most of the founders belonged to the urban, educated, English-speaking group and, except for the founder of India Resists, all had a journalistic education and/or experience. The age group was the early 20s to the late 50s. The general narrative acquired from interviews with them regarding their digital news startups is that they wanted to reclaim journalism (Chaudhry 2016; Harlow and Chadha 2018) or 'alter the manner in which media is run in the country' (Khan 2017). The founders of NewsLaundry, *Scroll.in*, and Janta ka Reporter primarily highlighted reasons for starting their news sites such as 'look at what is happening in the news',[3] or 'not a single TV channel is owned by an independent person who is only bothered about guarding the interest of journalism'.[4] The founders of ScoopWhoop and Youth ki Awaz said they started their websites because they did not see themselves or their generation reflected on the net. Founders of the Daily Pao wanted to simply fill a void in the coverage of Mumbai city culture and create jobs for themselves after the outlet covering the issue closed. The founder of Edit Platter wanted to address the issue of information overload by providing audiences with a selection of what the founder, with previous professional experience, thought was the important news of the day from various domestic and international news outlets. In all these reasons, probably the common denominator is that the founders wanted to provide the kind of journalism they thought mainstream media had failed at. Their goal was to cover the stories that ought to be covered but were not, and they wanted to give voice to the common man, a generation or even a demographic that was not allowed to speak its mind. Thus, even within digital startups, the founders were committed to the 'logic of responsibility' (Peterson 2015) that seems to be inbred in Indian journalists, given the Indian press's history of collaboration with the government.

Looking to the West, but Speaking for the East

In terms of the social references or positive and negative examples (Child et al. 2015) for their startups, the digital founders sought mostly American digital outlets as exemplars for their venture design and editorial input. The Indian founders referred to sites such as RealClearPolitics, Mic, Vox News, the *Huffington Post*, BuzzFeed, UpWorthy, and Medium in the initial stages. Arguably this was also the founders' way of gaining legitimacy, by referring to sites that were already well established in the digital news startup sphere and, thus, identifying themselves with this group (Ashforth and Mael 1989). The founders are aware, however, that Indian audiences are different, and do not have access to the digital infrastructure that American audiences take for granted. Thus, they adapt to their readers. As the founder of Youth ki Awaz explicated:

> We have identified elements which different platforms have which we associate with already and there is a lot of learning in how they do it

already.... So you know what a typical millennial in the US is doing today, a typical millennial [in India] will do next year. We are anyway about a year behind in terms of taking to technology. People are still joining Facebook for the first time and Facebook has a massive potential in India even today while it is getting saturated in the US. So you know it's a very different kind of market but obviously, there is a lot of learning as to how they do it, what is it that we can do here and can we replicate, can we learn from them, can we make our own model around it and so on.[5]

These founders are also aware that simply applying an idea without taking the Indian media market context into account is not feasible, and they adapt their editorial content accordingly. For example, the founder of Edit Platter 'really liked' the RealClearPolitics site in the US but believes he must tweak the model to comply with Indian media laws. The founder of the *Quint* said she researched the field by going on a 'digital pilgrimage' and visiting newsrooms such as Mic and Vox News, as well as those who were creating digital products such as Prismatic and Circa (both no longer exist) to see where digital news and publishing was headed. She stated that they knew, however, that 'the strength of the product would lie in our individual voice.'

Interestingly, the founder of India Resists used an Indian website as a negative example of what he did not want his site to be. Arguably, that site is a direct competitor in the Indian market and, therefore, it makes sense that the founder would want to provide something different to the audience. American websites, on the other hand, are not competing for the same eyeballs and therefore could be used as more positive examples.

Role Identity: The Bigger, the Clearer

Of all the founders, the ones who embraced the identity of the entrepreneur as central to their role had removed themselves from the day-to-day editorial responsibilities of the site. This role prioritization emerged in how they described their daily routines. For example, the co-founder of the *Quint* said she was 'less journalist', and, in her description of her regular day, managerial issues seemed to take precedence over editorial.

I begin the day with of course monitoring the site and looking at analytics etc.... 10 am in the morning, Raghav [co-founder] and Rohit [executive editor] and I and the Hindi senior editor meet with the entire team.... we go through all the ideas that come in and make a day plan so I am in on that and my rest of the day is ... split up between the site, product, looking at running these two floors, from kitchen towels to coffee to analytics site, hygiene, young team, lots of angst, lots of issues, lots of that, constant meeting candidates for fresh hiring....

The co-founder of ScoopWhoop identified herself as a 'content creator' and described her regular day as involving strategizing for the kind of content that should be posted on the site as well as the story design, based on audience analytics. The founders of Youth ki Awaz and NewsLaundry had internalized the separation between editorial and business responsibilities. As they focused on site growth and business duties, they did not call themselves journalists. The co-founder and editor of *Scroll.in* also believed in keeping the two sides separate and, as he was the editor, he had nothing to do with advertising and revenue earnings. These sites, however, are big in size and have a dedicated advertising team as well as a separate editorial desk.

In the smaller startups, such as Edit Platter, Janta ka Reporter, and the Daily Pao, the founders had to juggle their business and editorial roles as they worked in the capacities of both business and editorial heads. Thus, the work they did regularly influenced their role identity as being journalists before being entrepreneurs. It is telling that these sites had an established editorial staff but not necessarily an advertising section. With limited resources, their priority lay in creating and publishing original news stories. Thus, these sites displayed formational myopia (Naldi and Picard 2012) as their prior experience influenced venture design and business strategy. The founders of these three sites were professional journalists before launching their news ventures, and the emphasis on editorial is an extension of that experience. It also translated into long hours spent covering news or leading coverage of news. For example, the founder of Janta ka Reporter said:

What we do is we'll be here [office] until 6–6:30 [pm] depending on how many stories we are inundated with and we'll shut shop here, we all go.... I go back home, I've converted one of my rooms into a nice office with all kinds of facilities and everything. I'll start working just keeping an eye on what is happening, talking to my contributors, talking to my sources, talking to other stakeholders like bloggers…. I wake up at 6 o'clock and go through the newspapers before these guys [editorial staff] come in the office. I crack on with some writing … so that's what I do…. Essentially, I end up working 16–17 hours every day.

While they wanted to make their business sustainable and raise revenue, the editorial role was central to their identity. The founder of Edit Platter also claimed that he was working harder than he ever had, to run his news venture. This is similar to the self-exploitation that Harte et al. (2016) found among hyperlocal founders in the UK. Indian entrepreneurs, at least the smaller ones, also showed a certain amount of formational myopia as well as strong identification with the role of journalism rather than entrepreneurship in the planning and working design of their startups. Hyperlocal founders in the US have realized that they need to focus on business strategies as much as they do on editorial; this sensibility, while adapted by founders of the smaller Indian startups, is not one they seem to prioritize.

Eye on Sustainability

To examine if the sites were serious about longevity and had devised a strategy for sustaining their startups, the founders were asked about plans for their sites in the next five years. Most of the founders spoke of achieving milestones related to content creation and distribution of the content to get more audiences. The founder of India Resists firmly rejected advertising and, therefore, he focused on a two-year plan rather than a five-year plan. His immediate concern was to use social media more extensively to distribute content. Founders of the smaller sites—Janta ka Reporter and the Daily Pao—said they wanted to grow their sites and expand into other cities, events, and achieve a level of sustainability. The founder of the smaller site Edit Platter said he did not have a business plan because audience numbers were at the core of achieving advertising revenue and, consequently, sustainability. Incidentally, founders of the bigger sites, namely ScoopWhoop, the *Quint*, and Youth ki Awaz also said they did not have a business plan. Their reason for not having one, however, was the dynamic, ever-changing medium they were on—the internet. The bigger startups said they were evaluating their strategies all the time to keep up with the changing affordances of the digital space. The *Quint* founder was most representative of this group when she said, 'I am a little weary of saying what our next one-year mission is cause things are changing so, if you had asked a year back about the same time what my next year's mission was, I would not have been able to foresee half the things we are doing right now, they didn't exist, they weren't born.'

The *Quint* is at an advantage: the founders were paid well for exiting their last media venture and these funds keep their new digital venture afloat. They have not felt the need to get funding for any strategy they wanted to pursue. They have also invested money in Youth ki Awaz, the other site featured here. ScoopWhoop received investor funding and, therefore, they have the financial ability to experiment, fail, change, and move forward. NewsLaundry as a non-profit has received funding from consortiums dedicated to promoting free speech as well as other sources. With a dedicated partner who is focused on the business aspects of the site, *Scroll.in* is also at a distinct advantage, with the founder claiming that he wanted to focus on expanding editorial coverage to more issues, such as business, and across neglected states, such as in the North-East. The bigger sites talked about broad goals and revisiting their strategy and experimenting with new methods of content production and revenue generation. The smaller ones, however, were hesitant to think too far, even though they were self-funded and had received advertising revenue. They had definite timelines for turning things around and receiving external funding.

* * *

The founders featured in this chapter belong to an exclusive class: they work for English-language digital media in the two biggest metro cities in India on a digital platform. These three factors already separate them from the vast populations who live in smaller towns or rural areas, do not speak English, and do not have internet access. The narrative around the reasons why these sites were started revealed that the founders would like to publish stories that mainstream media failed to produce, and thus target the very audiences the latter already catered to. About three-fourths of the founders interviewed had a professional journalistic background, and thus prior experience in mainstream media, explaining why they chose to stay in the field they knew best and cater to the same audience as their previous organizations (Child et al. 2015).

The sites looked to Western exemplars—primarily in the US—as positive examples and did not mention any Indian exemplars when designing their news startups and editorial content. The founders were clear, however, that they would have to work towards developing a voice, brand, and content that specifically resonated with their own audiences. This phenomenon is akin to that of 'cultural modernity' that Neyazi (2010) found among Hindi newspapers in India. These vernacular publications had embraced the technological advances and methods of content production and distribution offered by Western media companies. A similar process was professed by the founders. They looked to digital news pioneers in the West but developed and maintained an independent voice that their Indian readers identified with.

In terms of their work on a regular basis, founders of the bigger sites embraced the role of entrepreneur more easily and their daily routine incorporated strategizing and thinking about business and revenue growth. The founders of smaller sites, however, worked longer hours and suffered from 'formational myopia' to the extent that their prior experiences in the news media industry influenced their behaviours when establishing their news startup and focusing on editorial growth more so than business growth opportunities. Thus, how clearly founders embrace their central identity as entrepreneurs indeed influences which aspects of the startup they are more likely to focus on (Hoang and Gimeno 2010). However, this needs to be studied in greater depth across a greater number of startups. Finally, founders of the bigger startups were aware of how quickly technology disrupted content production and dissemination routines, and therefore were more likely to revisit and revise their business strategies moving forward. Ideally, having a business plan is a good thing. Digital technologies, however, are disrupting industries and reinventing them at lightning speed, thus posing the important question for digital startups: should they have a plan?

Within the Indian news industry, these digital startups are positioning themselves as alternatives—in terms of choice rather than as unconventional—to English-language mainstream media. More research, however, needs to be done on vernacular-language news startups that may approach these issues differently. Focusing on news startups other than those published in English is even more important now, as a study conducted by Google with accounting firm KPMG in India said that the Indian-language internet user base is likely to cross the half billion mark by 2021 (KPMG and Google 2017). The lure of these growing markets has already led to several Indian startups—including some of those featured here such as the *Quint*, Youth ki Awaz, Janta ka Reporter, and NewsLaundry—offering content in Hindi and other Indian languages (Pandit 2018).

Given the ease with which digital news startups launch and fold, and no central body or group keeping track of their operations, researchers must rely on their personal networks and knowledge of the Indian news industry to conduct any research related to this topic. Additionally, not being multilingual in a country that has 20 major languages (Rao and Wasserman 2015) creates hurdles in tracking all the active Indian-language, independent news sites. These deficiencies mean that sites equally worthy of study, such as the Gaon Connection and Khabar Lahariya (Hindi-language print and digital outlets that focus on rural news from Hindi-speaking states in north India), Samachara (an independent news site published in the Kannada language spoken in Karnataka), Dool News (a self-described news portal that publishes content in the Malayalam language, spoken in Kerala), and Marathi-language independent news sites, such as Bigul and Aksharnama in Maharashtra, slip through the sampling cracks.

Thus, an effort needs to be made on the part of researchers to look beyond the known names and analyse the work being done by Indian language startups. It would be worthwhile to collaborate with researchers within India to get a broader sample that includes such examples. Additionally, the reporters who work at these startups should be studied to understand the journalistic norms and routines they follow. They must also be asked if they feel the pressure of publishing news that gets more clicks and, hence, more revenue, or if they are allowed to pursue less popular stories that nonetheless are informative and promote civic discourse. A content analysis would also help identify the different kinds of stories that are published on Indian news startups. Then one would truly learn whether these founders are successful in their efforts to offer choice to the Indian news consumer and are supporting the country's democratic processes.

NOTES

1. This study was funded by an internal grant by Florida State University and conducted in collaboration with Assistant Professor Summer Harlow in December 2016.
2. We were unable to meet with the founders of IndiaSpend when we were visiting Mumbai, so the site has been excluded from the discussion.
3. Sekhri, Newslaundry, personal interview.
4. Jawaid, JKR, personal interview.
5. Interviews cited in this chapter were conducted in New Delhi and Mumbai in December 2016.

REFERENCES

Achtenhagen, Leona (2017). 'Media Entrepreneurship: Taking Stock and Moving Forward'. *International Journal on Media Management*, 19(1): 1–10. doi: 10.1080/14241277.2017.1298941.

Aldrich, H. E. and C. M. Fiol (1994). 'Fools Rush In? The Institutional Context of Industry Creation'. *Academy of Management*, 19(4): 645–70.

Ashforth, B. E. (2001). *Role Transitions in Organizational Life: An Identity Based Perspective*. Mahwah, NJ: Lawrence Erlbaum Associates.

Ashforth, B. E. and F. Mael (1989). 'Social Identity Theory and the Organization'. *Academy of Management Review*, 14(1): 20–39.

Barry, E. (2017). 'Raids in India Target Founders of News Outlet Critical of Government'. *New York Times*. Retrieved from https://www.nytimes.com/2017/06/05/world/asia/india-ndtv-raids-narendra-modi-prannoy-roy.html?_r=0 (accessed on 17 August 2018).

Benton, J. (2015). 'Who's Making Money—and Who Isn't—in Local Online News?' NiemanLab. Retrieved from http://www.niemanlab.org/2015/07/whos-making-money-and-who-isnt-in-local-online-news/ (accessed on 17 August 2018).

Bhattacharya, A. (2017). 'India's Internet Users Have More Faith in Content That's Not in English'. *Quartz India*. Retrieved from https://qz.com/972844/indias-internet-users-have-more-faith-in-content-thats-not-in-english-study-says/ (accessed on 17 August 2018).

Cardon, M. S., J. Wincent, J. Singh, and M. Drnovsek (2009). 'The Nature and Experience of Entrepreneurial Passion'. *Academy of Management Review*, 34(3): 511–32.

Carlson, M. and N. Usher (2015). 'News Startups as Agents of Innovation'. *Digital Journalism*. doi: 10.1080.21670811.2015.1076344.

Carr, David (2014). 'Local Papers Shine Light in Society's Dark Corners'. *New York Times*, 9 February. http://www.nytimes.com/2014/02/10/business/media/local-papers-shinelight-in-societys-dark-corners.html.

Chadha, M. (2016). 'What I Am Versus What I Do'. *Journalism Practice*, 10(6): 697–714. doi: 10.1080/17512786.2015.1046994.

Chaudhry, L. (2016). 'Can the Digital Revolution Save Indian Journalism?'*Columbia Journalism Review*, Fall/Winter. Retrieved from http://www.cjr.org/special_report/india_digital_revolution_startups_scoopwhoop_wire_times.php (accessed on 17 August 2018).

Chen, C. C., P. G. Greene, and A. Crick (1998). 'Does Entrepreneurial Self-Efficacy Distinguish Entrepreneurs from Managers?' *Journal of Business Venturing*, 13: 295–316.

Child, C., E. M. Witesman, and D. B. Braudt (2015). 'Sector Choice: How Fair Trade Entrepreneurs Choose between Nonprofit and For-Profit Forms'. *Nonprofit and Voluntary Sector Quarterly*, 44(4): 832–51. doi: 10.1177/0899764014542688.

Deuze, M. (2005). 'What Is Journalism? Professional Identity and Ideology of Journalists Reconsidered'. *Journalism*, 6(4): 442–64. doi: 10.1177/1464884905056815.

Downie, L. Jr, and M. Schudson (2009). 'The Reconstruction of American Journalism'. *Columbia Journalism Review*, 48(4): 28–51.

Fauchart, E. and M. Gruber (2011). 'Darwinians, Communitarians, and Missionaries: The Role of Founder Identity in Entrepreneurship'. *Academy of Management Journal*, 54(5): 935–57.

Hanitzsch, T. (2007). 'Deconstructing Journalism Culture: Toward a Universal Theory'. *Communication Theory*, 17: 365–85.

Harlow, S. and M. Chadha (2018). 'Indian Entrepreneurial Journalism'. *Journalism Studies*, Online first. doi: 10.1080/1461670X.2018.1463170.

Harte, D., J. Turner, and A. Williams (2016). 'Discourses of Enterprise in Hyperlocal Community News in the UK'. *Journalism Practice*, 10(2): 233–50. doi: 10.1080/17512786.2015.1123109.

Hoag, Anne (2008). 'Measuring Media Entrepreneurship'. *International Journal on Media Management*, 10: 74–80. doi: 10.1080/14241270802000496.

Hoang, H. and J. Gimeno (2010). 'Becoming a Founder: How Founder Role Identity Affects Entrepreneurial Transitions and Persistence in Founding'. *Journal of Business Venturing*, 25: 41–53. doi: 10.1016/j.jbusvent.2008.07.002.

Ibarra, H. (1999). 'Provisional Selves: Experimenting with Image and Identity in Professional Adaptation'. *Administrative Science Quarterly*, 44: 764–91. doi: 10.2307/2667055.

Jarvis, J. (2009). 'The Future of News Is Entrepreneurial'. Buzzmachine. Retrieved from http://buzzmachine.com/2009/11/01/the-future-of-journalism-is-entrepreneurial/ (accessed on 17 August 2018).

Khan, S. A. (2017). 'Pankaj Pachauri to Launch Mobile-Only Channel, Go News'. Exchange4media.com. Retrieved from http://www.exchange4media.com/digital/pankaj-pachauri-to-launch-mobile-only-channel-go-news_67486.html (accessed on 17 August 2018).

Kohli-Khandekar, V. (2015). 'The Online News Experiment'. *Business Standard*. Retrieved from http://www.business-standard.com/article/opinion/vanita-kohli-khandekar-the-online-news-experiment-115111001461_1.html (accessed on 17 August 2018).

Konieczna, M. (2014). 'Do Old Norms Have a Place in New Media?' *Journalism Practice*, 8(1): 49–64. doi: 10.1080/17512786.2013.793511.

KPMG and Google (2017). 'Indian Languages—Defining India's Internet'. Retrieved from https://assets.kpmg.com/content/dam/kpmg/in/pdf/2017/04/Indian-languages-Defining-Indias-Internet.pdf (accessed on 17 August 2018).

Mathias, B. D. and D. W. Williams (2017). 'The Impact of Role Identities on Entrepreneurial Evaluation and Selection of Opportunities'. *Journal of Management*, 43(3): 892–918. doi: 10.1177/0149206314544747.

Meeker, M. (2017). '2016 Internet Trends'. Kleiner Perkins Caufield Byers. Retrieved from https://www.slideshare.net/kleinerperkins/internet-trends-2017-report/234 (accessed on 11 September 2018).

Metzgar, E. T., D. T. Kurpius, and K. M. Rowley (2011). 'Defining Hyperlocal Media: Proposing a Framework for Discussion'. *New Media and Society*, 13(5): 772–87. doi: 10.1177/146144810385095.

Minniti, M. and C. Nardone (2007). 'Being in Someone Else's Shoes: The Role of Gender in Nascent Entrepreneurship'. *Small Business Economics*, 28: 223–38.

Naldi, L. and R. G. Picard (2012). 'Let's Start an Online News Site: Opportunities, Resources, Strategy and Formational Myopia in Startups'. *Journal of Media Business Studies*, 9(4): 69–97.

Nee, R. C. (2013). 'Creative Destruction: An Exploratory Study of How Digitally Native News Nonprofits Are Innovating Online Journalism Practices'. *International Journal on Media Management*, 15(1): 3–22. doi: 10.1080/14241277.2012.732153.

Neyazi, T. A. (2010). 'Cultural Imperialism or Vernacular Modernity? Hindi Newspapers in a Globalizing India'. *Media, Culture and Society*, 32(6): 907–24. doi: 10.1177/0163443710379664.

Painter, J. (2013). 'Introduction'. In *India's Media Boom: The Good News and the Bad*, ed. J. Painter, pp. xi–xv. Reuters Institute for the Study of Journalism. Retrieved from http://reutersinstitute.politics.ox.ac.uk/publication/india%E2%80%99s-media-boom.

Panagariya, A. (2004). 'India's Trade Reform'. Report by Brookings Institution. Retrieved from https://www.brookings.edu/wp-content/uploads/2016/07/2004_panagariya.pdf (accessed on 17 August 2018).

Pandit, V. (2018). 'Indian Start-Ups Add Vernacular Languages to Expand Reach'. *Hindu BusinessLine*. Retrieved from https://www.thehindubusinessline.com/companies/indian-startups-add vernacular-languages-to-expand-reach/article10012197.ece (accessed on 17 August 2018).

Peterson, M. A. (2015). 'Speaking of News: Press, Democracy and Metapragmatics in a Changing India'. *American Ethnologist*, 42(4): 673–87. doi: 10.1111/amet.12163.

Rahman, M. (2010). 'India: Paid News Scandal Hits Major Newspapers'. *Guardian*. Retrieved from https://www.theguardian.com/media/2010/jan/04/india-paid-news-scandal (accessed on 17 August 2018).

Ramachandran, S. K. (2016). 'NDTV India Ban: First Time a News Channel Barred over National Security'. *Hindustan Times*, 4 November. Retrieved from http://www.hindustantimes.com/india-news/ndtv-india-ban-not-the-first-time-a-channel-has-been-taken-off-air/story-8B0kY8CiWYGttC46qrb6gO.html (accessed 11 September 2018).

Ramaprasad, J., N. Gudipaty, and R. K. Vemula (2015). 'Indian Journalists: Personal Passion, Organizational Dynamics and Environmental Forces'. *African Journalism Studies*, 36(3): 61–86. doi: 10.1080/23743670.2015.1073932.

Rao, S. (2008). 'Accountability, Democracy, and Globalization: A Study of Broadcast Journalism in India'. *Asian Journal of Communication*, 18(3): 193–206.

Rao, S. and N. S. Johal (2006). 'Ethics and News Making in the Changing Indian Mediascape'. *Journal of Mass Media Ethics*, 21(2): 286–303.

Rao, S. and H. Wasserman (2015). 'A Media Not for All: A Comparative Analysis of Journalism, Democracy and Exclusion in Indian and South African Media'. *Journalism Studies*, 16(5): 651–62.

Reporters without Borders (2017). *India*. Retrieved from https://rsf.org/en/india.

Roberts, P. W., S. Klepper, and S. Hayward (2011). 'Founder Backgrounds and the Evolution of Firm Size'. *Industrial and Corporate Change*, 20(6): 1515–38. doi: 10.1093/icc/dtr026.

Robinson, J. J., K. Grennan, and A. Schiffrin (2015). 'Publishing for Peanuts: Innovation and the Journalism Start-Up'. Report by Columbia University School of International and Public Affairs. Retrieved from http://www.

cima.ned.org/wp-content/uploads/2015/11/PublishingforPeanuts.pdf (accessed on 17 August 2018).

Roy, P. (2013). 'More News Is Good News: Democracy and Media in India'. In *India's Media Boom: The Good News and the Bad*, ed. James Painter. Report by Reuters Institute for the Study of Journalism. Retrieved from http://reutersinstitute.politics.ox.ac.uk/publication/india%E2%80%99s-media-boom.

Saeed, S. (2015). 'Phantom Journalism: Governing India's Proxy Media Owners'. *Journalism Studies*, 16(5): 663–79. doi: 10.1080/1461670X.2015.1054174.

Scroll.in (2017). 'CBI Raids on NDTV Should Worry Us All, Fali Nariman Tells Journalists Gathered at Delhi Press Club'. Retrieved from https://scroll.in/latest/840189/cbi-raids-on-ndtv-should-worry-us-all-fali-nariman-tells-journalists-gathered-at-delhi-press-club (accessed on 17 August 2018).

Sen, A. and R. K. Nielsen (2016). 'Digital Journalism Start-Ups in India'. Report, Reuters Institute for the Study of Journalism. Retrieved from http://reutersinstitute.politics.ox.ac.uk/publication/digital-journalism-start-ups-india (accessed on 17 August 2018).

Shane, S. and S. Venkataraman (2000). 'The Promise of Entrepreneurship as a Field of Research'. *Academy of Management*, 25(1): 217–26.

Sonwalkar, P. (2002). '"Murdochization" of the Indian Press: From By-Line to Bottom-Line'. *Media, Culture and Society*, 24(6): 821–34.

Sorensen, J. B. (2007). 'Bureaucracy and Entrepreneurship: Workplace Effects on Entrepreneurial Entry'. *Administrative Science Quarterly*, 52(3): 387–412.

Sylvie, G. and P. D. Witherspoon (2002). *Time, Change, and the American Newspaper*. Mahwah, NJ: Lawrence Erlbaum Associates.

Thussu, D. K. (2005). 'Adapting to Globalization: The Changing Contours of Journalism in India'. In *Making Journalists*, ed. Hugo de Burgh, pp. 127–41. Abingdon, Oxon: Routledge.

Vos, T. P. and J. Singer (2016). 'Media Discourse about Entrepreneurial Journalism: Implications for Journalistic Capital'. *Journalism Practice*, 10(2): 143–59.

CHAPTER TEN

Mapping the News App Ecosystem

Indian General Elections, Mobile Apps, and Emerging News Culture

SAAYAN CHATTOPADHYAYA

. . . .

A number of important attributes characterize the mobile phone as an increasingly important communication device in a wide variety of contexts. The mobile phone is evidently an essential constituent of information communication technology; it is certainly very portable; besides being completely open to commodification and considerable personalization, mobile phones are also becoming ubiquitous nodes of computational technology and frequently turning out to be platforms for intriguing techno-cultural and social practices (Hooker and Raby 2000). In developing countries, mobile phones, especially smartphones, are usually identified as emerging technologies, and, as telecommunication devices, they are continuously being upgraded, transformed, and redesigned. The market economy and the business strategies revolving around these mobile phones are also witnessing significant alterations and negotiations. While mobile phones, tablets, or phablets in the developed nations are gradually forging the internet of things, the developing nations are also witnessing how cheap smartphones and rapidly reducing bandwidth charges are enabling hundreds of millions of people to connect to a range of information, services, and interactions.

Consequently, the rising popularity of mobile applications or 'apps' at this particular period is crucial to understand. There is a small but growing academic literature on mobile phone use in India; however, specific studies on mobile apps and their implications are particularly limited (Chakraborty 2006; Kumar and Thomas 2006; Steenson and Donner 2009; Rai 2012; Doron and Jeffrey 2013).[1] While these studies highlight the numerically persuasive empirical narratives of mobile phone use in India, sociological theory and technology studies have failed to come to a consensus on understanding the democratic potential of new media technologies including cell phones (Sreekumar 2015: 287). Although scholarly attention to mobile apps is fairly recent, it is important to critically engage with such new media practices to explore what kind of techno-cultural paradigm they constitute and, in particular, what kinds of uses, practices, intentions, and individuals may access apps—and what would be the socio-economic and cultural implications of that intervention. These are fundamental cultural, political questions that are necessary to put forward for a better under-standing of any emerging communicative technologies; hence, the purpose of this chapter is to flag the complexity of such a condition. With that intention, this chapter concentrates on a relatively narrow aspect of apps, albeit one with significantly wider ramifications. With reference to the 2014 Indian general elections or Lok Sabha elections, this chapter discusses the use of mobile apps, particularly news apps, to examine the power relationships that are implicit in the emerging techno-cultural matrix of a developing country.

It must be noted at the onset that the electoral population of India is the largest in the world, and the 2014 general election was the longest and the most expensive general election in the history of the country. At present, there is a range of different kinds of mobile apps available across a number of apps stores and handset types that directly relate to the different aspects of the Indian general elections. The Google Play Store alone lists more than 200 apps specifically developed for the general elections in 2014. Different political parties, the Election Commission of India, a number of news media organizations, not to mention individual citizens are developing, promoting, and using these mobile apps in relation to the elections. Information about constituencies, schedule, profiles of candidates, trivia, results of past elections, media reports, games, and entertainment based on the 2014 general elections are available through these applications, which can be downloaded from the application market, mostly free of cost. These mobile apps exploit the power of social media, big data, analytics, and mobility to give the user a sense of control and authority on what seems to be a complex web of information. Moreover, the apps allow the individual to participate in the entire process through its gamified and interactive features. The 2014 general elections are widely touted as the first proper digital elections in India, as the total expenditure on campaigns on digital platforms reportedly reached a staggering $300 million, out of the total of more than five million dollars spent on advertisement and publicity by different political parties. Predictably, the youth, many of them first-time voters, were the primary target audience for the wide use of mobile phones in disseminating political messages, updates, and information. All these developments point to a significant transformation from the 2009 general elections, which witnessed moderate use of social media and mobile communication.

The emergence of news apps provokes us to map a substantially new realm of emerging journalistic practices and evolving news paradigms, indicating not only new centres of agency, interactions, and desires, but also towards the consolidation of a system for societies of control. In this chapter, I seek to explore some of these aspects, pointing towards specific attributes of this emerging techno-cultural practice that may offer a fresh perspective on the cultural work of technology, away from the much-cited tropes of modernity, development, and autonomy. In the next section of the chapter, I provide a brief outline of the rise of mobile apps in India; the subsequent section explains in what way mobile news apps have been used in the 2014 general elections, followed by a section describing a theoretical matrix to locate the specificity of mobile news apps, using the 2014 general elections as a case in point. Finally, I identify three different modalities through which mobile news apps function as a techno-cultural apparatus: as sites of control, as forms of agency, and as systems of knowledge.

MEDIATED ELECTION AND MOBILE APPS IN INDIA

The mobile phone in India functions within an array of cultural and symbolic registers. Instead of being simple electronic telecommunication devices, mobile phones are rich sites of cultural production. Hence, rather than exclusively focusing on the hegemony of Western, developed countries as a pivot of innovation, production, and consumption, a closer examination of mobile phone culture in emerging economies like India may reveal distinctive, albeit complicated insights. The developing countries are characterized by a particular mode of social mobility that is essential to recognize to understand the ways in which mobile phones have been adopted and used. The rapid acceptance of mobile phones in India is deeply influenced by the traditional patterns of social mobility outside of the home. The notion of 'mobility' is invested with cultural specificity, and the nuances of being mobile have specific cultural underpinnings. Mobile apps are increasingly being developed, distributed, and consumed within these different and shifting cultures of mobility.

Even in the early 1990s, owning a telephone was considered a sign of lavishness, and to obtain a new fixed phone connection one had to go through an exceedingly complicated process, at times with waiting periods of more than a year for a landline, even after paying substantial application fees (Kumar and Thomas 2006). Until 1994, the simple task of owning a phone with buttons or an extension cord or even getting a coloured phone would involve waiting in endless queues or obtaining a recommendation from a member of Parliament or minister (Chowdary 2004: 2085). According to the Telecom Regulatory Authority of India (TRAI 2017), in 2016, more than one billion subscribers had phone connections including 1,078.42 million wireless subscribers. Hence, mobile phones have rapidly become a popular consumer item adopted by a wide segment of Indian consumers. Mobile phones first arrived in the Indian market in the mid-1990s. Although, due to the high cost of the handset and call charges, in addition to limited availability of mobile network, the initial response was relatively slow, their adoption has grown exponentially over time, with an average annual growth of more than 80 per cent. While multimedia phones were available in India since early 2000, from 2010, with the introduction of Android's open-source platform, smartphones started to gain widespread popularity. Although 81 per cent of people own a mobile phone, a mere 17 per cent use smartphones and 61 per cent own a non-smartphone cell phone or feature phone. This is in stark contrast to China or Brazil, where smartphone users comprise 58 per cent and 41 per cent of the population respectively (Poushter 2016).[2] However, India is considered one of the fastest-growing markets for smartphones. The smartphone user base in India crossed 300 million as shipments grew 18 per cent annually in 2016, compared to the global smartphone market which grew only 3 per cent (Mukherjee 2017). In 2011, the census revealed that nearly half of India's 1.2 billion people (46.9 per cent) did not have a toilet at home, but 53.2 per cent owned a mobile phone (BBC 2012). However, because of enduring prejudices and structures of authority, the mobile phone has proved even more disruptive in India than elsewhere (Doron and Jeffrey 2013: 2).

Considering the vast market potential, smartphones offer a range of opportunities and options to marketers, manufacturers, and advertisers. Surveys by Nielsen Informate Mobile Insights (Singh and Pant 2014) have also recorded an exceptional rise in smartphone usage among the under-18 and 25–30 age groups in India. Hence, being early adopters, it is obvious that these groups are eager for new technological innovations and seem prepared to become engaged and consume products and services targeted to them. With smartphone penetration growing at an unprecedented pace and the range of content, apps, and social media persistently rising, it is apparent that this new media space is equipped with prospects for marketers.

In the last few years, India has witnessed steady growth in the development, distribution, and consumption of mobile apps, which does not only open up a thriving socio-cultural arena but also points to the lucrative economic aspect. Parallel to the rapid proliferation of touchscreen mobile devices, third-party content producers such as news media organizations have witnessed a tremendous growth of mobile apps. Although limited in contrast to the West, traditional news media continues to experiment with how to make mobile news provision more user-friendly through dedicated services. At the end of 2012, the *Times of India*, the leading English broadsheet daily, started using QR code next to the news articles so that the reader could scan the code with their mobile app and instantly connect to video and other online content on the website through their mobile phone. This was aimed at providing a direct and user-friendly transfer from print to mobile that stimulated complementary news accessing.

Nonetheless, smartphone owners in India are the least likely to use all categories of apps on a regular basis; the most popular tend to be more entertainment-driven, like social networking and games. According to surveys, 39 per cent of Indian app users use mobile apps for gaming; while 29 per cent use apps for social networking; the same percentage also use apps for watching online videos, and a mere 13 per cent access news using mobile apps in India (Nielsen 2013). Even though at the moment, the popularity of news apps is more limited than that of games or entertainment apps, it is essential to observe that news content often acquires a place within business, entertainment, social media, lifestyle, and a variety of other more popular categories as well.

MAPPING THE NEWS APPS ECOSYSTEM DURING ELECTIONS

The Indian general election of 2014 was held from 7 April to 12 May 2014, to constitute the 16th Lok Sabha by electing members of Parliament for the parliamentary constituencies of India.[3] Spread over nine phases, this was the longest election in the country's history and, according to the Election Commission of India, 814.5 million people were eligible to vote, making this the largest-ever election in the world. The results were declared on 16 May 2014, announcing that the National Democratic Alliance led by the BJP had won, after the counting exercise was completed at 989 counting centres. The Internet and Mobile Association of India estimated that a well-executed social media campaign could swing 3 to 4 per cent of votes. Being second only to the US presidential election in terms of expense, the Indian general election in 2014 witnessed a spurt in digital campaigning, from 3D holographic speeches to simple text messages, through which politicians were hoping to connect to a younger generation and first-time voters. Politicians participated in Google+ Hangouts, televised interviews arranged by Facebook, and used the Facebook-owned smartphone messaging app WhatsApp to connect with millions of technologically enabled urban voters. Two of the foremost parties, the Indian National Congress and the BJP, allocated 2–5 per cent of their election budgets for social media (Patel 2014). Hence, the elections marked India's late arrival at the spectacle of 'mediated elections' familiar to observers of American-style mediated democracy. 'The Indian elections took place in the glare of close to 800 television channels (of which 300 are twenty four-hour news channels) and 94,000 plus newspapers across twenty languages alongside one of the fastest growing advertising industries in the world' (Chakravartty and Roy 2015: 312).

The 2014 general elections witnessed an unprecedented engagement with mobile apps, with a range of different kinds of mobile apps available across a number of apps stores and handset types that directly related to the different aspects of the elections. Google Play Store or the Windows phone apps section list more than 200 apps specifically developed for the general elections in 2014. Most of the major news channels and newspapers published stories that discussed the most popular or must-have 'apps across platforms that are working towards empowering the voter' (Swamy 2014). While almost all the major mobile networks in India provided SMS- or MMS-based election news alerts to their subscribers, which are available on basic mobile phones as well, the use of mobile apps in the distribution and consumption of election-related news, information, and entertainment was truly unprecedented.

During the months of the elections (April–May 2014), the Google app store listed more than 167 mobile apps directly related to the general election. Moreover, a keyword search with 'Indian News' within the app store listed 240 apps. These apps are developed and distributed by emerging apps entrepreneurs, political parties, news media organizations, and of course the Election Commission of India. However, a closer look at these apps would illustrate that although each one of the apps is not specifically related to news reports per se, or standard journalistic writings on the general elections, the majority of the apps included 'news' and information regarding the elections in some from or the other. It needs to be mentioned that a number of mobile apps on election news were either removed from the app stores or renamed to keep them relevant even after the elections were over. To make sense of the emerging news app ecosystem in India, in reference to the general election, it can be useful to categorize these apps broadly into five different categories: first, the official 'news media apps'; second, 'news aggregator apps'; third, 'independent news apps'; fourth, 'social media news apps'; and fifth, mobile journalism or 'MoJo apps'.

To engage their audience, the majority of leading news media organizations in India launched their own mobile apps. Times Now, one of the leading English news channels, collaborated with Nokia to develop the General Elections 2014 app that provides real-time information through video, image, and text feeds on the general elections. The app integrates video and text and allows users to watch streaming videos of the special election programming as well as a live feed of events as they happen. Linking with leading social media sites, the app also offers options to share feeds and to chat with each other while the show is on air. On the other hand, BBC News India, motivated by the popularity of WhatsApp in the 2013 coverage of Typhoon Haiyan in the Philippines and the coverage of pre-election campaigning in India, made use of WhatsApp and WeChat to circulate BBC content in both Hindi and English in addition to sourcing substantial user-generated content. ABP News, in a similar manner, under its flagship election programme *Kaun Banega Pradhanmantri* (Who's Going to Be the Prime Minister), introduced the KBPM app to connect with viewers on mobile platforms. The KBPM app displays sections like latest news, videos, polls, live TV, and includes interactive features, particularly targeted towards a young audience. It also offers continuous real-time update of news content, and users may also customize the content according to their preferences. Some of the leading magazine publishers, like *Outlook Magazine* and *India Today*, developed election news apps in different languages, offering long-form feature stories, columns, and opinion pieces; however, these apps offered limited interactive features apart from the usual integration with social media sites. Similarly, the *Hindu, Indian Express, Hindustan Times, Zee News, IBN Live, Times of India*, and other news media organizations including regional channels also introduced their own mobile apps providing a range of information and options for personalization.

It is necessary to underline the increasing presence of news aggregators during the general elections. A number of mobile apps function as tools for news provisioning by content aggregators, such as Flipboard, Indian Newspaper app, News Hunt, India Online Newspaper app, among many others. These apps allow users to personalize their news consumption, and during the elections most of them provided elaborate categories of news related to the elections. These news aggregator apps access either the mobile site or the basic website of the official news media and then categorize and filter content according to the user's preferences. Therefore, the audience of news media is extended through mobile platforms beyond the native apps of particular news media houses.

Independent apps developers or small-scale digital entrepreneurs launched another segment of apps that offered news and information related to the elections. While these apps do not exclusively offer news content, in most of these apps the user is provided with news articles, statistics, profiles, and quotations in a highly customizable and interactive method on their smartphones. India Elections, iCitizen-India Elections, and India Elections 2014 are some of the mobile applications that provide information mostly free of cost about the profiles of candidates, political meetings, controversies, often through links to news reports published by legacy news media. For instance, most of these apps feature 'in the news' or 'trending' sections relating to a particular party, a political leader, or an event, and the content of these sections is often sourced from the constantly updated news feeds of leading Indian news websites. A number of independent news apps like Election News, Breaking News, and Election Samachar operate similar to news aggregator apps. The main difference is that while the news aggregator apps aggregate news in widely diverse categories and are usually not centred on a single topic, independent news apps only assembled news related to the 2014 general elections from different sources and presented it in a personalized manner.

This brief outline of new apps related to the general elections would remain incomplete without mentioning the social media apps which also played an important role in the dissemination of news related to the elections. While these apps are not directly related to news media, a considerable percentage of their content on the elections is actually crowdsourced from videos, articles, and photographs that individuals share on their social media accounts, which in turn are often produced by both mainstream or alternative news and information websites. India's largest software services firm, Tata Consultancy Services, worked together with Twitter to develop the iElect app that aggregates content from Twitter and presents it in the form of visually engaging infographics, so that users may get a comprehensive idea about the social media conversations revolving around the general elections. Similarly, Facebook India launched a 'tracker' to engage users interested in the general elections, offering links to the latest news and feature articles. The India Election Tracker offered a new dashboard that tracked mentions of candidates and parties throughout the election period. Google Elections Hub, developed by Google, was also created for news, information, and updates about the elections. The site also included features such as election-related news videos and search trends. Interestingly, Google also provided audio access to people to listen in on Hangouts over the phone so that the majority of the population, which still did not have access to computers, could also participate in this process. As mentioned earlier, in all these cases, a large segment of the content is in fact sourced from mainstream or alternative news and information websites that individuals share as links on their social media accounts.

A number mobile apps also offered citizens the technological tools and connections to report corrupt practices during election by using their smartphones to capture photographs and videos of such incidents. Promoted by the advocacy group for good electoral practices, Association of Democratic Reforms, the Election Watch Reporter app gained wide media coverage for enabling common people in their struggle against corrupt political practices, using mobile technology. While there are a few experimental and isolated instances of citizen journalism through mobile phones in India, citizen reporting practices through mobile phones or mobile apps in particular are yet to be implemented in India, as there are hardly any such apps that specifically facilitate these efforts (Ghosh 2014).

Thus, unlike the legacy news media, the portable, ubiquitous mobile applications, such as news apps, allow individuals to interact with one another, share videos, images, or other kinds of feed and participate in discussions, and create conversations on election-related issues. Within these emerging conditions, it is important to question in what way the rise of the mobile apps is shaping the traditional means of news access in India, and whether new forms of participation and sources of accountability may emerge through mobile apps.

SOCIETIES OF CONTROL AND THE 'NEW' FREEDOM

Mobile phones and the internet have been studied by scholars primarily to theorize the notions of ubiquity, innovation, and openness and to understand how, as digital networked technology, they have contributed to the formation of decentralized, user-driven techno-culture (Brynjolfsson and Saunders 2010; Pascal et al. 2010; Stoneman 2010; Lemstra et al. 2011). In contrast to the internet, mobile phones emerged from more conventional structures and conditions of innovation organized through large multinational corporations. However, it can be useful to turn to the idea of 'arenas of innovation' to make sense of the proliferation of mobile apps, which are also critically dependent on a set of 'enabling' or 'soft infrastructures' for participation. Thus, simply offering a broadband network is not adequate; rather, what is required is the 'soft infrastructure' that includes mechanisms for authentication, micro-payments, and digital rights management that facilitate the development of a broadband economy (Sawhney 2009: 113). This is an issue that points to a very critical inadequacy in the capacity of transformative cultures of mobile ubiquity within which mobile apps may develop. Moreover, to identify the ways news apps function as the new circuits of cultures, it is necessary to distinguish their difference from the hegemonic internet culture. Often the issues of ubiquity and openness are discussed in comparison to the apparently unparalleled potentials and socio-cultural influences connected with dominant internet cultures. Hence, the assumption that the mobile is considered derivative of the internet calls for a more critical consideration. The difference between 'app ecology' and 'mod ecology' is important to emphasize, as the possibility for a thriving app culture seems more significant through the mod ecology and much less through the app ecology, which is considered a shallow form of creative making (Powell 2011).[4] It is also necessary to examine the conceptual issues upon which the apps culture flourishes: what kinds of power relations exist, and what kind of freedom is allowed.

While these news apps give a sense of ever-expanding possibilities and opportunities, their specific location within the global economy reminds us of Gilles Deleuze's notion of societies of control. Deleuze reminds us that disciplinary societies emerged after the 'sovereign' societies, and that they focused on the organization of life and production rather than the exercise of arbitrary entitlements in relation to these two domains. Disciplinary societies produced sites and institutions within which individuals were located, trained, or punished at various times in their life, like prisons, hospitals, schools, or the family. Through this process, the category of the 'population' emerged as a quantifiable, measurable object, which is open to various kinds of manipulation. In other words, the disciplinary system is one of contiguity, since the individual is transferred from one site to another, beginning again each time. On the contrary, societies of control—which emerged particularly after the Second World War— are continuous in form and mark the present conditions of life. The different forms of control comprise a network of 'inseparable variations'. The individual, in a disciplinary society, is placed in various 'molds, distinct castings' at different times, whereas the individual in a contemporary control society is in a constant state of modulation 'like a self-deforming cast that will continuously change from one moment to the other, or like a sieve whose mesh will transmute from point to point' (Deleuze 1992: 5).

It is important to note that in control societies, the dominant model is that of the 'market', in which it is more frequently the task of the individual to engage in forms of competition and numeration in order to attain a certain level of profit. 'We no longer find ourselves dealing with the mass/individual pair. Individuals have become "dividuals", and masses, samples, data, markets, or "banks"' (Deleuze 1992: 6). In contrast to disciplinary individuals, who produced quantifiable and discrete amounts of energy, 'dividuals' are engaged in a process of constant modulation. In the case of news apps, which seem to be moving towards a system of a high degree of personalization and customization with advanced news-filtering processes and geo-tagging, this means that the figure of the individual is replaced by a dividual segment of coded matter to be controlled. This technological evolution must be, even more profoundly, 'a mutation of capitalism' as this is no longer 'a capitalism for production but for the product, which is to say, for being sold or marketed' (Deleuze 1992: 6).

In this age of ubiquitous computing, globally networked mobile devices can track every move, in which every touch, every comment, every interaction, even expressions of emotions can be tracked, and not only tracked but modified moment to moment through modulated control mechanisms which in turn constitute the market. Thus, the society of control offers a 'new freedom', and while freedom seems to be increased, the control of our activities widens. Rather than a panopticon, one is situated within a diffuse matrix of information-gathering algorithms. It is redundant to say that these mobile apps often covertly monitor online activities and share this information with third-party businesses, which then channel particular advertisements to the mobile or modify the content of certain web pages; they can also post on behalf of the owner on a number of social media sites, thus complicating the notions of freedom and empowerment.

What distinguishes internet-enabled computers from mobile apps, particularly in developing countries, is that mobile is perceived to be a social technology in contrast to the computer or laptop, which produces a lesser degree of social association. In addition, mobile news apps assign the apparently boundless interactions and sharing a fixity, since it is necessary to download and install each app in the mobile device itself. This process, first, makes it easier to monitor and codify, and second, it becomes easier to target and deliver. This fixity posits the user within the ambivalence of the mass/individual binary. The user imagines each interaction within an otherwise shared, stable, and continuous world; a temporal flow from which they have abstracted their point of interactions. However, it is capitalism that necessitates the fixed territory, the unit of capital, and imagines all possible beings or deterritorializations as measured through capital. Even concepts become 'information' to be marketed (Colebrook 2002: 64).

Elections become an emblematic instance to understand the political economy of news apps, since during elections the discourse of the 'informed voter' and 'empowered citizen' gains prominence. This is the period when active participation promises to have a substantial impact, especially in a vast democratic country with a large electoral population like India. The news apps related to the Indian general elections become a part of this larger discourse that constitutes the hegemonic identity of the voter who has to 'perform', and apps provide a sense of empowerment to the individual citizen through technologically facilitated control and agency. Furthermore, as mentioned earlier, in control societies the dominant model is that of the 'market', and naturally the process of election itself is heavily imbued with marketing strategies and motivations, where news apps play a significant role. As election campaigns become exceedingly similar to product promotion and brand management, mobile news apps offer new ways of 'modulation'.

MODALITIES OF TECHNO-CULTURE

Within this context, it is important to study the reciprocal relation between the use of news apps and social contexts, leading to transformations in a variety of forms of engagement with technology, especially the shifting everyday practices of news distribution and consumption as more digital technologies are made accessible and affordable. Such a viewpoint illustrates the interpretive flexibility of technology in various ways: that the meanings and uses of a technology or system are not fixed by the form alone, but come to be identified in distinctive ways by different users. To make sense of the individual's encounter with the mobile apps, this chapter draws from critical theories of identity and subjectivity to come up with three different modalities in which mobile apps function as techno-cultural objects: as sites of control, as forms of agency, and as systems of knowledge, and explores how news apps have been distinctly appropriated by a range of social and electoral circumstances.

Sites of Control

Sites of control can be defined, first, by the promise of instantaneous interaction and by a sense of temporality where the present continuously endures; and second, the capacity of customization and personalization that produces an assemblage that is ideally productive. Naturally there is a mutually constitutive relation between the two.

Extending the Deleuzian framework, it can be suggested that instead of placing emphasis on the expropriation and appropriation of an outside through an exercise of control, we may focus on the process of convergence and assemblage between heterogeneous elements. Hence, there is a sense of dual control: first, understood as the control over time and space, as manifested by rapidly updated information, statistics, and data into a historical succession, represented through such apps like Vote-India 2014, Election Info India, Indian Poll Results 2014, Indian Elections 2014, Vote-Box, and iCitizen-India to mention a few; second, defined as an articulation of control in terms of productive assemblage through customization that engenders new ways of expression, a new spatial arrangement, a new performative practice. News apps that provide election statistics, reports on candidate profiles and quotations, and election results in a highly customizable and interactive form on the user's smartphone embody such attributes. Therefore, mobile news apps may point in two directions; first, they offer a kind of order or consistency vis-à-vis an excess of information and data which assumes a significant complexity, but they also enable—from that order—the production of supplementary and more complex networks.

Forms of Agency

Agency is defined by the capacity of interaction and participation in the production of an event that is also the site of the participant's own becoming. While considering agency, it is also important to take into consideration the news apps' coded abilities to manage users. Agency comprises a number of different uses and agents, and has a deep association with cultural specificity. While there is a rising demand for greater autonomy in content production, consumers are anxious about algorithms tracking their behaviour and reshaping their profile. Hence, in terms of agency engendered by interaction and participation, the triad of apps developers, advertisers, and consumers has turned out to be ever more important in present conditions. Mobile apps about the Indian elections, developed in collaboration with social media sites, such as the iElect app that aggregates content from Twitter, the India Election Tracker from Facebook, and Google Elections Hub are ideal examples. This structuring of mobile apps reminds us of the notion of the actor network, where objects constitute multiple proscriptions, affordances, and allowances, and that concerns itself with what a device allows or forbids in relation to the actor (Latour 2005). Often these news apps act as non-human moral agents; they embody a local cultural condition and a sense of ordinariness that shape the interrelation between the agent and the technology. Apps like Election Watch Reporter that utilize the built-in recording features of the smartphone to help citizens report violations of election regulations exemplify such a modality.

Systems of Knowledge

Systems of knowledge are constituted by a decentralized, to a certain extent open, networked, and participatory structure of managing information. Further, it is possible to identify the origin of this mediated participatory practice in the idea of the information society. However, as Headrick (2000) explains, what is commonly known today as the 'information age' is merely the beginning of another period in a long history of information ages. The present information age began as early as the eighteenth century with the philosophical shift towards empiricism. Significant transformations, in both the public and the governmental appetite for information along with technological development, resurface throughout history. Hence, Headrick suggests, instead of engaging with the study of information, it would be reasonable to focus on a more convenient concept, the study of information systems. By systems are meant the methods and techniques by which individuals organize and manage information, rather than the content of the information itself. In other words, the production of knowledge and social reality become collaborative effects achieved with other non-human partners, in such a way that humans are not the only actors in that production. 'Information systems were created to supplement the mental functions of thought, memory, and speech. They are, if you will, the technologies of knowledge' (Headrick 2000: 5). Mobile apps, particularly mobile news media apps, function as technologies of knowledge and in turn invest in the technologies of the self, in other words, the specific practices by which subjects constitute themselves within and through systems of power. However, I must hasten to add that the modalities of control, agency, and knowledge are typically juxta-posed and interspersed and, hence, difficult to identify separately in the mobile apps culture.

* * *

This exploration of mobiles app in the context of the 2014 Indian general elections has shown that the ways in which the news apps connect to new streams of content have produced new experiences and also new patterns of engagement and imagination. As mobile news apps increasingly become pivotal in our daily experiences, we need to significantly reshape our understanding of how the mobile apps culture represents an event-oriented and transformative form of relationality and interaction. New media ecologies, even in developing countries like India, have produced new opportunities in the distribution of and access to news within a rising culture of mobility. Such potentialities have been the result of interrelated fac-tors, including the availability of cheap mobile devices, significant reduction in mobile internet data charges, and the rising demand for mobile-ready regional content backed by emerging app entrepre-neurs in India, making India one of the top-ranking countries across app stores. However, the political economy of news apps has received scant academic attention, and there has been a lack of scholarly work, mainly perhaps because of the historically specific domain of tele-communications technology and media policy from which mobiles developed. Nonetheless, new forms of collaboration, significantly distinct from the older organizations of networks, are being devel-oped at the intersections of mobile hardware, software codes, and the internet, with important social implications.

This chapter has attempted to put forward a broad view of the complex ways in which relationships of control are implemented through the use of mobile news apps in a range of electoral cir-cumstances, which may act as an incentive for further studies and research on the increasingly complex news culture in India. I have argued that the emergence of mobile news apps provokes us to map a substantially new realm of emerging practices and evolving para-digms of news dissemination and news consumption, indicating not only new centres of agency, interactions, and desires, but also the consolidation of a system for societies of control. Identifying three different modalities in which news apps function as techno-cultural objects—as sites of control, as forms of agency, and as systems of knowledge—this study has sought to widen the existing interdisciplinary frameworks and concepts so that more exhaustive future research on mobile news apps culture, particularly in developing countries, can help lead to the development of a practical, unifying theoretical matrix that might broaden our understanding of the attributes of this new techno-cultural practice and offer fresh perspectives on wider journalistic practices.

NOTES

1. A number of significant studies on mobile phone use in India have explored different aspects of mobile phone culture, including: how it supports alternative political patterns and rejuvenates networks of kinship and village sociality; the sending and receiving of 'missed calls' as a way of economical communication; the gendered aspect of mobile phone use has also been explored referring to issues of access and ownership of mobile phones and their relation with increased mobility (Donner 2008; Tenhunen 2008; Zainudeen et al. 2010; Tacchi and Chandola 2015). Thus, the mobile phone has been theorized from various approaches but a particular focus on mobile applications or apps has so far been considerably limited.

2. Smartphones include devices with or without touchscreen, but obviously with an advanced operating system. Multimedia phones may or may not include touchscreens and/or QWERTY keypads, but they do not run on an advanced operating system. Basic feature phones do not have touchscreens, QWERTY keypads, or advanced operating systems.

3. The Lok Sabha or House of the People is the lower house of the Parliament of India. The Parliament comprises two houses: the Lok Sabha and the Rajya Sabha or Council of States. Representatives of the people from 543 constituencies, chosen by direct elections (the Indian general elections) constitute the Lok Sabha.

4. 'Mod ecology' is marked by individuals taking apart, replacing, or putting back together mobile hardware or software, which is increasingly becoming a crucial part of engaging with technology. The 'mod ecology', as Powell notes, can be an immersive, creative, and collaborative endeavour—but needs high technical knowledge, social capital, financial

capital, time, and interest (like most other forms of open-source innovation). In contrast, the 'app ecology' offers a shallow form of engagement because building an app does not necessarily contribute to the stock of knowledge held in common.

REFERENCES

BBC (2012). 'India Census: Half of Homes Have Phones but No Toilets'. BBC Asia, 14 March. Retrieved from http://www.bbc.com/news/world-asia-india-17362837 (accessed on 17 August 2018).

Brynjolfsson, E. and A. Saunders (2010). *Wired for Innovation: How Information Technology Is Reshaping the Economy*. Cambridge, MA: MIT Press.

Chakraborty, S. (2006). 'Mobile Phone Usage Patterns amongst University Students: A Comparative Study between India and USA'. MS thesis, University of North Carolina.

Chakravartty, P. and S. Roy (2015). 'Mr. Modi Goes to Delhi: Mediated Populism and the 2014 Indian Elections'. *Television and New Media*, 16(4): 311–22.

Chowdary, T. H. (2004). 'Telecom Reforms: A Decade On'. *Economic and Political Weekly*, 39(21): 2085–7.

Colebrook, C. (2002). *Gilles Deleuze*. New York: Routledge.

Deleuze, G. (1992). *Postscript on the Societies of Control*. Cambridge, MA: MIT Press.

Donner, J. (2008). 'Research Approaches to Mobile Use in the Developing World: A Review of the Literature'. *Information Society*, 24(3): 140–59.

Doron, A. and R. Jeffrey (2013). *The Great Indian Phone Book: How the Cheap Cell Phone Changes Business, Politics, and Daily Life*. Cambridge, MA: Harvard University Press.

Ghosh, A. (2014). 'CGNet Swara: Shifting the Power of Journalism to the Mobile Phone for Adivasis'. *LiveMint*, 20 March. Retrieved from http://www.livemint.com/Consumer/Bj8phV6COEqlGMp3HhIuuL/CGNet-Swara-Shifting-the-power-of-journalism-to-the-mobile.html (accessed on 17 August 2018).

Headrick, D. R. (2000). *When Information Came of Age: Technologies of Knowledge in the Age of Reason and Revolution, 1700–1850*. New York: Oxford University Press.

Hooker, B. and F. Raby (2000). *Project #26765 FLIRT: Flexible Information and Recreation for Mobile Users*. London: Art Books International.

Kumar, K. and A. Thomas (2006). 'Telecommunications and Development: The Cellular Mobile "Revolution" in India and China'. *Journal of Creative Communications*, 1(3): 297–309.

Latour, B. (2005). *Reassembling the Social: An Introduction to Actor-Network-Theory.* Oxford: Oxford University Press.

Lemstra, W., V. Hayes, and J. Groenewegen (eds) (2011). *The Innovation Journey of Wi-Fi: The Road to Global Success.* Cambridge: Cambridge University Press.

Mukherjee, W. (2017). 'India's Smartphone User Base Topped 300 Million in 2016'. *Economic Times,* 24 January. Retrieved from http://economictimes.indiatimes.com/tech/hardware/indias-smartphone-user-base-topped-300-million-in-2016/articleshow/56759056.cms (accessed on 17 August 2018).

Nielsen (2013). 'The Mobile Consumer: A Global Snapshot'. Retrieved from http://www.nielsen.com/content/dam/corporate/us/en/reports-down-loads/2013%20Reports/Mobile-Consumer-Report-2013.pdf (accessed on 17 August 2018).

Pascal, L. M., B. Weil, and A. Hatchuel (2010). *Strategic Management of Innovation and Design.* New York: Cambridge University Press.

Patel, A. (2014). 'India's Social Media Election Battle'. *BBC,* 31 March. Retrieved from http://www.bbc.com/news/world-asia-india-26762391 (accessed on 17 August 2018).

Poushter, J. (2016). 'Smartphone Ownership and Internet Usage Continues to Climb in Emerging Economies'. Pew Research Center. Retrieved from http://www.pewglobal.org/2016/02/22/smartphone-ownership-and-internet-usage-continues-to-climb-in-emerging-economies/ (accessed on 21 December 2016).

Powell, A. (2011). 'The "Mod" Ecology and the "App" Ecology'. Retrieved from http://www.alisonpowell.ca/?p=434 (accessed 11 September 2018).

Rai, A. (2012). 'On the Jugaad Image: Embodying the Mobile Phone in India'. *Postmodern Culture,* 23(1). Retrieved from https://muse.jhu.edu/article/513307 (accessed on 11 September 2018).

Sawhney, H. (2009). 'Innovations at the Edge: The Impact of Mobile Technologies on the Character of the Internet'. In *Mobile Technologies: From Telecommunications to Media,* eds G. Goggin and L. Hjorth, pp. 105–17. New York: Routledge.

Singh, P. and S. Pant (2014). 'Unstoppable! Smartphone Surge in India Continues'. Nielsen Informate Mobile Insights. Retrieved from http://www.nielsen.com/in/en/insights/reports/2014/unstoppable--smartphone-surge-in-india-continues.html (accessed on 17 August 2018).

Sreekumar, T. (2015). Review of *The Great Indian Phone Book: How the Cheap Cell Phone Changes Business, Politics, and Daily Life* by Robin Jeffrey and Assa Doron. *Mobile Media and Communication,* 3: 287–9.

Steenson, M. and J. Donner (2009). 'Beyond the Personal and Private: Modes of Mobile Phone Sharing in Urban India'. In *The Reconstruction of Space and Time: Mobile Communication Practices*, eds R. Ling and S. Campbell, pp. 231–50. Piscataway, NJ: Transaction.

Stoneman, P. (2010). *Soft Innovation: Economics, Product Aesthetics, and the Creative Industries*. Oxford: Oxford University Press.

Swamy, R. (2014). 'Eight Apps to Stay on Top of Lok Sabha Elections 2014'. *NDTV Gadgets*, 9 April. Retrieved from http://gadgets.ndtv.com/apps/features/eight-apps-to-stay-on-top-of-lok-sabha-elections-2014-506324 (accessed on 17 August 2018).

Tacchi, J. and T. Chandola (2015). 'Complicating Connectivity: Gendered Mobilities in an Urban Slum'. In *Routledge Handbook of New Media in Asia*, eds L. Hjorth and O. Khoo, pp. 179–88. Abingdon: Routledge.

Tenhunen, S. (2008). 'Mobile Technology in the Village: ICTs, Culture, and Social Logistics in India'. *Journal of the Royal Anthropological Institute*, 14(3): 515–34.

TRAI (Telecom Regulatory Authority of India) (2017). Highlights of Telecom Subscription Data as on 31st December 2016. Retrieved from http://www.trai.gov.in/sites/default/files/Press_Release_11_17_Feb_2017_Eng_0.pdf (accessed on 17 August 2018).

Zainudeen, A., T. Iqbal, and R. Samarajiva (2010). 'Who's Got the Phone? Gender and the Use of the Telephone at the Bottom of the Pyramid'. *New Media and Society*, 12(4): 549–66.

PART THREE

Marginalization and Journalism

CHAPTER ELEVEN

Gender and Journalism

Selection and Framing of Rape News in Indian Media

DHIMAN CHATTOPADHYAYA

. . . .

'Is there nothing brother, not even a small little rape?' I remember the words from that late-night conversation ever so clearly. This story is a little old, though—over two decades old. The year was 1996. I was a trainee journalist for a national newspaper's Kolkata edition, being mentored by a senior colleague on the many responsibilities of a night-shift reporter. We'd finished our work that night—mostly keying in copies faxed by regional correspondents and helping sub-editors double-check headlines—when we received an SOS from the news desk: a front page news brief (news items that are short, typically 100 words or less) had fallen through and there was a hole to be filled. My senior was overjoyed. This was (he said) a golden opportunity for me to learn the main job of a night reporter, calling up the fire and police departments every hour to check for any late-night fires, accidents, or crimes. We called the fire department first. There were no fires to report. The city police too had nothing to share. In desperation, my 'mentor' decided to torment the officer on duty at the suburban police headquarters. The officer on duty must have mumbled something, since I could not hear his reply properly (I was on a parallel line, listening to the conversation so that I could take notes), but I remember my colleague's question very well: 'Is there nothing brother, not even a small little rape?'

I said nothing. Maybe I was too shocked. After all, I was fresh out of university, and still not used to being a thick-skinned journalist. I remember feeling rather disturbed at rape being referred to as 'small little'. As I gathered experience over the next few years, heading news bureaus and editing newspapers and websites for different organizations across India, I did become thick(er)-skinned, but that night's memory returned like a bad penny every time I edited a copy on gender-related crimes—whether they dealt with domestic violence, workplace harassment, or the growing number of rape and molestation stories that seemed to pile up on my editing table every evening. In different newsrooms where I worked, crime reporters would routinely file rape stories. The rising number of such reports concerned me. But as a journalist what bothered me equally was the criterion we would use sometimes to select or reject news, and the factors that seemed to influence our decisions to select and frame the rape news stories to our readers. Often, only the most sensational items were considered newsworthy enough to make it to the front page (who were the people involved, where did it occur, how did it happen, was anyone famous involved, rich or poor, and so on), while others were relegated to inside pages, crime briefs, or left out entirely because there was no space for a story about the molestation of a slum dweller or college students crying harassment on a day when too many rapes and assaults had happened in urban sprawls. Perhaps, I told myself, I was overreacting. Common consensus seemed to suggest that journalists in India were doing exemplary work when it came to reporting sexual assaults and rapes, often acting as champions of social justice (Nargunde 2013), helping survivors record police cases and even making the judiciary sit up and take notice.

Journalism in India is indeed coming of age. The growth pangs are proof of that. Being sensitive to the sufferings of fellow humans and being known for conscientious reporting are among the surest signs of maturity. The volume of rape reportage is a welcome development. Volume alone, however, is not a measure of progress. How much has really changed in newsrooms since that night in 1996, about how gender-related issues, especially how news about sexual assaults and rapes, are reported and presented? More is being done in newsrooms across India to ensure that gender-related issues, from coverage of female athletes and LGBTQ rights to news of domestic violence, sexual harassments, and rapes, find a place in newspapers, TV news shows, and on news websites. But is the language of rape news coverage living up to these noble intentions? Are the processes by which news items are selected being affected by tectonic changes in news sharing and consumption habits?

In an interview to the Poynter website in 2013, journalist Sameera Khan, co-author of the book *Why Loiter? Women and Risk on Mumbai Streets* (Phadke et al. 2011), argued that while rape coverage in India had increased in recent years, the coverage was still mostly uneven (Tenore 2013). 'It is often class-biased (that is if the rape survivor is middle-class it gets more media play than if she is working class or tribal, rural, etc.); intrusive and violative of the privacy of the survivor; and often takes on a moral stance ("what was she doing there so late?" or "what was she wearing?")', Khan said in her interview to Poynter, adding that 'usually police make moral judgements and the media simply echo what they say without questioning them' (Tenore 2013: 1).

Similar themes emerged in an online content analysis of Indian newspapers and news sites in 2015—a study that examined the framing of rape news in Indian media. While examining one such incident of rape, where a woman was raped by a man in Delhi, I analysed 50 news reports in 15 English newspapers and websites on 27 February 2015—all of them being reports of the incident. Even though medical examination had confirmed rape, 46 of the reports referred to the incident as 'alleged rape' (for example, *Indian Express* 2015a; Zee News 2015). Almost an equal number thought it was important to mention the woman's/survivor's ethnicity and profession (for example, *Northeast Today* 2015; *Telegraph* 2015), and several news reports included a quote from a police officer on how women from this particular region of India were routinely coming to Delhi, working in beauty parlours, and being driven to prostitution (Chattopadhyaya 2015). The headlines or the opening sentences in the body copies sounded eerily similar (and no, they were not agency copies). If one headline screamed 'Woman from Northeast Allegedly Raped by Doctor in Delhi', another echoed 'Married Woman Alleges Rape', while still another mentioned in the copy: 'She is an army man's wife and her husband, is posted in Rajasthan, far away from where she had come.' A police officer was quoted in several news stories, such as the *Tribune*, saying: 'After a while, the woman allegedly agreed somehow and they indulged in a physical relationship, the investigating officer said.' Another publication, the *Telegraph*, wrote: 'He told us he had contacted a pimp who supplies girls.... He said after having sex, he had let the woman go.'

I realized, as I examined the news reports, that in describing a single incident where a man had raped a woman, many of the reports had not only framed the survivor as possibly dishonest by referring to her statements as claims and her complaints as allegations—but also framed an entire ethnic group as likely to enter prostitution (for example, this report that stated: 'Police are investigating whether they had brought other women from Northeast to Delhi and forced them into prostitution') and sullied the reputation of an entire profession! As I examined the framing of several other rape reports over a three-year period, I found the themes being, with unerring regularity: reports highlighting the ethnicity and professions of perpetrators and victims in reports, especially when they did not belong to the same linguistic group or city where the incident occurred (for example, *Times of India* 2015; *Mid-Day* 2017); mentioning the marital status of victims as a critical element in the report (for example, *India Today* 2014; NDTV 2016; *Hindu* 2011); and almost always using a doubt frame—referring to a survivor's statements as claims and complaints as allegations—even in instances when perpetrators had been arrested (for example, *Indian Express* 2015b), medical tests had confirmed rape (for example, *Hindustan Times* 2017), and in one instance, after perpetrators had confessed to the crime (ANI 2017). The last-mentioned news report, for instance, started with this sentence: 'the Gurugram police on Wednesday arrested the accused who has admitted to the crime,' but three sentences later mentioned: 'Sketches of the three

men who allegedly gang-raped the woman ...' (ANI 2015). The
Indian Express (2015b) report similarly mentioned:

> A sticker on the back of the mini bus that she was raped in and three
> digits of the vehicle's registration number that she remembered
> helped the Bengaluru police arrest the two men who allegedly sexu-
> ally assaulted a BPO employee in the city.... Police Commissioner
> N S Megharikh on Tuesday said the two are Suneel Omkarappa (23)
> and Yogesh Malleshappa (27), both drivers by profession. They have
> confessed to the crime.

Clearly, the facts that the culprits had been arrested and had confessed,
did not have any impact on the rape being referred to as an 'alleged'
incident. The words 'allege' and 'claim' both indicate that a statement
has been made without proof. The reports suggest that the arrests and
confessions are not proof enough.

I mention these examples—both anecdotal and empirical—not
to show Indian journalism in a poor light. Indeed, journalists in
other nations too are faced with similar uncomfortable questions of
how they frame rape news or any gender-related news, wittingly or
unwittingly. I use the stories to illustrate the difficult juncture, the
crossroads that India's journalists and newsrooms find themselves
in today, especially when selecting and framing gender-related news
such as rapes. The advent of social media as a source of breaking and
sharing news, and the growing perception in newsrooms that consumers will switch to competing websites, channels, or newspapers
unless breaking news does not reach them in real time, have made
matters more complex.

RAPE AS A GLOBAL ISSUE OF CONCERN

The role of India's media in selecting and reporting stories about crimes
such as rapes assumes critical significance today, given the growing
number of rape cases reported annually in India—34,771 rapes were
reported in 2015 alone (NCRB 2015: 161). A rape is reported every
21 minutes but even this number is just the tip of an iceberg by the
National Crime Records Bureau's (NCRB's) own admission, since
most incidents go unreported (Raj and McDougal 2014). In addition,

marital rape is not considered 'rape' under Indian laws, unless the couple is separated, nor are rapes of men or transgender individuals included in this list (Rath 2007; BBC.com 2013). The Government of India, its minister of state for home affairs to be precise, categorically stated in 2015 that since marriage in India is considered a sacred union, marital rape cannot be included under rape laws (Agnes 2015). Given this political and social background, the time has never been this crucial for the mainstream media in India to take a leadership role in creating mass awareness and influencing attitudes about rapes and rape culture in India.

The growing number of sexual attacks and rapes, of course, are not just a problem that India and the Indian media are faced with, but a problem in many developed economies as well. According to the 2012 US Bureau of Justice Statistics report, for instance, a person is raped every 90 seconds in the United States. The National Intimate Partner and Sexual Violence Survey in 2013 found that, on average, 20 people per minute are victims of physical violence by an intimate partner in the United States. Over the course of a year, that equals more than 10 million women and men. Those numbers only tell part of the story—nearly two million women are raped in a year and over seven million women and men are victims of stalking in a year (CDC 2014) in the United States.

The United States sees many more cases of rapes reported every year compared to India. But the situation in India could well be as grave, even though the reported numbers do not suggest so. The NCRB admits that less than 1 per cent of all rapes are reported. Several studies have shown that the police are not always keen to record rape cases. And I am being polite here. The political classes in India are notorious for their complete lack of empathy for women's rights (Ahmed 2016), safety, and gender equality (BBC.com 2012), often ending up defending rapists instead (Al Jazeera 2014; Neelakantan 2016). A few admittedly unscientific surveys of the general public in some Indian cities have also thrown up curious results. One *Wall Street Journal* survey of 100 men in Delhi, for instance, asked male respondents across Delhi to indicate the main reason rapes happened. While 33 of them said lack of respect for women was the main cause and 34 blamed gaps in law enforcement, 26 of them believed 'Western influence' was to blame for rapes, with several of them saying rapes would stop if women stopped wearing skimpy clothes (*WSJ* 2013).

The media has the potential to not only tell the audience what to think about, but also how to think about that issue (Scheufele 1999). If Indian journalists need to uphold their role as responsible members of a powerful fourth estate, and truly honour the journalist's creed (Williams 1914) that tells them to be unafraid, be indignant at injustice, and not to be swayed by either the privileged or the mob, then it is time they took stock and introspected on how they select and frame rape news. It is in this context that India's newsrooms must examine two time-honoured practices—how they frame news about rapes and gender-related crime stories, and how they select or gatekeep such stories.

FRAMING OF RAPE NEWS IN INDIAN MEDIA

Why is the framing of a news report critical to how a story is read, seen, or perceived by audiences? Just like how the frame of a photograph, or a certificate—its shape, size, positioning within a room—can all influence how that image is interpreted (Tewksbury and Scheufele 2009), the manner in which a news report, photograph, or a headline is framed can guide audiences to 'define problems, or make moral judgments' (Entman 1993: 52) based on the manner in which that information or image is worded, described, and contextualized (Matthes 2009). In other words, a frame is that combination of information provided in a specific manner or package in a way that can influence audiences and make them 'think about an issue in particular ways' (Tewksbury and Scheufele 2009: 19).

The meaning of a frame has definitive cultural roots in the sense that the wording of a message may refer to a notion that is understood in the local culture, and the presence of the specific frame influences consumers or audiences to read the information and interpret meanings from the information in a way that reflects existing local cultural beliefs (van Gorp 2007). As is often the case with journalism, especially with journalists working in a cultural milieu they are accustomed to for years, the familiarity of frames means that bias in information framing may go unnoticed by journalists and the public alike, and therefore influence audiences without them being fully aware of it.

In the United States, for instance, studies have found news organizations using biased frames to report rape cases (Carter 1998; Durham 2015), including a preference to select and present rape news in a manner that blames the victims, mostly women (Ardovini-Booker and Caringella-Macdonald 2002), cast aspersions on the character and credibility of women/victims (Cuklanz 1996), or show empathy for male perpetrators (Taylor 2009). Some recent studies (for example, Durham 2013; Rao 2014) have examined the framing of gender-related news such as rapes in Indian media and different forces that may or may not influence these frames. However, much more focus is needed (from both academics and journalists) to study how Indian journalists select and frame gender-related news such as rapes.

One reason for this relative lack of research on the selection and framing of rape news in India could be the historically limited coverage given to incidents of rape in India's news media (Dreze 2013) till recently (Drèze and Sen 2013). Even the more liberal English-language press had largely stayed away from covering rape incidents till the first decade of the twenty-first century, apparently because the subject was inappropriate for mass consumption (Bhattacharjee 2008). However, after the 2012 gang rape and murder of a woman in New Delhi 'shook the conscience of a nation' (*India Today* 2013), the volume of coverage of rape news in Indian media has significantly gone up (Raj and McDougal 2014; Rao 2014). The English news media, in particular, have been hailed for playing a leading role in heralding this change, consistently covering news about rapes and sexual assaults and giving rape news prominent space (Nargunde 2013).

Increased coverage, however, may not have led to increased focus on how these stories are reported or even what is reported (Rao and Wasserman 2015). Even the so-called liberal English media have been guilty of using blame frames to describe incidents of rape, indicating subtly in their reports that the victims or survivors are to blame for being raped (Bhattacharjee 2008), thus 'inflicting more suffering on the victim than on the perpetrator' (Bhattacharjee 2008: 23). The perception that laws in India are still unclear about sex without consent, often ignoring or condoning sexual violence against spouses, partners, family members, and even strangers (Belair-Gagnon et al. 2014), has only muddied the waters. The news media is not divorced from this social reality, and reinforces these dominant social perceptions through the framing of rape news in a manner that perpetuates rape myths and stereotypes (Drache and Velagic 2014). Some recurring frames include rape as just another form of sex, women as provocateurs whose attitude and behaviour force men to commit rape (Fadnis 2017), and women as vindictive liars seeking revenge (Sen 2013). Some other reports also frame victims and perpetrators according to perceived social norms and beliefs (Bedi and Bedi 2017). So, while media reports may not directly comment on the truth of the victims' statements, mistrust is subtly indicated when stories are selected or presented by introducing words and phrases such as *alleged* and *claimed*, or mentioning a victim's profession (for example, she worked night shifts in a call centre), age, marital status (for example, a married woman was in a pub when she was raped), habits, or attire (for example, they were dressed to provoke, they were drunk, or they lured the perpetrators).

Once again, Indian media are not unique in the way they frame rape news. In Sweden, a nation with one of the world's highest incidents of rapes (Matharu 2016), the mainstream media have been found to employ concepts of 'foreign culture and jet-set drinking culture' (Bernhardsson and Bogren 2012: 3) to describe incidents of rapes, reproducing stereotypical discourses on gender, sexuality, and ethnicity/nationality. Similar frames of women who drink or frequent pubs as provoking rape, or being responsible for their own plight, can be seen in several instances of rape reportage in the United States (for example, Abrahamson 2006; Finch and Munro 2007), and in the United Kingdom (for example, Day et al. 2004; Lyons et al. 2006).

It is probably easy to put the blame entirely on how headlines are given for such news items and how the copies are written and rewritten to provide that frame. However, it may be wiser to step back and address the problem at the earlier step—news selection. How do journalists select rape and other gender-related crime stories? What factors influence these selection or gatekeeping decisions? Identifying possible issues in the selection process may help us better understand the problem areas so that journalists can address the problems and find solutions—for identifying problems without identifying or discussing possible solutions serves no good purpose. This brings us to the domain of the journalist as a gatekeeper, and the demands of speed-driven, online-first news on journalistic norms and practices.

GATEKEEPING CRIME NEWS IN AN ONLINE-FIRST ERA

Who is a gatekeeper? The answer to this question is becoming more and more ambiguous today. Editors, news editors, bureau chiefs, producers, news directors, online editors, content managers, and others who occupy strategic decision-making positions within news media organizations are all gatekeepers (Schwalbe et al. 2015) who decide at various stages which news item is to be selected and how it is to be presented to the public. Even the reporter on the ground is a gatekeeper for it is s/he who takes that first decision: which parts of a quote to mention in his/her report and which aspects of the story to leave out. Journalists at all levels then, work together to select, shape, and present news content in a systematic process, 'by which billions of messages that are available in the world get cut down and transformed into the hundreds of messages that reach a given person on a given day' (Shoemaker and Reese 1995).

Every time a news breaks, editorial selections and prioritizations are made at different levels, from the junior reporter who uses individual judgement (Shoemaker and Reese 2013) to decide whether a story is important and relevant, the bureau chief who runs fact checks and considers the story's timeliness and newsworthiness, to the pages editor who perhaps considers if the news item is consistent with organizational dictates, to the editor who may finally consider how the news may impact both advertisers and interest groups as well as potential consumers. Taken together these factors are referred to as the *Hierarchy of Influences* (Shoemaker & Reese 2013). In classical newsrooms in newspapers and television channels, these five *hierarchies of influences* (Shoemaker and Reese 1995) or factors are important to every gatekeeping decision—making gatekeeping one of the most complex processes in mainstream news organizations.

Nowhere has the effect of social media been felt more than in the crime news genre, especially in the reportage of gender-related news such as rapes—genres where journalistic codes, especially ethical codes for writing news reports, are almost absent for Indian journalists (Rao 2014). The speed-driven nature of new media technology has significantly changed the way news organizations conceptualize the gatekeeping role (Lee 2015), with most organizations paying more attention to speed than ever before (Thurman and Walters 2013). For example, almost every major news channel or newspaper in India, or any other democracy, now updates its websites every few minutes and round the clock, while simultaneously disseminating breaking news alerts through its official Twitter or Facebook accounts (Ju et al. 2014). An increasing number of news organizations acknowledge that they favour speed-driven journalism because they believe faster updates translate into more eyeballs, which equate to more profit (Lee 2015).

The quest for speed does not always work as a boon. While the advent of social media and online updates of websites has meant that journalists can now share every development in a story, such as an incident of sexual attack (Hermida 2012), a political election, or a tennis match, the craze for instant updates can seriously undermine journalistic credibility. For example, with the drive to constantly publish and to keep news current, speed-driven journalism discourages investigative or in-depth journalism, which takes more time to produce, but is critical to keep powerful institutions and individuals in check (Silverman 2007). Also, the retroactive correction (upload first and correct later) mentality often leads to a higher number of errors, contributing to misinformation (Lee 2015) and potentially eroding audiences' trust in the press (Maier 2005).

These new challenges mean that journalists across democracies need to reflect afresh on the twin issues of authenticity and accountability of news selection (Singer 2008) in an environment dominated by speed and multiple gates. This is particularly relevant in socially sensitive topics such as sexual assaults and rapes. For instance, do journalists have enough time to authenticate information about an alleged rape that has been tweeted or posted on social media, before such news is uploaded to their news organization's official website? What gatekeeping norms are exercised when selecting news from social media to run on the next news show, or upload on the web?

When it comes to political news, most news organizations have political leanings (Scherr and Baugut 2015) or have well-defined norms and conventions on what to report and how to report an event. A Republican-leaning American news channel such as Fox News, for instance, is highly unlikely to telecast a show in support of Hillary Clinton. A left-leaning TV channel in India, such as NDTV or a magazine such as *Frontline*, is likely to be more critical of a decision taken by the BJP-led Narendra Modi government than the right-leaning Republic TV. However, when it comes to the crime genre, rape reportage in particular, very few organizational gate-keeping norms are in place apart from standard ethical practices of not naming a victim.

When a story of a sexual crime breaks, the mainstream journalist may receive the news from a personal source (such as a friend who works in the victim's office), an official source (such as the police), or via social media. According to the hierarchy of influences model (Shoemaker and Reese 2013), journalists keep individual, routine, organizational, social institutional, and social structural factors in mind when selecting certain news items over others and deciding how to present those news items to audiences.

When the news of a rape breaks, therefore, particularly if it is a sensational case (for example, the New Delhi gang rape of a woman in 2012 or the gang rape of a journalist in the heart of Mumbai in 2013), a news organization has only a few minutes to upload the breaking rape story, complete with relevant links, visuals, accounts, or statements before competitors do so. The person sitting behind the online desk may be a junior reporter or sub-editor on the night shift. The news item needs to be uploaded within minutes. How does the journalist in such a scenario follow gatekeeping norms? The issue of account-ability of journalistic ethics when reporting rapes is another area where gatekeeping faces a challenge in the digital era. Ethical practices and reporting methods of journalists may vary across the world (Correa 2009), and although there are similarities (for example, in most cultures, journalists do not reveal confidential sources), differences do exist based on 'newsroom experience, family upbringing, religious values, journalism education, news media managers and the size of the newspaper where the reporter works' (Correa 2009: 656).

Where there seems to be some common ground, however, is in the rising influence of powerful individual journalists (Singer 2014) on social media, with the number of their followers often bettering those of their organization's official handles and sites (celebrated journalists such as Barkha Dutt and Rajdeep Sardesai, for instance, have over four million Twitter followers each, and many senior editors also have over a million followers, or at least a few hundred thousand). They are also more engaged with followers on social media than the official organizational pages or handles (Al-Rawi 2016). Greater engagement has been shown to result in greater trust (Al-Rawi 2016), and journalists in India too are taking advantage of Twitter, Facebook, and other platforms to get their personal or organizational opinions on most major issues across to their followers—often in a more effective way than the parent organizations manage to do online.

Under such circumstances, when journalists tweet or post their opinion about an incident of rape, do they follow the same gatekeeping norms as their organizations? Do they apologize, for instance, if they post or tweet inaccurate news about a sexual assault or state clearly their political or religious biases when posting an opinion on an incident of rape that may have religious or political overtones? Some scholars have argued that such transparency can weaken the authority of journalists who once held relatively unchallenged jurisdiction in information delivery (Lowrey and Anderson 2005). Journalists may be unaccustomed to or uncomfortable with the sort of transparency that is expected online. How they negotiate gatekeeping steps in an online environment with regard to posting or tweeting on sensitive topics such as rapes, and whether news organizations can exercise any influence on their employees in the social media space—these are matters that need serious thought from both editors as well as the leadership teams in Indian news organizations.

WHAT JOURNALISTS THINK THEY ARE DOING

It may be interesting to discuss briefly here the early findings from an ongoing project that examines Indian journalists' own perceptions of how rape news is selected and presented to their audiences, and what factors affect their selection and presentation decisions. I conducted a survey of a little over 300 journalists from 15 Indian cities was conducted for this purpose. The respondents were asked two sets of questions. The first set examined their perceptions of social media as a useful professional tool, and as a source for breaking news. The second set of questions examined the factors that they believed influenced journalistic decisions to select/share or reject breaking rape news story to an online audience. Since almost all Indian newspapers and television channels now have their own official websites and social media handles, the survey was open to journalists of all hues and colours.

I intend to briefly discuss just a couple of the key findings in this chapter. One interesting revelation, for instance, indicated that while most journalists did not seem to have faith in social media as a source of breaking crime news, they reposed a high level of trust in social media as a platform for sharing and monitoring news. While only 47 out of the 302 respondents found it a trustworthy or very trustworthy source (201 said it was somewhat or totally untrustworthy as a source of accurate, unbiased, and genuine news about crimes such as rapes; the rest were non-committal), an overwhelming number (over 200) found social media to be a very useful or somewhat useful tool to share breaking crime news, monitor such news, and even use it as a means to get hold of quotes. This seems to suggest that journalists in India are very likely to share news about rapes on the official social media handles of their news organizations, as also to upload the news on the organizational websites—both of which are usually done within minutes of a news reaching the reporter. What does this mean for accuracy and authenticity of news? What can be done to ensure accuracy is not sacrificed at the altar of speed?

Equally importantly for this chapter, a significant number of journalists (187/302) thought their organizations were very likely to verify breaking news on incidents of rape before sharing it with audiences on websites or social media posts—but they also believed their organizations would 'immediately upload' such news since it was of the utmost importance that audiences received such news 'as soon as possible'. This finding again reinforces the idea of a conflict between the need for verification—a time-honoured journalistic routine—and the need-for-speed, a market-driven factor central to the success of online news business. Many senior editors across platforms seemed concerned with these results or findings, and, over several hours of formal and informal conversations, discussed possible solutions or plans of action to tackle this broad issue.

SOLUTIONS TO PROBLEMS: SOME THOUGHTS

To dive deeper in to the issue, I interviewed senior editors and seasoned journalists from across India. The well-thought-out strategies of the 20 editors I interviewed led to the emergence of six broad themes. It may be pertinent to mention that all editors interviewed had a minimum of 15 years of experience in Indian journalism and were eminently qualified to speak on the subject. The list included editors, news editors, online editors, and senior editors from publications such as the *Hindu*, the *Telegraph, Mid-Day, Mumbai Mirror*, and *Times of India*; TV channels such as Zee News, Times Now, and CNN IBN; and websites such as *FirstPost, Scroll.in, Nyusu*, and others.

Codified Rules for Reporting Gender Issues

One theme that emerged was the need to create a guide for journalists who report on crime, on the lines of the 66-page guide for journalists who report on crime and crime victims published by the US Department of Justice (Bucqueroux and Seymour 2009). The Press Council of India (PCI) code book for journalists barely touches upon how to select or report news about incidents of rapes. The US guide, for instance, mandates: 'It is important for reporters and editors to under-stand that sexual assault is not a crime about sex but about violence, power, and control. Journalists should avoid reporting details about the assault in ways that imply the victim's behavior caused the crime (walking alone at night, drinking alcohol)' (Bucqueroux and Seymour 2009: 15). In another instance, the guidelines warn that editors can introduce problems.

> People outside the news business often hold reporters accountable for decisions that were made by the editors. For example, many victims report that the headline bothered them the most because it was too sensational, misleading, or flatly wrong. At most newspapers and magazines, copy editors write the headline, not the reporter. Copy editors also change parts of stories, sometimes without conferring with reporters, which can result in errors or insensitivities. It is best to ensure that the

system allows reporters who cover victims the opportunity to check headlines, corrections, and changes before the stories are aired or published. (Bucqueroux and Seymour 2009: 16)

One editor from Kolkata, for instance, suggested the formal inclusion of some key Supreme Court (SC) judgments regarding rape reporting into the PCI guidelines. He said that SC rulings, such as the 1994 judgment making it mandatory for the police to inform every woman who approached them with an allegation of rape that she was entitled to legal counsel to help file a case, be included in the journalistic routine code, so that reporters routinely sought proof from police officers to check if the process had been followed for each case they were reporting. Similarly, another editor from Pune cited a 2000 SC ruling that made it mandatory for all hospitals to immediately treat a woman for 'physical injuries and collect evidence, whether or not she decides to report the allegation (of rape) to police. Doctors should treat the victim before insisting that she file a police report' (*State of Karnataka v. Manjanna* 2000). As a senior editor of a leading Mumbai-based TV channel summed up: 'we need to question and verify each time if these steps have been followed. This is part of our responsibility as members of the fourth estate, to keep an eye on the other three estates. We should be watchdogs and not lapdogs.'[1]

Correct the Gender Imbalance in Workplaces

In an interview to a *New York Times* reporter in 2013, Usha Rai, who had worked in the Indian print media for 37 years, does some plain speaking about the position of women in many newsrooms even today, when she says: 'Women were not taken seriously in journalism.... Men thought that beat reporting was their preserve' (Raina 2013). Writing in the *Media Magazine*, scholar Shoma Chatterji gives several examples from Indian newsrooms to argue that matters have

> not changed much from the time women could not access top jobs in media organizations in spite of their expertise and their qualifications. Even today, in most newsrooms across the world the leaders who head media organizations or edit news channels or papers are men. Though women comprise more than half the world's population, men routinely decide what news they should hear and read. (Chatterji 2017)

While more and more women are joining media organizations, as both male and female editors I spoke to acknowledged, most of them join either the news desk or the feature and lifestyle teams. The two areas where women are employed the least are in crime reporting and sports journalism. As one editor pointed out, 'unless we have a gender balance in newsrooms across all sectors, news stories will continued to be told from a male point of view. We need to make a conscious attempt to encourage and train more women journalists to be crime beat reporters and join the online news teams who both report and upload stories.'

More Research Teams

Speed is of the essence in all forms of online journalism—whether it deals with news websites or social media platforms. The journalists who are receiving, writing, uploading, or posting a rape news story, probably have less than 30 minutes from the time they receive the first information, till the time the first version of the story is shared with consumers over multiple online platforms. As the editor of a Delhi-based newspaper's online edition argued,

> where is the time for that poor reporter to conduct any research or even detailed verifications about a news when the total time to write, run a grammar check and a basic fact-check is less than 30 minutes? You cannot run 10 verification filters in that short a time. What we need is a research team to assist all online news teams. These should be journalists, who have specific training in running background checks, verifying facts and providing further information including historical facts when a report is being filed. For instance was this the first time a college student had been raped in college X? Is that a genuine fact or something the reporter wrote because a source told him so? A research team can look these up even as the reporter is filing a story.

Privileging Accuracy over Speed

Several editors stated that they were of the firm belief that the craze for speed was just a temporary phase, and management teams, marketing teams, as well as editorial leaderships would soon realize that *being correct* would not just earn public loyalty and trust, but also translate into profit compared to *being first*, which may bring in advertisements and page views in the short run but only drive away customers and advertisers over time. The editor of a relatively new Mumbai-based online news site for instance said that all editorial staff had been instructed not to upload any story unless and until it had been 'properly verified'. Another editor said:

> Proper verification does not mean checking Twitter feeds of trustworthy sources alone. We also insist that a confirmation be taken from a trustworthy source such as a senior police official via phone, email or in a face-to-face meeting when possible, in instances where a reporter is unable to reach the scene of the crime quickly. We would rather be late by 30 minutes than be wrong.

Need for Greater In-House Sensitization Training for Reporters and Sub-editors

Editors across platforms and cities also stressed the importance of in-house training for journalists, especially those who were on online teams, as well as reporters, sub-editors, photographers, and editors, on how to handle rape news stories. One editor from Bengaluru cited the Guide for Journalists in the United States. Indeed, the guide mentions:

> Online articles (and mistakes) can live forever. News organizations and victims will not always agree on what should or should not be printed. But online articles can remain infinitely retrievable through search engines. Victims in particular can have concerns that someone who searches for their name years later may learn about their victimization even though the victim wants to move on. This can be of particular concern if the original article contained errors. News organizations should consider including victims and victim organizations in their discussions on developing these policies. (Bucqueroux and Seymour 2009: 26)

Many recent studies have found that the process of selecting and rejecting news of rapes involving members of marginalized or minority groups may not always be a deliberate result of male conspiracy (Durham 2013), but a reflection of a significant public opinion that prevails in the social milieu in which the news organization functions

(Lewis 2008; Gibson 2009) and where reporters and editors themselves are often unaware of their embeddedness in a social and political context that shapes their reporting (Shoemaker and Reese 1995). Editors also stressed the need for media organizations to conduct regular sensitization workshops with journalists to sensitize them to some of the stereotypes they may have grown up with, ones they needed to be aware of as journalists, so that they would not fall prey to them.

Greater Transparency and Accountability to Gain Credibility

Editors agreed that journalists, like those in any other profession, were likely to make errors of judgement from time to time. However, many, including online editors, were concerned that the ease with which errors could be constantly corrected and news stories updated on online platforms was leading to a breach of ethics, possible a breach of trust with customers. While journalists in India may be familiar with various journalistic ethical codes, they may not be sufficiently exposed or encouraged to discuss ethical codes with colleagues, editors, or owners (Rao and Johal 2006). While journalism and media education in India has exploded over the past two decades, ethics education remains largely absent.

The 111-page PCI code titled *Norms of Journalistic Conduct*—the code of ethics, for instance—makes little direct reference to covering or reporting on rape or sexual violence, and provides few guidelines for discussing such topics. A subsection under the discussion of the right to privacy simply states: 'when reporting crime involving rape, abduction or kidnap of women/females or sexual assault on children, raising doubts and questions touching the chastity, personal character and privacy of women, the names, photographs of the victims or other particulars leading to their identity shall not be published' (PCI 2010, 2016).

Editors suggested a two-pronged solution to this issue. At the first level, they stressed the need for mass communication schools across India to include journalism ethics as a part of the core curriculum in media studies courses. 'It should not just be a few classes. This should be a core class that runs through a full semester. Students should be made to do projects that incorporate different elements of journalistic ethics,' one Delhi-based editor argued. Another, a Kolkata-based television channel editor, concurred. 'It is not sufficient to know that rape victims cannot be named. Reporters and editors need to be accountable to the families of the victims and perpetrators, and to the public at large, for their actions.'

Being accountable also means journalists need to maintain a level of transparency with the consumer that was almost impossible in traditional newsrooms where audience members and journalists seldom interacted or engaged with each other. One editor remarked:

> On online platforms, consumers can see the news at any time. Merely correcting inaccurate news a few minutes later is not enough. Consumers are highly unlikely to return to a website every few minutes to check for updates. What if we report that a person has been accused of raping a woman and correct it 20 minutes later stating that the person's name was not X but Y? Is that sufficient?

Her argument: that journalists and news organizations should have a written policy making it mandatory for them to preface every update or correction on a news story with an acknowledgement that an error had been made in the previous version, and to highlight the corrected part of the story for people to see. 'Being transparent and owning up to mistakes may see some politicians or fringe elements taking a potshot at you. But you will earn the respect of the masses, you will be known as someone who strives to provide honest and accurate news,' the editor observed.

Evidently the solutions offered by the editors are not exhaustive by any means, nor are they foolproof. They are what they are: the opinions of a few very senior journalists/editors. This is only a start, an appetizer so to speak, to hopefully initiate a process of introspection and further research on how India's newsrooms treat stories about gender-related crimes such as rapes, and possibly to extend the discussion to the larger issue of gender imbalance in India's newsrooms. Indian journalism has undoubtedly taken rapid strides in many areas. There are many challenges before it too, not least of which is the new ownership patterns of media houses and the aggressive bid by some politicians, political parties, and industrialists to take control of or gain ownership of major media houses. Some of these challenges that Indian journalism faces today are discussed in other chapters. Gender and the coverage of news stories about gender-related crimes such as rapes are one of the major issues that Indian journalism must deal with if journalism in India has to retain, possibly regain, public trust as a source of timely, accurate, and unbiased information. As we write, trust in media is globally at an all-time low (Karainan 2017; Swift 2016). In India, the media is the least trusted institution—trusted even less than the government, business houses, and NGOs. If public trust has to be regained, it has to start now.

NOTE

1. The in-depth interviews were conducted across a two-month period during the summer of 2017 (May–June 2017). Interviews were conducted with editors of newspapers, magazines, TV channels, and news websites across five Indian cities—Kolkata, Delhi, Mumbai, Bengaluru, and Pune. They were conducted either face-to-face or over Skype.

REFERENCES

Abrahamson, M. (2006). 'Young Women's and Men's Different Worlds of Alcohol, Fear, and Violence in Focus Group Discussions with 18 Year-Olds in Stockholm'. *Contemporary Drug Problems*, 33(1): 3–28.

Agnes, F. (2015). 'Section 498A, Marital Rape and Adverse Propaganda'. *Economic and Political Weekly*, L(23): 12–15. Retrieved from http://majlislaw.com/file/2015_06_06_Section_498A__Marital_Rape_and_Adverse_Propaganda_EPW_Jun_2015.pdf (accessed on 17 August 2018).

Ahmed, S. (2016). 'Safety Tip from India's Tourism Minister: Don't Wear Skirts'. Retrieved from http://www.cnn.com/2016/08/29/asia/india-skirt-safety-advice-women-trnd/index.html (accessed on 17 August 2018).

Al Jazeera (2014). 'Indian Leader Castigated for Rape Remark'. Retrieved from http://www.aljazeera.com/news/asia/2014/04/indian-leader-castigated-rape-remark-201441175838318816.html (accessed on 17 August 2018).

Al-Rawi, A. (2016). 'News Values on Social Media: News Organizations' Facebook Use'. *Journalism*. doi:1464884916636142.

ANI (2017). 'Gurgaon Gangrape: After Sketches Released, 1 Arrested Confesses to Crime'. Retrieved from http://www.deccanchronicle.com/nation/current-affairs/070617/gurugram-gangrape-after-sketches-released-1-arrested-confesses-to-crime.html (accessed on 17 August 2018).

Ardovini-Booker, J. and S. Caringella-Macdonald (2002). 'Media Attributions of Blame and Sympathy in Ten Rape Cases'. *The Justice Professional*, 15(1): 3–18.

BBC.com (2012). 'India President's Son Apologises over Rape Comments'. Retrieved from http://www.bbc.com/news/world-asia-india-20852513 (accessed on 17 August 2018).

——— (2013). 'Explaining India's New Anti-Rape Laws'. Retrieved from http://www.bbc.com/news/world-asia-india-21950197 (accessed on 17 August 2018).

Bedi, A. and S. Bedi (2017). 'Indian Woman Representation: The Male Eye and the Media Lens'. *Indian Journal of Health and Wellbeing*, 8(3): 206–10. doi:ISSN-p-2229-5356,e-2321-3698.

Belair-Gagnon, V., S. Mishra, and C. Agur (2014). 'Reconstructing the Indian Public Sphere: Newswork and Social Media in the Delhi Gang Rape Case'. *Journalism*, 1059–75.

Bernhardsson, J. and A. Bogren (2012). Drink Sluts, Brats and Immigrants as Others: An Analysis of Swedish Media Discourse on Gender, Alcohol and Rape. *Feminist Media Studies*, 1–16.

Bhattacharjee, S. (2008). 'Rape, Retribution and Beyond: Understanding the Problem of Rape in the Indian Context'. In *A Unique Crime: Understanding Rape in India*, pp. 1–52. New Delhi: Oxford University Press.

Bucqueroux, B. and A. Seymour (2009). 'A Guide for Journalists Who Report on Crime and Crime Victims'. Retrieved from http://www.mediacrimevictimguide.com/journalistguide.pdf (accessed on 17 August 2018).

Carter, C. (1998). 'When the "Extraordinary" Becomes "Ordinary": Everyday News of Sexual Violence'. In *News, Gender and Power*, eds C. Carter, G. A. Branston, and S. Allen, pp. 219–32. New York: Routledge.

CDC (Center for Diseases Control) (2014). 'The National Intimate Partner and Sexual Violence Survey'. Retrieved from http://www.cdc.gov/ViolencePrevention/NISVS/ (accessed on 17 August 2018).

Chatterji, S. (2017). 'Indian Women in Journalism'. Retrieved from http://mediamagazine.in/content/indian-women-journalism (accessed on 17 August 2018).

Chattopadhyaya, D. (2015). 'Young Wife from Sikkim Allegedly Raped: Understanding the Framing of Rape Reportage in India's English Language Media'. AEJMC Annual Convention 2015, San Francisco.

Correa, T. (2009). 'Does Class Matter? The Effect of Social Class on Journalists' Ethical Decision Making'. *Journalism and Mass Communication Quarterly*, 86(3): 654–72.

Cuklanz, L. (1996). *Rape on Trial: How the Mass Media Construct Legal Reform and Social Change*. Philadelphia: University of Pennsylvania Press.

Day, K., B. Gough, and M. McFadden (2004). 'Warning! Alcohol can Seriously Damage your Feminine Health'. *Feminist Media Studies*, 4(2): 165–83.

Drache, D. and J. Velagic (2014). 'Sexual Violence Journalism in Four Leading English Language Indian Publications before and after the Delhi Rape'. *Journal of Research in Gender Studies*, 4(2): 11–38.

Drèze, J. and A. Sen (2013). *An Uncertain Glory: India and Its Contradictions*. Princeton, NJ: Princeton University Press.

Durham, M. G. (2013). 'Vicious Assault Shakes Texan Town: The Politics of Gender Violence in the *New York Times*' Coverage of a Schoolgirl's Gang Rape'. *Journalism Studies*, 4(1): 1–12.

——— (2015). 'Scene of the Crime: News Discourse of Rape in India and the Geopolitics of Sexual Assault'. *Feminist Media Studies*, 15(2): 175–91.

Entman, R. (1993). 'Framing: Toward Clarification of a Fractured Paradigm'. *Journal of Communication*, 43(4): 51–8.

Fadnis, D. (2017). 'Uncovering Rape Culture: Patriarchal Values Guide Indian Media's Rape-Related Reporting'. *Journalism Studies*, 19(12): 1–17. doi:http://dx.doi.org/10.1080/1461670X.2017.1301781.

Finch, E. and V. Munro (2007). 'The Demon Drink and the Demonized Woman: Sociosexual Stereotypes and Responsibility Attribution in Rape Trials Involving Intoxicants'. *Social and Legal Studies*, 16(4): 591–614.

Gibson, Katie L. (2009). 'Undermining Katie Couric: The Discipline Function of the Press'. *Women and Language*, 32(1): 51–9.

Hermida, A. (2012). 'Tweets and Truth: Journalism as a Discipline of Collaborative Verification'. *Journalism Practice*, 6(5–6): 659–68.

Hindu (2011). 'Minor Girl and Married Woman Raped in Capital', 9 April. Retrieved from https://www.thehindu.com/todays-paper/tp-national/tp-newdelhi/Minor-girl-and-married-woman-raped-in-Capital/article14676229.ece (accessed on 12 September 2018).

Hindustan Times (2017). 'Delhi: Man Arrested for Luring Uzbek Woman to India, Raping Her over Six Months'. Retrieved from http://www.hindustantimes.com/india-news/delhi-man-arrested-for-luring-uzbek-woman-to-india-raping-her-over-six-months/story-UWPX0fnbxoWbr7cvk5GXWO.html (accessed on 17 August 2018).

India Today (2013). 'Delhi Gangrape Shocked the Collective Conscience of the Nation, Says Judge in His Verdict', 13 September. Retrieved from https://www.indiatoday.in/india/north/story/delhi-gangrape-shocked-the-conscience-of-nation-judge-210889-2013-09-13 (accessed on 12 September 2018).

——— (2014). 'Married Woman Gangraped in South-West Delhi'. Retrieved from http://indiatoday.intoday.in/story/gangrape-rape-married-woman-dwarka-delhi-police-vikas-anil-ramesh-meerut-gangrape-lisadi-gate/1/400117.html (accessed on 17 August 2018).

Indian Express (2015a). 'AIIMS Doctor Held for Rape of Sikkim Woman'. Retrieved from http://indianexpress.com/article/cities/delhi/sikkim-woman-raped-in-delhi-aiims-doctor-4-others-arrested/ (accessed on 17 August 2018).

———— (2015b). 'Two Arrested for Raping BPO Employee in Bengaluru'. Retrieved from http://indianexpress.com/article/india/india-news-india/bpo-employee-raped-in-bengaluru/ (accessed on 17 August 2018).

Ju, A., S. H. Jeong, and H. I. Chyi (2014). 'Will Social Media Save Newspapers? Examining the Effectiveness of Facebook and Twitter as News Platforms'. *Journalism Practice*, 8(1): 1–17.

Karainan, J. (2017). 'The Results Are In: Nobody Trusts Anyone Anymore—The Edelman Trust Barometer', 16 January. Retrieved from https://qz.com/886054/the-results-are-in-nobody-trusts-anyone-anymore/ (accessed on 12 September 2018).

Lee, A. M. (2015). 'Social Media and Speed-Driven Journalism: Expectations and Practices'. *International Journal on Media Management*, 1(4): 217–39.

Lewis, N. (2008). 'From Cheesecake to the Chief: Newspaper Editors' Slow Acceptance of Women'. *American Journalism*, 25(2): 33–55.

Lowrey, W. and W. Anderson (2005). 'The Journalist behind the Curtain: Participatory Functions on the Internet and Their Impact on Perceptions of the Work of Journalism'. *Journal of Computer-Mediated Communication*, 10(3). https://doi.org/10.1111/j.1083-6101.2005.tb00261.x.

Lyons, A., S. Dalton, and A. Hoy (2006). 'Hardcore Drinking: Portrayals of Alcohol Consumption in Young Women's and Men's Magazines'. *Journal of Health Psychology*, 11(2): 223–32.

Maier, S. R. (2005). 'Accuracy Matters: A Cross-market Assessment of Newspaper Error and Credibility'. *Journalism and Mass Communication Quarterly*, 82(3): 533–51.

Matharu, H. (2016). 'Sweden and Denmark Have Highest Rates of Sexual Harassment in Europe'. *Independent*, 7 January. Retrieved from https://www.independent.co.uk/news/world/europe/sweden-and-denmark-have-highest-number-of-sexual-assaults-in-europe-a6800901.html (accessed on 12 September 2018).

Matthes, J. (2009). 'What's in a Frame? A Content Analysis of Media Framing Studies in the World's Leading Communication Journals'. *Journalism and Mass Communication Quarterly*, 349–67. doi:10.1177/107769900908600206.

Mid-day (2017). 'New Delhi: Northeast Woman Raped Near Hauz Khas Village', 20 February. Retrieved from https://www.mid-day.com/articles/new-delhi-northeast-woman-raped-near-hauz-khas-village-crime-news/18010163 (accessed on 12 September 2018).

Nargunde, R. (2013). 'The Delhi Gang Rape: The Role of Media in Justice'. *International Journal of Research*, 1(8): 869–81.

NCRB (National Crime Records Bureau) (2015). *Crime in India 2014*. New Delhi: National Crime Records Bureau.

NDTV (2016). 'Married Woman Allegedly Gangraped in Mathura'. Retrieved from http://www.ndtv.com/cities/married-woman-allegedly-gangraped-in-mathura-1477063 (accessed on 17 August 2018).

Neelakantan, S. (2016). 'Indian Politicians' Revolting Comments about Rape'. Retrieved from http://timesofindia.indiatimes.com/india/Indian-politicians-revolting-comments-about-rape/articleshow/53512298.cms (accessed on 17 August 2018).

Northeast Today (2015). 'Sikkim Woman Raped in Delhi, AIIMS Doctor Held'. Retrieved from https://www.northeasttoday.in/sikkim-woman-raped-in-delhi-aiims-doctor-held/ (accessed on 17 August 2018).

PCI (Press Council of India) (2010). 'Norms of Journalistic Conduct'. Retrieved from http://presscouncil.nic.in/Content/6_1_Norms.aspx.

——— (2016). 'Press Council of India: Principles and Ethics'. Retrieved from http://www.presscouncil.nic.in/Content/62_1_PrinciplesEthics.aspx (accessed on 17 December 2016).

Phadke, S., S. Khan, and S. Ranade (2011). *Why Loiter? Women and Risk on Mumbai Streets*. New Delhi: Penguin.

Press Trust of India (2016). 'Woman Allegedly Raped by Ashram Head in Vrindavan'. Retrieved from http://www.ndtv.com/cities/woman-allegedly-raped-by-ashram-head-in-vrindavan-1621612 (accessed on 17 August 2018).

Raina, P. (2013). 'Why Female Journalists in India Still Can't Have It All'. Retrieved from https://india.blogs.nytimes.com/2013/09/02/why-women-journalists-in-india-still-cant-have-it-all/ (accessed on 17 August 2018).

Raj, A. and L. McDougal (2014). 'Sexual Violence and Rape in India'. *Women*, 383(March): 865.

Rao, S. (2014). 'Covering Rape in Shame Culture: Studying Journalism Ethics in India's New Television News Media'. *Journal of Mass Media Ethics*, 29(3): 146–62.

Rao, S. and N. Johal (2006). 'Ethics and News Making in the Changing Indian Mediascape'. *Journal of Mass Media Ethics*, 21(4): 286–303.

Rao, S. and H. Wasserman (2015). 'A Media Not for All: A Comparative Analysis of Journalism, Democracy and Exclusion in Indian and South African Media'. *Journalism Studies*, 16(5): 651–62. doi:10.1080/1461670X.2015.1054173.

Rath, P. (2007). 'Marital Rape and the Indian Legal Scenario'. *India Law Journal*, 21–4. Retrieved from http://www.indialawjournal.org/archives/volume2/issue_2/article_by_priyanka.html (accessed on 17 August 2018).

Scherr, S. and P. Baugut (2015). 'The Meaning of Leaning: The Impact of Journalists' Political Leaning on Active Role Perception and Satisfaction with Audiences and Editorial Policy'. *Journalism and Mass Communication Quarterly*. doi:1077699015606678.

Scheufele, D. A. (1999). 'Framing as a Theory of Media Effects'. *Journal of Communication*, 49(4): 103–22.

Schwalbe, C. B., B. W. Silcock, and E. Candello (2015). 'Gatecheckers at the Visual News Stream: A New Model for Classic Gatekeeping Theory'. *Journalism Practice*, 9(4): 465–83. doi:10.1080/17512786.2015.1030133.

Sen, A. (2013). *Press Freedom: What Is It Good For?* New Delhi: Index of Censorship.

Shoemaker, P. J. and S. D. Reese (1995). *Mediating the Message: Theories of Influences on Mass Media Content*. New York: Longman.

——— (2013). *Mediating the Message in the 21st Century: A Media Sociology Perspective*. New York: Routledge.

Silverman, C. (2007). *Regret the Error: How Media Mistakes Pollute the Press and Imperil Free Speech*. Toronto, Ontario: Penguin.

Singer, J. B. (2008). 'The Journalist in the Network: A Shifting Role for the Gatekeeping and Objectivity Norms'. *Tripodos*, 23: 61–76.

——— (2014). 'User-Generated Visibility: Secondary Gatekeeping in a Shared Media Space'. *New Media and Society*, 55–73. Retrieved from http://openaccess.city.ac.uk/3445/7/User-generated%2520Visibility.pdf (accessed on 17 August 2018).

State of Karnataka v. Manjanna, Appeal (Crl.) 1911/1966 (Supreme Court of India May 4, 2000).

Swift, A. (2016). 'Americans' Trust in Mass Media Sinks to New Low'. Retrieved from http://www.gallup.com/poll/195542/americans-trust-mass-media-sinks-new-low.aspx (accessed on 17 August 2018).

Taylor, R. (2009). 'Slain and Slandered: A Content Analysis of the Portrayal of Femicide in Crime News'. *Homicide Studies*, 13(1): 21–49. https://doi.org/10.1177/1088767908326679.

Telegraph (2015). 'AIIMS Doctor Held for Rape of Woman Snared into Flesh Trade'. Retrieved from https://www.telegraphindia.com/1150228/jsp/nation/story_5993.jsp (accessed on 17 August 2018).

Tenore, M. (2013). 'Why Journalists Are Covering Rapes Differently in New Delhi & Steubenville'. Retrieved from http://www.poynter.org/2013/why-journalists-are-covering-rapes-differently-in-new-delhi-steubenville/200119/ (accessed on 17 August 2018).

Tewksbury, D. and D. Scheufele (2009). 'News Framing Theory and Research'. In *Media Effects: Advances in Theory and Research*, eds J. Bryant and M. Oliver, pp. 17–33. New York: Routledge.

Thurman, N. and A. Walters (2013). 'Live Blogging—Digital Journalism's Pivotal Platform? A Case Study of the Production, Consumption, and Form of Live Blogs at guardian.co.uk'. *Digital Journalism*, 82–101. doi:10.1080/21670811.2012. 714935.

Times of India (2015). '25-Year-Old Trafficked Woman Raped by AIIMS Doctor, 5 Held'. 28 February. Retrieved from https://timesofindia.india-times.com/city/delhi/25-year-old-trafficked-woman-raped-by-AIIMS-doctor-5-held/articleshow/46402558.cms (accessed on 11 September 2018).

van Gorp, B. (2007). 'The Constructionist Approach to Framing: Bringing Culture Back In'. *Journal of Communication*, 57(1): 60–78. https://doi.org/10.1111/j.1460-2466.2006.00329_3.x.

Williams, W. (1914). 'The Journalist's Creed: Missouri School of Journalism'. Retrieved from https://journalism.missouri.edu/tabbed-content/creed-2/ (accessed on 7 January 2017).

WSJ (2013). 'Poll of Delhi Men: What Causes Rape'. Retrieved from https://blogs.wsj.com/indiarealtime/2013/01/29/poll-of-delhi-men-what-causes-rape/ (accessed on 17 August 2018).

Zee News (2015). 'Delhi: Sikkimese Girl Allegedly Raped by AIIMS Doctor'. Retrieved from http://zeenews.india.com/news/videos/top-stories/delhi-sikkimese-girl-allegedly-raped-by-aiims-doctor_1553419.html (accessed on 17 August 2018).

CHAPTER TWELVE

Media and the Existing News Narratives in Kashmir Conflict

ARIF HUSSAIN NADAF

. . . .

The political crises in a conflict situation are 'demonstrated' through the narratives of media (Cottle 2008). The media in a conflict situation facilitates the dissemination of existing political ideologies, has a profound impact on policy-making and influences the process of conflict escalation and resolution (Seib 2005). The conflict in Kashmir region is often presented with three distinctive narratives in the news media in India, Pakistan, and the local media in the region. In a protracted conflict like Kashmir that involves persistent competing political rhetoric, it becomes essential to understand the dynamics of news narratives that position themselves in the existing political situation.

Ever since the beginning of media's evolution in Kashmir region, the regional political dynamics have played a determinant role in shaping the local press in the region. The decentralized political regionalism has been one of the fundamental characteristics of politics in the Jammu and Kashmir State since 1947 and the local media have followed the suit by embedding themselves in the socio-political ethos of the region. The local media in the region have evolved through the decades of violent conflict in the region and have faced the wrath of violence through intimidation, threats, and even assassination of journalists (Jeffrey 2003; Tekwani 2008). The chapter discusses the role of the local press in the region, the impact of violence on media and, the representation of conflict through distinctive and diverse news narratives in the national (Indian media), Pakistani, and the regional media.

REGIONAL MEDIA IN THE STATE

The 'regionalization' of news media vis-à-vis political regionalism and the localization of news content are inherent characteristics of Indian media systems (Chakravartty and Roy 2013; Jeffrey 2003; Neyazi 2011, 2014). The regional political narrative has strengthened the role of local media in India and the news discourse remains highly local-ized in Indian states (Jeffrey 2003; Neyazi 2011; Stahlberg 2013). The dominant discourse about politics in Kashmir is powered by region-alized political identities and *Kashmiriyat*[1] as a historical entity that embodies the idea of Kashmiri's own version of nationalism (Zutshi 2004). The local media in Kashmir strongly adheres to political regionalism that stems from the regional identity politics.

Regional and socio-political environment prevailing in the state of Jammu and Kashmir has been largely determined by the histori-cal circumstances in the region (Snedden 2013). The regional press in Kashmir traces its roots in pre-1947 nationalist movement when political activists began publishing newspapers as a means to promote dissent (Bamzai 1994). Ever since the beginning of the conflict in Kashmir, the local newspapers have consolidated their role by taking a 'pro-people' position throughout the course of conflict (Singh 1995). Local newspapers adhere to internal dynamics of conflict in the region and often antagonize the establishment by reflecting on regional aspi-rations, whatever they might be (Joseph 2000). The local news narra-tive on politics is fundamentally built on the discourse of contestation between the two existing dominant narratives of regional politics; pro-India mainstream politics and the politics of separatism in the region. The reportage reflects on the regional political discourse and local newspapers tread a fine line between the above two dominant narratives of politics in Kashmir. The vernacular press which played a crucial role in pre-1947 nationalist movement in Jammu and Kashmir continued to dominate the news discourse for decades (Sofi 1973). The Urdu news publications were leading the regional journalism in Kashmir region. However, after the escalation of armed violence in the region, English newspapers started gaining ground. English language newspapers like *Kashmir Times, Greater Kashmir, Kashmir Images*, and *Daily Excelsior* began growing during the late 1980s and early 1990s. Due to strong political regionalism, the local newspapers continued to influence the conflict discourse. With the outbreak of militancy in the late 1980s, the journalism in the region became vulnerable to the dictates of guerrilla groups and security forces operating in the region (Tekwani 2008).

Over the decades, newspaper publications have mushroomed in the state. According to the statistics provided by the Registrar of Newspapers for India (RNI 2017),[2] the number of registered publications in the state is increasing at a remarkable speed (Table 12.1). As per RNI data, there has been a rapid growth of newspaper publications in last six decades in the state of Jammu and Kashmir and the total number of registrations from the region has reached to a spectacular mark of 1,191 publications. However, this growth does not seem to make any impact on the ground as not all the registered titles appear in print versions and are available to readers.

Table 12.1 Distribution of the Number of Registered Publications in J&K, 1961–2011

Decade	Number of Publications Registered
1961–1970	68
1971–1980	125
1981–1990	76
1991–2000	108
2001–2010	278
2011 Onwards	499
*NA	37

Source: Registrar of Newspapers for India.

The data provided by Jammu and Kashmir Directorate of Information and Public Relations (JKDIPR), show only 372 registered functional news publications [Jammu (201) and Kashmir (171)] in the state, among which 139 publications, mainly newspapers are empanelled with India's Directorate of Advertising and Visual Publicity (DAVP) for the release of Government advertisement.[3] This extraordinary difference in the statistics about newspaper publications in the region between RNI and the State Information Department reveals the prevalence of defunct news publications in the state. According to JKDIPR, there are 31 English, 59 Urdu, two Kashmiri language newspapers in Kashmir region. Although the news dailies registered in Kashmir region are predominantly in Urdu language, only a couple of old Urdu newspapers like *Srinagar Times, Aaftaab*, and *Kashmir Uzma* are widely read and have a consistent readership. On the other hand, the news dailies in Jammu are predominantly in the English language. There are 49 English, 23 Urdu, 20 Hindi news dailies published in Jammu region. Interestingly, there are only two registered Kashmiri language newspapers and only one Dogri language newspaper in Kashmir and Jammu regions, respectively despite the fact that Kashmiri and Dogra are the two dominant ethnicities in Jammu and Kashmir.

The state-owned Doordarshan, run by Indian Information and Broadcasting Ministry, started television broadcasting in the region in early 1990s and continued to have a monopoly over local news broadcasting throughout the militancy period with an exclusive pro-government narrative on the events. The Government of India introduced *DD Kashmir* in 2000 as a subsidiary of Doordarshan Television Network to promote 'Kashmiri culture' and 'counter the Pakistani propaganda' in the Kashmir valley (Mahajan 2017). Due to the volatile situation during the peak of militancy in the region, the channel was run from New Delhi until 2006. In 2006, the Ministry of Information and Broadcasting decided to shift the operations to Srinagar to help the local government to 'stop any misinformation being spread by extremist outfits' (Mahajan 2017).

The local cable television networks that began operations in the early 2000s paved the way for small private local news channels beyond Doordarshan. However, during the mass demonstrations and violent protests that erupted in 2010, the state government enforced a complete ban of private news channels in the region. The local news channels were accused of broadcasting provocative speeches by secessionist elements, which according to the national government was dangerous to law and order in the region ('Govt bans SEN TV network' (*Greater Kashmir* 2010). In the absence of private news broadcasters, the local newspapers continue to dominate the media sector in the region.

MEDIA AFTER THE RISE OF CONFLICT

The local media in Kashmir, especially the local newspapers have survived through the peak of violence and facing the wrath from state and non-state actors, the journalists in the region have reported under persistent threats (Tekwani 2008). In 1987, the infamous rigging in State Assembly elections that were orchestrated to keep away separatist elements from making inroads to the state legislature, led to state-wide demonstrations subsequently, the outbreak of armed militancy (Schofield 2003). The shift from regular deliberative politics to the armed violence had a profound impact on the discourse of conflict in the region. During this period, journalists were under heavy pressure from both the government forces and militant groups operating in the region using tactics to discipline the journalists to promote their ideologies and policies (Jeffrey 2003). The context of armed violence fostered the culture of journalistic loyalties with physical intimidation from state and non-state actors (Jamwal 2014).

The violence in the region broke out with the assassination of Lassa Kaul, then director of Doordarshan in Srinagar in 1990 (Evans 2000). This high-profile assassination sent ripples across the political landscape in the region and the local news media. A year later, Mohammad Shaban Waqil, editor of one of the leading Urdu daily *Alsafa*, who was involved in six legal cases for 'objectionable writing' was shot dead by masked gunmen in his office on 23 April 1991 (Jeffrey 2003). Yousuf Jameel, the BBC journalist in Kashmir, was severely injured when a letter bomb addressed to him exploded in his office at Srinagar in September 1995, killing his colleague Mushtaq Ali who was then a cameraman with Asian News International: Yousuf Jameel (*Kashmir Life* 2010).

The commissioning of counter-insurgency by the Government of India in the wake of increased insurgent activities turned out to be the worst time for local journalism leading to an increase in assaults on media persons in the Kashmir region (Jamwal 2014). During the heightened tension between counter-insurgents and bourgeoning militant groups, Zafar Mehraj, a senior journalist then working with Zee Television, a national channel, was shot thrice by unknown gunmen, injuring him severely (HRW 1996). Zafar was returning from an interview with Kuka Parray, then head of the counter-insurgent group: Ikhwan-ul-Muslimoon (HRW 1996). The pro-India militia group: Ikhwan-ul-Muslimoon in July 1996 abducted nineteen journalists in Kashmir region, including correspondents working with international news agencies like *Reuters, The Associated Press*, and *Agence France-Presse* (IFEX 1996). The group that initially threatened to kill six of them demanded a meeting with the editors of leading Urdu language dailies as a pre-condition for the release of captured journalists (IFEX 1996). During the last three decades, ten journalists have been assassinated in the ongoing violence in the Kashmir region: '10 journalists killed in Kashmir insurgency' (Kashmir Newz 2008).

The resurgence of violence in recent years in the form of mass demonstration and the continuous civilian killings at the hands of security forces has reinvigorated the media discourse on the conflict in the region. The recent crisis in the region received an extensive coverage in the local, national, and international media, however, the conflict narratives varied across media. The unrest in the region after 2008 Amarnath land row, the Shopian double rape, and murder case in the 2009 and 2010 summer unrest attracted international media attention (Kazi 2009). The international newspapers like the *New York Times*, the *Guardian*, and the *Wall Street Journal* and, the international news channels like *BBC, Al Jazeera*, and *Press TV* started sending in correspondents and covering civilian demonstrations and human rights violations in the region. *Al Jazeera* started an exclusive web section on Kashmir conflict in 2011 following the civilian deaths: 'Kashmir the Forgotten Conflict' (*Al Jazeera* 2011). During the 2016 violence in the region that escalated in the aftermath of the killing of local militant commander, Burhan Wani, the international news media showed a renewed focus towards the Kashmir conflict. The issue of the excessive use of pellet guns on protesters by the security forces found frequent coverage in international media with headlines such as: 'Cruelty and Cowardice in Kashmir' (*New York Times* 2017) and 'India Kashmir: The Teenager Blinded by Pellets' (*BBC* 2016a). However, the international media coverage of the conflict in the region has primarily been 'episodic' and they are attracted only during the time of heightened violence in the region.

The discourse on Kashmir conflict, ever since its origin, is constituted of three different narratives projected by the local, Indian, and the Pakistani media. While the local media predominantly stick to regional politics in isolation from Indo-Pakistani rhetoric, the media in India and Pakistan reflect 'nationalistic' narratives while covering the conflict in Kashmir. To understand the media-conflict relationship in Kashmir region, it is essential to analyse all the three narratives.

REGIONAL MEDIA NARRATIVE

The regional politics in the state of Jammu and Kashmir exists in two domains: mainstream politics represented by local 'pro-Indian' political parties and leaders and, politics of separatism represented by 'pro-Pakistan' and 'pro-independence' parties (Chowdhary 2008). Ever since the eruption of violence in the region, 'separatism continues to be the focal point of Kashmir politics' (Chowdhary 2008: 23). The local newspapers which are the primary sources of internal politics in the region adhere to covering regional politics which predominantly reflect on the domains of mainstream and separatist politics by its extensive coverage to the day-to-day politics and crises (Joseph 2000; Khalid 2016; Nazakat 2012; Singh 1995). The separatist leaders having gained strong relevance and political space in recent years of turmoil get lion's share of coverage in local newspapers. The local newspapers, therefore, are often 'accused of spreading "pro-Pakistan" and "pro-militant" propaganda when reporting the facts pertaining to the conflict and history of Kashmir' (Khalid 2016; Sreedharan 2009).

The cycle of violence and mass demonstrations in the last decade mobilized the local media in consolidating its role in influencing the regional political discourse. The local newspapers gave exclusive coverage to the civilian killings, the families of victims, impunity of armed forces, and denial of human rights during mass demonstrations. The overwhelming coverage given to the narratives of resistance and conflict in the region by local newspapers antagonised state authorities and security forces which resorted to warnings, restrictions, and complete bans of the newspapers: 'Kashmir Newspaper Ban Criticised' (BBC 2016b). In 2016, the Jammu and Kashmir Government's spokesperson and then Education Minister, Naeem Akhter ordered a complete crackdown on local newspapers (Masood 2016). The newspaper printing presses were raided, the published newspapers were seized, and some reporters were detained (Masood 2016). The leading local daily *Kashmir Reader* was banned for three months during the peak of violence in 2016 by the state government on the allegations that the paper 'contained such material and content which tends to incite acts of violence and disturb public peace and tranquillity' (*Al Jazeera* 2016). The regional media's coverage of the crisis reflected the local political aspirations and mass mobilization in the region, the reason these newspapers were able to retain their readership. The anti-establishment stance in the coverage stemmed from the belief among the readers and media consumers that they faced unabated civilian killings and marginalization in the Indian state (Jamwal 2014).

'Jammu' and 'Kashmir' are the two main administrative regions of the state. Although the regional politics dominate the local media in both Kashmir and Jammu regions, there exist two sub-national media narratives of internal politics; pro-India Jammu and pro-separatist Kashmir (Nazakat 2012). The newspapers in Muslim dominated Kashmir region predominately reflects on the resistance movement, politics of separatism and human rights violations by security forces while the media in Hindu dominated Jammu region is primarily pro-Indian in its coverage of the conflict. This regional distinction of media narratives becomes more intense during the times of heightened crisis in the state (Nazakat 2012). The resurgence of violence and mass alienation in recent years has sharpened regional polarization between Jammu and Kashmir (Tremblay 2009). During the 2008 summer unrest, the local newspapers in Jammu and Kashmir regions displayed sharp 'Jammu' versus 'Kashmir' discourse with both fanning communal fire and becoming the agents of provocation (Jamwal 2014). The news stereotypes found in local newspapers reflect the sub-national regional narratives of the conflict. For instance, the local newspapers in Kashmir region use the terms like, 'resistance movement', 'resistance leaders', and 'militants' while newspapers from Jammu would use terms like 'terrorists', 'anti-nationals', 'army jawans', and 'secessionists'. During the recent killings of a militant commander-Abu Dujana, the leading Kashmir daily *Greater Kashmir* carried the banner headline; 'Funeral prayers in absentia held for Abu Dujana, aide in Kashmir: Joint Resistance Leadership had appealed to people to offer funeral prayers for the slain militants' (*Greater Kashmir* 2017). The leading newspaper in Jammu *Daily Excelsior* carried the following headline for the same incident: 'Top Lashkar terrorist Abu Dujana killed in encounter in Pulwama' (*Daily Excelsior* 2017). The news narratives about the crisis in the region reveal the regional divergences existing within the state.

NATIONAL MEDIA NARRATIVE

The national media coverage of the conflict is contextualized within the parameters of 'national interest' (Joseph 2000; Singh 1995). The news narratives about the day-to-day politics in the region, found in national newspapers and television channels, generally reflect on the idea of 'nationalism' and persistent contestation with Pakistan (Nazakat 2012). Unlike local media narratives of the crisis, national media ignores the political realities on the ground, toes the government's line of national integration and Pakistan's role in destabilizing the 'peace' in the region (Jamwal 2014). The issue of 'cross border terrorism' is an embedded value of Indian news discourse on issues related to Pakistan or the politics of separatism. The national media coverage of diplomatic deliberations with Pakistan vis-à-vis the Kashmir dispute is primarily seen through the reality of sovereignty and security of India, not human rights or regional concerns.

The former Editor-in-Chief of leading national newspaper, *Indian Express*, Shekhar Gupta stated that while covering Kashmir 'the national media has never been truthful with the place as truth was considered against national interests': 'Media was Never Honest with Kashmir' (*Kashmir Life* 2015). The human rights abuses, civilian killings, and the most importantly the resolution of the conflict in the region continue to remain offbeat issues or find a passing reference in the national media (Nazakat 2012). During recent years, the national media's treatment of the political discourse was presented as a concern of 'threat' and mass demonstrations were mostly considered as a threat to the regional peace as this headline suggests: 'Indian Soldiers Are Victims Of Stone Pelters' (*Times Now* 2017). The TRP-driven (Television Rating Points) national news channels have turned television studios into the broadcast War Rooms with cherry picked experts discussing Kashmir problem as the violence continues (Wani 2016). The issue of trending television debates on national channels have been blamed for polarizing the situation in the region by further galvanizing both sides. For instance, while covering the state-wide demonstrations during the peak of the crisis in 2016 unrest, leading national news channel *Times Now* ran a debate on Kashmir crisis titled 'How to Deal With Pro-Pakistanis & Anti-Indians' in its top show *The Newshour*. Such debates have been very frequent across national news channels and are widely watched which is evident from the higher TRPs of these channels. In May 2017, the Chief Minister of the state Mehbooba Mufti openly criticized the national media coverage by saying that 'National media must stop spreading hatred against people of Kashmir' (*The Indian Express* 2017).

The last decade witnessed the revival of separatist politics as the dominant political force in the region and one which receives massive popular support (Chowdhary 2008). The national media's obsession with 'Pakistan factor' while engaging with regional politics in the state has set the discourse based on a perception of 'Pakistan supported' separatism in the region as the main reason for the crisis. This narrative is reflected in the headlines of the national newspapers and television channels: 'How ISI funds stone-pelters via Hurriyat in Kashmir' (*The Times of India* 2017), 'ISI's budget for Kashmir stone pelting is Rs 1,000 cr' (*Sunday Guardian* 2017), 'Pakistan's desperate moves in Kashmir Valley' (*Business Standard* 2016). The senior broadcast journalist, Rajdeep Sardesai, while writing about Indian media's treatment of the conflict in Kashmir argued: 'In a polarised, toxic environment, journalists are being asked to take sides, to state their preferences, to place opinion ahead of facts, to show off their macho "nationalism", to be part of a "them" versus "us" battleground in TV studios and beyond.' (Sardesai 2016)

During the devastating flood in the region in 2014, the national media switched over to embedded reporting by glorifying the rescue operations by Indian Army in their exclusive coverage. Khalid (2016), while preparing a report on media during 2014 Kashmir floods, found that the national media remained entirely busy in covering the crisis from the perspective of 'Indian Jawans saving helpless Kashmir's' while all the human-interest stories regarding victims and local volunteer rescue efforts were completely obscured. During floods, the famous TV journalist, Barkha Dutt tweeted: 'Army & Air Force are risking their own lives to save lives in #JKfloods. Separatists who have only abused the Fauj should feel chastened now' (@BDUTT 2014). The *Al Jazeera* reported that while international media gave reasonable coverage to human interest stories and the survival stories of the victims, Indian news channels 'came under fire for "politicising" the rescue efforts launched by thousands of its soldiers stationed here to quell an armed rebellion that erupted in 1989' (Kanjwal 2014). The flood scenario was a typical case to understand how nationalism and national interest turn out to be the main lens through which the national media covers Kashmir.

PAKISTAN'S MEDIA NARRATIVE

During the 1999 Kargil war, a low level war between India and Pakistan over Kashmir territory, the swarming Indian news channels turned international opinion against Pakistan by 'squeezing out the Pakistani point of view' (Page and Crawley 2005). Pakistan's lone state-sponsored news channel, PTV (Pakistan Television), failed miserably to make any impact in countering Indian media's narrative that was fervently covering and vilifying Pakistan and its strategic position on Kashmir during the war. The then President of Pakistan, General Pervez Musharraf, liberalized the country's broadcast media structure in 2002 to create a 'media deterrent' and counter the onslaughts of Indian media (Jabbar 2003; Siddiqa 2017). For the period between the years 2002 to 2009, a total of 77 new private television channels were launched in Pakistan and 26 foreign channels were allowed to broadcast in the country (PEMRA 2009).

While Indian media which mainstreams Pakistan's role in nurturing regional terrorism and inciting violence in Kashmir region, the media in Pakistan predominantly focuses on what it perceives to be suppression of Kashmiris under 'Indian occupation'. Take for example this headline, 'Kashmir unrest: Pellet Guns usage by Indian forces causes "Dead Eyes" epidemic' (*Pakistan Today* 2016). The distinctive feature of Pakistan's media coverage is that, unlike India, they do not have correspondents on the ground in the region and they mostly rely on news agencies and secondary sources while covering the conflict. Pakistan's media coverage of Kashmir's politics is not consistent or continuous and the media reports only when the violence erupts in the region. The dominant discourse in the news narrative reflects Kashmir as a 'disputed territory' and the internal political elements of the region like state ministers, officials, and other mainstream political actors find no coverage in Pakistani media.

Pakistani media approach to the crisis in Kashmir is mostly historical and the news narratives are mostly thematic which banks on the disputed nature of the region since 1947 and people's repressed right in the region. However, when it comes to the stance on issues of violence, the coverage is pro-national, similar to Indian media, and reflecting on the country's official stance. The discourse found in the news reports is often blended with the nationalist idea of Kashmir's liberation from India. The *Urdu* language dominates the national news media in Pakistan and news media reportage on Kashmir conflict often finds frequent usages of value-laden terms like *Tehreek e Azadi* (freedom movement), *maqbooza Kashmir* (occupied Kashmir), *bharati afwaaj ke mazzalim* (oppression by Indian forces). The militancy in Kashmir finds prominent significance in news narratives with militants being called as 'free-fighters', '*shaheed*' (martyr), '*Jung e Azadi*' (war for freedom) and receive headlines such as 'Top freedom fighter killed in Kashmir' (*Dawn* 2008). The reportage on guerrilla groups is often related to the indigenous struggle for the right to self-determination in the region. During the killing of local militant commander Burhan Wani in 2016, Pakistani news media gave an in-depth coverage to subsequent events in the region with nationalist headlines like 'First martyrdom anniversary of Kashmiri freedom fighter Burhan Wani today' (*Pakistan Today* 2017).

One of the key features of the Pakistani media's approach towards Kashmir is to locate international relevance in the existing political instability in the region that reflects on the country's official diplomatic strategy in the international arena. The news narratives on Kashmir tries to set an international agenda by advocating people's rights and evoking discussions on the United Nations resolutions (UN 1948) on the dispute in the region. The news reports focus on the magnitude of human rights violations in the region to discredit India's legitimacy and attract international attention towards the problems faced by the people in the region (Syed and Naqash 2016).

In 2008, the Jammu and Kashmir government and the Government of India agreed to lease 99 acres of land to Amarnath Shrine Board, a functionary responsible for managing the annual Hindu pilgrimage to Amarnath shrine in the mountains of south Kashmir (Ishfaq ul Hassan 2008). The move was condemned in the local media with separatist groups in the region calling it a 'nefarious' move to dilute state's autonomy and an open violation to the provisions laid under Article 370 of the constitution that stipulated 'provision prohibiting non-Kashmiris from acquiring land in the state' (Ganguly 2009: 44). However, the issue found a communal voice in Pakistani news media, with least focus on the violation of state autonomy. Instead, headlines read, 'Muslims vow protests as Hindus clinch Kashmir land accord' (*Dawn* 2008). This whole issue was seen from the perspective of mounting communal tensions between Muslims and Hindus rather than the issue of land grab by the state. For instance, one of the Pakistani leading news channel's headline read, 'Two dead as Hindus protest over occupied Kashmir land: Report' (*AAJ News* 2008).

Another important characteristic of Pakistani media's coverage of Kashmir issue is their overwhelming support of separatist politics. In Pakistani media narratives on Kashmir conflict, the separatist leaders in the region find great stature and important voice as '*Kashmiri rehnuma*' (Kashmir's leaders), while regional mainstream political parties are brushed off as 'pro-Indian'. The separatist groups operating in the region are projected as the only political 'representatives' of the people with newspaper headlines like: 'Kashmiri leader Geelani placed under house arrest' (*Dawn* 2009), 'Release of Kashmiri pro-freedom leader creates hurdles for Modi' (*Pakistan Today* 2015).

* * *

The coverage of Kashmir conflict involves elements of Indian nationalism, Pakistani nationalism, and bourgeoned local dissent. The diversity in news narratives reflects the contesting political discourses which have further complicated the dimensions of the conflict. The news coverage by Indian and Pakistani media contain value-laden narratives of contestation, demonisation, and victimization that according to Galtung's (2002) classification of conflict reporting encourage 'war journalism'. Moreover, the news reports produced by the media in Indian and Pakistan also promote alienation as they present the conflict with negative linguistic orientation. The ideal news narratives identified by Lynch and McGoldrick (2005) to promote peace and facilitate conflict resolution are absent in the news narratives of India and Pakistan. This argument is also validated by the study conducted by Sreedharan in Kashmir region who found a predominance of 'anti-peace coverage and negative portrayal of the other sides' in the national news media which according to him 'played a destructive role in the Kashmir conflict' (2009: 219).

The media in both the countries approach Kashmir problem with conflict as 'news value' and the coverage is directly proportional to the level of crisis in the region. The narrative during the recent years of violence has been overwhelmingly state-led with pro-government framing. The Indian media while upholding it's nationalistic' and 'patriotic' approach to the conflict in the region, frames the political crises to portray Pakistan as the sponsor of violence in the region while turning a blind eye to state-sponsored repression and human rights abuses by its own security forces. Moreover, due to Indian media's preoccupation with blending Kashmir issue with 'national integration', the regional politics vis-à-vis its relationship with the center continues to remain a news interest for media in the country. One of the intriguing insights from Indian news media is that the rights abuses and the sufferings of the common people in the region are overshadowed by 'anti-Pakistan' narrative and doesn't find any space in the news reports. On the other hand, Pakistani media also has been approaching the crisis only within the context of the country's official stance without any serious deliberations over the resolution of the conflict. They try to benefit from covering violence in the region and promoting the narrative of victimhood to counter India, diplomatically. The media in Pakistan sees the violence in Kashmir as newsworthy but during times of normalcy, Kashmir doesn't find much space in the news media.

However, the local newspapers in the region have survived and evolved through the periods of oppression and intimidation and despite being 'disciplined' time and again, have emerged as the main and most reliable source of news in the region. The local newspapers reflect political ground realities. Unlike, the news coverage of Indian and Pakistani media, the local newspapers have positioned themselves in a way that their coverage reflects a relatively more nuanced and deeper understanding of the politics and conflict. The local news narrative goes far beyond the Indian-Pakistani nationalism binaries to provide coverage to the widespread dissent and human rights violations. The newspapers have a pro-people stance in covering the crisis which is reflected in their human-interest reportage and it is the local media persons who are most often intimidated, threatened and killed and newspapers banned by state and central government.

NOTES

1. The term *'Kashmiriyat'* signifies the ethno-national and socio-cultural consciousness and values of Kashmiri people. The term is often identified with secular and distinct indigenous socio-cultural identity of Kashmir.
2. Registrar of Newspapers for India (2017) Govt of India, New Delhi. Available at http://www.rni.nic.in/registerdtitle_search/registeredtitle_ser.aspx.
3. List of Approved and non-Approved Daily/Bi-weeklies/Weeklies/Fortnightlies/Monthly/Quarterly Newspapers/Magazines of Jammu Division and Kashmir Division. Available at http://www.jkdirinf.in/NewsPapers.aspx.

REFERENCES

Aaj News (2008). 'Two Dead as Hindus Protest over Occupied Kashmir Land: Report'. Retrieved from http://aaj.tv/2008/07/two-dead-as-hindus-protest-over-occupied-kashmir-land-report/ (accessed on 17 August 2018).

Ahmad, Khalid Bashir (2016). 'Kashmir's Media Experience Continuum'. *Kashmir Reader*, 23 August. Retrieved from http://kashmirreader.com/2016/08/23/kashmirs-media-experience-continuum/ (accessed on 17 August 2018).

Al Jazeera (2011). 'Kashmir the Forgotten Conflict'. Retrieved from http://www.aljazeera.com/indepth/spotlight/kashmirtheforgottenconflict/2011/7/2011715143415277754.html (accessed on 11 January 2017).

Al Jazeera (2016). 'Kashmir Newspaper Banned for "Inciting Violence"', 3 October. Retrieved from https://www.aljazeera.com/news/2016/10/kashmir-newspaper-banned-inciting-violence-161003061348246.html (accessed on 12 September 2018).

Bamzai, Prithivi Nath Kaul (1994). *Culture and Political History of Kashmir*, vol. 1. New Delhi: MD Publications.

BBC (2016a). 'India Kashmir: The Teenager Blinded by Pellets'. Retrieved from http://www.bbc.com/news/world-asia-india-37773759 (accessed on 17 August 2018).

———— (2016b). 'Kashmir Newspaper Ban Criticised'. Retrieved from http://www.bbc.com/news/world-asia-india-37559679 (accessed on 17 August 2018).

Business Standard (2016). 'Pakistan's Desperate Moves in Kashmir Valley'. Retrieved from http://www.business-standard.com/article/news-ani/pakistan-s-desperate-moves-in-kashmir-valley-116072000131_1.html (accessed on 17 August 2018).

Chakravartty, Paula and Srirupa Roy (2013). 'Media Pluralism Redux: Towards New Frameworks of Comparative Media Studies "Beyond the West"'. *Political Communication*, 30(3): 349–70.

Chowdhary, Rekha (2008). 'Electioneering in Kashmir: Overlap between Separatist and Mainstream Political Space'. *Economic and Political Weekly*, 43(28): 22–5.

Cottle, Simon (2008). 'Reporting Demonstrations: The Changing Media Politics of Dissent'. *Media, Culture and Society*, 30(6): 853–72.

Daily Excelsior (2017). 'Top Lashkar Terrorist Abu Dujana Killed in Encounter in Pulwama'. Retrieved from http://www.dailyexcelsior.com/top-lashkar-terrorist-abu-dujana-killed-in-encounter-in-pulwama-2/ (accessed on 17 August 2018).

Dawn (2008a). 'Muslims Vow Protests as Hindus Clinch Kashmir Land Accord'. Retrieved from https://www.dawn.com/news/319233 (accessed on 17 August 2018).

———— (2008b). 'Top Freedom Fighter Killed in Kashmir'. Retrieved from https://www.dawn.com/news/955366/top-freedom-fighter-killed-in-kashmir (accessed on 17 August 2018).

———— (2009). 'Kashmiri Leader Placed under House Arrest'. Retrieved from https://www.dawn.com/news/912466/kashmiri-leader-geelani-placed-under-house-arrest (accessed on 17 August 2018).

Dutt, Barkha (@bdutt) (2014). 'Army & Air Force are risking their own lives to save lives in #JKfloods. Separatists who have only abused the Fauj should feel chastened now'. Twitter post. Available at https://twitter.com/BDUTT/status/509220895550742529 (accessed on 17 August 2018).

Evans, Alexander (2000). 'The Kashmir Insurgency: As Bad as It Gets'. *Small Wars and Insurgencies*, 11: 69–81.

Galtung, Johan (2002). 'Peace Journalism: A Challenge'. *Journalism and the New World Order*, 2: 259–72.

Ganguly, Sumit (2009). 'India in 2008: Domestic Turmoil and External Hopes'. *Asian Survey*, 49(1): 39–52.

Greater Kashmir (2010). 'Govt Bans SEN TV Network'. Retrieved from http://www.greaterkashmir.com/news/news/govt-bans-sen-tv network/ 80239.html (accessed on 17 August 2018).

———— (2017). 'Funeral Prayers in Absentia Held for Abu Dujana, Aide in Kashmir'. Retrieved from http://www.greaterkashmir.com/news/kashmir/ funeral-prayers-in-absentia-held-for-abu-dujana-aide-in-kashmir/ 256484.html (accessed on 17 August 2018).

Hassan, Ishfaq ul (2008). 'Amarnath Land Transfer Order Revoked'. *DNA*, 2 July. Retrieved from http://www.dnaindia.com/india/report-amarnath-land-transfer-order-revoked-1175009 (accessed on 17 August 2018).

HRW (Human Rights Watch) 1996. 'India's Secret Army in Kashmir: New Patterns of Abuse Emerge in the Conflict'. Retrieved from https://www. hrw.org/reports/1996/India2.htm (accessed on 17 August 2018).

IFEX (1996). 'Indian-Backed Militia in Kashmir Abducts and Detains 19 Journalists for over Seven Hours'. Retrieved from https://www.ifex.org/ india/1996/07/09/indian_backed_militia_in_kashmir/ (accessed on 17 August 2018).

Indian Express (2017). 'National Media Must Stop Spreading Hatred against People of Kashmir'. Retrieved from https://indianexpress.com/ article/india/national-media-must-stop-spreading-hatred-against-people-of-kashmir-cm-mehbooba-mufti-4645621/ (accessed on 17 August 2018).

Jabbar, Javed (2003). 'To Ban or Not to Ban?' *Newsline*. Retrieved from http:// www.newsline.com.pk/newsSep2003/guestsep.html.

Jamwal, Anuradha B. (2014). 'Kashmir's Media History'. *Himal Magazine*, 18 July. Retrieved from http://himalmag.com/kashmirs-media-story/ (accessed on 17 August 2018).

Jeffrey, Robin (2003). *India's Newspaper Revolution Capitalism, Politics, and the Indian Language Press, 1977–99*. London: C. Hurst and Co.

Joseph, Teresa (2000). 'Kashmir, Human Rights and the Indian Press'. *Contemporary South Asia*, 9(1): 41–55.

Kanjwal, Hafsa (2014). 'India Turns Kashmir Flood Disaster into PR Stunt'. *Al Jazeera*, 20 September. Retrieved from http://america.aljazeera.com/ opinions/2014/9/kashmir-floods-indiarescuereliefeffort.html (accessed on 17 August 2018).

Kashmir Life (2010). 'Yousuf Jameel, 2010'. Retrieved from http://kashmirlife. net/yusuf-jameel-srinagar-10863/ (accessed on 17 August 2018).

———— (2015). 'Media Was Never Honest with Kashmir: Journalist Shekhar Gupta'. Retrieved from http://kashmirlife.net/media-was-never-honest-with-kashmir-journalist-shekhar-gupta-87403/ (accessed on 17 August 2018).

Kashmir Newz (2008). '10 Journalists Killed in Kashmir Insurgency'. Retrieved from https://www.kashmirnewz.com/n000366.html (accessed on 12 September 2018).

Kazi, Seema (2009). 'Shopian: War, Gender and Democracy in Kashmir'. *Economic and Political Weekly*, 44(49): 13–15.

Khalid, Wasim (2016). 'Media Propaganda and the Kashmir Dispute: A Case Study of the Kashmir Floods'. Report, Thomson Reuters Foundation, UK, August.

Lynch, Jake and Annabel McGoldrick (2005). *Peace Journalism*. Stroud: Hawthorn Press.

Mahajan, Nitin (2017). 'DD Kashir Revamp Aims to Counter Propaganda', *Asian Age*, 26 June. Retrieved from http://www.asianage.com/india/all-india/260617/dd-kashir-revamp-aims-to-counter-propaganda.html (accessed on 17 August 2018).

Masood, Bashaarat (2016). 'Kashmir Gagged: Newspaper Presses Raided, Editors Say Staff= Held'. *Indian Express*, 17 July, Retrieved from http://indianexpress.com/article/india/india-news-india/kashmir-violence-protest-burhan-wani-killing-media-blockade-newspaper-raid-staff-held-2918852/ (accessed on 17 August 2018).

Mishra, Abhinandan (2017). 'ISI's Budget for Kashmir Stone Pelting is Rs 1,000 Cr'. *Sunday Guardian*, 2 April. Retrieved from http://www.sundayguardianlive.com/news/8956-isi-s-budget-kashmir-stone-pelting-rs-1000cr (accessed on 17 August 2018).

Nazakat, Syed (2012). 'Indian Media Coverage of Kashmir When Stories Clash with National Interest'. *Asia Pacific Media Educator*, 22(1): 69–74.

New York Times (2017). 'Cruelty and Cowardice in Kashmir'. Retrieved from https://www.nytimes.com/2017/04/21/opinion/cruelty-and-cowardice-in-kashmir.html?mcubz=3 (accessed on 17 August 2018).

Neyazi, Taberez A. (2011). 'Politics after Vernacularisation: Hindi Media and Indian Democracy'. *Economic and Political Weekly*, special article, 46(10): 75–82.

———— (2014). 'News Media and Political Participation: Re-evaluating Democratic Deepening in India'. In *Democratic Transformation and the Vernacular Public Arena in India*, eds Taberez A. Neyazi, Akio Tanabe, and Shinya Ishizaka, pp. 76–94. London: Routledge.

Page, David and William Crawley (2005). 'The Transnational and the National: Changing Patterns of Cultural Influence in the South Asian TV Market'. In *Transnational Television Worldwide: Towards a New Media Order*, ed. J. K. Chalaby, pp. 128–55. London: I.B. Tauris.

Pakistan Today (2015). 'Release of Kashmiri Pro-freedom Leader Creates Hurdles for Modi'. Retrieved from https://www.pakistantoday.com.pk/2015/03/10/release-of-kashmiri-pro-freedom-leader-creates-hurdles-for-modi/ (accessed on 17 August 2018).

———— (2016). 'Kashmir Unrest: Pellet Guns Usage by Indian Forces Causes "Dead Eyes" Epidemic'. Retrieved from https://www.pakistantoday.com.pk/2016/08/29/kashmir-unrest-pellet-guns-usage-by-indian-forcs.causes-dead-eyes-epidemic/ (accessed on 17 August 2018).

———— (2017). 'First Martyrdom Anniversary of Kashmiri Freedom Fighter Burhan Wani Today'. Retrieved from https://www.pakistantoday.com.pk/2017/07/08/first-martyrdom-anniversary-of-kashmiri-freedom-fighter-burhan-wani-today/ (accessed on 17 August 2018).

PEMRA (2009). *Annual Report, 2009*. Retrieved from http://www.pemra.gov.pk/pdf/Annaul_Report.pdf.

Sardesai, Rajdeep (2016). 'Stop Questioning Media's "Patriotism" in Covering Burhan Wani's Death'. *Dailyo.in*, 11 July. Retrieved from http://www.dailyo.in/politics/burhan-wani-kashmir-militancy-tral-kokernag-azaadi-kashmiri-pandits-journalism-twitter-trolls abuse/story/1/11676.html (accessed on 17 August 2018).

Schofield, Victoria (2003). *Kashmir in Conflict: India, Pakistan and the Unending War*. London: IB Tauris.

Seib, Philip (ed.) (2005). *Media and Conflict in the Twenty-first Century*. New York: Springer.

Siddiqa, Ayesha (2017). *Military Inc.: Inside Pakistan's Military Economy*. New Delhi: Penguin Random House India.

Singh, Tavleen (1995). *Kashmir: A Tragedy of Errors*. New Delhi: Viking Books.

Sofi, Mohiuddin G. (1973). *Jammu-Wa-Kashmir Meen Urdu Suhafat*. Srinagar.

Sreedharan, Chindu (2009). 'Reporting Kashmir: An Analysis of the Conflict Coverage in Indian and Pakistani Newspapers'. PhD dissertation, Bournemouth University.

Stahlberg, Per (2013). *Writing Society through Media: Ethnography of a Hindi Daily*. New Delhi: Rawat.

Syed, Syed B. and T. Naqash (2016). 'Pakistan, India Set to Clash on Kashmir at UN'. *Dawn*, 17 September. Retrieved from https://www.dawn.com/news/1284310 (accessed on 17 August 2018).

Tekwani, Shyam (2008). *Media & Conflict Reporting in Asia*. Singapore: Asian.

Times of India (2017). 'How ISI Funds Stone-Pelters via Hurriyat in Kashmir'. Retrieved from http://timesofindia.indiatimes.com/india/how-isi-funds-stone-pelters-via-hurriyat-in-kashmir-times-now/articleshow/58546402.cms (accessed on 17 August 2018).

Times Now (2016). 'How to Deal with Pro-Pakistanis & Anti-Indians'. Retrieved from https://www.youtube.com/watch?v=M8jtVBt28nU (accessed on 17 August 2018).

——— (2017). 'Indian Soldiers Are Victims of Stone Pelters'. Retrieved from https://www.youtube.com/watch?v=YCcJpqEMgcg (accessed on 17 August 2018).

Tremblay, Reeta Chowdhari (2009). 'Kashmir's Secessionist Movement Resurfaces: Ethnic Identity, Community Competition, and the State'. *Asian Survey*, 49(6): 924–50.

UN (United Nations) (1948). 'Resolutions Adopted by Security Council in 1948'. Retrieved from http://www.un.org/en/ga/search/view_doc.asp?symbol=S/RES/47(1948) (accessed 21 January 2017).

Wani, Gull (2016). 'Kashmir and the National Media'. *Greater Kashmir*, 3 June. Retrieved from http://www.greaterkashmir.com/news/op-ed/kashmir-and-the-national-media/219409.html (accessed on 17 August 2018).

Zutshi, Chitralekha (2004). *Languages of Belonging: Islam, Regional Identity, and the Making of Kashmir*. London: Hurst.

CHAPTER THIRTEEN

Covering the Green Beat

Environmental Journalism in India

RAM AWTAR YADAV
AND KANCHAN K. MALIK

. . . .

India has witnessed incredible and enduring environmental struggles, such as the Chipko Movement, Silent Valley Project, Navdanya Movement, Narmada Bachao Andolan, and more. At the same time, there is also a history of toil by celebrity journalists who have dedicated themselves to development reporting and to campaigning against the degradation of the environment. Environmental journalism got a boost with the formation of the Forum of Environmental Journalists in India (FEJI) in the 1980s. However, with the advent of liberalization in India in the 1990s, the predominance of economic concerns led to a shrinking of space for environmental issues in news reports. While India, even today, grapples with serious environmental concerns—climate change, deforestation, air and water pollution, increasing frequency of floods, droughts, and hailstorms, and so on—media coverage of these subjects appears to have dwindled.

The attempt of this chapter is to explore the journalistic traditions of environmental journalism in India, and to map the visible current trends in covering the green beat. In doing so, the authors also attempt to explain the role that journalists are playing, against all odds, in setting the public agenda for discussions on current and emerging environmental themes—both locally and nationally.

The chapter draws attention to the complexity of environmental reporting and how it is not just about covering natural disasters. There are challenges and difficulties that journalists encounter in crafting accurate narratives on contested topics that sometimes require interdisciplinary expertise for a penetrating analysis, comprehensible to readers. The authors also attempt to summarize ethical, political, economic, and professional constraints that drive media coverage of the environment in India.

THE BEGINNINGS

Human civilizations across the world have always longed for better living, in every age. And to attain a better quality of life, they have always explored new things around them. In the process, they kept inventing and discovering new things that would fulfil their varied needs. In doing so, they seemed to have become so obsessed that their longing for more of everything does not seem to have an end. This obsession has, today, become a new culture called 'consumerism', which means ever-increasing demands for goods and services. The seeds of this culture were sown more than 200 years ago with the beginning of the Industrial Revolution, which had a tremendous impact on all spheres of human life (Fine and Leopold 1990; Dancea and Merce 2009). Like many Western nations that blindly adopted the industrial growth models for economic development, especially in the eighteenth century, ignoring its harmful effects on the environment, India too witnessed ecological innocence after independence as the urge, then, was to industrialize to catch up with the developed world where environmental concerns were never a priority (Guha 2006). Therefore, in the quest for development, the relentless exploitation of nature began only to be noticed in India a few decades later.

With the process of industrialization and ruthless exploitation of natural resources like forests, land, and water for the next few decades, issues related to environmental degradation started coming to light, forcing affected and concerned people to spring into action. The rapid exploitation of natural resources like forests resulted in some resistance in the early part of 1970s, which later took the shape of a crusade called Chipko Andolan, where Himalayan women launched a movement to hug the trees as timber producers engaged in persistent felling of trees in the Garhwal region of Uttar Pradesh (now Uttarakhand). The movement set the tone for other environmental movements in the country. It was during this movement that environmental reporting gained tremendous momentum in India. If one has to talk about environmental journalism in India, one would have to locate it against the backdrop of such environmental movements between 1970 and 1985, according to Shah and Shah (2008). The Chipko Movement in the Himalayan mountain range got international attention because of the extensive media coverage it acquired.

Many prominent figures emerged after these movements who communicated environmental concerns and brought them to the locus of environmental discourses India. Anil Agarwal, Ramachandra Guha, Sunita Narain, Madhav Gadgil, Vandana Shiva, and others are a few among them. These environmental writers were instrumental in building some pressure on the government to act to protect nature and people. Although they contributed in communicating environmental messages to the society in their own different ways, their actions towards the protection of the environment and, hence, for people's future saw the emergence of a community of environmental communicators which only kept growing with the passage of time.

The formation of FEJI in the late 1980s gave momentum to the process of communicating environmental crises, as it helped journalists across the country reporting on environmental beats to join hands to deal with a complex situation which was posing a severe threat to human existence. The forum, with its regular workshops, training programmes for environmental journalists, publications, and newsletters on environmental matters gave a further push to the field of environmental journalism in India during the 1990s and 2000s.

Organizations like the Centre for Science and Environment (CSE), The Energy Research Institute (TERI), the Indian Environmental Society, Centre for Environmental Education, and others have also contributed deeply in producing literature, revealing the worrisome state of India's environment, raising awareness among people, and also suggesting ways to the government to draft new policies and introduce new laws to protect the environment. The publication of *Down to Earth*, a science and environment fortnightly that CSE initiated in partnership with its sister organization, the Society for Environmental Communications, in May 1992 sought to create awareness about the challenges of local and global environmental management, and was a big step forward in the field of environmental journalism.

Meanwhile, even as the number of environmentally dedicated institutions, groups, activists, and concerned individuals was increasing, paradoxically, environmental crises seemed to be worsening. The devastating flash flood in Uttarakhand in 2013 that claimed thousands of lives; recurring droughts in several parts of the country including the Bundelkhand region in central India and Vidarbha in Maharashtra; other frequent weather events like hailstorms, floods, extreme heat waves, and hurricanes; dying water bodies leading to severe water scarcity in many parts of India; increasing pollution levels in air and water; deforestation; as well as relentless urbanization causing ecological imbalances—are challenges that the present human society is already coping with. These, and other harsh realities such as global warming, environmental migration, and fatal diseases caused by pollution, point towards the environmental concerns that future generations will have to gear themselves up to face.

Environmental journalism's trajectory in India has seen a frequent rise and fall in different periods. While media coverage of environmental campaigns, especially the *padyatras* (foot marches) and rallies led by prominent environmental activists like Sunderlal Bahuguna and Baba Amte, did help build some environmental consciousness among citizens in the late 1980s, economic liberalization in 1991 caused a drastic change in the media landscape of the country. The sudden transformation in the political economy of media organizations witnessed in the 1990s was certain to make a huge impact on how environmental issues were reported in media.

254   *Ram Awtar Yadav and Kanchan K. Malik*

Most media houses came to be either owned or controlled by corporate houses with vested interests, posing a grim challenge to environmental journalists in covering and dealing with numerous environmental threats.

ENVIRONMENTAL COVERAGE IN THE 1970s AND 1980s

The origin of some sort of environmental journalism in India might be traced to the 1920s, when environmental thinkers and writers like J. C. Kumarappa, a Tamilian economist, social scientists like Radhakamal Mukherjee, and Albert Howard, a dissident colonial scientist, in their writings talked about nature's conservation even as the country was stepping up to become an industrialized society (Govindu and Malghan 2005). Their writings, in that era, were considered as nature writing, as the field of environmental journalism was yet to evolve properly.

If we talk about the beginning of environmental reporting in India, it too began in 1920 when the Tatas were building a dam on a river in the Western Ghats near Lonavala, which resulted in a protest led by the socialist and nationalist Pandurang Mahadev, also popularly known as Senapati Bapat, as the dam was going to displace around 15–20 villages in the region. The agitation was prominently covered in newspapers like *Times of India* and the *Bombay Chronicle*, with their reports and articles generating debates on topics like power for Bombay versus land for peasants (Shah and Shah 2008). In the late 1930s, another writer, S. G. Warty, wrote several articles in the *Bombay Chronicle* on different issues, ranging from flaws in the colonial forest policy to peasants' needs and forest management to benefit the peasants. In the 1950s and the following decades, another prominent naturalist, M. Krishnan, wrote extensively on nature and its conservation in the *Statesman*. Recognized for his deep understanding and observations of nature and its fascinating aspects, reflected in his writings on a wide range of topics like preserving indigenous breeds of cattle, the significance of neem, and so on, Krishnan is considered one of the pioneers among environmental journalists in India.

After India won independence in 1947, like many Western nations, it too saw a debate between modernizers and the conservationists.

While the conservationists advocated the idea of respecting the natural wealth and coexisting with it, the former believed that advocating the idea of natural conservation was an impediment towards attaining economic growth and becoming an industrially strong nation. Unfortunately, the modernizers emerged victorious in the debate, as environmental considerations were kept on the back burner after the country's achievement of freedom.

But environmental concerns kept growing among ecologically responsible people, and resurfaced in the form of people's movements, as evident in struggles like the Chipko Andolan (1970s), Appiko movement (1980s), the fisherfolk movement in Kerala (1977–94), the forest movements in Bihar, Jharkhand, and Madhya Pradesh (1980s), the anti-dam movement in the Narmada valley (1985), Koel Karo resistance (1980s), Tehri Dam movement (1980s), and many others. Interestingly, when one tries to trace the beginnings of active environmental journalism in India, one finds that the media started taking an interest in environmental issues in the early 1970s (Mahapatra 2010), which was a time when environmental movements were gaining ground in the country. So, it could be said that environmental journalism in India started alongside the movements in the 1970s which caught the attention of the people and helped in shaping a consciousness and awareness among them about the model of development that was unsustainable.

During the mid-1970s, owing to these movements and struggles by the people, there was a kind of explosion in environmental writing that was reflected mostly in print media, as radio and television were controlled by the state (Gadgil and Guha 1994). The Chipko Movement, being of a very unique kind, got widespread coverage in the media not only within the country but also in the West, where people came to know of it as the 'tree-hugging movement'. This was one of the first movements in developing nations to protect forests. Besides the emergence of several people's movements of this kind for the protection of natural resources and to save the ecology in the mid- and late 1970s, the Bhopal gas tragedy in 1984, considered one of the biggest industrial catastrophes on earth, also resulted in extensive coverage of environmental issues in the media. The Bhopal gas leakage disaster that claimed thousands of lives immediately and affected tens of thousands in the aftermath, not only attracted the attention of the national media, but also got extensive coverage in global media, and for a long period of time. Therefore, the decade from 1975 to 1985 seems to have been an alive phase of environmental coverage in the media.

The establishment of the CSE in 1980 by the late Anil Agrawal was actually the beginning of a new era of green journalism in India. Similarly, the formation of FEJI in 1988 gave a further impetus to the field by offering a platform to all environmental communicators to come together and write about environmental issues.

Then came liberalization in the 1990s, which was all set to bring about a drastic change in how environment-related issues were reported in the media, with 'growth' suddenly becoming the buzzword (Mahapatra 2010). This was the time when the sharp contrast between the traditional lifestyle (considered typical of the rural way of life) with its belief in the judicious use of natural resources, and the new economic model (considered indicative of urban living) looking to exploit available resources for economic growth, came to the fore like never before. Consequently, the emergence of the new economic growth model also brought with it a stronger environmentalism in India, which saw the participation of the middle-class population of the country, especially those residing in urban areas, in environmental struggles— a population that, until then, had been hardly bothered about environmental issues.

The personal sympathy and sensitivity of many journalists and columnists were among the major factors that helped the people's protests for environmental protection gain significant space in the mainstream media. While environmentalism in India got recognition internationally because of the above-mentioned movements, and the widespread media coverage they received, CSE's campaign against the use of pesticides in bottled water, soft drinks like Pepsi and Coke, and so on, gave a further push to the practice of environmental journalism in the country. The fast and prominently emerging environmental degradation concerns resulted in some environmental awareness and a national consciousness which was, to a great extent, a result of these issues being represented by the media, involving various activists, environmentalists, and institutions working in the sector.

GREEN JOURNALISM IN THE LIBERALIZATION-PRIVATIZATION-GLOBALIZATION ERA

The biggest challenge for the field of environmental journalism after economic liberalization in 1991 was to strike a balance between two streams of thought, wherein the economic model based on local ecology and its judicious use stood in conflict with the priorities of the government, which envisioned that bringing in investments in the private sector would help in attaining prosperity (Mahapatra 2010). As the new economic development model was becoming the accepted mode of development in the country, the environment seemed to be fast losing its relevance as a public good, and hence, the relentless exploitation of natural resources was on the cards. According to a senior journalist, Lyla Bavadam (2010), the present economic model of development which treats everything else in nature as a thing to be utilized by human beings for their consumption, is an important challenge. It is a big hurdle not only in any kind of environmental movement, but in environmental reporting as well. Therefore, for Mahapatra (2010: 21), 'this conflict of interests of perspectives and modes of development' is the greatest challenge to environmental journalism in India after liberalization.

The challenge posed by the economic model to the green beat is further described by Mahapatra (2010: 21) when he says:

> The challenge is more daunting as economic liberalisation is the accepted mode of delivering economic goods. From the prime minister to public relation officers of corporate houses, environment reporters are the most debated species. Policy makers often term environment journalists as 'people practicing socialism as time pass'. Industries see them as 'less progressive'. Even inside national media houses, environment as a subject of reportage is reserved for 'old school students'. An environment reporter occasionally celebrates his or her existence in case of an extraordinary environmental event. The rest of the time they just remain in the margin, waiting for the next big event.

The newly emerged economic model in the country also brought drastic changes in the ownership patterns of the media industry, and most media houses came under the complete ownership or control of the corporate houses. This, coupled with cross-ownership in business, were among the factors that led to the dwindling of environmental coverage in the media and to the curtailing of the freedom of the press in writing on contentious issues like the environment. A palpable example of such constraints came to the fore when the national Hindi daily, *Dainik Bhaskar* in Chhattisgarh, turned a blind eye towards the protests and agitations of the local people against a coal mine project, and remained sympathetic to the interests of the industry, as its parent organization DB Corp. Ltd had major stakes in the power and mining sector (Sharma 2013). While the liberalization that attracted innumerable foreign firms to invest in India saw economic growth go up almost twofold, the issues of environmental degradation, poverty, displacement, pollution, and so on started aggravating at a faster rate. But unfortunately, the relationship between environmental problems and poverty and migration were neither understood nor represented properly in the media, as a result of which they did not receive much favour in the public sphere.

The new economic policies and the changing media landscape also saw the shrinking of the news hole for environmental issues in media. Many journalists covering the environment or related beats faced difficulties in finding spaces for their stories within their media organizations. The squeezing of the space in the media has been aptly described by Warrier (2010: 33) in the following manner:

> The marginalisation and loss of space for environmental discussions in the national consciousness had its impact on environmental journalists. They too felt the squeeze for space to express themselves in their publications and TV and radio channels, a decade after the economic liberalisation process had started. 'No, not another environment story,' is usually the refrain that many environment journalists heard.... Baptised into the world of classical environmental controversies, many of these journalists failed to see the space closing. However, there were some who saw the changes coming and had started reporting on the emerging environmental issues such as the green markets and green diplomacy. Unfortunately they were unable to convince their seniors of the growing significance of these areas. Editors and managements considered anything green as peripheral to journalism. And many environmental journalists moved away from actively reporting the subject.

Another consequence of liberalization, however, was that the middle class suddenly acquired an important role in the society as consumers. Mahapatra (2010) suggests that a parallel shift also happened in environmentalism, from being driven by common people's movements to the middle class talking about environmental issues. As the middle class was a beneficiary of the new economic boom, their debates did not necessarily pin the moral authority for environmental degradation on the government or corporates.

Warrier (2010) observes that with this shift of the environmental discussion in the country from the communities to the middle-class urbanite, the tools also changed, from those of the slogan-shouting, fasting members of environment movements 'to fighting legal cases, media campaigns, lobbying with parliamentarians, policy advocacy and warfare through email and the Internet' (Warrier 2010: 32). This middle-class-centred environmentalism in India thus took on a new language, more in sync with the global trends of green diplomacy, and one that was spurred on by a growing market for environmental goods and services. The media also bought into such trends and some of these more global, but passive, characteristics started manifesting themselves in environmental reporting in India.

The 1990s also saw the Indian judiciary playing a crucial role in the protection of the environment and natural resources. Activist lawyers like M. C. Mehta filed several cases against industries and the government who were responsible for large-scale pollution of the environment (Warrier 2010). Justice Kuldeep Singh, who was popularly known as the 'Green Judge', hearing the cases filed by Mehta, gave several historic verdicts, like ordering the closure of 84 plants in Uttar Pradesh for polluting the environment and the holy river Ganges, and of 30 plants in West Bengal, besides asking many of them to pay for the environmental damages already inflicted, observing, 'We are conscious that the closure of the tanneries may bring unemployment, loss of revenue but the life, health and ecology have greater importance' (Houck 2010). The court especially emphasized the dissemination of environmental messages through media and the production of documentaries on environmental issues like pollution, nature, and so on, saying it was important in the first place to make citizens aware of the ill impacts of pollution to solicit their support for initiatives to protect the ecology.

These remarkable environmental cases and verdicts kept the environment in media focus from the mid-1980s through the entire decade of the 1990s and into the next century, as the hearing of the cases went on for years. The strong verdicts that admonished the central and the state governments, pollution control boards, and others for pollution, illegal mining, and other issues, pronounced by the apex court of the country in the following years while hearing the PILs (public interest litigations) filed by various individuals, saw the rise of judicial activism in India. Apart from these, there were also judgments on several so-called development projects, asking them to be suspended looking at the potential risks they posed to the ecology, especially in the coastal region; for example, the Goshree project in Kochi.

Similarly, hearing a petition filed by M. C. Mehta in 1998, the Supreme Court ordered that all the buses in New Delhi running on diesel be converted to CNG (compressed natural gas). This did not go down well with the government or the affiliated agencies, but the apex court was stern, looking at the amount of air pollution caused by the buses in the national capital. Heavy fines were also imposed on operators who failed to abide by the mandate. The PIL proved to be an empowering tool for the common people especially, when it came to identifying environment-related problems and seeking their redressal from the courts (R. Jain 2014). This way, issues related to the environment, the trials, and the court's decisions kept appearing in the media, particularly in newspapers, off and on.

PROSPECTS AND CHALLENGES FOR ENVIRONMENTAL JOURNALISM IN THE TWENTY-FIRST CENTURY

The judicial activism which started during the last decade of the twentieth century, continued into the next century. One of the major developments owing to the Supreme Court's clear and stern approach towards protecting the environment and safeguarding people's right to healthy living, was its directing the union government to set up an environmental regulatory body with branches in all the states to look after the cases related to environmental clearances and monitor the conditions according to the provisions of the Environmental Impact Assessment Notification of 2006.

The apex court of India played a crucial role in several high-profile cases like Vedanta's bauxite mining project in the Niyamgiri Hills and a steel plant proposed by South Korean firm Posco in the Khandadhar Hills near Paradeep in Odisha. While Vedanta's mining project was rejected outright by the Union Ministry of Environment, in January 2014, Posco's steel plant was given a green signal after delinking other components of the integrated project, including the port and the mining works, abiding by the directions issued by the Supreme Court and the National Green Tribunal (NGT). These proceedings at the Supreme Court saw issues like ecology, forest, and environment continuously featuring in the mainstream media. Reports of other cases at the Supreme Court, such as the Kudankulam nuclear plant in Tamil Nadu, persistent pollution in the Yamuna river regarding which the central as well as the state governments of Delhi, Haryana, and Uttar Pradesh were reprimanded by the apex court for their failure to curb pollution in the river, illegal mining in Odisha and Jharkhand, and recently, the odd–even scheme for road rationing in Delhi, have kept environmental coverage afloat in the national media.

The other important factors that gave a substantial amount of media coverage to environmental and climate change were global environmental concerns as well as politics in the form of international conventions and conferences on the environment, like the Conference of Parties (COP) under the United Nations Framework Convention on Climate Change; international summits on the environment, sustainable development, and so on; natural disasters and weather events which have increased manifold in frequency in the last two decades or so (Boykoff and Roberts 2007–8; Boykoff 2009; Banholzer et al. 2014). A good thing about Indian media is that, unlike scepticism in the North American and European media, the Indian media completely endorses climate change as a reality and most media reports directly attribute anthropogenic activities as the cause of climate change (Billet 2009).

Several significant developments took place in India with the onset of the twenty-first century that brought about remarkable changes in the way journalism was practised. The flow of information was faster compared to the 1980s and 1990s on environmental issues, thanks to the various active civil society groups and individual activists. Besides, the rapid growth in information technology and increasing affordability of the internet, computers, and so on, among the middle-class population have made a vast resource of information accessible to people across borders. The journalistic community across the world, including India, has fast adapted to the new technological developments, which, in a way, have revolutionized the way journalism is practised. The sources of news stories are becoming more reachable with new means of communication like mobile, e-mail, text messages, and so on. These technological developments in the society and media industry have helped journalists to work on their stories and assignments more efficiently and enabled them to collect background materials and other related information with greater ease. The Right to Information (RTI) Act further empowered journalists with a tool which enabled them to collect crucial information from government departments and agencies with great ease, for which they had had to toil hard earlier (Mahapatra 2010).[1] The development of the internet and the world wide web and its fast evolution also enabled many institutions and individuals to start their own websites and blogs and share their own stories, observations, and experiences about the earth and its environmental health.

With the passage of time, activists, civil society organizations, and various institutions like CSE and TERI continued producing literature that underlined the stresses on the earth's ecology due to the relentless exploitation of natural resources, increasing atmospheric pressure, rising sea level, melting glaciers, changing rainfall patters, failing agriculture, drying water bodies, polluted rivers, drought, floods, and so on. Also, FEJI produced relevant literature in the forms of books and newsletters apart from holding training and workshops for environmental journalists for the effective dissemination of environment-related stories to the masses in a way that could build opinion in favour of the earth and its environment.

The NGT, set up in 2010 for effective and expeditious disposal of cases related to environmental protection and conservation of forests and other natural resources, had its branches opened in various state capitals and other cities, which turned out to be one of the important sources for environmental news stories for journalists. The journalists in the national capital as well as the state capitals covering the green beat have found some kind of story or the other originating from here almost every day. Recently, in March 2016, the NGT slapping a fine of Rs 5 crore on Sri Sri Ravishankar's Art of Living Foundation for organizing a three-day 'World Cultural Festival' on the floodplains of the Yamuna was an event covered widely by Indian media. The Art of Living Foundation was also directed by the NGT to bear the cost of restoring the area as a biodiversity park after the event, as it held the foundation responsible for damage to the ecology, environment, biodiversity, and aquatic life. All these developments offered a huge prospect for environmental journalists to delve deeper into the field and write and present insightful and analytical environmental stories for their respective media houses.

However, studies suggest that the space for environmental reporting has been shrinking in many countries including the USA, UK, and India, even as environmental crises are only getting worse with the squeezing of the news hole for the beat, as most journalists report on the environment only during events like conferences, seminars, or conventions; or at a time of natural disaster or weather events like a flood, tsunami, hurricane, drought, hailstorm, and so on (Acharya and Noronha 2010; Friedman 2004, 2015). Many of the reports also lacked the idea of using the information for shaping public opinion and raising national consciousness on environmental stresses, as seen during the media coverage of the Paris Agreement during COP 21 in November–December 2015, where the media reported widely on the target set by the countries involved to prevent rise in temperature beyond 2 degrees Celsius, but did not delve deep into the complexities and challenges (Jayaraman and Kanitkar 2016). And this shows the lack of ability among most journalists in the national media to critically look at the national and international discourses around the environment and climate change.

Another serious point of concern for the green scribes is the physical threats they receive from different individuals and organizations indulging in activities like illegal mining, land encroachments, and other projects degrading the environment. Those working from small towns and remote areas, especially as stringers or freelancers, face more risks compared to those working in cities where they have organizational backing. According to the annual Impunity Index of the Committee to Protect Journalists (CPJ), India ranked quite high at 13 and 14 in 2014 and 2015, respectively, as 11 journalists were killed in India between 1 September 2005 and 31 August 2015 without a single perpetrator being convicted (CPJ 2015). All these 11 murders, the CPJ report confirmed, were work-related killing with complete impunity. Murders of UP-based local journalist Jagendra Singh, and of Sandeep Kothari, a local journalist from the Balaghat district of Madhya Pradesh, both of whom reported on illegal mining in their respective areas, were examples of such killings with impunity. Singh, in a statement made before his death, alleged that he was set on fire by the police at the behest of a state government minister. A few days after Jagendra's death, another journalist, Haider Khan, was thrashed and dragged behind a car in Pilibhit district of Uttar Pradesh, allegedly for his reports on dubious land deals.

According to a report, in total, 8 journalists were killed in 2015 while there were 30 cases of attacks and 27 threats reported from various parts of the country (*Hoot* 2015). The recent incidents of the murders of Hindi daily *Hindustan* bureau chief of Siwan in Bihar, Rajdev Ranjan and a TV journalist, Akhilesh Pratap Singh in Chatra district of Jharkhand, who were shot dead within a span of 24 hours, manifest the dangerous terrain in which journalists operate in India. The nexus of politicians with criminals, mining mafias, other influential industrialists, and businessmen has always posed a threat to journalists covering sensitive beats like environment, crime, politics, and so on.

Amidst this threatening landscape for journalists, some ethical issues too have emerged with the steady rise in the number of pseudo-journalists working to gain access to power, positions, institutions, and the privileges that come with the press card and press stickers on vehicles. Unfortunately, many such journalists are indulging in corruption, false stories, downplaying issues, blackmailing, and so on, while many have stakes in different kinds of businesses and projects (Rashid 2015). Similarly, the issue of corruption and paid news in media too has surfaced as one of the major challenges coming in the way of environmental journalism in India. Many individual journalists as well as media houses have started planting reports and views in exchange for different kinds of favours or cash (Lloyd 2013). Citing Paranjoy Guha Thakurta's report on paid news, Lloyd highlights the issue of corruption in the Indian media industry, wherein newspapers and television channels are publishing or broadcasting stories in favour of corporate houses, individuals, political parties, and others. Such unsolicited practices in the field of journalism have led environmental journalism to dwindle, as many journalists who have become a part of such nexuses have compromised with regard to the environmental threats caused by many corporate entities for whom they write.

Therefore, the major challenges facing twenty-first-century environmental journalists are going to be addressing these ethical issues as well as understanding the complexities behind the different environmental problems surfacing within the country, for which some specific training and workshops may be continuously provided to even those reporting for small newspapers and local television stations in rural areas or tier-three towns. It will also be important for organizations like the Press Council of India, the Information and Broadcasting Ministry, and other national-level media organizations like the All India Freelance Journalists Association, the News Broadcasters' Association, All India Newspaper Editor and Publishers Association, and others to take measures that will ensure the safety and security of journalists covering crucial, contentious beats like climate change and environment, and also to develop mechanisms to deal effectively with the pseudo-journalism being practised by many media professionals today.

Even today, the growth of environmental journalism in India is considered to be occurring at a slow pace, unlike Western nations where this beat of media reporting is given ample importance, because of multifarious factors like complexities in environmental issues, corruption, conflicts of interest, growth and development issues, and so on (A. Jain 2010; Rajeesh 2012). So, it is time for us in India to realize the importance of environmental journalism, and speak and write for safeguarding our ecosystems and protecting the forest cover that is fast disappearing, rivers that are drying, and call attention to the pollution levels in the air, water, and soil that are continuously increasing with every passing day.

NOTE

1. The RTI Act, which was introduced in 2005, mandates timely response to citizen requests for government information.

REFERENCES

Acharya, K. and F. Noronha (2010). 'Preface'. In *The Green Pen: Environmental Journalism in India and South Asia*, eds K. Acharya and F. Noronha. New Delhi: Sage.

Banholzer, S., J. Kossin, and S. Donner (2014). 'The Impact of Climate Change on Natural Disasters'. In *Reducing Disaster: Early Warning Systems for Climate Change*, eds Z. Zommers and A. Singh, pp. 21–49. Dordrecht: Springer Science+Business Media.

Bavadam, L. (2010). 'Environmental Stories, among the Most Challenging'. In *The Green Pen: Environmental Journalism in India and South Asia*, eds K. Acharya and F. Noronha, pp. 3–11. New Delhi: Sage.

Billet, S. (2009). 'Dividing Climate Change: Global Warming in the Indian Mass Media'. *Climatic Change*, 99(1): 1–16. 10.1007/s10584-009-9605-3.

Boykoff, M. T. (2009). 'We Speak for the Trees: Media Reporting on the Environment'. Annual Review of Environment and Resources, Center for Science and Technology Policy Research and Environmental Studies Program, University of Colorado, Boulder, Colorado.

Boykoff, M. T. and J. T. Roberts (2007–8). 'Media Coverage of Climate Change: Current Trends, Strengths, Weaknesses'. New York: United Nations Development Programme.

CPJ (Committee for the Protection of Journalists) (2015). 'Getting Away with Murder'. Retrieved from https://cpj.org/reports/2015/10/impunity-index-getting-away-with-murder.php (accessed on 17 August 2018).

Dancea, L. and I. Merce (2009). 'The Quality of Human Life under Industrial Revolution'. *Research Journal of Agricultural Science*, 41(2): 67–70.

Fine, B. and E. Leopold (1990). 'Consumerism and the Industrial Revolution'. *Social History*, 15(2): 151–79.

Friedman, S. M. (2004). 'And the Beat Goes On: Third Decade of Environmental Journalism'. In *The Environmental Communication Yearbook*, ed. S. L. Senecah, pp. 175–88. Manwah, NJ: Lawrence Erlbaum Associates.

——— (2015). 'The Changing Face of Environmental Journalism in the United States'. In *The Routledge Handbook of Environment and Communication*, eds A. Hansen and R. Cox, pp. 144–57. Oxon: Routledge.

Gadgil, M. and R. Guha (1994). 'Ecological Conflicts and the Environmental Movement in India'. *Development and Change*, 25(1): 101–36.

Govindu, V. M. and D. Malghan (2005). 'Building a Creative Freedom: J. C. Kumarappa and His Economic Philosophy'. *Economic and Political Weekly*, 40(52): 5477–85.

Guha, R. (2006). *How Much Should a Person Consume?* Ranikhet: Permanent Black.

Hoot (2015). 'Free Speech in India, 2015'. Retrieved from http://www.thehoot. org/research/special-reports/free-speech-in-india-2015-9091 (accessed on 27 July 2016).

Houck, O. A. (2010). *Taking Back Eden: Eight Environmental Cases That Changed the World*. Washington, D.C.: Island Press.

Jain, A. (2010). 'The Need for Environmental Journalism'. Retrieved from http://theviewspaper.net/the-need-for-environmental-journalism/ (accessed on 17 August 2018).

Jain, R. (2014). 'The Indian Supreme Court as Environmental Activist'. *Diplomat*. Retrieved from http://thediplomat.com/2014/01/the-indian-supreme-court-as-environmental-activist/ (accessed on 17 August 2018).

Jayaraman, T. and T. Kanitkar (2016). 'The Paris Agreement: Deepening the Climate Crisis'. *Economic and Political Weekly*, 51(3): 10–13.

Lloyd, J. (2013). 'A Personal Journey through India's Journalism'. In *India's Media Boom: The Good News and the Bad*, ed. J. Painter, pp. 19–26. Oxford: Reuters Institute for the Study of Journalism.

Mahapatra, R. (2010). 'Environmental Journalism at the Time of Economic Liberalisation'. In *The Green Pen: Environmental Journalism in India and South Asia*, eds K. Acharya and F. Noronha, pp. 20–27. New Delhi: Sage.

Rajeesh, S. (2012). 'In Advocacy of Environmental Journalism'. Retrieved from http://mediamagazine.in/content/advocacy-environmental-journalism (accessed on 17 August 2018).

Rashid, O. (2015). 'For Regional Journalists, It's a Fight for Survival'. Retrieved from http://www.thehindu.com/opinion/op-ed/For-regional journalists-it%E2%80%99s-a-fight-for-survival/article10899626.ece (accessed on 17 August 2018).

Shah, I. K. and H. Shah (2008). 'Environmental Journalism: Concept and Scope in India'. *Indian Journal of Science Communication*, 7(2): 25–30.

Sharma, S. (2013). 'Guns and Protests: Media Priorities in Chhattisgarh'. In *India's Media Boom: The Good News and the Bad*, ed. J. Painter, pp. 27–42. Oxford: Reuters Institute for the Study of Journalism.

Warrier, S. G. (2010). 'Environmental Journalism since Economic Liberalisation'. In *The Green Pen: Environmental Journalism in India and South Asia*, eds K. Acharya and F. Noronha, pp. 28–34. New Delhi: Sage.

PART FOUR

Ethics, Pedagogy, and the Public Sphere in Journalism

CHAPTER FOURTEEN

Principle or Practice? Pedagogic Challenges in Indian Journalism Education

USHA RAMAN

· ·

It is a conflict as old as the oldest journalism department in any part of the world, and it's been no different in India.[1] The same old questions echo around the discussion table every time journalism academics meet, and even more so when they sit across from practitioners. What is the theory–practice balance, and which is more important? Should journalism education be about building skills for the newsbeat and newsroom or is it about building a perspective about society, culture, and life? Or even more fundamental: can journalism be taught in a classroom? Working journalists would largely disagree, one famously stating that it would be akin to 'learning swimming by postal tuition' (newspaper editor K. M. Roy, quoted in Sanjay 2012: 119).

Academics of course would defend the importance of a good liberal arts education for those who perform the civic duty of interpreting the world for the general public. Across time, the contours of this debate have remained unchanged, touching issues of quality of curriculum and infrastructure, almost always ending in that contentious question of what counts as an adequate level of preparedness. The question of pedagogy—how that preparation is to be effected—is rarely examined from the inside out. In this chapter, after laying out some of the main criticisms levelled against the journalism academy in India, I attempt to unpack the nature of journalism skills pedagogy and argue that we need to shift our attention from the often-discussed *functional* gap (or skills gap) that both academics and practitioners bemoan, to the less discussed *critical* gap that exists between the space of instruction/learning and the space of practice. I draw from an examination of newswriting/reporting syllabi from major institutions around the country and discussions with journalism educators and recent graduates to argue for the need for a more reflective, experience-based pedagogy and classroom practice that avoids divorcing skill from concept and builds in a keen appreciation of context.

JOURNALISM EDUCATION IN INDIA: A BRIEF OVERVIEW

The landscape of journalism education in India has been charted multiple times in the seven decades since the first university-based department was established in 1941 in Punjab University, with several renewed attempts at taking stock in the current century (Karan 2001; Desai 2008; Muppidi 2008; Sanjay 2012; Thomas 2016; CMS 2015; Raman 2015). These scholars describe the various forms that education programmes take, and the range of curricular designs generally adopted. These programmes fall into two broad categories: university-based graduate and undergraduate degree programmes, and diploma courses at standalone media schools, run either by private entities or media organizations. The first construct journalism as an academic discipline within the humanities or social science framework, with core journalism subjects forming one segment of the mandated coursework and combining media critique with production training. The second set focuses almost exclusively on skills and technique, complemented by some exposure to media laws and ethics and specialized reporting topics.

University-based programmes at both the graduate and undergraduate level are accredited by the governmental body that oversees higher education in India—the University Grants Commission (UGC)—and must submit themselves to periodic external scrutiny. Such programmes are offered through a network of private and public colleges that are affiliated to degree-granting universities, or, in the case of master's level programmes, at the university itself. A 2015 survey by the Delhi-based Centre for Media Studies listed 310 schools of journalism fitting various descriptions, with roughly half being UGC-recognized university programmes (CMS 2015). Many university programmes offer journalism (or practice orientation) as an option within a broader communication and media studies graduate curriculum that is increasingly seen as an avenue to an academic career. This chapter focuses on university-based journalism education, as these are the programmes which, despite a variety of acknowledged limitations in terms of resources and infrastructure, offer the richest possibility for critique, review, and reshaping. In a country like India, where access to higher education is still limited to few, such public institutions play an important role in broadening its reach to new constituencies from hitherto excluded communities.

Journalism education in the country has been heavily influenced by the American model of professional education, as has been pointed out by many of the scholars listed above, as well as in more recent works (Bockino 2017). Taking their cue from established skills-focused schools, such as those at Columbia University and the University of Missouri, the journalism departments that were set up in the post-independence years drew on curricula that aimed to create news professionals who would uphold the values of an idealized fourth estate. Professor K. E. Eapen, one of the pioneers of media education in the country, noted that there was a 'fixation with the US model' of journalism education (quoted in Sanjay 2012: 120). This has resulted in a highly normative approach to teaching the skills of reporting and editing with little media critique, combined with a healthy dose of such topics as news values and newsroom structure, techniques of information gathering and writing, and the basics of editing. Discussion and introspection made an appearance mainly in the obligatory media laws and ethics course and possibly to some extent in development journalism, if included. The values of the news business were celebrated and the focus of most such programmes was to create professionals who would fit into the industry.

An international expert panel constituted by UNESCO and chaired by Indian journalist Chalapathi Rao in 1956 recommended that 'journalism education should be of a comprehensive character' (UNESCO 1956: 2). However, this commission also affirmed that such an education must 'emphasize the practical side of training' (UNESCO 1956: 2). Close to 20 years later, a panel constituted by the UGC recommended that journalism curricula should blend the art and craft of journalism with the social sciences, a directive that was repeated by the UGC's Curriculum Development Committee in 2000 (Sanjay 2012; Thomas 2016).[2] Thus, UGC-approved curricula consciously incorporated some aspects of media criticism, but stopped short of including elements of social sciences. In 2007, UNESCO held consultations in 60 countries across the world, including India, and put forward model curricula that could be adapted to local needs. These were reviewed and revised in 2013 and formed the basis for the formulation of curricula in several new university departments that were established in India in the new millennium. The model curricula have proved a useful starting point for young faculty recruited by these new departments, with many adopting them with little or no change, although localization and contextualization were recommended by the expert committee (Claussen 2007).

MAPPING THE CRITIQUE

Despite the UGC's repeated attempts to bring about a standardization of journalism education in India, Kavita Karan (2001) points to a continuing unevenness in curriculum and content. This is certainly not unique to the country and seems to be echoed in neighbouring Bangladesh and other countries in the region (Ullah 2013) that have either followed India's lead or have drawn from the UNESCO initiative. Bockino (2016) however finds that there is a 'façade of isomorphism' across journalism programmes in India, with a similar emphasis on skills over theory.

The continuing dissatisfaction with journalism education is not unique to the Indian media space. The widely discussed Bollinger Report commissioned by the Knight Foundation and Columbia

University (Bollinger 2015) prompted some deep reflections on the purpose and form of university-based journalism programmes in the United States. While such an exercise has not yet been undertaken in India, there have been periodic commentaries in the trade and popular press that express a similar concern with the perceived gap between the 'classroom and newsroom' (Rath 2012; Raman 2015).

The introduction to the UNESCO Model Curriculum acknowledges the need to produce graduates with keen analytical skills and an understanding of the context within which journalism operates, but the course outlines themselves tip the balance towards the 'doing' of journalism (UNESCO 2013). Sanjay (2012: 115) acknowledges the problematics of situating journalism and communication education 'in the academic world with stated aims for nomenclature, curriculum inputs, etc.', referring no doubt to the conflict that arises when such departments are required to serve the dual purposes of scholarship and skill building.

Kavita Karan, in her critique of journalism and mass communication programmes in the country, notes that few formal studies of journalism education have been conducted in India since Eapen and Thakur's 1989 survey for the UGC (Karan 2001: 297). My own readings of these reviews suggested that they are largely descriptive and based on secondary data, apart from Muppidi's (2009) interview-based report and the CMS study that drew on a survey of faculty, students, and industry professionals to understand the gaps in journalism education (CMS 2015). They comment mainly on the scope of curricula and materials, such as Pradip Thomas's (2016) wide-ranging review of journalism education in India, where he notes that 'much of what is being taught today is sourced from aging textbooks, there is little connection to context, and the results are top-down models that do not account for the many political, economic, cultural and social shapings that have impacted on communication for development or its extraordinarily diverse manifestations in civil society in India' (Thomas 2016: 445).

The critiques are all strikingly similar, and have remained so in the three decades since Eapen and Thakur's review in 1989. There is agreement that journalism training needs to combine critical thinking and an understanding of social, political, and economic realities with building strong skills in fact finding, interviewing, writing, and editing.

There is also agreement that the location of journalism as an academic discipline is crucial to achieving the larger democratic purpose of the fourth estate. There seems to be a concurrence—and an assumption—about having faculty who can deliver these twin objectives of critical thinking and skills. And this is where the problem arises. The most recent UGC hiring and career advancement norms (UGC 2016) make it difficult for lateral entry of experienced journalists into academia, and with more and more young people choosing to go straight into higher education without acquiring industry experience, there is low representation of faculty members who have substantial journalistic experience that can help in delivering a convincing skills course. The CMS (2015) survey found that most faculty who responded to the survey had no industry experience and a small percentage had less than five years of experience. The other major criticism is that public universities and colleges have found it difficult to keep up with the rapid changes in technology, that the modes and methods of journalism taught in universities are out of sync with contemporary newsrooms. A less acknowledged but widely experienced issue is the absence of evidence-based or thoughtful strategies to address the needs of a socially, culturally, and linguistically diverse student body that enters higher education with an often inadequate level of undergraduate preparation.

EXAMINING SYLLABI: THE ARTICULATION OF PRINCIPLE

Newswriting and reporting are perhaps the cornerstone of any skills-oriented journalism programme, in any part of the world, and an examination of how these subjects are taught in university departments could possibly give us a clue about where—as has been charged—the classroom is falling out of step with industry expectations. I examined newswriting and reporting syllabi from 15 university departments from around the country that offer graduate (master's level) programmes in journalism and mass communication approved by the UGC. The foundation-level course, usually offered in the first year of the programme, is variously titled 'Reporting and Writing for Print Media', 'Basics of Print', 'Writing for Print', or 'Reporting and Feature Writing'. Writing as a journalistic process is explored through several courses, usually in a series, from a basic reporting course to feature writing to specialized reporting and writing. A few universities combine two or more of these into a single course. In all cases, the syllabi attempt—on the face of it—to combine an understanding of process with skill, with some units focusing on such topics as 'organization of the newsroom' and 'determinants of news' and others focusing on structural elements of a news/feature story and newsgathering techniques.

The reporting and writing courses are seen as working within the larger print journalism programme, which includes courses on media ethics, editing, production and media technology, media history, and media management, and possibly development and social change processes as they interface with journalism. A few university programmes also offer students the opportunity to take one or two electives from other departments, so students may take courses from social sciences and humanities fields such as political science, sociology, anthropology, and literature. The journalism-specific skills, thus, are acquired—in principle—along with an understanding of the larger socio-political milieu within which these skills must be applied. The increasing establishment of single-discipline universities, though, limits this possibility of interdisciplinary learning. Even in the West, as Jackie Harrison notes, while there is widespread agreement on the topics that must be included in a skills curriculum (the inverted pyramid, news values, 5 Ws and H, as well as media ethics and laws), there is 'less agreement about which other disciplines should play a part in a broader news journalism curriculum' (Harrison 2007: 176). While diversity in curricular approaches is to be welcomed, what is important is for students to have access to ideas from a wide range of relevant disciplines that can strengthen their understanding of life in a manner that leads to better journalism.

Where specified, learning objectives in these writing courses mainly have to do with 'developing writing and reporting skills' and also 'to make students understand the nuances of news'. The pedagogic approach is rarely mentioned, except in two instances, one of which simply lists 'discussions, practical work and lectures' and another, which describes it as follows:

> This course takes a skills oriented approach to train students in the basics of reporting and news writing. To move students as close as possible to the real world of journalism where they will report and write on

deadline, as well as work through editing process with their professor. The main objective is to help develop a clear, concise writing style and a passion for thorough, accurate reporting. (MA course on Reporting, Writing and Editing for Print Media, Pondicherry University)

By and large, there is uniformity of purpose and content in these syllabi, which differ, if at all, only in the manner of breaking up units or distributing topics across related courses. Almost all reporting and writing courses offered in Indian universities have a practical component in the form of a printed lab journal or online publication. One thread that seems to run through all these syllabi is the desire to create students who can fit into the media industry—to socialize and normalize according to the dominant, widely accepted tenets of a kind of journalism that has for years been idealized in Western democracies. Is there a problem with this? Perhaps not, unless one remembers Professor Eapen's exhortation to 'break free' of the American model and attempt to create a journalism practice that was responsive to the needs of the Indian context—or contexts. The nod to this may be seen in courses that aim to expose students to media history (usually a conventional, linear approach) and to social change processes (often still referred to as 'development' communication). In any case, these ideas exist in other courses, and the students are generally expected to make the connections and stitch together a conception of skills-within-context on their own.

The other problem, one that is less tangible and perhaps more problematic, is the schism between the frame of media critique/analysis and that of media production. A skills course such as reporting and writing teaches just that: it gives you a toolkit and practice in applying the tools to telling news stories whose relevance is judged by applying news values. In theory and critique courses, students are encouraged to look beyond and underneath these stories, to understand how they work within and mesh with the socio-cultural fabric. But how does this critique influence production? How does one gain media literacy—the capacity to analyse and deconstruct—and set that aside to 'reproduce' media in its own image, as skills courses teach us to do? How do students take this skill set and make it work in the confusing, politically charged space of the newsroom? What learned rules does one hold on to in a shifting, changing context that contemporary media organizations work within? Such concerns and possibilities lie in the space between the syllabus and its delivery, and making them visible and dealing with the complexities and confusions that might arise is an important pedagogic project.

INSIDE THE CLASSROOM

The Bollinger Report (Bollinger 2015) noted that the goals of journalism and journalism education are similar—to facilitate an informed citizenry and enable participation in a democracy, among other things—and both groups would agree on the skills required to achieve this. The hand-wringing by the committee that produced the Bollinger Report is no different from what goes on among those interested in journalism education in India and, likely, elsewhere. Deuze (2006: 22) observes that journalism educators across the world face similar challenges:

> So journalism educators and scholars face similar struggles all over the world, having to defend their curriculum, methods and theories against industry-wide shared notions that the academy is not the place to teach students how to get a job in the media, and that journalism is not the place to thoroughly reflect on the roles and functions of news media in society. Journalism education, in other words, must negotiate rather essentialist self-perceptions of both industry and academy, while at the same time finding ways to navigate the inconsistencies of its own field (e.g. negotiating a tradition in both the humanities and the social sciences).

How exactly does this gap arise? What are the dynamics of teaching journalistic skills that give rise to this perceived gap? How do journalism teachers, many of whom are only too keenly aware of such a critique, having heard it repeatedly from old students and practitioners, attempt to bridge this gap? 'Syllabi are representative of outwardly facing curricular structure; they tell us little about day-to-day maneuverings', notes David Bockino, in his examination of teaching at three professional journalism schools in India (2016: 277). Bockino proceeded to examine the teaching culture in three private media schools, emerging with the key finding that the curriculum was seen as 'incredibly dynamic', with plenty of room for the individual teacher to work in contextual and need-based interpretations.

This is of course the ideal situation in any teaching space. Curriculum should be no more than a framework, a suggestive outline for the broad goals of a particular programme. But in the skills classroom, this assumes a certain level of what we might call 'interpretive aptitude' in the teacher/facilitator, which might be acquired through experience—over time in the classroom, or from first-hand exposure to the field of practice.

Teaching of skills, particularly in today's complex media environment, can be a fraught exercise. Those who have no media experience, or who connect with media primarily as critics, take a critical approach to the process of media production, teaching to an (mostly non-existent) 'ideal type', while those who come with substantial media experience focus on 'fitting in' to media industries with an acceptable level of skill and an understanding of newsroom politics. Andersson and Wiik (2013) describe the tension between what they term as the 'discourse of organizational professionalism' (that aligns itself with the institutional structure) and 'occupational professionalism' (an alignment with the larger goals of a profession) that is often not discerned by those without media experience and is treated as an individual rather than systemic issue by those from the media. They also note that these two types of teachers may represent a 'discrepancy in the perceptions of what journalistic quality really means and how it should be achieved' (2016: 706).

The 15 syllabi reviewed for the purposes of this chapter offer a screened view into the reporting and writing classroom. They list topics and themes neatly divided into units, and in a few cases list assignments and evaluation criteria. But there is no sense of how this syllabus might unfold in the classroom, what the texture of those discussions might be. Five faculty members from among those who volunteered syllabi were interviewed via e-mail to understand how they managed their classes and balanced practical and conceptual elements in their reporting/writing course. To get some insights into how graduates managed the classroom to newsroom transition, five young journalists with an experience of two to five years, were also interviewed via e-mail.

Young teachers who come into the classroom with little or no journalistic experience are very conscious of their lack of first-hand knowledge of the field, and attempt to fill this gap by inviting working journalists to interact with their students, and building in a number of hands-on assignments that will give students an exposure to the field. 'I keep the course outline flexible and somewhat open-ended, so that I can bring in these additional inputs,' said an assistant professor at the state university, who has worked briefly in the industry. Of the four other teachers, only one had some media experience, while another had done two short internships when she was a graduate student. Their focus, thus, tends to be normative, aiming to 'coach' students in the skills required in the ideal Indian newsroom. When asked about challenges, two of the five teachers pointed to lack of infrastructure and the heterogeneous nature of the student body. Another teacher who came into academia after working for more than a decade as a journalist, across print and broadcast media, spoke at length about her lack of preparedness for teaching. 'Ask me to write or produce a news story, I have no problem, but teaching others how to do it was an entirely different issue.' This points to a related issue: the lack of any serious discussion of or mentoring in classroom practice. This is of course a more general problem in higher education, the lack of peda-gogic preparation for faculty recruits. Very few doctoral programmes offer opportunities for supervised teaching, and there is no formal effort to expose new faculty to the principles of pedagogy. And as for the complicated and nuanced issue of teaching skills for contextual application—it is prominent by its absence. The UGC does require assistant professors to complete what is called an 'orientation' course followed by a 'refresher course' before they become eligible for pro-motion to the next level. But these are more often than not general courses that do not address discipline-specific concerns.

The teachers' responses also reflected a point made earlier by B. P. Sanjay (2012), that journalism departments must 'serve two masters'—academia and industry—but this search for balance is expressed more at the macro level of programme design rather than the micro level of course syllabi and delivery. One teacher noted that 'students get the critical and theoretical inputs in other courses, so I don't bother with that in the reporting and writing course—it's more important that I focus on skills.'

While almost all university departments make an effort to include working journalists on their Boards of Studies, practitioners often cannot make it for the meetings. One faculty member from a state university remarks:

> There exists a HUGE gap between the industry and the academia. Many of them feel that the syllabus is outdated. The requirements of the industry is varying and needs more standardization.... we need to change the syllabus at least once in two years. Though it's on paper, it's not practised all over. Many of the journalists who are there in the BOS [Board of Studies] never attend or give [practical] suggestions for improvement [and] later blame the institutions.

Even discounting the implied criticism of practitioners who 'blame' without providing constructive suggestions, what becomes clear is the pedagogic gap between intention, as written into the syllabus, and action as expressed in its delivery. Even practitioners who understand the nuances of newsroom work find it difficult to translate it into their teaching, as mentioned earlier by the practitioner-turned-teacher. In recent years, the rapid infusion of technology into reporting and news dissemination has required journalists to quickly adapt to digital reporting and writing tools, and so the divide between what students are exposed to in the classroom and what they need to do when they join the industry becomes even wider. This also complicates the curriculum delivery, since, lacking first-hand exposure to such newsroom changes, teachers are unable to convincingly discuss how core skills need to be adapted to a digital environment.

Students, on the other hand, while pointing to the fact that academic training does not get them '100 per cent ready' for the job, believe that extensive discussions about the ethical and cultural climate of the newsroom can help them find their feet in the industry. 'We do acquire the ability to adapt quickly to the situation,' said one reporter, who works as a sports writer for an English-language daily. 'Entering into the job from campus gives you that confidence that you can do the job given your whatever experience you had in campus. But you will have a lot to learn in the job and that makes you feel that you did very little in the campus.'

Another reporter, who graduated from an elite private media school and now works at a major English daily, said: 'I believe my first job didn't require a journalism degree at all. Any graduate who understands English, has a little bit of news sense and knows how to use a computer would fit the bill.' Developing this 'news sense' then becomes the key ingredient in delivering a reporting and writing course, and such a sensibility can only be built by continually blending discussions of ideas with demonstration of and exposure to skills.

A young woman who graduated in 2013 and now works with a national business daily, pointing to the emphasis on the idealistic, normative approach, and the day-to-day conflicts that arise, said:

> Workplace scenario is very different from what we learn in journalism school. Journalism education, I feel, is still very idealistic in its approach. For example, in classrooms, a favourite topic of discussion is how advertisements eat into the news space and there is constant tussle for space between editors and advertisers. In reality, when we are faced with an ad-free page in which we have to edit and accommodate 7–8 stories within a given time, we ourselves beg for ads on the pages.

While the students appreciate the effort to bring practitioners to speak to classes, two students observed that most speakers tend to focus on the exciting and successful aspects of their careers. One young woman who works with the City Bureau of a large English daily remarks,

> it shouldn't just be limited to sharing of experiences but reflections that include dealing with daily pressures maybe even tough bosses while delivering a story. Being a journalist is taxing and all these aspects influence an individual's work. Sharing failures is also important. If someone has left journalism and moved on to something, that individual's experience will help much more than someone who is happy with the job, I believe. It helps students understand harsh realities of the job, as the job is nothing but harsh.

The situation is confounded further when one considers the gap between such a normatively oriented journalism education and the field of regional-language journalism. Textbooks—and teachers— hardly present any examples from smaller newspapers, and only rarely are practitioners from small publications or rural media invited to speak to students. Discussions tend to focus on the spectacular rather than the mundane, thus invisibilizing the messy, tedious everyday routines that can vary widely across media contexts.

Practitioners also tend to be dismissive of classroom learning, as one newbie described, 'The first day that I stepped into the office, my then boss had told us, "Forget all that you have learnt in college and start unlearning." And that was quite true, from preparing rundowns to handling instructions of the talkback, we learnt everything on the job.'

Clearly, it helps no one to get into a blame game. Every industry has its differences with the structure of the corresponding academic discipline, and fields of practice tend to be particularly problematic, where standards of ethics and professionalism may be perceived differently by either side. The discussion above only serves to point to the nature of the divide in a manner that might help journalism academics rethink their approaches to teaching—not necessarily to address the divide itself, but to better equip their students to manage the transition to the workplace and to encourage a reflective practice.

THINKING ABOUT JOURNALISM PEDAGOGY

Over the seven decades since journalism was formalized as an academic discipline, there have been many discussions around curriculum development, with much thought given to the balance of practice and theory both in programmatic structure and within the syllabi of individual courses. However, there has been little or no discussion around teaching practice, on the nitty-gritty of how a course outline should be translated into classroom interaction. Therefore, an artificial and unproductive divide has emerged between 'theory' courses and 'skills' courses, and those who teach the latter have little guidance in terms of how to teach so that students build reflection into practice or use skills to respond to critique.

Media education is dominated by the discourse of professionalism, where the goal is to reproduce the dominant modes of professional practice. Curricula are designed specifically to prepare students to fill particular job slots in the industry, 'not unlike the process of training workers to fill the slots on an assembly line' (Shoemaker 1993: 150). As a result, there is a schism between the theory of media studies, which tends toward the critical (even in approaches outside the critical-cultural paradigm), and the teaching of media skills, which tends to emphasize a professional approach that is artificially stripped of cultural and ideological context.

We teach our students to emulate 'successes' in the field without simultaneously looking at their impact and cultural context. We teach them to be critical of institutions outside the media but, in skills classes, rarely teach them to be critical of the media themselves, or even to look at media as producers of culture and meaning. At the same time, we cannot abdicate the responsibility we have to produce 'employable' communicators. Our students must be able to write clearly and produce efficiently, while taking into account the relationships their work has to other aspects of the media business and to the world at large.

I argue that to create a more reflective, intellectually informed journalism pedagogy, we need to focus on two sets of questions: one, how do we grapple with the messy space between idealized journalistic norms and values and the constraints of structure and culture in media organizations? How do we equip young academics—with or without media experience—to teach skills courses in a reflective, context-sensitive manner that resists both 'standardization' and extreme relativism? And how do we bring together the practice of critique and the practice of journalism—in our teaching—without descending into negativity and cynicism about the industry? How do we encourage our students to become agents of transformation in an industry that we too often criticize without offering solutions? In other words, is it possible to move from teaching to an 'ideal type' that does not exist, to a focus on critical skills that build flexibility, resilience, and reflection into journalistic practice?

Ralph Beliveau (2009: 336), arguing for a literacy-based approach to teaching skills, points to the dangers inherent in a decontextualized approach: 'A skilled journalist is able to integrate professional practices with the meanings behind and circumstances surrounding their use. If skills training is not combined with a critical understanding of the contexts that make journalism meaningful, the effect is to essentially "de-skill" that individual.'

Sheridan Burns (2004: 95) further outlines the need for teachers to build a 'cognitive bridge' between theory and practice, offering reflective practice as a model for teaching journalism, with students knowing what to do, how to do it, and being able to demonstrate the ability to do:

> It is through critical self-reflection that journalists develop self-reliance, confidence, problem solving, cooperation and adaptability, while simultaneously gaining knowledge. Perhaps more importantly, it develops in students a sense of professional efficacy in their ability to negotiate the dilemmas and complexities that are inherent in their practice. Reflection is also the process by which journalists learn to recognize their own assumptions and understand their place in the wider social context.

Stephanie Craft (2014) notes, in her introduction to a special collection of essays on the future of journalism studies, 'Just as practitioners have held onto old ways of doing things in that new space, researchers have held onto old theories and methods for understanding it.' This is also true of educators, I would argue. Are we also not using old methods and old frameworks to teach students who will join a vastly changed industry? We have studied how journalism production, practice, business, and consumption have changed, but have we brought this understanding into the classroom to prepare students, in different ways, to adapt to these changes?

It would help to ease the way for new faculty members to discuss their own concerns about teaching and their expectations. Seminars should provide space for discussion on 'theoretical development within the practical domain' (McLaren et al. 1995). In such a meeting, they may be encouraged to develop ways of bringing their critiques to bear on the training of future communicators, not just on media products, processes, or impact. While there are numerous opportunities for us to engage in intellectual discussions revolving around our research interests, there are few organized events within which we can similarly address our concerns relating to teaching, particularly as novice academics. In the Indian context, this becomes even more urgent, given the diversity of our classrooms and the uneven nature of the undergraduate education that precedes a journalism degree.

In my experience, skills instructors seldom engage in serious discussion about pedagogy. We rarely question our methods or look to colleagues for ways to change our syllabi in these classes. The pragmatic nature of the topics covered seems to supersede intense pedagogical engagement. These courses tend to be considered assembly lines that feed industry (and, as one colleague remarked, 'pay the bills'), requiring little thought or didactical restructuring. Since most schools offer multiple sections of basic skills courses (which are much in demand), there is a wide range of teaching styles used and specific content addressed. My reviews and interviews also indicate that journalism education could do with more study, perhaps more classroom ethnographies and examinations of individual teaching philosophies, to give us further insight into how it unfolds and where the possibilities of enhancement lie. More dialogue among teachers of skills courses can lead to recognition of where and how critical approaches can be incorporated. At the very least, it will encourage us as pedagogues to reflect on our own work, that part of our work that is usually relegated to the bottom of our own intellectual priorities.

NOTES

1. Many of the thoughts presented in this chapter have evolved over cups of tea and lunchtime conversations with fellow travellers in media education, beginning from my days as a journalist-turned-graduate student and continuing through my career as a practitioner-cum-teacher, and finally in my current role as a full-time academic. Special thanks to Elfriede Fursich, with whom I first exchanged anguished notes about bringing critique into the skills classroom, and to my many students, who have helped me strike some balance, from year to year.
2. See http://www.ugc.ac.in/oldpdf/modelcurriculum/masscomm.pdf for the report of the UGC's Curriculum Development Committee constituted in 2000.

REFERENCES

Andersson, U. and J. Wiik (2013). 'Journalism Meets Management: Changing Leadership in Swedish News Organizations'. *Journalism Practice*, 7(6): 705–19. http://dx.doi.org/10.1080/17512786.2013.790612.

Beliveau, R. (2009). 'Literacy Problems within Skill Solutions: Index, Contexts and Critical Journalism Education'. *Journalism Practice*, 3(3): 335–46.

Bockino, D. (2017). 'Indian Field Notes: New Institutionalism and Journalism Education'. *Asian Journal of Communication*, 27(3): 267–84. doi:10.1080/01292986.2016.1257646.

Bollinger, L. C. (2003). 'Statement on the Future of Journalism Education'. Retrieved from http://www.columbia.edu/cu/president/docs/communications/2002-2003/030415-journalism.html (accessed on 22 July 2017).

Burns, S. L. (2004). 'A Reflective Approach to Teaching Journalism'. *Art, Design and Communication in Higher Education*, 3(1): 5–16.

Claussen, D. S. (2007). 'Editor's Note: A Model J&MC Curriculum for Developing Countries Is Progress for Them, Perhaps at Least Reminders for "Developed" U.S. J&MC Education'. *Journalism and Mass Communication Educator*, 62(3): 237–40.

CMS (Centre for Media Studies) (2015). 'Study Finds Many Gaps in Indian Journalism Education'. *Vidura*, 7(3): 1, 3–5.

Craft, S. (2014). 'Trajectories: An Introduction'. *Journalism Studies*, 15(6): 689–710. http://dx.doi.org/10.1080/1461670X.2014.952971.

Desai, M. K. (2008). 'Reviewing Communication/Journalism Education in India: Many Players, Diverse Directions but Lost Focus … ?!' *Journal of Global Communication*, 11(2): 118–31.

Deuze, M. (2006). 'Global Journalism Education: A Conceptual Approach'. *Journalism Studies*, 7(1): 19–34.

Harrison, J. (2007). 'Critical Foundations and Directions for the Teaching of News Journalism'. *Journalism Practice*, 1(2): 175–89.

Karan, K. (2001). 'Journalism Education in India: Debate: Journalism Education'. *Journalism Studies*, 2(2): 281–99.

McLaren, P., R. Hammer, D. Sholle, and S. S. Reilley (eds) (1995). *Rethinking Media Literacy: A Critical Pedagogy of Representation*. New York: Peter Lang.

Muppidi, S. (2008). 'Journalism Education in India'. *Media Asia*, 35(2): 67–83.

Raman, U. (2015). 'Failure of Communication: India Must Face Up to the Rift between Its Newsrooms and Classrooms'. *Caravan*, December 2015. Retrieved from http://www.caravanmagazine.in/perspectives/failure-of-communication-rift-between-india-newsrooms-clasrooms (accessed on 10 September 2016).

Rath, N. (2012). 'Wanted: Quality Media Education'. Retrieved from http://www.thehoot.org/media-watch/media-practice/wanted-quality-media-education-6216 (accessed on 15 April 2017).

Sanjay, B. P. (2012). 'Journalism and Mass Communication Education: An Assessment'. *Asia Pacific Media Educator*, 22(1): 115–26.

Shoemaker, P. (1993). 'Communication Is Crisis: Theory, Curricula and Power'. *Journal of Communication*, 43(4): 146–53.

Thomas, Pradip N. (2016). 'Observations on Journalism and Communication Education in India'. *International History of Communication Study*, eds Peter Simonson and David W. Park, pp. 435–51. New York: Routledge.

UGC (University Grants Commission) (2016). 'Gazette Notification'. Retrieved from http://ugc.ac.in/pdfnews/3375714_API-4th-Amentment-Regulations-2016.pdf (accessed on 1 July 2017).

Ullah, M. S. (2013). 'Halfway between Newsroom and Classroom: The Human Resource Development Strategy for Journalism in Bangladesh'. *Media Asia*, 40(2): 183–96.

UNESCO (United Nations Educational, Scientific and Cultural Organization) (1956). 'International Expert Group Meeting on Professional Training for Journalists. Trends in Journalism Education in India' (submitted by U. Chalapathi Rao). New Delhi: UNESCO House.

——— (2013). 'Model Curricula for Journalism Education'. UNESCO Series on Journalism Education. Paris: UNESCO. Retrieved from http://unesdoc.unesco.org/images/0022/002211/221199e.pdf (accessed on 15 July 2017).

CHAPTER FIFTEEN

The 24/7 English News Cycle as a Spectre of Neoliberal Violence

MOHAN J. DUTTA
AND ASHWINI FALNIKAR

. . . .

In this chapter, we will examine the ways in which the 24/7 English news cycle in India operates as the spectre of neoliberal violence, circulating as normal and necessary the various forms of violence that are integral to the neoliberal project being carried out across India, framed as development. The narratives of the free market and economic growth are picked up uncritically across news frames, offering as natural the framework of trickle-down economics and growth-driven everyday displacements, marking India as a site of monolithic aspirations toward the global free market, while simultaneously marking as the threatening 'other' the sites of resistance against this neoliberal onslaught (Dutta 2017). Debates and conversations on 24/7 news media are thus framed in assumptions of growth as integral to the alleviation of poverty, producing spectacles that reproduce the monolithic narrative of an aspiring India, juxtaposed against the backdrop of productions of stories of crime, corruption, and violence that individualize these sites of violence into demands for justice that punish the perpetrator. The accelerated pace of news production and the repeated recycling of packaged news leaves uninterrogated the interplays of gender, caste, class, religion, and minority position (such as in Manipur, Chhattisgarh, and Kashmir) as sites of state-corporate produced violence in neoliberal India, while at the same time producing spectacles that draw in publics in the production of individualized affect and mobilized into spectacular protests, such as hunger performances and candlelight vigils (marches on the capital, anti-corruption protests, sit-ins) (Udupa 2015). In this sense, 24/7 English-language news media, speaking to and producing an upwardly aspiring Indian middle-class neoliberal subject, frame, justify, and discursively enable the erasure of India's margins, repeating stories of great aspirations and marking the 'other' of these aspirations as the legitimate targets of state-sponsored violence (Rajagopal 2002). The apparition of neoliberal violence percolates through these stories in what they make visible, and more importantly, in what they make invisible. Voices of India's margins are erased systematically as the repetitions of the neoliberal tropes of aspirations, growth, and individualized problems concretize the grasp of the ideological apparatus of neoliberalism.

Starting with the economic reforms in the 1990s, the neoliberal transformation of news perpetuated as normative an overarching value system that framed the invisible hand of the free market as the solution to India's problems (Thussu 2007; Rao 2009). From Prannoy Roy's NDTV to the newly launched Republic TV, the aspiration for India is one of accelerated economic growth, industrialization, and urbanization, punctuated as the hegemonic pathway to development. The narratives of the free market as the source of miraculous solutions to India's problems of poverty and underdevelopment are circulated as the organizing tropes that frame India's news industry and its aspirations, depicting the overarching neoliberal ideology through which the industry approaches the production of news and the construction of social problems. The televised production of news attends to the spectacular as the site of dramatizing events, while at the same time obfuscating the structural contexts that constitute these events. News stories typically erase the everyday violence in the contexts of gender, caste, class, religion, and minority position, and when they do address one of these sites, put forth individualized frames in articulating questions of agency divorced from structures. In doing so, 24/7 cycles reproduce these sites of oppression in everyday life as individual problems and cultivate certain performances of individualized grievances strategically as catalysts for democratic engagement and for the production of public participation. Democracy and participation, thus rendered meaningless, are the new tools for the perpetuation of neoliberal India constituted through news, and commoditized in candlelight vigils and the spectacular marches of a homogeneously aspiring, economically interconnected, privileged public on the capital.

While news reportage requires facts to make it truthful, 24/7 TV news has changed the face of reporting, selectively presenting facts and distorting reality and framing the news to suit the neoliberal fantasy of India as an aspiring destination. In competition with other news channels, every TV news outlet widely uses audience-grabbing tactics, such as dramatization of news, aggressive debating, maximizing the shock value of a news piece, and unrestrained probing of victims, witnesses, and the concerned parties for the spectacular 'bite'. The reality is partially presented, and the nuances of what constitutes the reality are selectively erased in favour of the incessant production of a neoliberal fantasy, catalysed through twitter hashtags and Facebook engagements. The consuming publics of 24/7 news are constructed around a national imaginary where individualized aspirations for the market are realized through the free market/development/growth aspiration of the nation. The commoditization of the 'other' of the nation as a threat is integral to the generation of ratings. Events as spectacles emerge in these 24/7 news cycles as catalysts for grabbing audiences, congealing them into affective publics mobilized against injustices, individualizing problems as sites of justice while simultaneously obfuscating the structural productions of inequalities in neoliberal India. For instance, in most instances, the state-sponsored violence in Chhattisgarh and Kashmir is systematically erased, as these sites are constructed as terrorist threats to the sovereignty of the nation and to its agenda of development. In other instances, an incidence of violence say in Chhattisgarh is projected on the national imaginary to mark the terrorist other, building affectively charged publics that are offered glimpses into the threats to the nation, mobilized around the deployment of the military and paramilitary on the nation's sovereign subjects. On a similar note, the pivotal role of news productions in generating public protests against gender-based violence precisely serves to reproduce the neoliberal trope of Indian aspirations, divorced from the structural contexts of gender injustices that constitute the socio-cultural fabric of contemporary India. Everyday forms of injustices, such as caste, class, and religion-based injustices, are strategically obfuscated in the circulation of palatable spectacles for the aspiring classes.

NEWS INDUSTRY, GENDER, AND NEOLIBERAL FANTASY

Gender-based violence in contemporary India is marked by the various sites at which violence is routinized. From the urban sites of gendered violence to the semi-urban and rural peripheries of India, violence against women is as much a part of the national narrative as is its growth story. The Indian state is itself a site for perpetuating gendered violence, especially in the context of rapes and murders that are carried out by the Indian army in conflict zones and in the various sites of state-corporate land grab. In the 24/7 cycles of the national imagination, the free market has opened up opportunities of upward mobility and empowerment of women, and the individualized accounts of violence attend to the backward lower classes that have not yet caught up with the aspirations of a changing India, marking thus the fringes of the nation that need to be punished. The classed nature of the news stories on gender, therefore, attends to a particular form of gendered violence to narrate the spectacle, while simultaneously erasing the various forms of gendered violence that are produced by the very pathways of growth and development. The spectacles of gendered violence therefore mark the outside of the neoliberal mainstream as the threat to women's safety.

The news coverage of a rape/murder that took place in India's capital city, Delhi, is a particularly vivid example of this. On 16 December 2012, a 23-year-old woman was assaulted and gang-raped by six men on a moving bus between 9:30 p.m. and 11 p.m., and then thrown out of the bus along with her male friend in a brutalized state. The news media covered the event widely over the following weeks, recycling various images, sounds, and stories of the rape and the murder, recounting in detail the brutality of the murder. The woman, later identified as Jyoti Singh by the media with consent from her parents, went through over five surgeries, was later transferred to a hospital in Singapore, but lost her life due to multiple organ failure on 29 December.

GENDER AND ASPIRATION

In the 24/7 cycle, Jyoti, aka Nirbhaya (her mediated name), was repeatedly identified by her occupational and family background, depicted as a relic of the aspiring India. Jyoti's performance of identity as an aspiring woman in her journey towards upward mobility was the anchor to the media narrative. The news viewers were informed that she was a physiotherapy student whose parents were from small-town India, who themselves had had limited opportunities to get an education, and dreamt of giving their daughter a better education than themselves and the same educational opportunities as their sons. They had therefore sold ancestral land belonging to her father to send her to study physiotherapy, and worked double shifts to continue to pay for her schooling. Jyoti had completed her exams a few days before the incident, and was out with a male friend on the day of the incident to watch a movie at a cinema hall in south Delhi. The perpetrators on the other hand were identified as slum dwellers, one of them working as a fitness trainer–gym instructor, another a helper on the bus in which the crime took place; he was arrested in his native village in Bihar. The third accused was identified as a fruit seller. The fourth accused, who was driving the bus when the gang decided to pick up the couple on the day of the crime, worked as an occasional bus driver and cleaner, the fifth and prime accused was the elder brother of the driver, and lived with his brother in a room in a shanty area in Delhi. The sixth accused was a juvenile and was not identified. The 24/7 TV channels recreated the entire crime storyline minute by minute, tracing the exact same route as the two victims had taken from the cinema hall, while filling up the extra airtime with questions about the hobbies that the young woman had, her desires, and dreams. After his recovery, the male friend of the rape victim was made to relive the incident for TV news over and over again, with the repetition drilling into the audience the image of the spectacle. The repetition also worked to construct the image of Jyoti as the image of a modern India, carefully crafting her dreams that flowed seamlessly with the neoliberal narrative of gendered empowerment.

In their performance of the public spectacle, 24/7 news channels instantly took it upon themselves to galvanize the sentiment towards Jyoti as 'India's daughter'; the male friend of Jyoti became the one 'who stood up to the rapists'. Media played a role in mobilizing the sentiment of viewers and framing the anger and protests that followed as resulting from India's shaken conscience. The screening of affects mobilized public participation on the streets across various sites in urban India, demanding justice. The victim's professional and family background was repeatedly emphasized to appeal to the aspirational middle-class urban Indian who had similar narratives/sensibilities/aspirations of their own. The TV reporters covered the protests that followed as the 'nation coming together for justice'. A crime against a woman in Delhi, who was on her way to climbing out of her modest background and into the professional world, raped by men living in slums, uneducated, working as cleaners and bus drivers, was a narrative that the media played up as representative of the rot that India as a whole faces on its way to the global stage. The case instantly became a talking point to discuss 'women's safety' in India, marking the underclasses in urban sites of growth and development as threats to the national imaginary. What is critical here is to look at the erasures in this grand narrative about gender-based violence and women's safety, the structural features of the organization of cities, and the classed nature of disenfranchisements that are reproduced and normalized in urban spaces.

Criticism of the media reportage came from various sources. Some journalists criticized the media coverage on the grounds that this particular event was made to stand out as the single most horrific case. For example, the chief editor of *Times of Assam*, circulated in the North-Eastern state of India, cited several cases including the gang rape of a 14-year-old girl by men in the Indian army, to question why such a firestorm was not raised by the media in such cases (Zara 2012). Assam is one of the states in north-east India that is considered as a 'disturbed' area and is declared to be under the Armed Forces (Special Powers) Act, the act that grants special powers to the

Indian armed forces in order to crack down on the insurgent groups. According to National Crime Records Bureau statistics for 2014, 93 rapes are committed in India daily but not all get reported in the mainstream media that consist of English-language dailies and TV news channels (Maanvi 2016). This is so partly because when these outlets cater to the urban areas, the rapes committed in urban areas get greater coverage. The 'distance' from the urban area is a primary factor in deciding which crimes get higher media attention and which don't. An independent journalist, Kalpana Sharma, points out that 80–88 per cent of women experience violence within their homes, but reporting on violence against women focuses on public spaces, set within the ambits of the neoliberal city (Maanvi 2016).

MEDIATED JUSTICE

Demands for justice following the outrage in the Delhi rape case primarily consisted of the demand for the death penalty for the accused. The primary rationale behind the aggressive demand for the death penalty for rape heard on all media platforms, including newspapers, TV channels, and other platforms, was mainly that it would act as a deterrent. The criminal law was amended in 2013, without a thorough discussion on the recommendations of the Justice Verma Committee that had laid bare the philosophical arguments against the death penalty (Sharma 2013). In May 2017, after a speedy trial of the accused, four of the six accused were given death penalty, the juvenile accused was given three years in jail, and one of the accused had died earlier in jail in a possible suicide case. The Supreme Court cited the brutality of the case as a prime reason for awarding the death penalty.

What remains to be discussed is the continuing occurrences of brutal gang rapes that do not galvanize the same kind of media attention and demand for justice that the Delhi gang rape did. With each of these incidents, the question of 'women's safety in India' is discussed, which results in discussions about how India is not yet ready to give freedom to its women, and how the dreams of women to become independent are met with violence. This was the overarching argument of a documentary produced by BBC following the Delhi rape case, where one of the accused from the Delhi rape case and a lawyer speak about women's clothes that are provocative and how women staying out late in the evening are asking for trouble. Through these media discourses on violence against women in major metropolitan cities in India, which represent the opportunities that economically progressing India has to offer, a very large section of women employed in these cities are left out of the discussion (Rajkhowa 2016). Violence perpetrated by employers against women who work as house labourers, dowry-related killings, victims of cruelty by husbands or relatives, and the cases that go unreported are among those that remain out of the discussion that the news coverage demands justice for.

In the Delhi gang-rape case, capitalizing on the worldwide interest in this one event, news media took up the fight for justice into their own hands, driving the demand for the death penalty and individualizing the narrative of gender-based violence. By defining justice in this case as media-led public participation in large-scale protest, news discourse effectively dismissed ongoing collective and grassroots-based struggles, often led by women, against various forms of gender-based violence across classes, castes, and regions, perpetrated by various elements in power, in various parts of India. These erasures of the everyday forms of gendered violence in India's margins by a spectacular story of violence in the capital, constitute abetment to the violence of a neoliberal state that normalizes the violence perpetuated at the margins as a price that the marginalized must pay in return for national development and growth.

CASTE AND NEOLIBERAL DESIRE

Caste remains erased in India's neoliberal articulations. The desire for an aspiring neoliberal state reflects in the Indian media's denial of its caste system that in reality remains deeply entrenched in India's social fabric. The everyday occurrences of caste-based violence that are intertwined with the organization of India's social fabric mostly remain unarticulated in 24/7 news media. Stories of reforms point to the opportunities for the middle/upper middle classes opened up by the reforms, set against the backdrop of the barriers posed by caste-based affirmative action. In these instances, caste is seen as a barrier, framing the problem of caste as one of the lower castes 'taking up' positions, against the backdrop of which neoliberal reforms are constructed as opening up opportunities for employment and upward mobility. Caste as a category that organizes violence is obfuscated from media frames, and thus continues to perpetuate itself, adapting to the new terrains of the neoliberal imaginary. The entry of caste then into the 24/7 cycles takes place during spectacular outbursts of violence, framing these forms of violence as conflict. When these spectacular forms of violence do break into the 24/7 cycles, they are routinized into sensational narratives of conflict, and are framed as debates with hashtags, inviting audience members to share their opinions, obfuscating the structural features of caste injustice that are routinized into India's socio-cultural fabric. The erasure of the violence of the mundane and the repetition of the spectacular as conflict obfuscate conversations on the structural contexts of caste that perpetuate various forms of routinized violence.

A SUICIDE

Suicides or deaths of lower-caste individuals in specific urban contexts emerge as sites of news coverage, often against the backdrop of large-scale protests. Take, for instance, the media coverage of the spectacles of protest that emerged in the aftermath of the suicide of Rohith Vemula. In January 2016, Rohith Vemula, a Dalit (Scheduled Caste) PhD scholar from Hyderabad Central University (HCU) committed suicide after facing institutionalized caste-based discrimination at the university, a pattern that is systematically witnessed across universities in India. A year earlier in July 2015, the university had stopped paying the fellowship of Rs 25,000 per month to Rohith after he had raised issues under the banner of the university's Ambedkar Student's Association (ASA), an organization that fights for Dalit students' rights. Rohith and four other student members of ASA protested against the death penalty given to Yakub Memon, a convicted terrorist and conspirator behind the 1993 Bombay bombings. Rohith had also condemned the attack by a right-wing students' group Akhil Bharatiya Vidyarthi Parishad (ABVP) in Delhi University during the screening of the documentary *Muzaffarnagar Baqi Hai*. The ABVP had dubbed them as 'goons'. The ABVP leader had filed a complaint against the ASA students for having assaulted him, that had led him to undergoing a surgery the following day. But after the initial enquiry, the university cleared the students of any charges. Later, news reports revealed that the surgery that ABVP leader underwent had nothing to do with the conflict. However, ABVP wrote a letter to the union minister from Secunderabad Bandaru Dattatreya, alleging that the ASA students were indulging in 'casteist' and 'anti-national' activities. The letter was forwarded to Union Human Resource Minister Smriti Irani, and then to the university's vice chancellor. Thereafter the four ASA students and Rohith were suspended from the university. The five students set up a tent in the university campus and started a protest. Soon after the suspension, Rohith committed suicide by hanging himself in a friend's hostel room using the banner of ASA.

Rohith's suicide sparked protests across India as well as worldwide on the grounds of caste discrimination and human rights violations. In his suicide note, in order to take care of the 'formalities', he absolved anybody whatsoever from any responsibility for his act of killing himself. In the note, he also called his birth his 'fatal accident'. Exploring Rohith's family background and the meaning of the 'fatal accident' that Rohith had referred to in his suicide note, a report mentioned (Mondal n.d.) that Rohith's mother was born to a migrant labourer couple working on the railway tracks outside the house of a family that had adopted her. The woman in the family had recently lost a child and liked the baby and asked the couple for her. The couple agreed. The child, born to a Mala (Dalit/SC), was adopted into the house of a Vaddera (OBC, higher-caste) family, but was treated as a servant. She was married off at the age of 14 to a Vaddera man. Her caste was kept secret from the man. It was five years and three children later that somebody leaked the secret to him. Rohith's mother endured beatings from her husband much more now than before, spurred by the caste-based hatred stemming from being married to a woman from the 'untouchable' caste. This painful past and the struggles that followed were not known to Rohith's friends; he had preferred to keep them to himself. Coming from a financially backward family residing in Guntur village in Andhra Pradesh, Rohith had also written in his suicide note that he owed an amount of Rs 40,000 to a certain person and when his scholarship money is returned to him by the university, may the amount be paid to that person. The suicide as an act was mediatized through the 24/7 coverage of protests that emerged across campuses, invoking the conflict frame.

MEDIA OMISSIONS

The suicide of Rohith was a result of institutional discrimination, but it was aided by the media's neglect in giving coverage to caste-related issues. This was later acknowledged by reports in various news outlets. A report (Gopinath 2016) stated that the University of Hyderabad had a history of discriminating against Dalit students, and, in the last decade, there had been 10 suicides by Dalit students. If there had been proper media coverage of the expulsion of the students from the university and their sleep-in protest, it might have been a different issue, perhaps the suicide could have been avoided. 'Unfortunately there is a tendency to limit reporting on issues affecting Dalits to sensational stories in every media organization in the country' due to lack of diversity in the workforce, said a news portal (Damodaran 2016). Within local media in Hyderabad, there is a dominance of upper-caste editors and reporters in the newsroom. There is resistance from these authorities in the newsroom towards covering Dalit students' protests and matters affecting the Dalit community (Boruah 2016).

In attempts to downplay the role of caste discrimination and making the news palatable to the Brahminical sentiments of a consuming public, the dozen prior suicides in the university were referred to as students' suicides with 'Dalit' mentioned passingly. Questions were raised about why Vemula's death was more tragic and deplorable. Media reports brought up the mental fragility and depression Vemula faced for months and his fights with fellow Dalits, individualizing the locus of the suicide to Rohith's mental state. Rohith had made it amply clear in his suicide note that his dejection stemmed from his caste identity. But rather than sensing the need for comprehensive reportage on caste discrimination in the universities, hostels, and education in general, news reporters asked questions catering to those who suspected the suicide to be political.

A news magazine later ran a piece on the media reportage of the Dalit protests (Kaushik 2016) and contended that the news about Vemula's suspension from the University of Hyderabad had been on the online Dalit forums for months, but the issue was picked up by the mainstream media only after the protests broke out. The coverage of the protests on the campus by students demanding the resignation of the vice chancellor of HCU completely erased the demand of the students for justice against caste-based discrimination. Instead, the newsroom debates revolved around the legalities of whether the vice chancellor was allowed to be on campus on the day of the protests when a judicial enquiry was on, whether police beating of the protesting students was sanctioned, or whether the protests were not peaceful in the first place. Deflecting from the key issue of caste-based protests, the TV news capitalized on the presence of police on campus and the vandalism that ensued. The anger of the students and their demand for justice were rarely acknowledged as Dalit students' protest. It was simply framed as part of the student politics between ABVP and the Ambedkarite group, and the protests were framed as being against 'suicides', but not as 'a Dalit student's suicide'. The TV news channels predictably banked upon the sensationalism of the lathi charge and police dragging students by the hair.

The coverage of the protests after Rohith's suicide continued to circulate the conflict frame, attending to the different parties that were involved in the conflict, and depicting the politicization of India's universities. Televised images of protests, police action, and different groups in the conflict failed to catalyse public affect as the death of Jyoti Singh had. In the realm of caste, caste-based violence does not fit into the story of an aspiring India, and hence public sensibilities are captured in the suspended state of watching a conflict unfold, devoid of its roots in caste violence. Unless the news involves a sensational element of violence (such as a suicide or a murder), there is no attention given to the continual injustice meted out to Dalit communities. These omissions of caste-based violence abet and perpetrate the violence of a neoliberal state that fancies an aspiring India as a site for erasing differences while at the same time engraving them into the cultural fabric. The burying and denying of narratives of caste-based injustices silence the victims of such injustices in favour of a narrative of India that is casteless, driving the agenda of Brahminical supremacy dressed in the garb of neoliberal aspirations.

CLASS AND ITS ERASURE

The neoliberal story of India's aspirations systematically erases social class as a site for contestation, obfuscating the structural contexts and inequalities that constitute sites of contemporary structural violence in India (Fernandes 2000). Narratives of India's margins remain obfuscated in 24/7 cycles of growth and modernization. For instance, stories of the epidemic of farmer suicides across India or stories of the inequalities experienced in rural India remain erased from the upwardly aspiring frames (Rastogi and Dutta 2015). Class is relegated to a site of articulation in the old India, juxtaposed against the backdrop of a 'new India' that is charged with the effects of aspiration. When class-based conflicts do emerge at sites of capitalist accumulation, the classed nature of the events is usually obfuscated, erasing the underlying inequalities, instead framing the events as conflicts between tradition and modernity. When the classed nature of conflicts is indeed televised, the onus of conflict is placed on the deviant lower class that steals, and uses and threatens violence against the neoliberal inside of the nation. As opposed to the legitimized public anger of the middle classes demanding efficiency, growth, and democracy, the anger of the underclasses is circulated as a threat, tied to affective productions of fear and insecurity.

THE MARKED OTHER

Take for instance the 24/7 coverage of domestic worker protests at Mahagun Moderne, a gated community for the aspiring, English-speaking, middle/upper-middle classes in Noida, New Delhi. The protests of domestic workers and their families against the backdrop of the mistreatment, abuse, and forced imprisonment of a domestic worker were framed in the 24/7 cycle as an ongoing conflict. Images of protesting domestic workers and their families were deployed to mark the 'other', the 'outside' of the neoliberal imaginary, recycling images, and narratives of migrants from elsewhere as mobs threatening the security of the assumed mainstream (Muslim immigrants from Bangladesh). The constructions of the conflict then go back and forth between screening CCTV footage of protesting workers, stories of a mob attack, and the security threats to the housing community. The securitizing narrative foregrounds the voices of middle-class residents who discuss the threats posed by the mob.

The Twitter hashtag #MaldainNoida, referring to Malda in Bengal that is portrayed as the site of Islamic threats through open migration from Bangladesh, is repeated on the screen to recirculate the affect around the marked outsider/other threatening the sanctity of the neoliberal mainstream/aspiring middle class residing in the gated community. The voices of domestic workers are mostly absent from the presentation of news reports, and, when present, are talked down to, and drowned out by the voices of Mahagun residents. The everyday violence experienced by workers in India's informal sector are obfuscated from English-language, 24/7 news cycles.

On a similar note, 24/7 news coverage of class-based protests, such as the protests of Maruti workers, depicts them as a threat to the aspiring story of India's growth and development. For instance, the Times Now coverage of worker protests at a Maruti plant, followed by a conflict that resulted in the death of a manager, framed the protests as lawlessness that needed to be brought to justice. Pointing to the failure of the state and its political leadership to take adequate action against the protesting workers, the coverage recycled images of broken car windows and burnt office spaces to call for justice and accountability, hashtagging calls to public action. When the workers involved in the protests were jailed, English-language media coverage foregrounded the narrative of justice secured. Even as the anger of the English-language viewer was catalysed against the threats to law presented by workers, the plight of the workers and the structural violence they experience remained erased from the discursive space. In other words, the affects produced by 24/7 news frames are conditioned within the specific class interests of an upwardly aspiring urban middle class, whose interests are positioned in opposition to the interests of the lower classes.

The depiction of the underclasses as the violent 'other' is markedly exaggerated when portraying the indigenous communities of India that live in forests that are marked as sites for mining development. The marking of the protesting indigenous communities as the Maoist other invokes the terror narrative to justify state-sponsored violence in the form of military action. The 24/7 news cycles offering video montages of the Maoist jungles reproduce effects of insecurity that are deployed towards the reproduction of violence as a necessary response.

UNDOING WELFARE

The neoliberal imaginary of India is constructed around the promises offered by privatization, presenting privatized solutions of effective management and efficiency to India's problems of governance, juxtaposing privatization against political corruption (Dutta 2017). The state and politicians are presented as targets of English-language media coverage, in contrast to the promises of effective and rational management brought about by privatization. The 24/7 news cycles perform stings, orchestrate hashtag campaigns, and invite public participation to imagine India's governance in the framework of corporate management and consultancy. One of the sites of 24/7 coverage is the state-driven public welfare system addressing the basic needs (employment, education, and food security) of India's underclasses. Images of leakage reproduce the narrative of welfare rot. Media narratives of corruption in the delivery systems for public assistance are circulated as invitations to undoing these systems, reorganizing them through public–private partnerships, and substituting them with incentivized programmes that foreground responsibility and ownership. Undoing of welfare and public assistance is a fundamental site for the neoliberal reorganizing of India's political economy, with mediatized narratives working precisely to catalyse this transformation. The constitution of public affect around corruption and misspent taxpayer money reproduces the neoliberal ideology of privatization of everyday life and public resources.

RELIGION AS NEOLIBERAL CULTURE

The 24/7 news cycle on the one hand punctuates the story of an aspiring India, circulating stories and images of affect as aspiration, and on the other hand, manages the anxieties of the upwardly mobile middle classes brought about by the rapid transformation of India through narratives of traditional culture as a resource for healing and sustenance. Religion is intertwined with the narrative of 'new India', with the arrival of India storied as the arrival of its Hindu culture. The revival of India on the global stage is as much a Hindu arrival as it is an economic transformation. Hindu religion is narrativized as a new-age resource for healing, offering imaginaries of cultural revival and civilizational glory. The telling of the story of an aspirational India goes hand in hand with the story of a reviving India, where Indian traditions are reworked into the ambit of the modern market, while at the same time they are positioned in conflict with the market. Simultaneously, accounts of the large-scale and widespread violence against India's religious minorities mostly remain erased, although images of particular sites of violence work simultaneously to produce media spectacles. The Hinduized imagery of India mainstreams the Hindutva forces as the everyday cultural logics of the nation, married to the promises of delivering good governance and economic growth. For instance, the Hindutva ideologue Yogi Adityanath in Uttar Pradesh is mainstreamed as the chief minister, made palatable to the English-reading upwardly aspiring middle classes through his promises of good governance.

REVIVING CULTURE AND NATION

Religion is marked as the site of culture, and therefore, the images of cultural revival are also images of the revival of mainstream Hindutva. Hindutva is mainstreamed as the cultural logic of the nation through stories of cultural revival, publicizing images of the presence of India on global platforms, mainstreaming lessons on spirituality, and offering services from astrology to yoga. Stories of Hindu culture are packaged as cultural stories, formulated as signifiers of the market, and incorporated into the logics of the market. Paradoxically, for its English-speaking upwardly aspiring audience, the 24/7 media cycles articulate liberal values when Hindutva forces attack markers of neoliberal modernity (such as Valentine's Day or the public display of affection), projecting the attackers as backward underclasses. In other words, affect is strategically deployed, on the one hand speaking to the sensibilities of the upwardly mobile audience when positioning Hindutva forces as relics of tradition that are in the way of modernization, and on the other hand, commoditizing and making palatable cultural symbols as everyday relics of modern India. The 24/7 news cycle produces an English-speaking audience that can both have its Hindutva symbols and practices, and participate in the commodity culture brought about by India's neoliberal transformation.

The revival of culture is positioned against the articulations of attacks on Indian (read Hindu) culture from a plethora of external forces (terrorist threats that challenge the security and the sovereignty of the nation). Culture is juxtaposed against the backdrop of the nation, and is catalysed as a trope for the circulation of nationalism (Udupa 2012, 2015). The marking of the anti-national, thus, is a favourite prime-time pastime, often marking India's Muslim other as the anti-national, as the threat to the nation and its sovereignty. Media events are created around this marking and hunting down of the anti-national, performing televised debates to punish the anti-national. Twitter hashtags are rapidly deployed to catalyse public frenzy, which in turn builds the ratings of the televised programme. Similar markings of the other in contested spaces such as Kashmir and Manipur are carried out through depictions of the threats to the nation. Once the threatening other has been marked, violence on her/his body is implied as a justified response. The nation thus is drawn up in 24/7 news cycles to construct its hegemonic image set in opposition to the threats to it, rendering necessary violence as a natural response.

ERASING RELIGIOUS VIOLENCE

The 24/7 news cycles are marked by the systematic erasure of stories of religious violence, violence carried out by India's Hindu majority on its minority population. In the most recent incidents of lynchings of Muslims in the context of the beef ban imposed by the right-wing ruling BJP, the stories of everyday violence and the religious contexts of violence mostly remain erased in the mainstream English-language media. Similarly, the hate-inciting speeches and actions of elected political leaders of the BJP remain uninterrogated in the mainstream English-language news stories. The role of Prime Minister Narendra Modi in the Gujarat pogrom remains erased from the performed debates and sting operations of 24/7 cycles. Erasure of the underlying features of violence, its structural causes, and its everyday effects on India's minorities is juxtaposed against televised images that place the audience as a spectator, unable and unwilling to act.

When an incident of religious violence does appear on the 24/7 cycle, it does so as a spectacle, with images and sounds that put forth an overarching narrative of securitization. The violence itself is often projected as 'Islamic terror', enabled by the infiltration of Muslims from neighbouring Muslim countries. For instance, the media coverage of the riots in Basirhat, West Bengal, projected the forms of violence as products of Muslim infiltration. The Hindutva narrative of the BJP is held up and enabled through media portrayals of an India under threat. Moreover, 24/7 news cycles often reproduce violence through the production of staged events that are made for the media. The mediated construction of images of clashing mobs obfuscates the structural contexts of religious hate that have been normalized as the mainstream.

* * *

In conclusion, the 24/7 English-language news cycle produces, commoditizes, and speaks to an aspiring, upwardly mobile Indian middle class that sees the market as the panacea to India's problems of development. The images, sounds, and narratives circulated in 24/7 news cycles reproduce public affects of aspiration, juxtaposed against the effects of anger and insecurity, localizing neoliberal articulations in local values and norms (Rao 2009). The violence that makes up India's neoliberal imaginary is perpetuated and made palatable through the 24/7 cycle, through strategies of erasure and marking the 'outside' of the culture. The digital transformation of the 24/7 cycle, combined with Twitter hashtags and public engagements, catalyses this transformation, producing an upwardly aspiring middle class that unsees the everyday violence of neoliberalism, while paradoxically being immersed in the images and sounds of conflicts and security threats. The inequalities of gender, caste, class, and minority position that make up the fabric of modern India are normalized into the grand narrative of aspirations, obfuscating the violence that makes up the story of contemporary India.

REFERENCES

Boruah, M. (2016). '#JusticeForRohith: Why the Movement Is Not Well-Covered in the Media?' Retrieved from http://www.oneindia.com/india/justice-for-rohith-why-the-movement-is-not-well-covered-in-the-media-2096637.html (accessed on 17 August 2018).

Damodaran, K. (2016). 'The Media's Caste: How It's to Blame for Rohith Vemula's Death'. Retrieved from http://www.hindustantimes.com/analysis/the-media-s-caste-how-it-s-to-blame-for-rohith-vemula-s-death/story-iMkswsn297muC9fTJRimlN.html (accessed on 17 August 2018).

——— (2017). *Imagining India in Discourse: Meaning, Power, Structure.* Singapore: Springer.

Fernandes, L. (2000). 'Nationalizing the Global: Media Images, Cultural Politics and the Middle Class in India'. *Media, Culture and Society*, 22(5): 611–28.

Gopinath, V. (2016). '5 Ways Media Can Show It's Fair to Rohith Vemula'. Retrieved from http://www.dailyo.in/politics/rohith-vemula-dalit-politics-caste-atrocities-university-of-hyderbad-bandaru-dattatreya-smriti-irani-media/story/1/8552.html (accessed on 17 August 2018).

Kaushik, M. (2016). 'Missing the Story'. Retrieved from http://www.caravanmagazine.in/perspectives/missing-the-story-lessons-indian-journalism-dalit-mobilisation-online (accessed on 17 August 2018).

Maanvi (2016). 'Post Nirbhaya, Let's Rethink How the Media Reports Rape'. Retrieved from https://www.thequint.com/women/2016/06/30/rethinking-how-media-reports-rape-one-news-item-at-a-time-nirbhaya-uber-rape-case-suzette-jordan-jisha (accessed on 17 August 2018).

Mondal, S. (n.d.). 'Rohith Vemula, an Unfinished Portrait'. Retrieved from http://www.hindustantimes.com/static/rohith-vemula-an-unfinished-portrait/ (accessed on 17 August 2018).

Rajagopal, A. (2002). 'Violence of Commodity Aesthetics: Hawkers, Demolition Raids and a New Regime of Consumption'. *Economic and Political Weekly*, 37(1): 65–76.

Rajkhowa, A. (2016). 'Cultural Critique after Nirbhaya: Indian and Foreign Media Commentators Negotiate Critique of Culture and Masculinity Following the 2012 Delhi Rape'. *Writing from Below*, 3(1).

Rao, S. (2009). 'Glocalization of Indian Journalism'. *Journalism Studies*, 10(4): 474–88.

Rastogi, R. and M. J. Dutta (2015). 'Neoliberalism, Agriculture and Farmer Stories: Voices of Farmers from the Margins of India'. *Journal of Creative Communications*, 10(2): 128–40.

Sharma, K. (2013). 'Crime and Punishment'. Retrieved from http://www.the-hindu.com/opinion/columns/Kalpana_Sharma/crime-and-punishment/article4414590.ece (accessed on 17 August 2018).

Thussu, D. K. (2007). 'The Murdochization of News? The Case of STAR TV in India'. *Media, Culture and Society*, 29(4): 593–611.

Udupa, S. (2012). 'News Media and Contention over "the Local" in Urban India'. *American Ethnologist*, 39(4): 819–34.

———— (2015). *News, Publics and Politics in Globalising India: Media, Publics, Politics*. Cambridge: Cambridge University Press.

Zara, C. (2012). 'Delhi Gang-Rape Victim: Indian Media Slammed for "Bloodlust" News Coverage'. Retrieved from http://www.ibtimes.com/delhi-gang-rape-victim-indian-media-slammed-bloodlust-news-coverage-981656 (accessed on 17 August 2018).

CHAPTER SIXTEEN

Journalistic Subcultures

Rules, Values, Routines, and Norms of English-Language and Hindi-Language Media

ANUP KUMAR

. . . .

The Indian news media[1] space is crowded, diverse, and fiercely competitive. There are more than a hundred thousand print newspapers and magazines, a hundred-plus news television channels, thousands of web-only publications, and hundreds of radio stations.[2] Journalistic practices, professional and citizen-initiated, are continuously evolving as well.[3] Not least because of news disseminators that operate entirely out of websites including on social media services such as YouTube, Twitter, Facebook, and WhatsApp. On top of all this diversity, an additional layer of complexity in Indian journalism is that the news media operate in multiple Indian languages including the English language. Apparently, journalists and audiences of mainstream media, in the English language and other Indian languages, have been living in different socio-cultural worlds, experiencing different news cultures, and, that too, before the much talked about social media fostered news bubbles in academic discourse (Parameswaran 1997; Ganguly-Scrase and Scrase 2009).

Hence, the purpose of this chapter is twofold: One, to show how the diversity in journalistic subcultures influences rules of social production of news (newswork). Two, to discuss a conceptual framework to understand and interpret how ethnolinguistic diversity in Indian media and journalism fosters differences in subcultures of news, leading to differences in news values, routines, sources, and professional norms.

The differences are not superficial; they are more than just about language. Journalists and audiences of English media come largely from the middle or upper classes, live mostly in major cities including the national capital region of Delhi, and are likely to be exposed to a progressive secular cosmopolitan culture.[4] Whereas journalists and audiences of the Indian-languages media largely come from the lower and middles classes (the proverbial *aam admi*, or common people), live mostly in poorer parts of the metros, provincial capitals, small towns and villages, and are likely to be struggling with the remnants of feudalism and social prejudices of caste and religion. This suggests that differences between media in English and other Indian languages relate to social differences that in turn are tied to elite and vernacular subcultures of news. By news culture, I mean patterns of journalistic practices and rules that guide professional behaviour. I will elaborate on this momentarily.

Because of the limited space that we have here, it will not be possible to address the immense ethnolinguistic diversity that we find in Indian journalism. The arguments will primarily draw from past studies on media in English and Hindi languages that together are followed by an overwhelming majority of people in the country. I hope the readers will see that the arguments have significance and relevance for a wider application in comparative studies of vernacular news cultures and the universalizing news culture of the English-language media. Additionally, the English-language media is a reference point for comparison because of the hegemonic status it occupies in India, and in the world as well.

In the context of contemporary Indian politics, the Hindi media is the loudest voice in the Indian public sphere; and the English media relative to its audience size has disproportionate social capital and political power and influence over the state apparatuses (Parameswaran 1997; Ganguly-Scrase and Scrase 2009; Kumar 2011). Additionally, the journalistic practices and occupational ideology of English-language media in India are closest to the practices of journalism in the English-speaking world (Chaudhary 1974; Kumar 2011). A major factor in the spread of universalizing news practices and occupational ideology is the spread of a 'journalistic paradigm' that was first developed in the United States (Kumar 2013).

To understand Indian journalism in the context of all its diversity, especially ethnolinguistic diversity, we need more comparative and cross-cultural studies on the social production of news (newswork). Drawing from previous studies, again, the proposition I am making in this chapter is that the differences we see in media coverage of events, issues, and government policies—in English- and Indian-language media—can be explained by linking them to the differences in social production of news (newswork) and the underlying journalistic subcultures. Additionally, media power differs across journalistic subcultures because of differences in the social production of news.

The news, like all knowledge, is socially constructed and for its validity relies on internal social processes (Park 1940). Social processes of newswork have many similarities to the social production of knowledge in social sciences, although the processes may not be as rigorous because of the deadline pressures (Ericson 1999; Gans 1980; Harrington 2003; Kumar 2009; Schudson 1989; Tuchman 1976). Additionally, media's interstitial position cutting across social, political, cultural, and economic fields gives the news special power to influence discourse emerging from other fields (Benson and Neveu 2005; Bourdieu 2005; Kumar 2009). This interstitial position highlights an important dimension of media power that comes from the power to block communication (Breed 2005). The media's power in the shaping of public discourse, and even blocking communication, plays out in multiple dimensions (Lukes 2005; Kumar 2009, 2013).

Past studies have addressed how cultural differences in media, especially between English and Hindi media in the north, can help us understand differences in journalistic practices, interactions with politics, and media power in India (Jeffery 2000; Kumar 2011; Neyazi 2011; Ninan 2007; Rajagopal 2002; Stahlberg 2002; Rao 2009).

Additionally, we have studies from other parts of the world that have shown how differences in journalistic subcultures can explain variation in news values and processes (Hanitzsch 2006; Marr et al. 2001; Pritchard and Souvageau 1998; Weaver 1998). We have global studies as well that have highlighted how cultural, historical, and political differences across countries lead to differences in professional values underlying newswork (McLeod and Rush 1969; Patterson and Donsbach 1996; Shoemaker and Cohen 2006).

Again, it cannot be emphasized enough that we need cross-cultural or comparative approaches to interpret findings in their proper cultural and historical contexts. Existence of multiple journalistic subcultures in India should not mean that there isn't a shared professional identity and occupational ideology as well, among journalists working for the English- and Indian-languages media. Instead, similarities constitute a baseline for comparative research (Przeworski and Teune 1970). A comparative approach is 'not only indispensable for establishing the generalizability of theories and findings, it also forces us to test our interpretations against cross-cultural differences and inconsistencies' (Hanitzsch 2009: 413).

In the rest of this chapter, I will first briefly discuss how the differences between media in the English language and in the Indian languages, precisely speaking Hindi media, can be understood in the context of the *split* Indian public sphere that fosters a contestation between the culture of elites and vernacular cultures in the wider context of progressive cosmopolitan modernity and a reactionary conservatism. Then I will trace how the split in the Indian public sphere relates to journalistic *doxa* and *habitus*. Following which, I will discuss how journalistic subcultures foster differences in social production of news (newswork)—news routines, news values, and professional norms—in the English and Hindi media. Finally, I will conclude with what this means in terms of the journalistic power of English and Hindi media.

SPLIT INDIAN PUBLIC SPHERE

What is fascinating for anyone studying Indian journalism is that the presence of multiple news cultures is associated with ethnolinguistically organized public spheres. Looking through the theoretical prism of print capitalism,[5] media organized along ethnolinguistic lines, within a continental-size[6] Indian public sphere, should be a factor in the fostering of competing political identities. Nevertheless, the post-independence history of media politics shows that an aspirational framework of a constitutional democracy and a common Indian market have worked as centripetal forces that keep the centrifugal forces in check, and likely play a role in the spread of a universal capitalist ideology of journalism.[7] We will later return to how the state and market have structuring influence on news values.

While the market based political economy of media highlights the underlying similarities in social processes of newswork, a productive approach to understanding and interpreting the diversity of Indian media is to see it in the context of how subcultures of newswork foster a fragmented and fragmenting public sphere in India. The fragmentation exists along gender, caste, class, and religious dimensions as well. The implication of a fragmented and fragmenting public sphere is that it leads to fragmentation in civil society as well. Hence, fragmentation fostered by news cultures in the Indian public sphere is important, as well, to understand the role of journalism, compellingly advocated for by many scholars, in empowering civil society and deepening democracy in India (Rao and Mudgal 2016).

As mentioned above, the major fault line is between the media in English and that in Hindi. As dominant voices, media in English and Hindi cut across the immense diversity of ethnolinguistically organized sub-national media, and play a central role in constructing a fledgling national public sphere in which they compete in constructing and evoking alternative visions of India that we see in discourses surrounding 'ideas of India.'[8] For example, one vision, preferred by English media, is grounded in cosmopolitan liberalism and secularism that can be traced to ideas of modernity in the West, and the other vision, preferred by Hindi media, is grounded in progress and modernization with one foot in the past. Since the 1980s, the latter has been associated with the rise of the illiberal discourse of Hindu nationalism that has undermined India's pluralism.

In a path-breaking study on the rise of the politics of Hindu nationalism in the backdrop of the transformations taking place in the Indian media, Rajagopal (2002) had proposed the concept of a 'split' along linguistic lines to understand the fragmented and fragmenting Indian public sphere. The Indian-languages media foster the 'split' in the public sphere because of the power of linguistic ideologies to evoke specific responses from the respective epistemic communities. Rajagopal (2002: 25) in his study showed that Hindi-language newspapers and television shows such as *Ramayana* were important factors in the dissemination of Hindu nationalist ideas and the political sentiments of the Ram Janam Bhoomi Movement in the 1980s and 1990s because of the proximity of the 'inner codes of meaning' embedded in Hindi, in comparison to English, to the Hindu culture of north India. The Hindi media evoked responses that were specific to the cultural tradition of the north Indian Hindu community using Hindu religious idiom, imagery, and symbolism. However, journalists will not always succeed in fostering desired meanings merely because they share predispositions with their audiences. Meanings are the outcome of cognitive interactions where meanings encoded in news stories encounter cultural codes that readers bring to those stories (Hall 2006). Yet, what is fascinating is that the Hindu nationalist movement (Hindutva) demonstrated an uncanny awareness of this split between the English and the Hindi media in the Indian public sphere. The movement strategically carved out a discursive space that was sympathetic to the political project of Hindutva.

We can trace the split in the north Indian public sphere to the colonial period (Orsini 2009). In the 1920s and 1930s, in north India, we see a similar split between Hindi-language and Urdu-language newspapers—because of the proximity of the inner codes to the epistemic communities of Hindus and Muslims—on the demand for Pakistan and media discourses of the Partition. Further back, we can even trace the split to the nineteenth century in the public debate on social reforms in Indian society in the English- and Indian-languages newspapers in the nineteenth century. For the progressive-minded Indians, the English-language newspapers were better suited for dissemination of new ideas from the West to Indians who were educated through the medium of the English language. The traditionalists used the Indian-languages newspapers as their platform to suspect and resist the new ideas.

This 'split' in a large measure can explain the differences in how the media in English and Hindi have responded to the politics of nationalism and Hindutva in recent years. By strategically using the Hindi-language media, the proponents of the Hindu nationalist movement have been relatively successful in presenting journalists and other progressive voices in the English media as antagonistic to Hindu interests. The symbiotic relationship between Hindu nationalist politics and the Hindi media has been a factor in the politics of north India (Kumar 2011).

However, the split is not only about the rise of Hindu nationalist politics. As alluded to earlier, it is about contestation between ruling elites and vernacular classes over imaginations of India and ideas of modernity as either clearly breaking from the past, or alternative forms that project a conservative stance towards tradition and social difference. The split in the public sphere, and consequently in civil society as well, has led to competing discourses of pluralism and ethno-nationalism identified with metaphors of 'India' and 'Bharat' respectively. In a way, the discourses draw on cultural codes embedded in the language and constitute the ideological structures of the elite subcultures of the English media and the vernacular subculture of Indian-languages media.

ELITE AND VERNACULAR NEWS CULTURES

What makes the split Indian public sphere fascinating is the significant overlap between speakers of English and elite culture, and speakers of Indian languages and vernacular culture. Vernacular culture is a catch-all anthropological concept that incorporates commonly shared attitudes and sentiments about social organization, beliefs, and subjectively experienced social identities by the majority of ordinary people. It is distinct and in opposition to the beliefs, attitudes, and experiences of elites or ruling classes in any society. So, in its wider connotation, the use of the vernacular is not limited to language, although it is linguistically structured, and its most visible manifestations are in verbal and non-verbal communication practices (Lantis 1960). Vernacular cultures view and present the world differently from the dominant discourses of those who occupy positions of power (Hauser 1999, 2007). We find such alternative expressions of modernity in social movements on the margins and in ungoverned spaces against the institutionalized use of reason and the spread of the rational-bureaucratic authority of a high modernist state (Chatterjee 2004; Habermas 2006; Kumar 2011: 27–8; Scott 1998).

It will be an error to view vernacular cultures as being opposed to the use of public reasoning that we associate with the emergence of a public sphere (Habermas 1989). Hence, vernacular must not be equated with obscurantism, because even though it may draw on traditions, history has shown that it does foster the social production of alternative modernities. From India's past we have many examples of how vernacularization of public discourses in languages other than Sanskrit transformed the power relationship between the ruling elites and subaltern majorities, thereby giving rise to new political identities.[9] Even the emergence of Urdu as a vernacular—from the hybridization of Turkish, Persian, and Arabic with Hindavi, a precursor to modern Hindi in north India—played an important role in the transformation and creation of the syncretic identities of the new ruling classes of north India before British colonization (Rahman 2011).

Following colonization, the English language displaced Sanskrit, Persian, Urdu, and Hindi in the nineteenth century as the language of power,[10] primarily because it was the language of the new rulers. The hegemonic power of the English language in the public sphere can be traced back to its historical roots in the introduction of modern education in India. The British rulers made the English language the medium of instruction in high schools and colleges in 1835. It was a momentous decision in Indian history. Thomas Babington Macaulay, the man who is credited with the introduction of the English language, had predicted that it would produce new modern ruling classes in India, different from traditional feudal elites, who could be separated in their thinking from the majority of the masses who spoke and thought in Indian languages (see Viswanathan 1989).

About 90 years after introduction of English, Ganesh Shankar Vidyarthi, the founding editor of *Pratap*, a newspaper that has an iconic status in the history of Hindi journalism, lamented the state of public discourse in the country. He felt that most people had no say in it at all, and that too primarily because of language. He argued that what was being presented as Indian public opinion (*lokmat*) on issues such as social justice and anti-feudalism, was not a true reflection of what the common people thought, but was the opinion of a

Anup Kumar

minority of elites who were educated in the English medium, and likely read only English-language newspapers.[11] Macaulay could have never imagined how this seemingly cosmetic change in the language of instruction in educational institutions, after many decades, would transform the country in more fundamental ways by splitting the doxa and habitus of Indians working in all fields, including political, bureaucratic, corporate, academic, artistic,[12] and journalistic.

JOURNALISTIC DOXA AND HABITUS

In his sociological studies of the media, Pierre Bourdieu (1993, 1996, 2005) paid special emphasis on how social distinction, and its hierarchical manifestation, is a rather fruitful way to understand and explain differences in news decisions and other practices of the mainstream media organizations in France and elsewhere.[13] He advocated that to understand subcultures of news, we must study how the educational and social background of journalists and their audiences produce and reproduce journalistic doxa and habitus (Bourdieu 2005; Kumar 2009, 2011).

Doxa is a commonly held belief about society that members of a field of practice share with each other. Bourdieu (2005: 37) in his study of fields of practice, including the journalistic field, had argued that we must consider the 'specific doxa, a system of presuppositions inherent in membership in a field' to understand and explain cultural practices. There are presuppositions that are intuitively shared by members of a cultural group or intersectional subcultures within a larger social body that can be traced back to social distinctions.

Vernacular news cultures and ruling/elite news cultures differ in the doxa and habitus of journalists and their audiences. Journalists in their reporting draw on social sensibilities and codes of meaning making that resonate with the doxa of the respective cultural groups that in India constitute fragmented epistemic communities organized along languages. We may as well say that doxa is what separates the journalistic subcultures of English and Hindi media. The respective doxa of journalists shapes their view on the relationship between the press and other three constitutional branches of the government (executive, legislature, and judiciary), and how they view other institutions of society.

Like doxa, habitus predisposes how we see and react to the world, and is helpful in interpreting news cultures. The concept of habitus combines the materiality of economic classes with the non-material cultural attributes of social classes (or caste in India). It incorporates the subjectively experienced cultural features in a society because of who we are as consequence of what we inherit from our parents' class/caste,[14] where we come from (urban or rural India), where we go to school (English or Indian-languages medium; private/ government-run), and so on.[15]

Journalists working in the Indian-languages media mostly come from the non-elite social groups, they are likely to have gone to government-run schools where education is imparted in Indian languages; whereas, journalists working in the English media are more likely to have had an education in private schools where the medium of instruction is English. There are exceptions, but that does not undermine the overall pattern we find in the split public sphere of India. Compelling evidence for how much of a role social habitus plays in Indian media comes from the recruitment patterns for English-language media journalists in India. In India, the English-language journalists are not only recruited from the elite educational institutions in the country and abroad, but they often come from families with close links to bureaucratic, corporate, and political elites in the country.[16] The pedigree of elite English media may include a foreign education, especially an Oxbridge or Ivy League degree. This is no different from how journalists of elite news media of Britain and the US are recruited from elite educational universities.

The expectation from owners, editors, and audiences is that journalists will fulfil their professional roles without disrupting the dominant paradigm and breaching the consensus of the ruling elites. Even when journalists come from a different social and educational background or habitus, they often get 'socialized in the newsroom' to the dominant culture of the media organizations (Breed 1955). For example, even when women or Dalits are hired in elite media, they do not change the culture of the newsrooms; instead, it is more likely that they will be socialized into the dominant doxa. And if they don't, they feel out of place, and even tormented in doing their newswork.[17]

To sum up the above discussion, the doxa- and habitus-fostered split in the public sphere leads to the differences in the presuppositions about the society and the state among members of the vernacular and ruling cultures. The respective doxa shape journalists' views on the rational-legal authority of the state, its democratic institutions, and constitutionally guaranteed personal liberties including the freedom of speech and press. We often see this play out differently in media debates on gender rights and other issues of social discrimination in English and Hindi media. The habitus of journalists of the English-language and Hindi-language media shape differently the dominant doxa relating to the legitimacy of the modern Indian state and its relationship to the traditional Indian society; and it shows up in the differences that we find in news routines, news values, sources, and occupational ideologies.

NEWS ROUTINES, VALUES, AND SOURCES

Returning to what we had talked about in the introductory part, how the diversity in journalistic subcultures influences diversity in the social production of news (newswork)—news routines, news values, news sources, and occupational ideologies—we see that the societal, organizational, and cultural influences on newswork lead to differences in news decisions that reporters and editors make on what to report, who to quote as sources, and how to analyse events and issues in the news. What journalists report and who they empower to be heard in the news are important to our understanding of how news media play a role in agenda building and the distribution of political power. There are similarities and significant differences in newswork between the media in English and Indian languages. The following discussion on news routines, news values, news sources, and occupational ideologies are based on past studies, but they need further research so that they can be refined and contextualized with evidence from Indian media.

Routines

Modern social production of news in the mainstream media resembles to a large degree the production of other commodities in the modern industrial economy of a supply chain of aggregation of value. The routines are designed to produce efficiency in daily work that is done by journalists, news organizations, and audiences. To manage daily routines, the beat system evolved to bring about a level of certainty in the production of news as a commodity for audiences that were paying for the news and expecting to get it on time. By following certain beats in daily routines, journalists bring some certainty into newswork, which inherently is dependent on the unpredictability of newsworthy events and issues cropping up every minute. Although new media technologies have with regularity disrupted established routines, the overall structure has remained the same. For example, daily routines and deadlines have changed—first with broadcast media, then with the internet, and now with social media tools such as Twitter and Facebook—but the central feature of repeated practices in the repertoire of newsgathering and dissemination has remained the defining feature of news as a modern industrial commodity.

The basic structure of journalistic routines evolved in the West, as newspaper publishing transformed from a cottage enterprise into a large-scale commercial enterprise with mass audiences in the nineteenth century; and the routines further crystallized in the 1920s and 1930s, with bureaucratic rationalization and professionalization through education and the development of consensus over norms (Schudson 2003). Since then, the journalism as a social practice has evolved into an institution or a field of practice with the production processes becoming standardized. One of the important aspects of this standardization was how the processes are repeated every day out in the field where reporters hunt for stories, and back in newsrooms where the information gathered undergoes editorial treatment in a timely fashion to meet the deadline (Kumar 2009).

There are similarities in the routines and beats—such as government, crime, sports, and movies—of media in the English and Indian languages. There are similarities from the perspective of the production processes of news as an industrial commodity as well. The differences in routines emerge from geographical localities. The English media stick to beats in major cities, and the Indian-languages media cover beats in provincial capitals, small towns, and villages. A major difference has emerged as a result of the hyper-localization of news beats, which was one of the major innovations in routines introduced by the Indian-languages media, including Hindi media (Kumar 2011).

Hyper-localization was one of the major factors in what Jeffery (2000) had described as India's newspaper revolution. It should not be surprising that the beats of the media in English and Indian languages follow where their audiences are. The important thing to note is that differences in the beats not only lead to differences in what gets reported, but also who gets to be heard. Reaching out in the rural areas and the hyper-localization of news have led to innovations in news values that prompted some purist of professional journalism to remark that all that Indian-languages media is reporting does not even qualify as news.[18] This raises a more important question, per different journalistic subcultures in India, what is news?

News Values

News values work implicitly in the shaping of social processes involved in the production of news. When journalists are asked how they discriminate a newsworthy event from a mundane event, they often say that they cannot articulate it as the selection is largely an instinctive response. Journalists seem to think that they have a nose for what event or issue qualifies as newsworthy, which is likely true, metaphorically speaking. However, this 'gut feeling' can be traced back to journalistic doxa, a set of presuppositions, or news values, shared by all journalists within a national or cultural context (I. Schulz 2007).

Out of a continuous stream of events happening every day, only a few get through the gatekeepers of the news media (White 1950). A fascinating feature of this gatekeeping process is that there is a lot of similarity in daily headlines across mainstream news media organizations (Haque 1986). Although similarities in headlines do not mean that there aren't significant differences in treatments and abstractions in meanings. Treatment of news includes how news is structured, framed, contextualized, and analysed in its presentation with a view to evoking a desired meaning in the reader.

However, social scientists studying journalism look at news values differently, especially because they incorporate treatment as an added layer in selection decisions. The most important consequences of differences in the journalistic subcultures are for news values and news sources in terms of differences in treatment. Social scientists have found that news values that seem to be an instinctive response—having a nose for what qualifies as news—are cultivated through a process of socialization in the newsroom, education, and training (Breed 1955; Harrison 2006; Kumar 2009).

Many scholars have made attempts to tease out news values from what they see being reported in the media. An iconic study in typologies of news values was first carried out by Galtung and Ruge (1965). While looking for answers to explain how foreign events become newsworthy in Norwegian newspapers, they identified the following 12 factors as news values: frequency, threshold, unambiguity, meaningfulness, consonance, unexpectedness, continuity, composition, elite nations, elite people, reference to people, and negativity. The typology created by Galtung and Ruge served as a template for determining news values in other cultural and national contexts (Golding and Elliot 1979; W. F. Schulz 1982; Harcup and O'Neill 2001). Golding and Elliot (1979), using feedback from audiences (letters to the editor, circulation, ratings, and so on), proposed their own set of 11 factors: drama, visual attractiveness, entertainment, importance, size of audience, proximity of an event, negativity, brevity, recency, elites, and personalities (celebrities).

One of the issues with any typology of news values, apart from how likely it is that they will differ across cultures, is that these values not only influence selection, as a gatekeeping function of news, but influence treatment as well. One of the factors that likely has a major influence on how a news event gets treated is normative evaluation, morality, or value judgements that journalists make while selecting news (Donsbach 2004). Harcup and O'Neill (2001) carried out a content analysis of stories in the British media with the goal of clarifying the mixing of selection with treatment in Galtung and Ruge's 12 factors. After carrying out a careful content analysis of thousands of stories, Harcup and O'Neill refined the original typology for mainstream media in the United Kingdom: power elites, celebrity, entertainment, surprise element, bad news, good news, magnitude (affecting a large number of people), relevance (to respective audience), follow-up, and media's agenda.

In their authoritarian and propaganda model of the capitalist news media system, Herman and Chomsky (1988) have argued that there is a shared set of news values, which they described as media filters, in Western media. They offered five filters for a capitalist propaganda model of journalism: serving the owner's interest (ownership), serving the advertisers' interest (market), serving the interest of the ruling elites (government and corporate voices), blocking deviance (voices that disrupt the hegemony of the elites), and negative treatment of communism or socialism. The five filters may be equally applicable to any commercial media system around the world, including in India.

There is a 'double dependency' in media on news cultures and the market (Champagne 2005). James Hamilton (2004: 8), in his study of news coverage in the American media, argued that the market dictates news values in a capitalist society, and that 'all the news that is fit to sell' best describes the news values of the mainstream news media. Similarly, Robin Jeffery (1997, 2000) found that advertising being the primary source of revenue for news media in India, like in the West, market-based news value dictates news coverage when it comes to choosing between a sub-national and national perspective in political conflict. In a detailed study of Hindi news media, it was found that economic gain and market share were the pre-eminent factors that influenced news decisions (Kumar 2011).

So, if there is a universal set of news values in journalistic cultures across the world, then it is most likely the values of market capitalism. Stuart Hall (1973) had suggested that there is a 'deep structure' underlying the selection of all news. This deep structure not only influences selection, but the treatment of news as well. The structure is a doxa that journalists share with the society at large and with peers in the profession. The doxa may differ across nations, and may even differ across subcultures within a nation such as India.

Take, for example, a journalistic doxa, discussed above, with respect to news coverage of social protest. We also find differences in the doxa of journalists working in the English-language and Hindi-language media with respect to religious traditions and modern progressive values. As suggested above, education, training, and socialization in newsrooms lead to cultivation of news values as well. The English-language journalists who share an education and training with journalists in the West, not surprisingly profess similar news values; whereas Hindi-language journalists who are differently educated and trained get socialized into a different set of news values with respect to the cultural proximity of tradition and scepticism with regard to Western modernity.

Hyper-localization of news in Indian-languages media forced the owners to depend mostly on stringers and freelancers to fill the pages of newspapers, and airtime on television targeted lay audiences in small towns and rural areas (Kumar 2011: 65–6). The consequence was that hyper-localization upended the news values that until now had a professionalism bias. News coverage of mundane events that would have never made it into the daily news rundown in the past were now breaking news items. Superstition and sensationalizing of community oddities began to qualify as news. In a way, it was a return to the days before the professionalization and rationalization of newswork. There is an upside to this influence of hyper-localization on routines and alleged trivialization of news values. The people who never got be heard in the media were being legitimized as news sources.

As discussed above, scholars of journalism have argued among themselves on news values that journalists rely on to assess the newsworthiness of events and issues. On the other hand, journalism schools teach news values under the rubric of the following six news factors: timeliness, proximity, conflict, unusualness, prominence, and impact in terms of size of audiences and intensity of emotions felt. We are not likely to find discernible differences between English-language and Indian-languages media on the above-mentioned six news values. However, when it comes to conflict, we find fascinating differences between English and Hindi media. Conflict is a news value for both, yet there are differences in how conflict as a value gets deployed in different situations, such as class, gender, caste, and religious conflict. The overarching doxa that shapes the treatment of conflict as value is disagreement over progress, secularism, and modernity. To understand and interpret how differences in journalistic cultures foster differences in news values, we need to go back to differences in doxa and habitus.

News Sources

Who journalists pick as their sources is perhaps the most important factor in what news is. News sources are important to how journalists interpret facts. Leon Sigal (1973) argued that news was not what journalists thought happened, but what their sources said happened; and additionally, sources helped journalists weed out their personal biases. Sourcing seems to be mostly contingent on who journalists encounter on their beats in their routine work, but the subculture of the community from which journalists come and to which audiences belong matters in who gets to be heard in the media. Journalists have relative autonomy in the selection of news sources as well. They have options on who they choose to quote as sources in their stories. Again, the relative autonomy that journalists have in selecting their sources plays a central role in deciding who gets, or perhaps even deserves, to be heard in the public sphere.

Journalists go looking for sources that may help them present a preferred treatment of the story. The selection of sources is influenced by how journalists are socialized into accepting certain types of sources—for example, sources from government, corporations, and elite academic institutions—as legitimate and authoritative (Fishman 1988; Roscho 1975; Tuchman 1976). Not surprisingly, scholars in the West have extensively studied the relationship of sources and agenda setting and news framing in the media (Berkowitz 1987; Entman 2004; Gitlin 1980; Weaver et al. 1972; Youssef et al. 2014). However, despite the occupational norm of maintaining objectivity, journalists have their own interpretation of a news event, and when they encounter sources representing different sides of an issue, which side gets precedence and meaning must be negotiated between journalists and their sources (Awad 2006; Berkowitz and TerKeurst 1999).

The differences in news sources that media rely on relate directly to the differences treatment—presentation, analysis, and interpretation—of news events. Sources make a difference in how journalists of English and Hindi media put a news item in historical context, such as the freedom struggle, Emergency, or past incidents of communal violence in the country. The English-language and Hindi-language media have their own preferences for go-to sources that can provide treatments to a story that meets the expectations of the journalists and their audiences. The go-to sources provide some pre-packaged, preferred meanings representing the broad contours of the political divide in the country.[19] To see how this may play out in the English and Indian-languages media, we need to look closely at the selection and treatment of news sources. Unfortunately, research on news sources is still lagging in Indian journalism, but a few studies have alluded to how selection of news sources is crucial to our understanding of media coverage (Kumar 2011). One of the consequences of the split in the public sphere of India, discussed above, is that news sources in the English and Indian-languages media split along class, caste, and gender lines. For example, it is more likely that sources in English-language media will be from the English-speaking middle classes and elites in major cities, including the capital. Similarly, it is more likely that more women sources may appear in the English-language media, relatively speaking, as more women reporters work in the English media and they are more likely to give space to women's voices.

When it comes to access to sources, especially politicians and bureaucrats, in the domains of national and provincial politics, habitus shapes differences in socio-political power that journalists working for media in the English language and Indian languages experience. It is much easier for journalists working for the English-language media to get major politicians to give interviews or come on television shows than for journalists working for the Hindi media. Per Stahlberg (2002) in his study found that journalists in the Hindi media had better access to politicians in Lucknow, whereas in Delhi English media would have better access.[20]

The reporters carry the burden of interpreting what the source said, which makes them reluctant to directly quote Hindi or other Indian-language speakers on the record in their stories, especially if they can get English-speaking sources. By contrast, the cultural proximity of Indian-language journalists to people in provincial capitals, small towns, and even villages makes their job easier, especially when it comes to reliance on cultural idiom in the treatment of facts and meanings in news stories.

Occupational Ideology

There are some things that all journalists seem to agree on when it comes to practice and stance: journalists/news media have a watchdog function in any democratic political system, a witnessing role on behalf of the public, and the responsibility to be objective on facts and fair to all sides in the treatment of value judgements. Like most ideologies, the occupational ideology of journalism is like the North Star that keeps the news media on a relatively objective course while it navigates the fraught and partisan world of politics. Yet, from the discussion above, it should be clear as well that how the occupational ideology of journalism is interpreted in practice differs across cultures.

In a way, the socio-cultural milieu of cosmopolitanism fostered by education and training in elite Indian universities and Western academia is an important factor in the spread of a universalizing occupational ideology of journalism. Not surprisingly, journalists working for the English-language media in India share similarities with journalists working in British and American media in occupational ideology of objectivity, and the legitimacy and primacy of authoritative sources from government, corporates, and academia.

The social habitus of Indian-language journalists makes it relatively easy for them to embed themselves in communities, and often the view they present in their coverage of issues, events, and the state's policies is that from within communities, and not as a bystander who witnesses with a relatively objective stance. This subject position of Indian-languages journalists is a factor in shaping their occupational ideology. A good place to look for how journalistic subcultures influence occupational ideologies is the coverage of social protests in the media.

Activism appears to be a widely accepted journalistic norm in the mainstream media[21] in India, yet there are differences in how journalists of the English-language and Indian-languages media report on social protest (Kumar 2011). In treatment of news of social protest, the default stance in Indian media is that protesting government is a virtuous act taken up by aggrieved citizens. However, when a protest turns highly disruptive and violent, it is more likely that the Hindi-language media (and likely other Indian languages), compared to the English-language media, will still treat the protest as a virtuous act in democracy. In the mainstream Indian media, the journalists working for the English-language media show a stronger professional desirability for and self-awareness in maintaining objectivity when they report on disruptions and violence in social protests (Kumar 2014).

Media coverage of social protests is shaped by how cultures of protest[22] interact with occupational ideologies of objectivity, fairness, and legitimacy of sources. The colonial origin of the press and its role in the freedom struggle of India has produced a news culture among journalists, and even among their audiences, which is distrusting of government action when compared with the actions of social activists leading protests. There is an underlying tension between the desire for social change and social control in the media. In a post-colonial society such as India, with a long history of popular struggle, there is wider acceptance of the disruption of the normal day-to-day functioning of society because of social protest under certain circumstances. The implicit acceptance of social protest in *jan andolan*s (populist social mobilization) as being necessary for social change, and protesters as virtuous *andolankari*s (revolutionaries), is rooted in the history of a prolonged struggle against colonial rule and feudal oppression.[23] In the coverage of social protest in Indian-languages media, the rational-juridical authority of the police in riot situations is presented as evidence of an oppressive authoritarian government, and not a necessity for preventing disruption and maintaining social order. It is more likely that English-language media news decisions would present social protest as disruptive and anarchic.

It is likely that this is because in post-colonial societies such as India, hegemonic acceptance of the rational-legal authority of the state is at a lower threshold. The state's legitimacy in the eyes of the people is underdeveloped compared to the legitimacy of other institutions of traditional society. However, in addition to historical reasons, among certain sections of Indian journalists, their activist stance derives its legitimacy from an anarchist of view of society where statelessness is an ideal norm and communities must not require exercise of social control from either the state apparatuses or the media. This is quite unlike mainstream media news cultures in the West, especially in American journalism, where journalists of mainstream media tend to take official actions and accounts as legitimate on face value, whereas they treat actions and accounts provided by social activists with scepticism (Kumar 2009).

Additionally, an important source of differences in occupational ideologies is the over-reliance on contractual arrangements and use of freelancers and stringers in the Hindi-language media compared to English-language media. The hyper-localization of the news in the Indian-language media that goes deep into rural areas is not possible without the work being done by local newsgatherers in stringer and freelancer capacities. However, the reasons for excessive reliance on stringers and freelancers are primarily economic; many of these stringers and freelancers in small towns and rural areas lack any professional education and training in journalism. To supplement their income, many do double duty as advertising agents for media companies as well. This dual occupational role plays an important part in further diluting professional values and norms.

CONCLUSION: JOURNALISTIC POWER

The most significant implications of differences in journalistic cultures on social production of news lead to differences in the journalistic power of English-language and Indian-languages media in India. Journalism's primary power comes from its role as gatekeeper of what qualifies to be heard in the public sphere. Journalists have the power to establish facts from non-facts, and to legitimize certain voices as being worthy of hearing, and certain opinions as being worthy of considering. At a secondary level, the power comes from journalists' professional role in the production of news as public knowledge. At a tertiary level, journalistic power includes not only blocking communication, but a social sanction to investigate, evaluate, and critique the performance of other actors in the public sphere. Journalists not only help politicians in organizing public opinion and building consent; they also compete with politicians as well by selecting who they pick as sources in their stories and by introducing their own assessment of what is good for the country and its politics.

All the same, we cannot ignore that the Indian-language media have, relatively speaking, more power in fostering a predisposition for social action, especially in the context of mass protests and social movements. There is a convergence between the culture of news of the Indian-languages media and the culture of protest in India. The proximity of Indian-languages media, including Hindi media, to vernacular political idiom and culture has been an important factor in the leading role they have played in jan andolans.

Vidyarthi had identified the problem with the iron grip of the English-speaking elite on Indian public opinion at the turn of the last century. Yet, as we enter the second decade of the twenty-first century, the power of the English-language media on building agendas and framing issues seems to be more consequential in view of its proximity to the elite power structure. As we saw above, this proximity comes from the habitus of journalists and their sources. The power differential comes from the social capital that news organizations and journalists earn through sustained quality of reporting and trust among audiences as well. In the split Indian public sphere, the proximity of the English-language media to the elite power structure seems to suggest that they are predisposed both to a progressive modernity and to a status quo in the elite power structure of the country. Social change seems to be less about disrupting the power structure and more about disrupting traditional conservatism in society.

To conclude, there are not enough studies out there to generalize our findings on Indian journalism in all its diversity, but the field of Indian journalism is very promising for scholars interested in understanding and interpreting the social production of news (newswork) from a cross-cultural and comparative perspective.

NOTES

1. Although 'media' is a catch-all phrase to refer to news media, entertainment media, social media, community media, and so on, here in this chapter, I use the term 'media' to mean 'news media' or what has traditionally been described as 'the press'.
2. As of now, privately owned radio stations source their news content from the government-owned All India Radio.
3. Nonetheless, here we will restrict our discussion to professional journalism in the mainstream media. The alternative media organizations, and news on social media, do not follow the routines, values, and norms of the mainstream media. It is not that they do not work with a set of news values. They have alternative news values that privilege activism, subaltern voices, and concerns of the poor to determine what is newsworthy.
4. In some circles, a pejorative appellation of 'Lutyens' people' is used to refer to the English-speaking elite journalists and their audiences. The metaphor draws from the name of Edwin Lutyens who designed the architectural plan for New Delhi as the capital of colonial India.
5. See the discussion of print capitalism and imagined political communities in Anderson (1991), Chatterjee (1994), and Jeffery (2000).

6. India perhaps is not unique in this regard. The European Union is a quasi-federal super-state that has similar overlapping public spheres that are organized along respective ethnolinguistic national identities. The Canadian public sphere is similarly composed of overlapping spheres of English-speaking and French-speaking citizens.

7. See Jeffery (1997), Kumar (2011). The argument on the role of a common market in constructing a commonly shared public space is furthered supported by the discourse surrounding 'One India, One Market' in the context of a single tax regime in the country. See Adhia (2016).

8. For themes in a continuing debate, see Mantri and Gupta (2013). Also see Khilnani (1997).

9. The bhakti movement played an important role in the vernacularization of public discourse through the language of the common people, and thereby it fostered new political identities in north and south India. See Novetzke (2016) for the emergence of vernacular publics and shifts in power in the context of the nascent public sphere of the bhakti movement, and Pollock (2006) for the emergence of vernacular lanaguges in courtly settings in premodern India.

10. To further illustrate the point, I encourage readers to check out a scene in the movie *Guide* (1965), dir. Vijay Anand, based on a novel by Mulk Raj Anand. The scene starts 13:40 minutes. In the scene, seeing the ritual power shift away towards an imposter who is posing as a learned guru, the village priests challenge him to show his leaning of Sanskrit. The imposter responds by condemning in English the self-serving ways of the priests for ages, and counters by telling the people these pundits call themselves learned, but do not know English. (Watch here: https://www.youtube.com/watch?v=kfA9jjIjJu0.)

11. See a discussion of a radical new Hindi journalism, in Francesca Orsini's (2009) book on the Hindi public sphere, pioneered by men such as Ganesh Shankar Vidyarthi in the first quarter of the twentieth century.

12. Even in the Hindi film industry, the ability to speak English is a prerequisite to being counted among the elite of Bollywood. See the controversy around Kangana Ranaut's criticism of Bollywood elites (Pillaai 2013).

13. Also see Neveu (2007) for influence of Bourdieu in the subdiscipline of media sociology.

14. Caste hierarchy is not equivalent to the hierarchy of classes, but there is a correlation between the two. See Baviskar and Ray (2011).

15. Even economists seem to have accepted this wider definition of hierarchy in social difference in society. Ethnicity, where one lives, and where one goes to school determine one's chances of doing well economically in later life.

16. Based on interviews with journalists working in the elite news media and young journalists struggling to climb up the hierarchy of Indian journalism.

17. Author's interviews with many journalists working in the elite English-language television newsrooms who come from a rural background.

18. See the discussion of the influence of hyper-localization on news values in Kumar (2011: 69–70).

19. In the news on economy and business, reliance on pre-packaged meanings is a widespread practice (Turk 1985).

20. Also, see Rao (2009) on how Hindi journalism transformed both the culture of news and the culture of politics.

21. Here we must keep in mind that activism is more closely associated with alternative news media. Most online publications such as the *Wire, Scroll,* and *Catch* would fall into the category of activist alternative news media. See Atton (2002) for the conceptual difference between alternative press and mainstream press with respect to professional values, norms, and occupational ideology.

22. See Kumar (2011: 30–32). In India, disruption caused by social protest including *bandh*s (shutdowns of a city), *hartal*s (strikes), *chakka jam* (stopping of the flow of traffic), and other forms of obstruction of regular day-to-day activities has a higher threshold of acceptance.

23. For a discussion of jan andolans as 'populist social mobilization' and its relationship to Hindi media in north India, see Kumar (2011, 2014).

REFERENCES

Adhia, H. (2016). 'One India, One Market'. *Hindu*, 19 July. Retrieved from http://www.thehindu.com/todays-paper/tp-opinion/One-India-one market/article14497348.ece (accessed on 17 August 2018).

Anderson, Benedict R. (1991). *Imagined Communities: Reflections on the Origin and Spread of Nationalism.* London: Verso.

Atton, C. (2002). *Alternative Media.* London: Sage.

Awad, I. (2006). 'Journalists and Their Sources: Lessons from Anthropology'. *Journalism Studies*, 7(6): 922–39.

Baviskar, A. and R. Ray (eds) (2011). *Elite and Everyman: The Cultural Politics of the Indian Middle Classes.* New Delhi: Routledge.

Benson, R. and E. Neveu (eds) (2005). *Bourdieu and the Journalistic Field.* Cambridge: Polity.

Berkowitz, D. (1987). 'TV News Sources and News Channels: A Study in Agenda-Building'. *Journalism Quarterly*, 64: 508–13.

Berkowitz, D. and J. TerKeurst (1999). 'Community as Interpretive Community: Rethinking the Journalists–Source Relationship'. *Journal of Communication*, 49(3): 125–36.

Bourdieu, P. (1990). *The Logic of Practice*. Cambridge, UK: Polity Press.

——— (1993). *The Field of Cultural Production: Essays on Art and Literature*. New York: Columbia University Press.

——— (1996). *On Television*, trans. P. P. Ferguson. New York: New Press.

——— (2005). 'The Political Field, the Social Science Field, and the Journalistic Field'. In *Bourdieu and the Journalistic Field*, eds Rodney Benson and Eric Neveu, pp. 20–47. Malden, MA: Polity Press.

Breed, W. 1955. 'Social Control in the Newsroom: A Functional Analysis'. *Social Forces*, 33: 326–55.

——— (2005 [1958]). 'Mass Communication and Socio-cultural Integration'. In *Mass Communication and American Social Thought*, eds John D. Peters and Peter Simonson, pp. 417–25. Boulder: Rowman and Littlefield.

Champagne, P. (2005). 'The "Double Dependency": The Journalistic Field between Politics and Markets'. In *Bourdieu and the Journalistic Field*, eds Rodney Benson and Eric Neveu, pp. 48–64. Malden, MA: Polity Press.

Chatterjee, P. (1994). *The Nation and Its Fragments: Colonial and Postcolonial Histories*. Princeton: Princeton University Press.

——— (2004). *The Politics of the Governed: Reflection on Popular Politics in Most of the World*. New York: Columbia University Press.

Chaudhary, A. (1974). 'Comparative New Judgment of Indian and American Journalists'. *International Communication*, Gazette, 20: 233–48.

Donsbach, W. (2004). 'Pyschology of News Decisions: Factors behind Journalists Professional Behaviour'. *Journalism*, 5(2): 131–57.

Entman, R. M. (2004). *Projections of Power: Framing News, Public Opinion and U.S. Foreign Policy*. Chicago: University of Chicago Press.

Ericson, R. (1999). 'Routines and Making of Oppositional News'. *Critical Studies in Mass Communication*, 5: 3113–334.

Fishman, M. (1988). *Manufacturing the News*. Austin: University of Texas Press.

Galtung, J. and M. Ruge (1965). 'The Structure of Foreign News: The Presentation of the Congo, Cuba and Cyprus Crises in Four Norwegian Newspapers'. *Journal of International Peace Research*, 1: 64–91.

Ganguly-Scrase, R. and T. J. Scrase (2009). *Globalisation and the Middle Classes in India: The Social and Cultural Impact of Neoliberal Reforms*. London: Routledge.

Gans, H. (1980). *Deciding What's News*. New York: Vintage Books.

Gitlin, T. (1980). *The Whole World Is Watching*. Berkeley: University of California Press.

Golding, P. and P. Elliot (1979). *Making the News*. London: Longman.

Habermas, J. (1989). *Structural Transformation of the Public Sphere*. London: Polity Press.

—— (2006). 'Political Communication in Media Society'. *Communication Theory*, 16: 411–26.

Hall, S. (1973). 'The Determinations of News Photographs'. In *The Manufacture of News: Deviance, Social Problems and Mass Media*, eds S. Cohen and J. Young, pp. 176–90. London: Sage.

—— (2006 [1974]). 'Encoding and Decoding'. In *Media and Cultural Studies: Key Works*, eds Meenakshi Gigi Durham and Douglas Kellner, pp. 166–76. Malden, MA: Blackwell.

Hamilton, James T. (2004). *All The News That's Fit to Sell: How Market Transforms Information into News*. Princeton, NJ: Princeton University Press.

Hanitzsch, T. (2006). 'Mapping Journalism Culture: A Theoretical Taxonomy and Case Studies from Indonesia'. *Asian Journal of Communication*, 16(2): 169–86.

—— (2009). 'Comparative Journalism Studies'. In *Handbook of Journalism Studies*, eds Karin Wahl-Jorgensen and Thomas Hanitzsch, pp. 413–27. New York: Routledge.

Haque, M. (1986). 'News Content Homogeneity in Elite Indian Dailies'. *Journalism Quarterly*, 63(4): 827–33.

Harcup, T. and D. O'Neill (2001). 'What Is News? Galtung and Ruge Revisited'. *Journalism Studies*, 292: 261–68.

Harrington, W. (2003). 'What Journalism Can Offer to Ethnography?' *Qualitative Inquiry*, 9(1): 90–104.

Harrison, J. (2006). *News*. London: Baltimore.

Hauser, G. A. (1999). *Vernacular Voices: Rhetoric of Publics and Public Spheres*. Columbia: University of South Carolina Press.

—— (2007). 'Vernacular Discourse and the Epistemic Dimension of Public Opinion'. *Communication Theory*, 17(4): 333–9.

Herman, E. S. and N. Chomsky (1988). *Manufacturing Consent*. New York: Pantheon.

Jeffery, R. (1997). 'Advertising and Indian-Language Newspapers: How Capitalism Supports (Certain) Cultures and (Some) States, 1947–96'. *Pacific Affairs*, 70(1): 57–83.

—— (2000). *India's Newspaper Revolution*. New Delhi: Oxford University Press.

Khilnani, S. (1997). *The Idea of India*. New York: Farrar, Strauss and Giroux.

Kumar, A. (2009). 'Looking Back and Looking Ahead: Journalistic Rules, Social Control, Social Change and Relative Autonomy'. *Journal of Media Sociology*, 1(3): 136–60.

Kumar, A. (2011). *Making of a Small State: Populist Social Mobilisation and the Hindi Press in the Uttarakhand Movement*. New Delhi: Orient BlackSwan.

——— (2013). 'News Epistemology, Radical Journalism, and Disruption of Paradigm in WikiLeaks Phenomenon'. Paper presented in the Philosophy, Theory, and Critique division at the International Communication Association annual conference, London.

——— (2014). 'Vernacular Publics, News Media and the Jan Lokpal Andolan'. In *Democratic Transformation and the Vernacular Publics in India*, eds Tabere Ahmed Neyazi, Akio Tanabe, and Shinya Ishizaka. London.

Lantis, M. (1960). 'Vernacular Culture'. *American Anthropologist*, 62(2): 202–15.

Lukes, S. (2005). *Power: A Radical View*. New York: Palgrave.

Mantri, R. and G. Gupta (2013). 'Let Us Debate Ideas of India'. *LiveMint*. Retrieved from http://www.livemint.com/Opinion/V7b5nL25jmtHFatG3tS2UN/Let-us-debate-the-idea-of-India.html (accessed on 17 August 2018).

Marr, M., V. Whyss, R. Blum, and H. Bonfadelli (2001). *Journalism in der Schweiz, Eigenschaften, Einstellungen, Einflusse*. Konstanz, Germany: UVK.

McLeod, Jack M. and Ramona R. Rush (1969). 'Professionalization of Latin American and U.S. Journalists'. *Journalism Quarterly*, 46(3): 583–90.

Neveu, E. (2007). 'Pierre Bourdieu: Sociologist of Media or Sociologist of Media Scholars?' *Journalism Studies*, 8(2): 335–47.

Neyazi, T. A. (2011). 'Politics after Vernacularisation: Hindi Media and Democracy'. *Economic and Political Weekly*, 46(10): 75–82.

Ninan, S. (2007). *Headlines from the Heartland: Reinventing the Hindi Public Sphere*. New Delhi: Sage.

Novetzke, C. L. (2016). *The Quotidian Revolution: Vernacularization, Religion, and Premodern Public Sphere in India*. New York: Columbia University Press.

Orsini, F. (2009). *The Hindi Public Sphere (1920–1940): Language and Literature in the Age of Nationalism*. London: Oxford University Press.

Parameswaran, Radhika (1997). 'Colonial Interventions and Postcolonial Situation in India: The English Language, Mass Media, and Articulation of Class'. *Gazette*, 59(1): 21–41.

Park, R. E. (1940). 'News as a Form of Knowledge: A Chapter in the Sociology of Knowledge'. *American Journal of Sociology*, 45: 669–86.

Patterson, T. E. and W. Donsbach (1996). 'News Decisions: Journalists as Partisan Actors'. *Political Communication*, 13(4): 455–68.

Pillaai, J. (2013). 'I Couldn't Speak English—Kangana Ranaut'. *Filmfare*, 21 October. Retrieved from http://www.filmfare.com/interviews/i-couldnt-speak-english-kangana-ranaut-4433.html (accessed on 17 August 2018).

Pollock, S. (2006). *The Language of the Gods in the World of Men: Sanskrit, Culture, and Power in Premodern India*. Los Angeles: University of California Press.

Pritchard, D. and F. Souvageau (1998). 'The Journalists and Journalism of Canada'. In *The Global Journalists: News People around the World*, ed. D. H. Weaver, pp. 373–93. Cresskill, NJ: Hampton Press.

Przeworski, P. and H. Teune (1970). *The Logic of Comparative Social Inquiry*. New York: Wiley-Interscience.

Rahman, T. (2011). *From Hindi to Urdu: A Social Political History*. Karachi: Oxford University Press.

Rajagopal, A. (2002). *Politics after Television: Hindu Nationalism and Reshaping of the Public in India*. Cambridge: Cambridge University Press.

Rao, S. and V. Mudgal (2016). *Journalism, Democracy, and Civil Society in India*. New Delhi: Routledge.

Rao, U. (2009). *News as Culture: Journalistic Practices and the Remaking of Indian Leadership Tradition*. New York: Berghahn Books.

Roscho, B. (1975). *Newsmaking*. Chicago: University of Chicago Press.

Schudson, M. (1989). 'Sociology of News Production'. *Media, Culture and Society*, 11: 263–82.

——— (2003). *The Sociology of News*. New York: Norton Books.

Schulz, Ida (2007). 'The Journalistic Gut Feeling: Journalistic Doxa, News Habitus, and Orthodox News Values'. *Journalism Practice*, 1(2): 190–207.

Schulz, W. F. (1982). 'News Structure and People's Awareness of Political Events'. *International Communication Gazette*, 30: 139–53.

Scott, James C. (1998). *Seeing Like a State: How Certain Schemes to Improve the Human Condition Have Failed*. New Haven, CT: Yale University Press.

Shoemaker, P. and A. A. Cohen (2006). *News around the World: Content, Practitioners and the Public*. New York: Routledge.

Sigal, L. (1973). *Reporters and Officials: The Organization and Politics of Newsmaking*. Lexington, MA: D.C. Heath.

Stahlberg, P. (2002). *Lucknow Daily: How a Hindi Newspaper Constructs Society*. Stockholm: Stockholm Studies in Social Anthropology.

Tuchman, G. (1972). 'Objectivity as a Strategic Ritual: An Examination of Newsmen's Notions of Objectivity'. *American Journal of Sociology*, 77: 660–79.

Tuchman, G. (1976). 'Telling Stories'. *Journal of Communication*, 26: 93–7.

Turk, J. (1985). 'Information Subsidies and Influence'. *Public Relations Review*, 11(3): 10–25.

Viswanathan, G. (1989). *Masks of Conquest: Literary Study and British Rule in India*. New York: Columbia University Press.

Weaver, D. H. (ed.) (1998). *The Global Journalists: News People around the World*, pp. 373–93. Cresskill, NJ: Hampton Press.

Weaver, D. H., M. E. McCombs, and D. L. Shaw (1972). 'Agenda Setting Research: Issues, Attributes and Influences'. *Handbook of Political Communication Research*, pp. 257–81.

White, D. M. (1950). 'The Gatekeeper: A Case Study in the Selection of News'. *Journalism Quarterly*, 27: 383–90.

Youssef, M., H. Arafa, and A. Kumar (2014). 'Mediating Discourse of Democratic Uprising in Egypt: Militarized Language and the "Battles" of Abbasiyya and Maspero'. *International Journal of Communication*, 8: 1–20.

CHAPTER SEVENTEEN

Journalism and Ethics

India Media Mines the Private

GEETA SESHU

. . . .

Recent concerns over the media have centred on corruption in the media, paid news, corporatization, and cross-media ownership—all important and legitimate issues. While the latter two have not received the attention they deserve, considerable attention on corruption and paid news has contributed to the devaluing of news media in the eyes of the public. Coupled with the anger and distrust of the media is a disquieting sense of the powerlessness of citizens against a very powerful and omnipresent media. How much of this is due to an aggressive assertion of the media's 'right' to invade personal space in its quest for the 'truth'? And, along with the increasing intrusion of the news media into the private lives of people, what about the increasing technological surveillance of the state into the lives of its citizens? In both, the notion of 'public interest' is a contested terrain.

The Indian media has had a peculiar relationship with privacy. Earlier, the media generally adopted a 'hands-off' approach to the private lives of those in positions of power and authority in society—be they politicians, businesspeople, sports, or film celebrities. There were a few instances of media coverage of what was seen to be in the realm of the private but these seemed confined to the tabloid press. Indeed, the First Press Commission of 1954 did acknowledge the existence of 'yellow' journalism, but said that the well-established newspapers had, on the whole, maintained a high standard of journalism and avoided cheap sensationalism and unwarranted intrusion into private lives.

The late 1980s and the 1990s marked the liberalization of the economy and the subsequent opening up of the media space to market forces. These developments also led to changes in media practices. Much of what was seen to be out of bounds entered into the news media. There was steady erosion of the invisible boundaries between what was considered 'hard-core' news of political events and 'softer' news of celebrities from the world of cinema, sports (mainly cricket), and of society. Soon, what came to be known as 'lifestyle' journalism and 'infotainment' crept into the pages of mainstream newspapers and magazines. The Indian version of the paparazzi emerged from the shadows.

By 31 March 2017, according to the Registrar of Newspapers for India, the total number of registered publications in India was 114,820,[1] while the total number of news and current affairs channels by March 2017 was 392 (Ministry of Information and Broadcasting).[2] Today, the quantitative explosion as well as the demands of intensely competitive 24/7 news coverage has resulted in immense pressures on the media to sell their stories. There has been a shift in media responsibility away from news in the public interest and the dilution of its accountability to the ethical code on the reporting of the personal. Given the complexity of India's media terrain, an exhaustive monitoring of media content and reportage of day-to-day events across different languages, regions, and cultures would, no doubt, be very useful. However, for the purposes of this chapter, described are a few glaring instances of privacy violations by the media that acquired some measure of a pan-India impact. This chapter will also delve into the debates and discussions that surrounded these cases, in an effort to examine the sometimes incomplete discourse around privacy.

THE NEOLIBERAL NEWS MEDIA'S OBSESSIONS

In numerous instances, the news media is belligerent in setting aside basic ethics in its reportage of the 'personal'. Invariably, the media's notion of what is in the 'public interest' trumps the rest. And, when the media coverage is framed in a particular manner by disclosures of private information in the public interest, they can substantially change public opinion, as illustrated in what came to be known as the 'Jogeshwari nuns' murder case'.

The incident, which took place in November 1990, provoked widespread condemnation from the public and anger ran high against the police force for its inability to ensure the safety of citizens. The police were also under immense pressure to solve the case and arrest the accused. In this situation, four newspapers—*Times of India, Indian Express, Free Press Journal,* and *Saamna*—published reports of the post-mortem of the nuns, suggesting that they were 'habituated to sexual intercourse' and that one of them had a venereal disease. In the reports, the newspapers carried the post-mortem reports, which indirectly alleged that there was a sexual relationship between the nuns and the boys of the children's home. Almost immediately, public opinion on the murder changed and the focus shifted from the criticism of the police for its failure to book the culprits to the 'virginity' of the nuns.

A fact-finding report by citizens' groups interviewed forensic experts and discussed how the post-mortem report was hardly conclusive proof of venereal disease or sexual activity (Solidarity for Justice 1991). The Bombay High Court upheld the charge of violation of privacy and said 'the news reports in question, in our opinion, transcended both the bounds of decency and propriety' (*Catholic Association of Bombay v. State of Maharashtra and Ors* 27 February 1991). The court directed the PCI (the statutory, quasi-judicial body that governs the standards of print media in India) to investigate the complaint of violation of privacy and of journalistic ethics. The PCI investigated and upheld the complaint against the four newspapers. The council also formulated detailed guidelines on privacy that would be attentive to the public interest. These guidelines included the protection of identity and information about a person's home, family, religion, health, sexuality, personal life, and private affairs except where these 'impinge on the public'. Private activity, which may result in the commission of a crime or in the evasion of criminal liability, may also be exposed in the public interest.

Reportage can be intrusive and cause hurt, embarrassment, distress, or damage to the reputation of individuals. The law of defamation covers only certain aspects of privacy, the PCI said. What was of interest to the public, it added, was not always in the public interest. The guidelines were prescient, pointing out that intrusive reporting techniques like gate-crashing into a home, hospital room, or even publishing casual conversation overheard in a privileged gathering, intercepting mail, photographing, or phone tapping, were all examples of intrusive reporting which constituted an invasion of privacy. Besides, 'fair practice by one journal would not justify publication by another, as this would be beyond the realm of fair competition'.[3] However, the PCI's powers are limited to censure. Already seen as a toothless body, in the post-liberalization scenario, the PCI has been largely ignored and rendered ineffective.

The guidelines on privacy formulated by the News Broadcasting Standards Authority (NBSA), the non-statutory body set up by the News Broadcasters Association to monitor standards in member television channels, echo much the same principles, but they state that 'it is also understood that the pursuit of the truth and the news is not possible through the predetermined principle of prior permission; hence door stepping individuals or authorities for the purpose of newsgathering may be used only in the larger purpose of public interest.'[4] More than 10 years later, the Delhi High Court grappled with just this issue in a case where two television channels and a newspaper published reports of a minor's complaint of sexual abuse by her father (*ABC v. Commissioner of Police and Others*). Justice Vipin Sanghi of the Delhi High Court ruled that the privacy rights of a minor who alleged sexual abuse by her father were violated by the Delhi Police in leaking information filed in her FIR, and by Aaj Tak channel, which came to the home of the mother and the minor and 'attempted to interview them in a deceptive manner against their will'. The channel aired a programme on 7 August 2005, telecasting the intrusion and revealing the name, designation, and office of the father. Besides, it showed several images of the colony in which the girl and her family lived and an image of her doorstep.

It also aired her mother's recorded voice refusing entry to Aaj Tak crew members.

The channel maintained that the minor's mother had been interviewed by Star News earlier and was also similarly approached by their crew. The channel said that

> when the correspondent initiated talks with the petitioner, the recording mike and the camera were put into motion—which were made fully visible and of which the petitioner was duly informed and no attempt was made to hide or conceal the same. Since the petitioner refused to answer any of the correspondent's queries and had also refused to step out of the door and speak on the matter, neither was the face of the petitioner visible, nor was her child's interview recorded or photograph taken. But the judge held that Aaj Tak couldn't use the Star TV interview to pass the buck and 'wash away its hands' [*sic*]. (*ABC v. Commissioner of Police and Others*)

A legal notice sent to Star TV restraining it from telecasting the interview, alleged that it was obtained by sheer persistence and emotional blackmail. The judge held that the act of continuing to record the conversation with the mother, even when she expressed her reluctance to be interviewed, called for the strongest condemnation and displayed prurient or morbid curiosity.

The second respondent in the case was *Hindustan Times*, which published an article revealing the minor's age, the locality she lived in, the class she studied in, and her father's occupation. However, the judge accepted the argument that the article did not disclose the name of the victim and actually sought to highlight the issue of child sexual abuse as a duty of the press. Nevertheless, thanks to such publicity, the girl was unable to attend school and finally had to move cities. She and her mother literally disappeared and had to be traced by her counsel when the case came up for hearing, seven years later!

Yet another attempt to gloss over a clear privacy violation was evident in the attempt by two journalists of the *Times of India* who went to the residence of a journalist who was gang-raped in the deserted Shakti Mills compound in Mumbai in July 2013 when she was on an assignment. The complainant was under treatment in a city hospital, and her neighbours didn't even know that she had been attacked. Indeed, her family and friends were desperately engaged in trying to keep as much information about her out of the public domain as possible, frantically deleting Facebook pages and photographs and any other information that might reveal something about her identity (Khan 2014).

Incredibly, when the newspaper was criticized for its intrusive reporting, it went on the offensive. In an article in the newspaper's editorial pages, the *Times of India* columnist Bachi Karkaria (2013a) exhorted the rape survivor to 'reveal your identity and help cast aside the veil of misplaced disgrace'. In a spirited response, senior journalist, gender rights activist, and consulting editor of Himal Southasian, Laxmi Murthy, argued that Karkaria's position was disingenuous. Several rape survivors—from Suzette Jordan who eschewed the 'Park Street rape victim' tag to Rajasthan's Bhanwari Devi, Suman Rani, Bilkis Banu, and Soni Sori had decided to 'come out' with the support of the women's movement and civil rights activists and shed the protective veil of anonymity. But when and how a woman chooses to reveal her identity is a product of complex factors and the decision to do so must remain hers, not the media's, Murthy (2013) correctly pointed out. Refuting the charge, Karkaria argued that the rape survivor must jettison the 'anonymity' which reinforces the perception of 'dishonour'. She added quite inexplicably, that journalists, as a profession, had begun to appropriate too much self-importance (Karkaria 2013b).

Whether it was a display of self-importance or duty to its notion of public interest, *Mumbai Mirror*, the widely circulated tabloid daily from the *Times of India* group, printed the entire FIR in another case of rape in Mumbai, the Tata Institute of Social Science (or TISS) incident. It did proffer an apology for offending readers' sensibilities (*Mumbai Mirror* 2009). Defending its decision to print a 'public document', the editor said (in words that deserve quotation verbatim and in full):

> Our story on the TISS rape victim's statement to the police ('Vinamra kept kissing me though I told him to stop', April 17), has led to much consternation and anger. We have been flooded with letters, asking if it was indeed necessary to run the statement of the victim, a public document, in all its graphic detail. Some readers have accused us of sensationalism, others of harming the interest of the victim. Our intention was neither. As pointed out by one of our readers, Bibhasbaree Biswal,

in the last one year India has emerged as the third worst offender in rape cases. The TISS student was not abducted by strangers and raped, she was abused by men she knew, men she thought were her friends, men she implicitly trusted. We used her gruesome account of date rape as a cautionary tale. It made for disturbing reading; it was meant to be so. However, going by the response from readers—much of it is reproduced below—it seems we misjudged. If readers' sensibilities have been offended, we apologise for the same (Editor). (*Mumbai Mirror* 2009)

The questions that were raised by these controversies: Even if the FIR was a public document, what public interest did it serve to print it in its entirety? What journalistic purpose did it serve? And was it really just self-importance to raise these questions?

INTRUSIVE MEDIA FEEDS THE BEAST

Besides these issues of ethics that surface with depressing regularity, there were other serious violations, ranging from the shocking trespass in 2010, with tragic consequences, into the home of a university lecturer allegedly to expose his homosexual relationship, the staging of a sting in 2007 that falsely accused a school principal of running a prostitution racket, or, in 2003, the media trial of a young woman caught in a vortex of custom and religiosity because of a second marriage after her first husband went missing as a prisoner of war across the border.

Well before the advent of reality television, a media trial of sorts was conducted over the plight of Gudiya, the young woman who married a distant cousin, Taufeeq, in 2003 after her first husband, Mohammed Arif, disappeared after the Kargil conflict in 1999. She was eight months pregnant when Arif, who had been taken by Pakistan as a prisoner of war, returned to India. The panchayat, which said her second marriage was against Islamic law or the Shariat, decided Gudiya must go back to her first husband. The decision sparked a nationwide debate and Zee News, a television channel, conducted a mock panchayat in which Gudiya and Taufeeq were present, along with a number of clerics.

According to reports, none of the three—Gudiya, Arif, and Taufeeq—even knew they were being taken to the television studio for the purpose of a televised panchayat hearing. Taufeeq, who heard

Gudiya say she would go to the first husband in the television studio, was unable to ask her any questions or discuss the issue with her. Tragically, Gudiya died in 2006, after an illness following a stillbirth that she never recovered from. Media attention on her life after she moved back to her first husband and her death was negligible (Rediff.com 2006).

Clearly, besides making a spectacle of a relatively rare predicament, the channel played a very intrusive role in participating in the decision-making process of the persons involved. While her decision on whether to stay with her second husband or go back to the first was mediated by her family and religious leaders, the execrable role of the media robbed her of respect and the dignity of privacy. Sting operations that are ostensibly investigative have resulted in highly unethical and criminal acts in some instances. Whether it was the Uma Khurana sting case, where the court held that 'inducement or entrapping infringed the right to privacy', or the TV9 case which was on the channel's coverage of 'gay culture', the condemnation was strong and unequivocal. In a suo moto case, the Delhi High Court examined the Khurana case and proposed guidelines to check sting operations (*Court on Its Own Motion v. State* 14 December 2007).

On 30 August 2007, a television channel, Live India, broadcast a 'sting' on a Delhi schoolteacher that purportedly showed that she forced a girl student into prostitution. An incensed mob, on hearing the news, then attacked the teacher and she was subsequently removed from service. However, a report in the *Hindustan Times* on 7 September 2007 revealed that the girl student was actually a journalist and the 'sting' was actually engineered by Virendra Singh, who had a previous dispute with Uma Khurana and had sought to settle scores with her. The court's guidelines on how sting operations must be conducted included directives on privacy that emphasized invasions of the individual's privacy only for an 'identifiable larger public interest' (*Court on Its Own Motion v. State*, proposed guidelines nos 8[e], 11–12).

In another instance when TV9, a television channel in Hyderabad, aired a programme entitled 'Gay Culture Rampant in Hyderabad' on 22 February 2011, the NBSA took suo moto action and decided that TV9's show outing gays in Hyderabad needlessly violated the right to privacy of individuals with possible alternate sexual orientation, no longer considered taboo or a criminal act; and the 'Program misused the special tool of a "sting-operation" available only to subserve the larger public interest.'[5] It is pertinent to note that the NBSA's power includes imposition of a fine, but this is applicable to members of the News Broadcasters Association. In the case of the NALSAR students against television channels that photographed them when they emerged from a pub in Hyderabad, complaints could not be lodged against some of the channels as they were not members of the News Broadcasters Association! So what was the outcome of the censure from the NBSA or even the Delhi High Court's guidelines? Did they deter other media houses from excessive intrusion?

The case of the deceased Aligarh Muslim University (AMU) professor S. R. Siras provides a tragic answer. A case of criminal trespass, assault, and forcible disturbance of privacy rights was lodged against the proctor of the university, Zubair Khan, the media adviser to the university's vice chancellor, Prof. N. A. K. Durrani, the university's PRO Rahat Abrar, and Adil Murtaza and Shiraz, two media persons belonging to a private news channel. A tape recording the consensual sex between the professor and another person was circulated and the university suspended the professor. After a strong protest, the university withdrew the suspension but by then it was too late and the professor committed suicide. When the incident occurred in February 2010, the Delhi High Court's path-breaking judgment striking down Sec 377 of the Indian Penal Code that criminalized homosexuality was already in place, and the Supreme Court was yet to admit an appeal against it. Citing this, gay rights activists and lawyers had argued that the professor was doing nothing illegal and, in any case, trespassing into his private space was a violation of his privacy. In an order staying the suspension of the professor, Justices Sunil Ambwani and K. N. Pandey of the Allahabad High Court said,

> sexual preference of an adult may not amount to misconduct specially in the circumstances (in violation to the right of privacy) in which the act was alleged to be discovered. The right of privacy is a fundamental right, needs to be protected and unless the conduct of a person, even if he is a teacher is going to affect and has substantial nexus with his employment, it may not be treated as misconduct. (*Dr Shrinivas Ramchandra Siras & Ors v. the Aligarh Muslim University & Ors*)

But university officials denied any violation of privacy by the act of trespassing into the professor's private quarters. It was the media, the AMU vice chancellor said, which was the real culprit (Vats 2010). While the media's aggressive intrusion is criminal, there are, of course, other culprits. With Sec 377 criminalizing same-sex relationships back on the statute books after a Supreme Court judgment, the harassment of members of the LGBT community and the threat to violations of their privacy is ever present.

By the late 1980s, the HIV epidemic spawned a number of articles, mostly feeding into the fears of a panic-stricken public against 'high-risk' groups. Much of the media reportage was ill-informed and intrusive to the point of callousness towards victims and, later, with greater awareness and organizational support for medical care towards HIV-positive survivors. Following a case on a visual screening of two minors, the PCI formulated guidelines for coverage of HIV/AIDS-related news (PCI n.d.). But how much of these guidelines remain on paper? How conscious is the media in adhering to them? And more importantly, when the media does transgress, is the remedy before the public accessible and effective?

In 2007, the *Hindustan Times* did a photo feature on children of HIV-positive parents who had become orphaned and were being taken care of by their families (Ghosh and Uttamchandani 2007). The children lived in their village homes, commuted to school, and were cared for by their grandparents or by their parents' siblings. The non-governmental organization (NGO) that supported their care, SANGRAM, kept in touch with the caregivers and monitored their nutrition and medical care. Other than the caregivers, the NGO staff, and doctors, no one knew the children were also HIV-positive.

The photographer and reporter of the newspaper, excited at their story, photographed the children. When the caregivers and staff of the NGO realized that photographs were covertly being taken of the children, they protested and warned the newspaper's staff not to do so and were assured the pictures would not be used. However, the photographs were published, without any attempt to mask their faces or pixelate their features. In a strong protest letter to the newspaper, the NGO tried to take up the matter with the senior editorial staff of the newspaper. The letter said:

The plight of orphans of the HIV epidemic has been largely invisible in the mainstream media. Regrettably, your effort to redress this hidden story of the gritty survivors—which could have been a truly laudable one—has degenerated into a voyeuristic violation of their privacy. Besides, your article robs them of their dignity and leaves them dangerously exposed to discrimination and stigma from insensitive quarters. Moreover, you made no attempt to disguise their pictures or change their names and the villages they hailed from to protect their identities. By failing to do so, you have violated their human rights and given the go by to basic journalistic norms that govern protection to victims.[6]

The letter got no response.

In another instance in 2009, *Tehelka* magazine printed an article, with pixelated photographs of tribal women raped by the Salwa Judum, the vigilante army set up to combat the Maoist insurgency in the central Indian state of Chhattisgarh (Sahi 2009a). The publication evoked protests, both from academic and researcher Nandini Sundar, who said the publication was a breach of confidence as she had shared the information with the author of the article, Ajit Sahi, in trust. Journalists wrote to *Tehelka* to protest the manner in which the article pixelated only the faces of the rape survivors, keeping other markers of their identity like their homes, their children, the clothes they wore, and their belongings in sharp relief.

The protest letter sent to the magazine said,

It is appalling that basic journalistic ethics were flouted by your publication. The identities of the women, clearly revealed by name and village, and even photographs (the pixelation is insufficient to ensure masking the identity). This was done in the face of an express undertaking to maintain confidentiality. Besides being explicitly prohibited by law, revealing the identities of survivors of rape not only severely compromises their attempts to cope with the assault, but also jeopardizes their security. In the highly polarized environment of Chhattisgarh, amidst documented atrocities by the Salwa Judum, seeking justice for these women will be that much more difficult. They are now vulnerable to harassment and pressure to retract the testimonies, with no protection being offered by the journalist concerned or your publication. Not only does this irresponsible report have severe consequences for these women, it also has an impact on other women in the area who might want to file cases of rape or other atrocities in future.[7]

Sahi, who was the magazine's 'editor-at-large', denied that Sundar was the source of his information and maintained that he had not committed any breach of journalistic ethics by carrying the story. The publication was in the public interest, he asserted. The magazine brushed aside its lack of sensitivity in dealing with the issue, and certainly could have done much more to protect the identity of the complainants. When does media coverage of victims and survivors of disasters, conflict, or tragedy become intrusive? Take the instance of the photograph of a tear-stricken Qutbuddin Ansari, a tailor from Ahmedabad, hands folded in a plea, which became what print and broadcast news media termed the 'face of the Gujarat riots' of 2002.

Widely circulated, the photograph resulted in instant recognition for Ansari, forcing him to relocate to Kolkata, where CPI(M) leader Mohammed Salim helped him to set up a tailoring shop. The latter, in turn, used Ansari's picture extensively during his parliamentary campaign against the Trinamool Congress candidate Ajit Panda, winning his seat into the bargain.

Unable to settle down in Kolkata, Ansari returned to Ahmedabad, only to find that he was recognized everywhere he went. The one photograph had achieved iconic status and was used by all factions. Ansari was shocked and disturbed that his photograph was used again in an e-mail sent out by the Indian Mujahideen after the 2008 bomb blasts in Delhi. Later, when then Gujarat chief minister Narendra Modi launched his *sadbhavna* (or harmony) rallies, Ansari was called to participate but refused. Ansari repeatedly told the media and anyone who cared to listen to 'leave him alone'. He finally wrote to the Commissioner of Police, Ahmedabad, on 9 June 2011 that he was living peacefully in Ahmedabad and that the police should restrain the media from using his photograph.

The complaint stated,

> On 28 February 2002, at around 3:00 pm, a mob attacked the building in which I was residing. In the nick of time police arrived and saved us. During the whole episode—my photograph with folded hands, terror reflecting in my eyes and begging for mercy was captured by some media person, which got wide publicity and was used by media, NGO & others as a face of 2002 riots. Various National and International NGO'S have

put my said photographs on their websites using it for publicity & donations in the name of helping riot-affected people. (Sahni 2012)

Should the photographer have taken the picture that overturned the life of a young tailor and forever embedded his identity in the collective memory in that split second as a tearful and pleading victim? The photographer who took the picture doesn't think he did something wrong (Sahni 2012).

But would he have had the time to stop and seek consent in a situation of conflict or natural disaster? Would this be a violation of privacy? Or would this have a chilling effect on the media? The media plays a vital role in shining a much-needed spotlight on tragedy or conflict and then transmitting it to a larger world. Clearly, however, there is a need for serious introspection on issues like consent while reporting disaster or tragedy. Can an increasingly commoditized media strike the fine balance? In crucial instances, it appears that the media fails in this basic responsibility. Nowhere was this more evident than in the extraordinary coverage of the killings of a 14-year-old schoolgirl Aarushi Talwar and the family's domestic help Hemraj Banjade in Delhi in 2008. In 2013, the girl's parents Nupur and Rajesh Talwar were convicted of the murders, but not before a series of twists and turns in the police investigation, including the accusation, later withdrawn, against three persons employed as house helps, allegations of suppression of evidence, and the handing over of the case to the Central Bureau of Investigation, and the accompanying media frenzy over details of Aarushi's life, her diary and Facebook entries, her relationship with her parents, the demonization of the parents, and allegations regarding their own personal lives.

All of this contributed to the shaping of public opinion on the case. Writing on the media coverage of the case, Shohini Ghosh warns,

> No matter how secure we may feel from our present vantage point, the predicament of the Talwars can visit any one of us. For no fault of ours, we could be caught in a vortex of malevolence as the combined force of failing institutions and a sensation-driven media bear down on us. And before we know it our lives and rights as citizens can be crushed by the new lynch-mob that masquerades as the 'collective conscience of society'. The Aarushi-Hemraj murder case is not about the Talwars but about each and every one of us. (Ghosh 2013)

STATE SURVEILLANCE

In the post–26 November 2008 scenario, after a 60-hour terrorist siege of the western commercial metropolis of Mumbai, surveillance by the state in the name of national security was accepted as being in the public interest. Public interest was an important issue that came under focus in the wake of the disclosure of the Radia tapes. The tapes, which comprised several hundred hours of phone conversations between lobbyist Niira Radia and industrialists, media persons, and political leaders, recorded by tax agencies during 2008–9, suggested that Radia had actively lobbied for the appointment of a person favoured by her corporate client as the minister for communications when the formation of the Union Cabinet was under consideration following the general elections in 2009.

Radia was a lobbyist for both Ratan Tata's Tata Group as well as Mukesh Ambani's Reliance Industries Ltd. Conversations between Radia and Tata were published by two magazines, *Outlook* and *Open*, while the recorded tapes were uploaded on the websites of both magazines. In a writ petition before the Supreme Court, industrialist Ratan Tata stated that his privacy was violated by the leak of tapes recording hundreds of conversations. He sought to know whether the leak was by the government agencies that did not take adequate safeguards to protect the tapes from falling into unauthorized hands. Despite early expressions of concern from the bench, the hearings have since followed a rather languid pace and are on even at this writing. It is pertinent to note that the industrialist did not challenge the right of the government to conduct surveillance, but said the release of the tapes was an infringement of his privacy. He sought to find out the source of the 'leak' and determine how the tapes entered the public domain, and to ensure that some of the conversations, the contents of which he described as personal, remained out of the public domain.

Tata's contention that his privacy was violated was refuted by the senior Supreme Court advocate Prashant Bhushan, who had filed a PIL on behalf of the Centre for Public Interest Litigation to seek the prosecution of former union telecom minister, A. Raja for his role in the 2G scam. Bhushan maintained that the disclosures were in the public interest and the public had a right to know about public policy (Seshu 2010).

Posing the right to privacy alongside the right to information, Bhushan pointed out that the information in the tapes would not fall under the exemptions laid down in Sec 8(1)(j) of the Right to Information Act, 2005, which creates the sole basis on which information could be denied on grounds of privacy. The law specifies that there can be no disclosure of

> information which relates to personal information the disclosure of which has no relationship to any public activity or interest, or which would cause unwarranted invasion of the privacy of the individual unless the Central Public Information Officer or the State Public Information Officer or the appellate authority, as the case may be, is satisfied that the larger public interest justifies the disclosure of such information.

The Indian media's concerns about a panopticon state in the making are nowhere as sharp as they should be. This is reflected in the seeming acquiescence of the public in the purported needs of national security by the state. While people are familiar with the draconian provisions of the amended Information Technology Act, 2000, like Sec 66A (since held unconstitutional by the Supreme Court and deleted from the statute books), there is less awareness of provisions like monitoring and interception of communication and rules on 'sensitive personal data' that can be accessed by an authority.

Fears of privacy violations are inherent in the Unique Identification Number 'Aadhaar' scheme, even as the government quietly rolls out a number of measures to increase monitoring and interception of all electronic communication. According to the Snowden revelations, India is the fifth most 'surveilled' nation in the controversial Prism programme and in the Boundless Informant programme, data-mining tools which track calls and e-mails collected by the security system (Greenwald and Saxena 2013). Of the 97 billion pieces of intelligence information gathered from computer networks worldwide, 6.3 billion pertained to India (Burke 2013).

Mass surveillance adversely affects privacy and freedom of expression. The report of the UN Special Rapporteur on Freedom of Expression, Frank La Rue, on surveillance, privacy, and freedom of expression lays down a number of recommendations on safeguarding both privacy and freedom of expression (Human Rights Council 2013).

Privacy and freedom of expression are interlinked, the recommendations said, adding that both must be safeguarded with adequate legislation and legal standards to ensure the privacy, security, and anonymity of communications, journalists, human rights defenders, and whistleblowers. Besides, communications surveillance networks must be regarded as highly intrusive acts that can potentially interfere with the right to freedom of expression and privacy. Recommendations include that legislation must stipulate that state surveillance of communications must only occur under the most exceptional circumstances and exclusively under the supervision of an independent judicial authority, illegal surveillance by public or private actors should be criminalized, and there should be transparency over communications surveillance techniques, public access to information, data protection should be ensured from corporates, and freedom of citizens to access communication services without disclosing their identities should be ensured.

However, even with the most stringent safeguards, there is an alarming dearth of public scrutiny of mass surveillance programmes in India and the resultant absence of accountability of these programmes. There is little information about the amount of money being pumped into various programmes for intelligence gathering, save for a few reports about the setting up of a Central Monitoring Scheme which is expected to monitor all online communication—including phone calls, chats, and SMSes, the NATGRID (National Intelligence Grid) which seeks to collect data ranging from tax and bank account details, credit card transactions, visa, and rail and air travel details and make these available to 11 security agencies.

PRIVACY IN THE DIGITAL AGE

An increasingly digital world has contributed to other invasions of privacy. Apart from state surveillance and media intrusions, there are privacy infringements from both corporate bodies engaged in data mining as well as private citizens who are wont to turn the recording device both onto themselves as well as on others. Digital media users, especially in social networks, have overturned earlier notions of privacy completely, in both positive and negative ways as they share personal details, even as they grapple with surveillance and stalking.

There are numerous studies on the impact of the merging of public and private domains in online media (Livingstone 2005). A 24/7 new media spawns other anxieties as it facilitates the quick and easy dissemination of information and opinion without any of the filters that were expected to operate in traditional media. Social media was the culprit, said an article lamenting the invasion of privacy of former prime minister, Atal Behari Vajpayee, after the death of a member of his adopted family (Haridas 2014). Other political leaders found it difficult to escape the digital media scanner. For instance, a video of Congress spokesperson Abhishek Manu Singhvi with a woman lawyer went viral and spawned a number of mirror sites amidst a flurry of take-down notices.

Even as society moves towards a relaxation of hitherto fixed notions of what could be aired and shared on social networks, the flip side is the increase in criminal acts like stalking and harassing, hacking of personal email addresses, and the transmission of photographs and videos of sexual encounters that may or may not be consensual, but could be used for extortion and blackmail. Women have used digital media as an imaginative and innovative space to express themselves and communicate freely. There are blogs, social media networks, websites, and e-groups, apart from the groups on mobile media. India, the global digital analysis firm comScore said, has the third largest number of internet users in the world, after USA and China. And a third of them are women.

For many, access itself is a major issue. Mobile telephones have helped women to connect and independently communicate without traditional barriers. For *khap* panchayats (the extra-judicial governing councils in some castes in parts of rural north India that exert considerable influence over social and political affairs), mobile media poses a threat to society. Periodically, there are calls from religious bodies or from khap panchayats to ban young women from using mobiles, but protests against these calls and Supreme Court observations that such 'diktats' are unlawful, may have had some effect (*Tribune* 2014).

For women who have found new expression in every public platform on social media, online gender harassment has spawned a veritable industry of trolls often forcing those targeted to seek legal redress from problematic laws like Sec 66A of the IT Act or to change accounts and even relocate to escape scrutiny and attack. Online harassment has become a weapon of censorship, often resulting in silencing them or forcing them to withdraw from public participation. Online harassment, which ranges from the most virulent threats of rape and assault to trolling, morphing, name calling, voyeurism, and stalking, affects the participation of women in the world of online media. In 2013, the NCRB, the centralized government agency that collates and analyses all available data on the incidence of crime in the country, classified 1,203 complaints under the cybercrime 'obscene publications/transmission in electronic form' section, with 737 arrests (*Times of India* 2014).

Twitter and Facebook are favoured sites for trolls, who target both well-known news anchors or writers and anyone else who may take a stand or speak up against misogyny. Arpita Biswas, who spoke out against singer Palash Sen, was trolled and given rape threats until she decided to speak out against it on Facebook (Index on Censorship 2014). Writer and poet Meena Kandaswamy said she received 8,000 tweets calling her a 'harlot, whore, bitch, terrorist', hours after tweeting that Dalits had a right to eat beef on a university campus.

In a 2013 study, the Internet and Democracy Project examined the experiences of women with online harassment and the techniques women use to deal with it (Padte 2013). Some have confronted or ignored their harassers, while others have had to change accounts, sought legal redress, and a few complained to cyber police about the harassment, despite misgivings about problematic provisions like Sec 66A of the amended IT Act, 2000.

In fact, the findings of the study, 'Don't Let It Stand: An Exploratory Study of Women and Online Verbal Abuse in India', found that women avoided legal recourse to deal with the threats and harassment they faced (Kovacs 2013: 36–44). Ironically, the issue of online gender harassment and the unmasking of trolls has also brought to the fore a paradoxical aspect of privacy: can people use the cloak of privacy and anonymity to harass and issue threats to others? And, if they are outed, can they cry foul? (Asher-Perrin 2012).

As the study of the Internet and Democracy Project pointed out, it was in 'the complexities of the virtual world comprising public streets (Twitter), backyards (Facebook—though not all of it) and houses (blogs) that discussions surrounding privacy, anonymity, families and access are held' (Kovacs 2013: 35).

PROPOSED LEGISLATION ON PRIVACY

In August 2017, a nine-judge bench of India's Supreme Court delivered a unanimous judgment that the right to privacy is a fundamental right under the Indian Constitution (*Justice K. S. Puttaswamy [Retd] and Anr v. Union of India and Ors*). The implications of this historic verdict are still unravelling in the arena of surveillance, data protection, freedom of expression, and so on. While India does not have a law on privacy, there have been attempts, largely fuelled by corporate interests, to formulate legislation to protect data and ensure that an authority is set up to deal with privacy issues. In 2012, the report of a Group of Experts on Privacy, chaired by Justice A. P. Shah and constituted by the Planning Commission, submitted its report suggesting a framework for a Privacy Act. The exhaustive report looked at international principles and examined the constitutional basis for privacy, laid down nine principles for privacy, and recommended the establishment of a Privacy Commissioner in a co-regulatory framework to deal with complaints. A privacy bill that was formulated in 2011 laid down some exceptions to acts that were not to be considered deprivations of privacy, including those for journalistic purposes. But it appears that another draft, circulated in 2014, has dropped this exception (CIS 2014). The drafts are not yet in the public domain, and there is little public discussion on their provisions.

* * *

As privacy is both used and abused in equal measure, the absence of any clear law on the right to privacy and on its protection, has made it all the more necessary to discuss and debate the contours of privacy. Should we have a law on privacy and what should its parameters be? How much can news media infringe upon privacy as a legitimate part of its coverage of events and issues? What are the safeguards against commodification of the personal and the sale of private information and trade in data? How can we protect the anonymity of the internet and guard against surveillance and intrusion? While a discussion on the nature of this legislation is beyond the scope of this chapter, it remains to be seen whether the proposed privacy law will affect news-gathering and news makers and provide protection against excessive media intrusions.

State surveillance and the increasing intrusion on privacy by established media has altered the larger contours of privacy rights of citizens. If digital media has ensured anonymous interaction between citizens and contributed to the protection of private spaces, it has also endangered private expression due to state surveillance and privacy intrusions by citizens on one another. Online gender harassment circumscribes the engagement of women with digital media. Any debate on privacy protections must take into account all these components, even as we remain vigilant about the twin dangers of an intrusive media and state surveillance.

NOTES

1. Registrar of Newspapers for India, http://rni.nic.in/all_page/press_india. aspx (accessed on 12 September 2018).
2. Ministry of Information and Broadcasting, https://mib.gov.in/broadcast-ing/uplinking-or-downlinking-tv-channels (accessed on 12 September 2018).
3. Press Council of India, *Norms of Journalistic Conduct*, http://presscoun-cil.nic.in/OldWebsite/NORMS-2010.pdf (accessed on 12 September 2018).
4. News Broadcasters Association (NBA), *Code of Ethics and Broadcasting Standards*, para 6, Privacy, p. 4, http://www.nbanewdelhi.com/assets/uploads/pdf/code_of_ethics_english.pdf (accessed on 12 September 2018).
5. See http://www.nbanewdelhi.com/assets/uploads/pdf/2011_2_ORDER_NO_5_DT__21_3_11.pdf (accessed on 12 September 2018).
6. Letter to the Editor, *Hindustan Times*, Mumbai, sd/- Meena Saraswathi Seshu, Secretary, SANGRAM, Sangli, NGO, Wednesday, 16 May 2007, 7:03 AM (copy of letter available with author).
7. Copy of the letter sent by women activists to *Tehelka* and shared with the author. Tehelka's response was carried in the magazine (see Sahi 2009b).

REFERENCES

ABC v. Commissioner of Police and Others, W.P.(C.) No. 12730/2005 and C.M. Nos. 9505/2005, 13315/2005 & 12222/2007. Retrieved from https://indiankanoon.org/doc/149860325/ (accessed on 12 September 2018).

Asher-Perrin, Emily (2012). 'You Are Not Anonymous: On Internet Privacy and the War on Trolls', 24 October. Retrieved from http://www.tor.com/

blogs/2012/10/you-are-not-anonymous-on-internet-privacy-and-the-war-on-trolls (accessed on 17 August 2018).

Burke, Jason (2013). 'NSA Spied on Indian Embassy and UN Mission, Edward Snowden Files Reveal'. *Guardian*, 25 September. Retrieved from http://www.theguardian.com/world/2013/sep/25/nsa-surveillance-indian-embassy-un-mission (accessed on 17 August 2018).

CIS (Centre for Internet and Society) (2014). 'Leaked Privacy Bill: 2014 vs. 2011'. Retrieved from http://cis-india.org/internet-governance/blog/leaked-privacy-bill-2014-v-2011 (accessed on 17 August 2018).

Court on Its Own Motion v. State, 14 December 2007. Judgment by Justice Mukundakam Sharma. http://indiankanoon.org/doc/45618/ (accessed on 17 August 2018).

Dr Shrinivas Ramchandra Siras & Ors v. the Aligarh Muslim University & Ors, Civil Misc. Writ Petition No. 17549 of 2010, Allahabad High Court, http://elegalix.allahabadhighcourt.in/elegalix/WebShowJudgment.do (accessed on 12 September 2018).

Ghosh, Aditya, and Ritesh Uttamchandani (2007). 'A Generation Orphaned'. *Hindustan Times*, 13 May.

Ghosh, Shohini (2013). 'The Talwars and Presumed Guilt'. *Hoot*, 15 November. Retrieved from http://www.thehoot.org/media-watch/media-practice/the-talwars-and-presumed-guilt-7127 (accessed on 17 August 2018).

Greenwald, Glenn, and Shobhan Saxena (2013). 'India among Top Targets of Spying by NSA'. *Hindu*, 23 September. Retrieved from http://www.the-hindu.com/news/national/india-among-top-targets-of-spying-by-nsa/article5157526.ece (accessed on 17 August 2018).

Haridas, Neena (2014). 'The End of Privacy: How Social Media Invaded Vajpayee's Personal Life'. *Firstpost*, 8 May. Retrieved from http://www.firstpost.com/living/the-end-of-privacy-how-social-media-invaded-vajpayees-personal-life-1514059.html (accessed on 17 August 2018).

Human Rights Council (2013). 'Report of the Special Rapporteur on the Promotion and Protection of the Right to Freedom of Opinion and Expression', 17 April. Retrieved from http://www.ohchr.org/Documents/HRBodies/HRCouncil/RegularSession/Session23/A.HRC.23.40_EN.pdf (accessed on 17 August 2018).

Index on Censorship (2014). 'Twitter Trolls in India: Sexist Abuse as a Tool to Muzzle Women', 1 April. Retrieved from http://www.indexoncensorship.org/2014/04/twitter-trolls-india-sexist-abuse-tool-muzzle-women/ (accessed on 17 August 2018).

Justice K. S. Puttaswamy (Retd.) and Anr. v. Union of India and Ors, Writ Petition (Civil) no. 494 OF 2012. Retrieved from https://www.sci.gov.in/pdf/LU/ALL%20WP(C)%20No.494%20of%202012%20Right%20to%20Privacy.pdf (accessed on 17 August 2018).

Karkaria, Bachi (2013a). 'Don't Make Her Lose Her Face'. *Times of India*, 2 September. Retrieved from https://blogs.timesofindia.indiatimes.com/erratica/don-t-make-her-lose-her-face/ (accessed on 12 September 2018).

———— (2013b). 'But I'm on the Same Page as You, Laxmi'. *Hoot*, 6 September. Retrieved from http://thehoot.org/media-watch/media-practice/but-i-m-on-the-same-page-as-you-laxmi-7019 (accessed on 17 August 2018).

Khan, Sonia (2014). 'That Hashtag Was My Colleague'. GristMedia, 18 August. Retrieved from https://in.news.yahoo.com/that-hashtag-was-my-colleague-060844991.html (accessed on 17 August 2018).

Kovacs, Anja (2013). *Don't Let It Stand: An Exploratory Study of Women and Online Verbal Abuse in India*. Internet Democracy Project, April. Retrieved from https://internetdemocracy.in/wp-content/uploads/2013/12/Internet-Democracy-Project-Women-and-Online-Abuse.pdf (accessed on 17 August 2018).

Livingstone, S. (2005). 'Mediating the Public/Private Boundary at Home: Children's Use of the Internet for Privacy and Participation'. *LSE Research Online*. Retrieved from http://eprints.lse.ac.uk/archive/00000506 (accessed on 17 August 2018).

Mumbai Mirror (2009). 'Mirror Is Sensational', 18 April. Retrieved from http://www.mumbaimirror.com/mumbai/others/Mirror-is-sensational/articleshow/15918433.cms (accessed on 17 August 2018).

Murthy, Laxmi (2013). 'Rape Victim's Identity: Disclosure for Whom?' *Hoot*, 9 September. Retrieved from http://www.thehoot.org/media-watch/media-practice/rape-victim-s-identity-disclosure-for-whom-7016 (accessed on 17 August 2018).

Padte, Richa Kaul (2013). 'Keeping Women Safe? Gender, Online Harassment and Indian Law', June. http://internetdemocracy.in/reports/keeping-women-safe-gender-online-harassment-and-indian-law/ (accessed on 17 August 2018).

PCI (Press Council of India) (n.d.). 'HIV/AIDS and the Media'. Retrieved from http://presscouncil.nic.in/OldWebsite/guidelines on HIVAIDS.pdf (accessed on 17 August 2018).

Rediff.com (2006). 'PoW's Wife Gudiya Dies', 2 January. Retrieved from http://www.rediff.com/news/2006/jan/02gudiya.htm (accessed on 17 August 2018).

Sahi, Ajit (2009a). 'The Evil That Men Do', parts 1 and 2. *Tehelka*, 6(28), 18 July.

———— (2009b). 'With Justice in Mind'. *Tehelka*, 6(30), 1 August.

Sahni, Diksha (2012). 'Picture Focus: Ansari and the Anatomy of Fear'. *Wall Street Journal*, 28 February. Retrieved from http://blogs.wsj.com/india-realtime/2012/02/28/picture-focus-ansari-and-the-anatomy-of-fear/ (accessed on 17 August 2018).

Seshu, Geeta (2010). 'The Right to Privacy Is Not Valid Because We Are Talking about Professional Conversations about Public Policy'. *Hoot*, 6 December. Retrieved from http://www.thehoot.org/web/freetracker/storynew.php?storyid=207&sectionId=10.

Solidarity for Justice (1991). Human Rights Issues Emerging from Investigation into the Murder of Sr Silvia and Sr Priya. Retrieved from http://www.unipune.ac.in/snc/cssh/HumanRights/07 STATE AND GENDER/08.pdf (accessed on 17 August 2018).

Times of India (2014). 'Cybercrimes Shoot Up by over 50% across India'. 2 July. Retrieved from http://timesofindia.indiatimes.com/tech/tech-news/Cybercrimes-shoot-up-by-over-50-across-India/articleshow/37627477.cms (accessed on 17 August 2018).

Tribune (2014). 'Haryana Khaps Bat for Gender Equality'. 10 August. Retrieved from http://www.tribuneindia.com/2014/20140811/main6.htm (accessed on 17 August 2018).

Vats, Vaibhav (2010). 'There Are No Homosexuals in AMU'. *Tehelka*, 24 April. Retrieved from http://www.tehelka.com/there-are-no-homosexuals-in-amu/.

INDEX

Bajrang Dal 116, 133n1
bandhs (shutdowns of a city) 333n22
Battle of Plassey (1757) 29
BBC 59, 107, 235, 296
Bengal Hurkaru 29–30
Bernstein, Carl 49
Beti Bachao Beti Padhao program of
    NDA 128
bhakti movement 332n9
bharati afwaaj ke mazzalim
    (oppression by Indian forces) 241
Bharat Itihas Sanshodhak Mandal
    (Pune) 21
Bharatiya Janata Party (BJP) 39, 101,
    103, 105, 110n8, 115, 117, 119,
    125, 131
    election budgets for campaigning
        in social media 185
    Hindutva or Hinduness
        campaign 116, 307
    leaders' hate-inciting speeches 306
    negative coverage by and its
        leaders 126–30
Bhaskar Group 102
Bhopal gas tragedy (1984) 255
Bibliothèque Nationale de France
    (Paris) 21
Bigul new site 173
Bloomberg India 85
Bollinger Report 279
Boundless Informant programme 353
Bourdieu, Pierre 318, 332n13
Brahmunical Magazine 19
Brazil, Russia, India, China, and
    South Africa (BRICS) 68
Breaking News mobile app 187
Broadband to Panchayats (white
    paper) 101
Buckingham, James Silk 26, 28
Bundelkhand region, drought in 253
Business India 43, 80–1, 83

Business Today 42, 80
Businessworld 80–1, 83
BuzzFeed 167

Calcutta Amusement 74
Calcutta Gazette 27
Calcutta Journal 26, 29–30
Cambridge Analytica 107
Caravan 81, 83, 87
caste 2, 4, 47, 74, 130, 291–3, 297,
    307, 355
    as category organizes violence 298
    discrimination 300–1
    hierarchy 332n14
    and neoliberal desire 297–8
    social prejudices of 311
    suicides and deaths among lower
        298–9
CCTV-9 57
Central Bureau of Investigation
    161, 351
Central Monitoring Scheme 354
Centre for Environmental
    Education 253
Centre for Media Studies 273
Centre for Science and Environment
    (CSE) 253, 256, 262
chakka jam (stopping of the flow of
    traffic) 333n22
Champak 87
Channel 4 News 63
China Central Television (CCTV) 57
China Daily 57
China Global Television Network
    (CGTN) 57–8
China Radio International 57
Chipko Andolan or Movement 250,
    252, 255
CNBC 56, 63
CNN 59, 63
CNNI 79

EDITOR AND CONTRIBUTORS

EDITOR

Shakuntala Rao is professor at State University of New York, Plattsburgh, USA. Rao has published extensively and influentially in communication, media, journalism, and various interdisciplinary journals. She is one of the most cited scholars in the areas of media ethics and South Asian journalism. She is co-editor of three anthologies with the most recent being *Media Ethics and Justice in the Age of Globalization* (2015). She has been a visiting research professor at Tsinghua University (Beijing) and at the University of Stockholm (Sweden) and is the recipient of the State University of New York Chancellor's award for excellence in research.

CONTRIBUTORS

Deb Aikat is associate professor at the School of Media and Journalism at University of North Carolina-Chapel Hill, USA. His research has been published in book chapters and in refereed journals such as *First Amendment Studies, Health Communication, Global Media and Communication*, and *Popular Music and Society*. His research has been funded by government agencies such as the US Department of State, US Department of Education, and corporate foundations such as the Freedom Forum and the Scripps Howard Foundation. Aikat earned his PhD in mass communication and journalism from Ohio University, USA. He has an MA and a BA from University of Calcutta, India, and has worked as a journalist in India for *The Telegraph*. Aikat completed in 1990 a Certificate in American Political Culture from New York University, USA.

Prashanth Bhat is a doctoral student at Philip Merrill College of Journalism at the University of Maryland-College Park, USA. His research interests include online hate speech, right-wing politics and media, and online political expressions. He has worked as a journalist for leading news organizations such as *Deccan Chronicle, Times of India*, and *China Central Television*.

Kalyani Chadha is associate professor at the Philip Merrill College of Journalism, University of Maryland-College Park, USA. Chadha received her BA from University of Delhi, MA from Jawaharlal University, Delhi, and her PhD from University of Maryland-College Park, USA. Her research broadly focuses on issues of media globalization, the implications of new media technologies with a particular emphasis on international contexts as well as the media and journalism landscape in India. Her work has appeared in leading journals such as *Media, Culture and Society, Journal of Broadcast and Electronic Media, Global Media and Communication*, and *Convergence*.

Monica Chadha is assistant professor at the Cronkite School of Journalism and Mass Communication, Arizona State University-Tempe, USA. Chadha spent more than a decade reporting from India for the BBC and *The Indian Express*. In over ten years of reporting, she produced multimedia stories for online, radio, print, and television. She completed her PhD at the University of Texas-Austin, USA, with a research focus in entrepreneurial journalism, newsroom convergence, and new technologies and media effects.

Dhiman Chattopadhyaya is assistant professor in the Department of Communication and Media at Lamar University, USA. He has published book chapters and articles in refereed journals such as *Journalism & Mass Communication Quarterly, Journal of Graphic*

Novels and Comics, and *Global Media Journal.* His research projects have won multiple awards at Association for Education in Journalism and Mass Communications (AEJMC), National Communication Association (NCA), and Broadcast Education Association (BEA). Chattopadhyaya earned his PhD from Bowling Green State University, USA. He has an MA from Calcutta University, India, and a BA from Presidency College, Calcutta, India. Before moving to academia, he worked as a journalist in India for 18 years and has been a former senior editor with *The Times of India, Mid-Day,* and *Business Today.*

Saayan Chattopadhyaya is assistant professor, Baruipur College, affiliated to University of Calcutta, India. After a stint as a journalist, he is currently engaged in research in postcolonial news culture, technoculture in developing nations, and south Asian masculinities. He has published research articles on various issues related to Indian media and culture in international journals including Studies in *South Asian Film and Media, Journalism Practice, South Asia Research, Sarai Reader, Journal of Boyhood Studies,* among others.

Sunitha Chitrapu is an independent media researcher in Mumbai, India. She was formerly head of the Social Communications Media department, Sophia Polytechnic, Mumbai, India. Chitrapu received her PhD in mass communications from The Media School, Indiana University, Bloomington, USA. Her research interests include the political economy of media in India and the economics of international media trade.

Mohan J. Dutta is Provost's chair professor and head of the department of Communications and New Media at National University of Singapore and Courtesy Professor of Communication at Purdue University, USA. At National University of Singapore, he is the Founding Director of the Center for Culture-Centered Approach to Research and Evaluation (CARE), directing research on cultural-lycentred, community-based projects of social change. He holds a Bachelor of Technology in Agricultural Engineering from the Indian Institute of Technology Kharagpur, India and a PhD in mass communication from the University of Minnesota, USA. Dutta has published over 170 journal articles and book chapters, and was recently noted as the most published scholar in health communication. He has authored *Communicating Health: A Culture-Centered Approach*, co-edited *Emerging Perspectives in Health Communication: Meaning, Culture, and Power*, and *Communicating for Social Impact: Engaging Communication Theory, Research, and Pedagogy*.

Ashwini Falnikar is a doctoral candidate at National University of Singapore, in the Department of Communications and New Media, Singapore. She has worked as a part-time research assistant with Center for Culture-Centered Approach to Research and Evaluation, and as a part-time teaching assistant. Ashwini's ongoing research contributes to global and social change communication and health communication scholarship.

Anup Kumar is associate professor of Communication at Cleveland State University, USA. Kumar received his MA in Communication Studies from the University of Northern Iowa and his PhD in mass communication from University of Iowa, USA. Before joining academia, he was a journalist for more than a decade. His academic interest falls in the interdisciplinary areas of media, politics, and international communication. He has published research articles in peer-reviewed journals including *Journal of Communication Inquiry, Newspaper Research Journal, International Journal of Communication, Journal of Media Sociology*, and *Javnost-The Public*. He is also the author of *The Making of a Small State: Populist Social Mobilization and the Hindi Press in the Uttarakhand Movement*.

Kanchan K. Malik is professor and department head at the Department of Communication, University of Hyderabad, India. She obtained her PhD in Communication from University of Hyderabad, India. She also holds dual master's degrees in economics and in mass communication from Panjab University, Chandigarh, India. She worked as a journalist with *The Economic Times* for two years before pursuing a career in the academy. Malik has worked on the project 'Religions, Ethics and Attitudes towards Corruption' as part of the Religions and Development project of the University of Birmingham, UK. Her scholastic interests include print journalism, community media, gender, media and development, and media law and ethics. She is the author of *Other Voices: The Struggle for Community Radio in India.*

Smeeta Mishra is associate professor of business ethics and communication at the Indian Institute of Management Calcutta, India. Previously, she had taught at IMT Ghaziabad, IIM Ahmedabad, and Bowling Green State University, USA. Mishra holds a PhD from University of Texas-Austin, USA, an MA from S.I. Newhouse School of Communication, Syracuse University, USA, and an MA from the Center for Political Studies, Jawaharlal Nehru University, New Delhi, India. Mishra has published research on new media, cyberpsychology, media representations, and gender studies. Her research articles have appeared in journals such as *International Journal of Cultural Studies, Global Media Journal, Journal of Communication Inquiry, Journal of Broadcasting and Electronic Media*, and *The Howard Journal of Communications.*

Arif Hussain Nadaf is a research scholar at the Centre for Culture, Media and Governance, Jamia Millia Islamia (University), New Delhi, India. Hailing from the conflict territory of Kashmir, he has reported the conflict in the region for the local press before formally joining the field of academic research in 2013. His research interests include political communication, conflict reporting, and new media research. He holds an MA in Mass Communication and Journalism from the University of Kashmir, India.

Taberez Ahmed Neyazi is assistant professor of political communication and new media at the Department of Communications and New Media, National University of Singapore (NUS). Before moving to NUS, he taught at Jamia Millia Islamia, Delhi, India. He has also held numerous fellowships including Japan Society for the Promotion of Science (JSPS) Postdoctoral Fellow at Kyoto University, visiting fellow at the East-West Center in Hawaii and Nanyang Technological University in Singapore, and German Academic Exchange Service (DAAD) fellow at Erfurt University. He has authored *Political Communication and Mobilisation: The Hindi Media in India* and co-edited *Democratic Transformation and the Vernacular Public Arena in India.*

Radhika Parameswaran is Herman B Wells Endowed Professor in The Media School, Indiana University, Bloomington, USA. Her research interests include feminist cultural studies, globalization and media, India, and postcolonial studies. She is the 2015 recipient of the Teresa Award for Outstanding Feminist Research from the International Communication Association. Her publications include a 2013 edited encyclopedic volume on global audience studies, monograph articles in journalism & communication monographs, journal articles (reprinted as book chapters), and book chapters. She was a visiting research professor at the Annenberg School for Communication, University of Pennsylvania; faculty-in-residence at University of Colorado, Boulder; and a faculty judge for the National Peabody Awards. She is a two-time recipient of the Journalism department's Gretchen Kemp Award for outstanding teaching, and she served as the editor of the International Communication Association's official journal Communication, Culture & Critique from 2014 to 2016.

Usha Raman is professor, Department of Communication, University of Hyderabad, India. Until September 2010, she headed the communications department at L. V. Prasad Eye Institute, where she was responsible for internal and external communications, and where she also played a role in adding a communications action and research perspective into public eye health and outreach activities. She has also been a freelance journalist for over three decades, publishing on topics related to health, technology, and women's issues in a range of mainstream newspapers and magazines. She currently is a columnist for *The Hindu*'s Education Plus, and edits a monthly magazine for school teachers, called *Teacher Plus*. Usha received her PhD in mass communication from the University of Georgia, Athens, Georgia, USA, in 1996. Her research interests include cultural studies of science, health communication, children's media, feminist media studies, and the social and cultural impact of digital media.

Geeta Seshu is an independent journalist, based in Mumbai, India. She is engaged in reporting and analysing media issues, in particular on freedom of expression, gender, media ethics, and working conditions of journalists in India. She began her career in journalism in 1984 and worked at *The Indian Express*, Mumbai, was editor of 'Soulkurry', an internet portal for women, and of the niche social issues magazine *Humanscape*. She coordinated the Free Speech Hub, an initiative of the media watch website, *The Hoot* (www.thehoot.org), to track freedom of expression in India. Currently, she is a consulting editor of *The Hoot*.

Prasun Sonwalkar is editor (UK and Europe), *Hindustan Times*, based in London. He previously taught in British universities after gaining a PhD from the University of Leicester on a Commonwealth Scholarship. His research has been published in several journals and edited collections. He has reported extensively on India's north-east, politics, government and sports for *The Times of India, Business Standard*, PTI, IANS and other news organizations.

Daya Thussu is professor of International Communication and co-director of India Media Centre at the University of Westminster, London, UK. Among his key publications are: *Communicating India's Soft Power: Buddha to Bollywood* (2013), *Media and Terrorism: Global Perspectives* (2012), *Internationalizing Media Studies* (2009), *News as Entertainment: The Rise of Global Infotainment* (2007), *Media on the Move: Global Flow and Contra-Flow* (2007), *International Communication-Continuity and Change*, third edition (2018), and *Electronic Empires-Global Media and Local Resistance* (1998). He is the founder and Managing Editor of the journal, *Global Media and Communication*.

Roshni Susana Verghese is currently a PhD candidate in The Media School, Indiana University, Bloomington, USA. Her research interests include media globalization, gender, South Asia, television, and youth and global popular culture. Most recently, she served as the editorial assistant of the journal *Communication, Culture & Critique*, an official journal of the International Communication Association.

Ram Awtar Yadav is a doctoral student at the Department of Communication, University of Hyderabad, India.